Perspectives on Cooperative Law

Willy Tadjudje · Ifigeneia Douvitsa
Editors

Perspectives on Cooperative Law

Festschrift In Honour of Professor Hagen Henrÿ

Springer

Editors
Willy Tadjudje
Université Catholique de Louvain
Ottignies-Louvain-la-Neuve, Belgium

Ifigeneia Douvitsa
Hellenic Open University
Athens, Greece

ISBN 978-981-19-1990-9 ISBN 978-981-19-1991-6 (eBook)
https://doi.org/10.1007/978-981-19-1991-6

This Springer imprint is published by the registered company Springer Nature Singapore Pte Ltd.
The registered company address is: 152 Beach Road, #21-01/04 Gateway East, Singapore 189721, Singapore

Preface

Cooperative law is a scientific subject with little or no academic recognition. One of the reasons for this paucity may be that, in most Universities around the world, it is not part of the teaching curriculum. As a result, it attracts little interest from the research community. Fortunately, despite the weak interest for cooperative law, researchers still work on it.[1]

Nevertheless, despite the relative interest in cooperative law in academia, such interest is even less visible at the international level. There are some references at national and regional levels,[2] but very little at international level. To our knowledge, the first time that cooperative lawyers from all regions of the world came together to present a comparative approach to cooperative law across the world was in 2013.[3] Since then, other opportunities may not have arisen until the advent of this project dedicated to an illustrious cooperative law scholar. The purpose of this book is not only to ensure the continuity of international research in cooperative law, remaining grateful to our forebearers for their efforts, but also to take some time to underline the work of one of our own: Professor Hagen Henrÿ.[4] Although this book is the second of its kind at the international level, i.e. the second to bring together cooperative law researchers from all regions of the world, it is the first in another respect. Indeed, to our knowledge, this is the first time that the international cooperative law community has paid tribute to a cooperative law scholar.

---

[1] For example, in recent years, an international association of cooperative lawyers has been created with members from all regions of the world. It is called Ius Cooperativum: https://iuscooperativum.org.

Similarly, the International Cooperative Alliance (ICA) now includes Cooperative Law Committees (CLC) at both global and regional levels, with lawyers from both the academic and practical spheres: https://www.ica.coop/en/welcome-webpage-ica-cooperative-law-committee-ica-clc.

[2] See in Africa Tadjudje (2020, 2021) and Theron (2010), in Europe Fajardo et al. (2017), in Asia FAO (1998) and in Latin America Cracogna (2013, 2015).

[3] Cracogna et al. (2013).

[4] For more details on Hagen Henrÿ, see below Preliminary Chapter (Background and Contribution of Hagen Henrÿ to the Development of Cooperative Law).

Cooperative law is unquestionably part of general corporate law, even if it introduces its own rules.[5] Such affiliation to corporate law, with a certain detachment to consider its authenticity, constitutes one of the greatest challenges of cooperative law. In this respect, the debate on the *companisation* of cooperative law,[6] dear to Hagen Henrÿ, recurs in most discussions on cooperative law. This challenge is revealed not only in general cooperative law, but also when dealing with sectoral issues (the law applicable to the sectors of activity that cooperatives may join) or crosscutting matters (notably tax law, competition law, accounting and auditing law, state aid law, etc.).[7] Similarly, a public international cooperative law has been developing over the years, with the aim of laying the foundations for an "autonomous" cooperative law.[8] Despite these developments, cooperative law is trying to find its way in an environment marked by hybridism, between belonging to corporate law and defending its authenticity.[9]

During his professional career, Hagen Henrÿ has made an essential contribution to the development of cooperative law by providing solutions to this main challenge: enabling cooperative law to flourish, keeping its specificity without drowning in general corporate law.[10] Through teaching, research, involvement in development projects, etc. he strived and is still striving his best to take cooperative law to the next stage. The present book brings together contributions from authors from all over the world to discuss various topics of cooperative law in order to acknowledge his contribution to the construction of cooperative law at the international level.

---

[5] Depending on the country, cooperative law is included in the general company law or is legislated separately in a specific law or laws. For an international overview, see Part III of Cracogna et al. (2013).

[6] Pönkä (2019).

[7] Henrÿ (2013b).

[8] Henrÿ (2013a).

[9] Fajardo et al. (2017); Münkner (2015).

[10] We believe that the most decisive of Hagen Henrÿ's contributions seems to be the Guidelines he published to support cooperative legislation processes. The latest version dates from 2013 (Henrÿ 2013b) within the framework of ILO publications.

The editors would like to thank all the organisations and individuals[11] who have supported the realisation of this honorary volume. In particular, we thank the authors of the contributions for the time they have devoted to this tribute to Hagen Henrÿ. They have shared their knowledge and the results of their research, without hesitation. We would like to thank all our reviewers[12] (technical and linguistic) for all the work they have done. Finally, we thank the readers. We hope that this book will reach as many people as possible, and we would like to receive their comments in order to improve the quality of this book.

Ottignies-Louvain-la-Neuve, Belgium — Willy Tadjudje
Athens, Greece — Ifigeneia Douvitsa

References

Cracogna D (2015) La legislación cooperativa latinoamericana en el marco del Plan para una Década Cooperativa de la Alianza Cooperativa Internacional, REVESCO Revista de Estudios Cooperativos: 12–33

Cracogna D et al (2013) International handbook of co-operative law. Springer, Heidelberg New York, Dordrecht, London

Fajardo et al (2017) Principles of European co-operative law—principles, commentaries and national reports. Intersentia, Cambridge—Antwerp—Portland

FAO (1998) A Study of Cooperative Legislations in selected Asian and Pacific Countries. Food and Agricultural Organization

Henrÿ H (2013a) Public international cooperative law. In: Cracogna D et al. (eds), International handbook of cooperative law. Springer, pp 65–88

Henrÿ H (2013b) Guidelines for cooperative legislation. International Labor Organization

Münkner H (2015) Co-operative principles and co-operative law. Lit Verlag

Pönkä V (2019) Are cooperative societies transforming into cooperative companies? reflections on the finnish cooperatives Act. Euro Bus Law Rev 1:77–99

Tadjudje W (2020) Standardization of cooperative law in Africa: a comparative analysis between the ohada act related to cooperative societies and the East Africa community's cooperative societies bill. Int J Cooperat Law 3:31–45

Tadjudje W (2021) Le droit des coopératives en Afrique—réflexions sur l'Acte uniforme de l'OHADA. Epure. Reims, France

Theron J (2010) Cooperative policy and law in east and southern Africa: a review, CoopAfrica Working Paper 18. ILO, Dar es Salam

[11] We extend our thanks to Mr. Ajibola Akanji for his assistance.

[12] Akira Kurimoto, Carlos Vargas Vasserot, Charles Gould, Clément Labi, Dante Cracogna, David Hiez, Deolinda Meira, Emanuele Cusa, Frank Lowery, Ger van der Sangen, Hans-H. Münkner, Ian Adderley, Ian Snaith, Itziar Villafáñez Pérez, Leonardo Rafael De Souza, Marina Aguilar Rubio, Mario de Conto, Santosh Kumar, Sofia Adam and Yiorgos Alexopoulos.

Contents

Editors and Contributors

About the Editors

Willy Tadjudje is a Cooperative Law Specialist with experience in teaching, research and consulting. He is an Associate Lecturer at the University of Luxembourg, a Lecturer at the University of Yaoundé II (Cameroon) and a Researcher at the Université Catholique de Louvain (Belgium). Apart from teaching and research, he usually works with international organisations for the promotion of cooperative law and social and solidarity economy. He is also a registered mediator in Belgium and Luxembourg. As such he has been supporting apex organisations in Africa on the establishment of Alternative Disputes Mechanisms. Willy Tadjudje is a member of several expert groups, and the authors of books and articles.

Ifigeneia Douvitsa is an Adjunct Professor Hellenic Open University in Greece. She is a Specialist of Cooperative Law in Europe. She provides advices to cooperative organisations in Greece and Europe. She is a member of expert groups including the Cooperative Law Committee of the International Cooperative Alliance (ICA).

Contributors

Marina Aguilar-Rubio Tax Law, Law School, Social Economy and Cooperative Law Research Center (CIDES), University of Almeria, Almeria, Spain

Orisel Hernandez Aguilar Legal Sciences, Law Department of the University of Pinar del Río, Pinar del Río, Cuba

Ajibola Anthony Akanji Faculty of Law, Lead City University, Ibadan, Nigeria

Dante Cracogna University of Buenos Aires, Buenos Aires, Argentina

Emanuele Cusa Business Law, Università degli Studi di Milano-Bicocca (University of Milano-Bicocca), Milan, Italy

Leonardo Rafael de Souza Pontifical Catholic University of Paraná, Curitiba, Brazil

Ifigeneia Douvitsa Hellenic Open University, Patra, Greece

Gemma Fajardo-García University of Valencia, Valencia, Spain

Antonio Fici Private Law, University of Tor Vergata, Roma, Italy

Yu. M. Goryachkovskaya Belgorod University of Cooperation, Economics and Law, Belgorod, Russia

Peter Herrmann Human Rights Centre, Law School of Central South University, Changsha, China

David Hiez University of Luxembourg, Esch-sur-Alzette, Luxembourg

Akira Kurimoto Japan Co-operative Alliance, Katsushika-ku, Tokyo, Japan

V. V. Kutko Belgorod University of Cooperation, Economics and Law, Belgorod, Russia

Tapani Köppä University of Helsinki Ruralia Institute, Helsinki, Finland

Deolinda Meira CEOS/ISCAP/Polytechnic of Oporto, São Mamede de Infesta, Portugal

Georg Miribung Faculty of Science and Technology, Free University of Bozen-Bolzano, Bolzano, BZ, Italy

Orestes Rodríguez Musa Legal Sciences, Law Department of the University of Pinar del Río, Pinar del Río, Cuba

Hans-H. Münkner University of Marburg, Marburg, Germany

Santosh Kumar Padmanabhan Director of Legislation, International Cooperative Alliance, Brussels, Belgium

Graciela Fernández Quintas Co-operatives of the Americas, Region of the International Co-operative Alliance, San José, Costa Rica

G. A. Semenenko Belgorod University of Cooperation, Economics and Law, Belgorod, Russia

Yifat Solel Law School, Haifa University, Haifa, Israel

Willy Tadjudje Université Catholique de Louvain, Ottignies-Louvain-la-Neuve, Belgium

Robby Tulus International Cooperative Alliance, Cooperatives in the Asia Pacific Region, New Delhi, India

G. J. H. van der Sangen Department Private, Business and Labour Law, Tilburg Law School, Tilburg, Netherlands

Itziar Villafáñez Pérez Faculty of Economics and Business, University of the Basque Country (UPV/EHU), Bilbao, Spain

Introduction

A General Introduction to Cooperative Law

Willy Tadjudje and Ifigeneia Douvitsa

Cooperative law is at a crossroads. It is trying to find its way, despite the pitfalls it encounters. The contributors to this honorary volume have underlined several of these difficulties, in particular when addressing issues related to the history or the hierarchy of legal norms (constitutionalisation of cooperative law). They have also highlighted some of them, by analysing the link between cooperative law and social and solidarity economy law, as well as the legal specificities and the very essence of cooperatives. Finally, they have highlighted it by examining cooperative law through the prism of sustainable development, and various issues related to the activities and governance of cooperatives.

Developments are uneven when compared from one country to another, and from one region to another. However, one convergence emerges: cooperative law is struggling to establish its authenticity. Cooperative lawyers have a lot of work to do, at the educational level, to raise the level of understanding of cooperative law in all spheres, including at the decision-making levels. Therefore, the idea of introducing cooperative law courses in education and training settings appears particularly urgent. It might be justified, on the one hand, by the fact that cooperatives can pursue not only economic but also social and cultural aspirations. It might also be justified, on the other hand, by the ability of cooperatives to engage in activities in all spheres of human life. This emergency has since been reported by the United Nations:

1. United Nations General Assembly, Economic and Social Council: "Given the important contributions of the cooperative movement to education, a number of enabling measures might be useful including the provision of public funds if they are made available to other forms of enterprise for educational programmes. Governments may also consider the inclusion within the national curricula at all

W. Tadjudje (✉)
Université Catholique de Louvain, Ottignies-Louvain-la-Neuve, Belgium
e-mail: willy.tadjudje@uclouvain.be

I. Douvitsa
Hellenic Open University, Athens, Greece

W. Tadjudje and I. Douvitsa (eds.), *Perspectives on Cooperative Law*,
https://doi.org/10.1007/978-981-19-1991-6_1

levels of the study of the values principles, history, current and potential contribution of the cooperative movement to national society; and encouragement and support of specialised studies in cooperatives at the tertiary level".[1]
2. ILO Recommendation 193 concerning the Promotion of Cooperatives (2002) paragraph 8.1.f: "National policies should notably: (…) (f) promote education and training in cooperative principles and practices, at all appropriate levels of the national education and training systems, and in the wider society".

1 Historical and Constitutional Developments in Cooperative Law

Research in cooperative law reveals that cooperatives, in their modern form, originated in Europe[2] and then were transported to other parts of the world.[3] However, in the territories where cooperatives were introduced, there were probably other forms of collaboration close to the cooperative form.[4] In any case, Dante Cracogna presents a 50-year history of cooperative law in Latin America. This is a fairly long period, with considerable developments and advances, both at national and regional levels. In the African context, the approach is national and Akanji Ajibola presents the evolution of cooperative law in the particular context of Nigeria. His analysis may have particular resonance for African countries that were colonised by the British.

Taking into account the colonial heritage and local specificities, Robby Tulus traces the history of cooperative law in Asia. Beyond that, he presents the role of the state, which at one time used cooperatives. Finally, he discusses the role, in more recent times, of ILO Recommendation 193 in clarifying the role of the state in the development of cooperatives.[5]

Historically, constitutions have remained an important source of law,[6] including for cooperative law. In most countries, the constitution is the fundamental norm and prevails even over international treaties and conventions.[7] It is in that dynamic that the mention or treatment of cooperative law in a country's constitution can have an impact on the strength of that law. Ifigeneia Douvitsa addresses the issue of the constitutionalisation of cooperative law. She points out that this phenomenon is very common in Latin American countries. She thus presents an overview of the incorporation of cooperative law into constitutions, and the legal consequences of such mechanism. In the specific context of Cuba, Orestes Rodríguez Musa and Orisel Hernandez Aguilar highlight an important innovation introduced by the 2019 Cuban

[1] Cooperatives in Social Development, Report of Secretary General (A/56/73–E/2001/68).
[2] Seeberger (2014).
[3] For the African context, see Tadjudje (2017).
[4] Lipeb (1984).
[5] See also Henrÿ (2018).
[6] Hardt and Heringa (2014).
[7] Merli (2015).

constitution. Indeed, it incorporates provisions of cooperative law that have helped to unify the field, as previously there were two statutes that seemed to be in conflict. In Cuba, the constitutionalisation of cooperative law would have changed the history of cooperative law in that country in a positive manner.

2 Cooperative Law and Social and Solidarity Economy Law

The social and solidarity economy (SSE) is institutionally defined as a sector including cooperatives, mutual societies, associations and foundations.[8] Depending on the country, other legal forms are also allowed. This is the case, for example, with social enterprises.[9] Moreover, depending on the legislation, the above-mentioned legal forms are either admitted automatically or, in some respects, subject to the fulfilment of a number of conditions.[10]

Cooperatives exist in all countries of the world,[11] but the same is not verifiable for other legal forms related to the SSE. They are the main legal form of the sector as the normative framework of cooperatives is the main sub-base of SSE law.[12]

David Hiez opens an interesting debate on whether cooperatives belong to the SSE or not. He acknowledges that in most countries with SSE legislation, cooperatives are included. However, he questions the situation in countries that do not recognise SSE, or in countries that do not provide a list of SSE entities. In the end, he presents the advantages of including cooperatives in the SSE sector.

Marina Aguilar Rubio discusses Agricultural Processing Companies in Spain, with a focus on their taxation. She shows that agricultural processing companies are civil companies with an economic and social purpose, established for the production, processing and marketing of agricultural; livestock or forestry products; the improvement of the rural environment and the promotion and development of agriculture and the provision of common services that serve this purpose. By definition, they are not cooperatives, but they have features that are shared by SSE entities. Marina Rubio believes that the Spanish legislator should promote agricultural processing companies, by using taxation.

Even if the terminology is different, Italy, through the reference to a "third sector" deals more or less with the same reality.[13] Antonio Fici places us at the heart of the latest innovations in Italian law. He explains, in particular, the transition from non-profit organisations governed by the civil code to third sector organisations (TSO)

---

[8] Caire and Tadjudje (2019).

[9] Defourny and Nyssens (2013).

[10] Hiez (2021).

[11] Henrÿ (2013b).

[12] Caire and Tadjudje (2019).

[13] Poirier (2014).

governed by the code of the third sector. Consequently, social enterprises and social cooperatives are particular types of third sector organisations.

3 Legal Specificities and the Essence of Cooperatives

At the international level, the Statement on International Cooperative Identity provides a definition, principles and values of cooperatives. This Statement is not a source of law, as its author, the International Cooperative Alliance (ICA), is only a private association. Nevertheless, the definition, principles and values of cooperatives as set out in the ICA International Statement have been incorporated into ILO Recommendation 193, which infuses them with a certain legal value in public international cooperative law.[14] However, cooperative laws are most often an interpretation of the principles and values of cooperatives.[15] Therefore, from one country to another, the laws are different insofar as the interpretation takes into account various economic, historical, social, political, or cultural parameters.

In Japan, Akira Kurimoto analyses the impact of cooperative legislation on cooperative structure and culture. He points out, firstly, that Japanese cooperative law is fragmented, with diverse laws governing a variety of cooperative sectors. On the other hand, he specifies that "the lack of a general or basic law on cooperatives is one of the reasons why the identity as a cooperative sector has not been nurtured". A general cooperative law, followed by specific legislation, would, in his view, better preserve the identity of cooperatives, and thus the specificities they embody.

The situation in Japan is mirrored in the Russian context. In Russia, there are general cooperative provisions in the constitution, as well as in the civil code. Above all, there are various special laws regulating sectors of cooperative activity. Yu. M. Goryachkovskaya, G.A. Semenenko and V.V. Kutko believe that " (...) the main problem concerning the legal regulation of cooperatives in Russia is the lack of a general framework law on cooperatives, which would enshrine the general legal framework for cooperatives, their legal status, the procedure for creation, reorganization and dissolution".

In a more general approach, Hans Münkner questions the management and regulation of the cooperative difference. In his contribution, he addresses different issues, notably the definition of the cooperative, the analysis of its operating principles, as well as the way in which these principles can be taken over by cooperative law to preserve such cooperative difference. He also discusses various challenges for the legislator and the thorny issue of the companisation of cooperative law. This last aspect is also addressed by Leonardo Rafael De Souza who presents the evidence in Brazil. Similarly, Ger J.H. van der Sangen addresses this issue in the Dutch context. It is true that he talks about the hybridisation of cooperatives, but this still refers to the notion of companisation as analysed by Leonardo De Souza in the case of Brazil.

---

[14] Henrÿ (2013a).

[15] Münkner (2015).

Yifat Solel also analyses the problem of companisation. Beyond that, she also deals with the issue of digitalisation which is extensively examined by Peter Hermann.

In a modern approach, Peter Hermann takes us into the field of technology and artificial intelligence (AI). He points out that: "Cooperatives are forms that, if combined with digitisation and AI, are well positioned to enhance the potentialities, providing a ground on which they can be transformed into real options and realities—in fact coops specifically define what a sufficiently wide and creative understanding of digitisation and AI means and *vice versa*, digitisation and AI grant a huge potential to elevate the idea of cooperatives on a larger scale. A central point, and with this a major challenge for economics and jurisprudence, is given by the fact of reshuffling the elements of the process of production, namely production in *strictu* sensu, consumption as productive process, distribution and exchange". In his view, digitalisation and AI can contribute to the broad dissemination of the message and specificity of cooperatives.

The specificity and essence of cooperatives is, depending on the country, also defended and protected by public policies, beyond the specific contributions of the law.[16] Public policies can be seen as important measures for the implementation of cooperative law. They are adopted by the state (in collaboration with the cooperative movement) as mechanisms to promote cooperatives.[17] Graciela Fernandez examines the relationship between the state and cooperatives in the specific context of Uruguay. She places particular emphasis on current public policies.

4 Cooperative Law and Sustainable Development

The approximation between cooperative law and sustainable development is a subject dear to Hagen Henrÿ.[18]

From the outset, Deolinda Meira makes the link between the cooperative principles and the notion of sustainable development in a specific European context. As she explains, cooperatives are best described as atypical business organisations, and this is evidenced by a set of features reflected in the PECOL (Principles of European Cooperative Law). More precisely, she underlines that the PECOL[19] related to cooperative governance are consistent with the concept of sustainability.

Santosh Kumar takes us to the heart of the notion of the intangible cultural heritage of humanity. He underlines that the United Nations Education, Scientific and Cultural Organization (UNESCO) included the "Idea and Practice of the Organization of Shared Interests in Cooperatives" on the Representative list of Intangible Cultural Heritage of Humanity based on the submission made by the

[16] Münkner (1973).

[17] Ingraham (1975).

[18] Henrÿ (2013c).

[19] For more details see Fajardo et al. (2017).

German Hermann-Schulze-Delitzsch-Gesellschaft e. V. and the Friedrich-Wilhelm-Raiffeisen-Gesellschaft in 2016.

Following Santosh Kumar, Tapani Köppä advocates for a more sustainable world. It is based on the contribution of cooperatives, as well as on certain values, notably *fraternité* with all its sisters, especially solidarity.

Georg Miribung tries to analyse the principle of sustainability by using the specific case of agricultural cooperatives in Italian private law. He points out that "Using agricultural cooperatives as an example, I argue that Italian private law contains some interesting features—specific constraints on the patrimony—that might help to better conceptualise legal rules that aim to make the principle of sustainability more concrete and—maybe—ultimately legally enforceable".

As Georg Miringung focusses on the agricultural cooperative sector to understand the concept of sustainable development, Emanuele Cusa is interested in the energy cooperative sector. He addresses the issue of energy through the lens of sustainable development and the cooperative legal form. He begins by linking the notion of sustainable development to that of energy consumption and to that of the cooperative. Subsequently, he analyses recent developments in European energy law, in particular, energy communities. He considers that the renewable energy communities, under the European model, are true energy cooperatives.

Finally, in a less systematic approach, Willy Tadjudje reflects on the potential of cooperatives to provide sustainable responses to rural development in Africa. He believes that the cooperative form has a lot of potential, in terms of sustainability, but that this potential is little used. In the end, he lays the groundwork for a cooperative revival in Africa, in which cooperatives can play a key role in sustainable development.

5 Legal Developments Regarding Cooperatives Activities and Governance

Depending on the country, cooperative law materialises itself with a particular physiognomy. Sometimes there is a general law, followed by specific laws depending on the activity. In other cases, there is only one or the other (a general law or special laws).[20] In any case, cooperatives are supposed to be allowed to engage in activities in all areas of human life. Such openness for the cooperative form may have managerial consequences, especially if cooperatives engage in a variety of activities at the same time. This is what Gemma Fajardo-García calls Multi-activity, Multi-stakeholder and Community Interest Cooperatives. According to her, multi-activity cooperatives provide services to the same homogeneous group of members (producers, consumers or workers). Multi-stakeholder cooperatives are differentiated by their provision of services to heterogeneous groups of members. Community interest cooperatives, in contrast, are those in which community interest holds a highly significant position in

---

[20] Henrÿ (2013b).

the cooperative and is even said to surpass the members' own interests. She presents the legal framework in a comparative and prospective approach.

Mobility is important for the human race and the cooperative movement can contribute to a qualitative and quantitative improvement of supply in the transport sector. Knowing that cooperatives can engage in activities in a variety of sectors, Itziar Villafáñez Pérez presents the case of transport cooperatives in Spain. She insists, in particular, on the complexity of the sector, the types of means of transport, while making proposals for a better regulation of the said sector.

References

Caire G, Tadjudje W (2019) Toward a global legal culture of the SSE Enterprise? Int Comparison SSE Legislation RECMA 353:74–88

Defourny J, Nyssens M (2013) L'approche EMES de l'entreprise sociale dans une perspective comparative », EMES Working Papers 13/02

Fajardo et al (2017) Principles of European co-operative law—principles, commentaries and national reports. Intersentia, Cambridge–Antwerp–Portland

Hardt S, Heringa AW (2014) Sources of constitutional law, Intersentia, 1st edn

Henrÿ H (2013a) Public international cooperative law. In: Cracogna D et al (eds) International handbook of cooperative law. Springer, Heidelberg, pp 65–88

Henrÿ H (2013b) Guidelines for cooperative legislation. International Labor Organization

Henrÿ H (2013c) Cooperative law and sustainable development match or mismatch? In: Draft paper prepared for the UNRISD conference potential and limits of social and solidarity economy 6–8 May 2013, Geneva, Switzerland. https://www.unrisd.org/sse-draft-henry

Henrÿ H (2018) Trends in cooperative legislation: what needs harmonizing? J Res Trade Manage Econ Dev 1(9):7–16

Hiez D (2021) Guide pour la rédaction d'un droit de l'ESS. Guidelines SSE-IF

Ingraham CH (1975) Policies—the key to a successful cooperative. The Ohio State University

Lipeb M (1984) Common and diverging elements of autochthonous self-help organisations and cooperatives—possibilities and problems of a synthesis. In: Münkner H-H (ed) Towards adjusted patterns of cooperatives in developing countries, Results of a Symposium towards an African cooperative, Friedrich-Ebert-Stiftung, pp 45–56

Merli F (2015) Principle of legality and the hierarchy of norms. In: Schroeder W (ed) Strengthening the rule of law in Europe: from a common concept to mechanisms of implementation. Bloomsbury Publishing PLC, pp 37–45

Münkner H (1973) La loi coopérative, instrument de promotion des coopératives par l'Etat. Inf Coopératives 1:27–43

Münkner H (2015) Co-operative principles and co-operative law. Lit Verla

Poirier Y (2014) Économie sociale solidaire et concepts apparentés. Les origines et les définitions: une perspective internationale, RIFRESS

Seeberger L (2014) History of the Evolution of Cooperative Law from Its Origins to the Present Day Recma 333:67–79

Tadjudje W (2017) L'évolution historique du droit des sociétés coopératives en Afrique. In: Hiez D, Kenmogne Simo A (eds) Droit des coopératives OHADA. Presses Universitaires d'Aix-Marseille, pp 89–105

Background and Contribution of Hagen Henrÿ to the Development of Cooperative Law

David Hiez

If I had to define Hagen Henrÿ, knowing that my perception is both partial and biased, I would say that he is characterized by two main features: a German man in the globalized world and a man conflicted between academy and practice. Culturally, he is German by his parents, his birth, his education, but he has lived most of his life in Helsinki, his wife is Finnish, and he spent between 1 and 7 years in the US, Madagascar, Switzerland, France, and Guatemala—leaving aside his many professional journeys around the world. In that sense, he is a very post-modern man. Meanwhile, from the beginning of his career to his retirement, he taught at the University, even if most of his time was dedicated to practitioner's activities.

Hagen Henrÿ was born in 1951 into the Deutsche Demokratische Republik, 2 years after its creation. His family moving to the West, he spent his 3 first years in a refugee camp, with the difficulties one can imagine. His education has been that of any German boy of that time. But soon he revealed his attraction to foreign countries. Actually, he spent 1 year studying in the U.S.A. before passing his Abitur, and traveled elsewhere after his Staatexam. During the 1970s, he was a perfect German law student, fully completing the tough German law courses, with their double examinations and legal practice training. However, his educational context was not purely German. He began in the border University of Saarbrücken, and quickly, at the end of the 1970s, moved on to Geneva and Paris to achieve post-graduate qualifications in development law. Later, he studied in Helsinki, in his new adopted country. That first orientation in comparative law and law and development, not always known to his current colleagues, remained for many years and made an indelible mark on his career and scientific publications. In 2004, he defended a PhD in comparative law, at the University of Helsinki.

I thank Dante Cracogna for his advice and Ian Snaith for his revision of English.

D. Hiez (✉)
University of Luxembourg, Esch-sur-Alzette, Luxembourg
e-mail: david.hiez@uni.lu

W. Tadjudje and I. Douvitsa (eds.), *Perspectives on Cooperative Law*,
https://doi.org/10.1007/978-981-19-1991-6_2

Like most academics, he started teaching during his student days. After his Staatsexamen, he became, and remained throughout the 1980s a legal adviser for both German public administration and Finnish economic organizations.

Meanwhile, he started to collaborate with Hans H. Münkner in Marburg during the 1980s, as comparativist and specialist in law and development. During that period, he came across cooperative law, but did not focus on it. Cooperative Law became a specialism after he left the Ministry of Employment, when Hans H. Münkner made that proposal to him in a telephone call. Even if it did not take the usual academic form, from that period a close and very respectful relationship developed between them, with Herr Münkner acting as a *Thesisvater*. It is not yet 30 years since Hagen Henrÿ first devoted himself to Cooperative Law, and yet we all think he was born into it, given all that he has achieved. Professionally, however, Hagen Henrÿ worked for many years as a freelance consultant and, separately, as a part time academic at the University of Helsinki. After a decade, he had become an excellent specialist in Cooperative Law, with worldwide experience. Based on that, he was appointed in 2007 as Head of the Cooperative Branch in the International Labor Office (ILO). When he left in 2011, he became Research Director at the University of Helsinki Ruralia Institute, where he was appointed as adjunct professor in 2004. There he acquired the academic position he needed to develop his scientific activities.

Throughout his career, his successes were punctuated by awards (Prize for the best teaching and research performance of the School for Cooperative Studies, doctorate honoris causà, etc.) and evidenced by scientific roles entrusted to him by his peers (editorial board membership for about ten journals, roles in diverse international academic associations, etc.). Having briefly described his professional life. It is enough to say in respect of his personal life that he and his wife have three children and are now grandparents. However, readers who don't know him personally may appreciate more information about his scientific work, since that is the main reason for the dedication of this book to him.

Hagen's academic activities have three pillars: law and development, comparative law, and cooperative law. This is true both for his teaching and for his publications. Certainly, his first productions did not concern cooperatives, and the later ones do not deal specifically with comparative law or law and development. However, the two latter topics still remain part of his concerns. I am not a specialist in either law and development or comparative law, and I have not read enough of Hagen Henry's writings in that field; therefore, I will not deal with them. However, from his publications on cooperative law, I think we can extract two main features and draw two major aspects of his legal thinking.

First of all, law and development is the basis of all his work. This assessment may surprise many, since Hagen Henry's publications on African property law are now rather ancient. Can we link that first research area with his recurrent interest for sustainable development? The linkage is, to me, rather superficial and looks more like an instance of a collective concern, particularly by the international organizations in which he has been involved. On the contrary, his familiarity with development and its importance for countries outside Western Europe and North America oriented his whole professional life but also his conception of cooperative law. Indeed, no other cooperative lawyer has such a wide knowledge of various cooperative laws, and this, to me, is Hagen's unique quality. Through his work with international organizations, and through his consultancy work for many legislators, he became familiar with many cooperative laws. That worldwide experience has been the basis for an incomparable network, but has also fed Hagen's thinking on cooperative law.

Then comes his comparative law approach. So strongly dedicated to his work of consultancy was Hagen that he did not always have time to produce extensive publications on the cooperative legislation on which he worked. In other words, he did not make systematic and dogmatic studies of national cooperative legislation. His approach has been more synthetic. Convinced that law is not autopoietic, probably because of his practical experiences, he usually mitigated his legal considerations with reasoning coming from economics, politics, and ethics. Therefore, his work calls for an open-minded conception of law, close to an inter-disciplinary method.

To conclude, although not perceptible at a first glance, Hagen's cooperative thinking has long been influenced by an intricate combination of action and research, and actors and thinkers. The thinking of Hagen Henrÿ is strongly influenced by his actions. He has not been a cooperator (his civic engagement has been to chair an association), but he has interacted with many of them. That creates a bias because he has not been a legal advisor to cooperators in their day-to-day life, but to legislators wishing to establish a framework for cooperatives. I can't measure the consequences of that bias, but I believe that there are some. Perhaps the most meaningful consequence is that his research has never been abstract or purely academic, but rather dictated by practical considerations.

If we jump from methodology to substance, I would personally note two main recurrent themes in his writings. The first is his demonstration of the existence of cooperative law as part of Public International Law. Inspired by his commitment to the implementation of ILO Recommendation R193 on support for cooperatives, he developed the firm conviction that the limited normativity or legal force of that Recommendation and other international sources of law in national legal systems should be overcome and that it is both important and urgent to make a systematic and dogmatic inquiry into the content of these sources. On that point, he remains the major academic reference.

The second axis of his research is about cooperative principles. He did not stop questioning the relationship between cooperative principles and positive law. This was the occasion for him to insist on the necessary coordination between international and national levels, and to emphasize how cooperative principles were a fruitful medium between abstract positive law and cooperative practice.

This analysis, if it is relevant at all, does not properly fit with Hagen Henry's achievements, since I focused only on his scientific publications, which represent probably less than one-quarter of his professional activity. Knowing that, I will nevertheless try to draw some key conclusions to describe his achievements in that field. Firstly, and all other outcomes flow from this, he has strongly contributed to the development of cooperative law during the last two decades. I can give two examples of that evolution, and Hagen was the main initiator for both. From the cooperative side, the creation of a law committee in the ICA evidences the growing attention paid by cooperatives to that question. From the academic side, Hagen was one of the founders of the first European network of cooperative lawyers (Study Group on European Cooperative Law, SGECOL) and then of the first worldwide network (Iuscooperativum), which publish the only International Journal of Cooperative Law (IJCL) and organizes the international forum on cooperative law, thanks to Hagen's energy and support. Of course, Hagen was not alone, and this evolution comes probably more from events than from individuals, but he has been clever enough to perceive the evolution and establish a framework to accompany and stimulate it.

The second treasure we owe to him is his academic output. The most famous is probably his guidelines on cooperative law, published several times. But he is also one of the editors of the only existing book which covers the cooperative law of most countries all over the world. Similarly, he is one of the drafters of the European principles of cooperative law and of the editors of the related book. But he has also written more than 100 articles, not forgetting all his lectures and speeches which were not always published. Partly because they were given in various languages in many countries and partly because cooperative law is only an emerging autonomous discipline, all these sources are widely dispersed and often not easy to access. If we could have a request to make to our friend and colleague, it would be to collect the most important ones and to publish them in a single volume.

To discuss my memories of working with Hagen, I must deal with courtesy, calmness, generosity, modesty and tenacity. Courtesy, since Hagen is always the same with everyone, with an immutable politeness, perhaps a little outdated. Calmness: I never saw him express anger, even when I knew he was irritated. These two features perhaps give him a something of the image of a protestant man, but without any puritanism and with perfect tolerance of the personality of others. Probably this is related to his generosity: simply always ready to pay the drinks, but also more academically the support to others' projects and development, dedicating his time and offering his network. Modesty: always ready to be behind others, always insisting on the merits of others, and that was not an affectation for he never denied his own merits when they existed, to the extent necessary to achieve the collective objective. And besides this, tenacity: he calmly, modestly, and politely sought the objective he desired and did not deviate from the route he had planned. We know the outcome. It was the number and the quality of the jewels he made.

All this belongs to Hagen Henrÿ, since he worked it out, but it belongs also to the scientific community, for which it is a legacy. It is now our common responsibility to cultivate it.

Historical and Constitutional Developments in Cooperative Law

Fifty Years in Latin American Cooperative Law

Dante Cracogna

To my friend Hagen Henrÿ, for his dream without borders.

1 Stages of Regional Cooperative Law

Initially, it would be convenient to put into an historical perspective the evolution of Cooperative Law in the region, in order to understand how it reached its present status, which is the result of a process that has undergone different stages. This contextualization allows for the appreciation of its evolutionary direction and a better understanding of its reality and current problems.[1]

As it may be logically inferred, Latin American cooperation—notwithstanding its background, which can be traced back to social organizations of peoples existing in the Americas prior to its Discovery—derives its existence from the European experiences of the mid-nineteenth century, which are the model for what we now know as cooperatives in the modern sense of the word. It is from then that we can speak of the origin of Cooperative Law.

The origins. The first manifestations of Cooperative Law are the legal provisions on cooperatives appearing in the commercial codes of Argentina[2] and México[3] of 1889. These pioneer stipulations show serious deficiencies in the characterization of cooperatives, which is not surprising considering their early emergence, when

[1] For an approach to this topic see: Cracogna (1992), p. 195.

[2] The Argentine Commercial Code included only three sections (392 to 394) referring to cooperatives, whereby it provided for the establishment of cooperatives under any of the forms set forth for business organizations, with open membership and withdrawal rights and under a one-member one-vote rule.

[3] On its part, Section 238 of the Mexican Commercial Code, following the French law of 1867, set forth that a cooperative company was "that which because of its nature proper is formed by members whose number and capital are variable."

D. Cracogna (✉)
University of Buenos Aires, Buenos Aires, Argentina
e-mail: dcracogna@estudiocracogna.com.ar

W. Tadjudje and I. Douvitsa (eds.), *Perspectives on Cooperative Law*,
https://doi.org/10.1007/978-981-19-1991-6_3

in Europe the legislation thereon was still at a very primitive stage. It should be pointed out that in both abovementioned countries there already existed embryonic cooperative experiences, so the legislation came to address a pre-existing reality. This stage carries onto WWI.

Specific legislation. In the period of time between WWI and WWII specific laws on cooperatives were enacted in different countries, some of which had background on that area—such as Argentina and Mexico (laws of 1926 and 1938, respectively)—and others had not, as was the case of Chile (1925), Colombia (1931), Brazil (1932), and Ecuador (1937). These laws, some of which were incorporated into existing codes, outlined cooperatives more accurately from a legal standpoint and are the foundation for the later evolution of Cooperative Law.

Promotion stage. Following WWII, cooperative legislation expanded in the countries of the region and even some provisions regulating cooperatives were included in several National Constitutions.[4] The Organization of American States (OAS), through its Cooperatives Section of the Department of Economic and Social Development, played a significant role in providing technical assistance and consulting services to governments in the drafting of cooperative legislation.[5] Also in this stage, which continued until the late 60s, cooperatives became relevant in the agrarian reform statutes enacted in different countries.

Consolidation stage. The subsequent stage, which continues today, began with the First Continental Congress on Cooperative Law held in Mérida in 1969, which is the starting point for a scientific approach to this matter. Even when prior to such Congress there already existed significant contributions made by different authors, it is after Mérida that the discipline was given a more serious theoretical approach and the results thereof incorporated into numerous national statutes. Moreover, during this stage, the existing legislation underwent an important process of modernization and considerable progress was made, such as with the Project for a Framework Law for Cooperatives of Latin America and the Statute of Mercosur Cooperatives, to both of which we shall refer hereinbelow.

2 The Legal Theory of Cooperation

It should be noted that, following the legislation on cooperatives enacted in different countries, scholarly works building a legal theory on this topic started to emerge, with a varying degree of intensity. The Argentinian case is revealing since, exception made

[4] It is interesting to remember that the Mexican National Constitution, considered one of the founders of social constitutionalism, makes express mention of cooperatives in Sections 28 and 123, whereby they are recognized as entities of collective benefit. Subsequently, the Constitutions of other countries started to acknowledge cooperatives, to different degrees. A remarkable example of this is the Federal Constitution of Brazil of 1988, which contains seven provisions on cooperatives.

[5] It needs to be highlighted that OAS Letter of 1948 acknowledges the importance of the contribution of cooperatives to society life and the development of nations.

of the first doctoral dissertation on cooperatives[6] submitted with the Law School of the University of Buenos Aires, the initial legal scholarly works on this matter were subsequent to the amendment of the Commercial Code of 1889, which introduced cooperatives into national statutes.

This is the way it happened in the other countries of the region, where, in general, the approach to the theoretical study of cooperatives was explanatory or reduced to mere commentary. However, this does not signify that the work done by pioneer legal scholars is without merit. Thanks to them, knowledge regarding the regulation of cooperatives was disseminated and it became possible to compare them to other civil and commercial organizations, thus resulting in the origin of their differentiation from the latter and in an emerging critical appreciation of their unique nature.

By mid-twentieth century some works that went beyond a descriptive approach and attempted at building a legal theory of cooperatives[7] became known. This endeavor was made in different countries, but we should highlight the cases of Mexico, Brazil, and Venezuela. In the first, a Mexican author made the initial approach toward the notion of "cooperative act" in his work titled, precisely, "Cooperative Law"[8]; in the second, Waldirio Bulgarelli and Walmor Franke made significant contributions in the 1960s and the beginning of the 1970s[9]; and in the third, Jaime Daly Guevara published his dissertation, which is also titled "Cooperative Law."[10]

These foundational landmarks evolved into an independent discipline of continental Cooperative Law, conceived with a scientific nature, and the subsequent congresses on Cooperative Law held after 1969 advanced its progress.

3 Congresses on Cooperative Law

In the 1960s, the Organization of the Cooperatives of America (OCA) worked intensely in promoting the progress of cooperative legislation in the Americas and in encouraging the study of Cooperative Law. To that effect, a Law Committee was created, which started by both bringing together legal scholars from different countries interested in this topic and raising awareness of it within the Organization.

One of the most consequential initiatives taken by the abovementioned committee was the call to the First Continental Congress on Cooperative Law held in Mérida

---

[6] Francisco Medina submitted his doctoral dissertation "Cooperative Companies" in 1887, that is to say, prior to the amendment of the Commercial Code of 1889, which included provisions on these legal entities for the first time. See Pastorino (1998), p. 49.

[7] García Müller (2009), p. 31 mentions that the expression "Cooperative Law" began to be used in the 1940s. Even if there exist different opinions in this regard, it can be unquestionably asserted that as from the 1950s the use of this expression was widespread.

[8] Salinas Puente (1954) did a true pioneer work, since it includes—for the first time in the American Continent-extensive analysis of Cooperative Law as well as of the cooperative act.

[9] Bulgarelli (1967), Franke (1973).

[10] Daly Guevara (1967).

in 1969, which was sponsored by the *Universidad de los Andes* and the Bar Association of the State of Mérida. This pioneer Congress brought together delegates from 11 countries who dealt with different topics, such as the relationship between the State and cooperatives, cooperative financing, cooperative integration, enterprise organization, and cooperative principles, but, among them, we must single out the "cooperative act." The closing document of such Congress, known as the "Letter of Merida," adopts and develops the notion of cooperative act in Chapter I, called General Principles.[11] This fundamental concept was formally acknowledged by the legislation of several countries in the region, thus becoming the subject matter of abundant jurisprudence.

After the Mérida Congress, several others were held in different countries and all of them dealt with the notion of cooperative act, since it was considered essential to Cooperative Law. The second congress took place in San Juan de Puerto Rico in 1976[12] and the next was held in Rosario (Argentina) in 1986, with the participation of delegates from 16 countries.[13]

In 1992, Brasilia hosted the IV Congress. Therefore, a special committee was created to deal with comparative Cooperative Law, with the participation of European specialists, and topics such as reserves, cooperative autonomy and self-control and the teaching of cooperative law were also part of the agenda.[14]

After a prolonged interregnum, caused due to the fact that OCA—which had called all previous congresses—had discontinued its activities, in 2013 a new congress was held in Guarujá (Brazil). This time the call was made by the Cooperatives of the Americas, the regional organization of the International Cooperative Alliance (ICA), and OCA's succeeding entity for continental cooperative integration affairs.[15]

Finally, the last congress held so far took place in Montevideo (Uruguay) in 2016, and it was also called by the Cooperatives of the Americas. This congress had as a distinctive feature the fact that it was held simultaneously with the 1st International Forum on Cooperative Law, organized by the Cooperative Law Committee of the International Cooperative Alliance, so it involved the presence of legal scholars from different parts of the world and not only from the American Continent.[16]

In recent years, the Cooperatives of the Americas have regularly included a forum on Cooperative Law among the activities held annually for its regional conference or cooperative summit, where current legal issues are discussed with the participation of the attending delegates. The last of said forums took place in Buenos Aires (Argentina), in October 2018, for the V Cooperative Summit of the Americas.

---

[11] Universidad de Los Andes (1971).

[12] The San Juan Congress approved as its closing document the Carta Jurídica de San Juan. See Administración de Fomento Cooperativo (1976).

[13] AA.VV (1987).

[14] See Organización de las Cooperativas de América (1993).

[15] See Cooperatives of the Americas (2014).

[16] See Cooperatives of the Americas (2018).

4 The Cooperative Act in the Legal Theory

Without a doubt, after the Mérida Congress, the notion of *cooperative act* became the core of Cooperative Law theory, even if, prior to that, such concept was already embryonic.[17] This notion tries to account—from a legal standpoint—for a unique social and economic phenomenon, that of the relationship between a cooperative and its members, which does not fall into the ordinary categories of legal acts since it has features that exceed them.

In broad terms, cooperation is a social phenomenon of unquestionable presence in multiple sectors of economic life and it adopts different forms of expression, which are embodied in a specific organization acknowledged and regulated in a unique manner: the cooperative. This social phenomenon differs from that which manifests itself through ordinary business activity, since the latter was born and operates in order for the people who engage in it to obtain profit or gain, measurable in money. On the contrary, cooperative activity aims primarily at rendering services to satisfy needs through the action of the interested parties properly.[18]

The uniqueness of the cooperative phenomenon becomes strikingly evident when we analyze the legal status of a member who obtains goods from its consumer cooperative and we compare it to that of a client who buys those same goods at a supermarket, or when we look at the legal status of a worker member of a worker cooperative and we contrast it with that of an employee of any certain company, or when we consider the legal status of a member who obtains his/her house from the housing cooperative he/she is a member of when compared to that of an individual acquiring a house through ordinary means. In all these cases, there exists an element in common among those mentioned in the first part of the comparisons made, which sets them apart from those described in the second, although—*prima facie*—it would appear that they are referring to equivalent situations. It is precisely that difference which gives rise to the notion of cooperative act, which is nothing but the proper basis and rationale for a legal theory of cooperation.

This notion arose in the legal field when the Law gave full recognition to a social phenomenon that, due to its unique features, could not be made to fall neatly and easily within traditional legal categories. This is how the notion of cooperative act came into existence in the legal field: not as a random and arbitrary creation of legal theory, but as the need of a new and different reality to be acknowledged as such.

In order to reach this conclusion, the proceeding to be undertaken needs to fulfill two requirements: first, cooperative activity as a fact of social reality needs to be strictly delimited, and then analyzed as a subject matter of legal regulation. The first stage, free from prejudice, needs to provide unbiased criteria that will allow for a later legal conceptualization in conformity to reality.

Once that stage has been completed, the resulting elements need to be contrasted to current legal provisions in order to ascertain whether the same are suitably applicable

---

[17] The first contributions were made by Salinas Puente (1954), p. 150; Daly Guevara (1967), p. 82 and Bulgarelli (1967), p. 91.

[18] Cracogna (2004), p. 45.

to such results or not. If it is determined that they are, then the task shall end there. For example, if it were to be concluded that the activity involved when housing cooperatives acquire real estate to build thereon is a sales contract, or that the activity involved when agricultural cooperatives acquire supplies to provide to their farmer members is a supply agreement, or that consumer cooperatives employ personnel under a labor agreement, etc.

Now, if it is noticed that the elements delimited in the first stage of the analysis do not fit neatly within traditional legal categories—this being either because they do not share all of their elements or because they show different ones—then it will become necessary to further the analysis, in order to determine as accurately as possible which are those relationships, business, or legal acts that are not commercial, civil, or labor in nature, but specifically cooperative. This occurs when members deliver their farm produce to the cooperative for commercialization thereof, or when they take out loans from their credit cooperative or when their car is insured with their insurance cooperative, etc.

In all the abovementioned cases, there appear certain elements that give shape to a legal actor business of a special nature, to wit: (a) certain legally relevant qualities of the subjects intervening in such act: the cooperative and its member; (b) a purpose which is specific to that of the cooperative in question (commercialization, credit, insurance, etc.); and (c) a strictly determined reason or motive: the service rendered to the cooperative member. With its elements so delimited, this legal act appears to be in a category of its own, that is to say, different from any other legal act or business. This is the reason why it is called *cooperative act*.[19] This notion is adopted, on general terms, by the Mérida Letter.[20]

5 The Cooperative Act in the Statutes

As it was mentioned above, after the Mérida Congress the concept of cooperative act started to be acknowledged by the cooperative statutes of many countries of the American Continent, until it practically became a common denominator. Notwithstanding, it should be noted that there exist differences as regards the scope given to such notion and its effects by the said national statutes.

The first case was the incorporation of the concept of cooperative act in Brazilian Law 5764 of 1971, in which Section 79 reads: "Cooperative acts are such acts performed between cooperatives and their members, between members and cooperatives, and between cooperatives when they are associated, for the fulfillment of their cooperative purpose."[21] This provision of Brazilian law may very well be considered

[19] Cracogna (1986), p. 13 where it is included a paper on this topic presented at the Mérida Congress.

[20] Universidad de Los Andes (1971), p. 508.

[21] An early comment on this notion can be found in Franke (1973), p. 23. For more recent works, see: Lopes Becho (2002), p. 148 and Krueger (2004) where there are also included other texts on the cooperative act in Brazilian law in reference to different types of cooperatives.

to be leading in relation to this topic because of the influence it exerted on the statutes of other countries and the scholarly works that originated therefrom.

Argentine Law 20337 of 1973 was the second to incorporate the notion of cooperative act; in this case, with a broader scope, since it considers as cooperative acts even those performed between cooperatives and other individuals (nonmembers) in fulfillment of their cooperative purpose. These are unilateral cooperative acts, that is to say, only for the cooperative.

These are some of the variations of the concept of cooperative act, which has been acknowledged by the statutes of approximately 20 countries of the region, though not without distinctions. Uruguayan Law 18407 of 2008—one of the most recent ones—affords extensive treatment to this topic, even when maintaining the scope of the cooperative act limited to the relationship between members and their cooperatives, and between cooperatives when they are associated. The legal theory developed by scholars, which reached a significant level of evolution, was built upon the guidelines originating from the congresses and the adoption of the concept of cooperative act by the statutes of the different countries of the region.[22]

6 The Project of a Framework Law for Cooperatives of Latin America

Among the promotion undertakings for the progress of Cooperative Law, in 1987 the Law Committee of OCA deemed it advisable to draw up a document that could be used as a guideline for the updating and improvement of cooperative legislation in the countries of the American Continent.

For that reason, a meeting of experts was called and held in Santa Cruz de la Sierra (Bolivia), with the attendance of specialists from different countries of the region. At such meeting, cooperative legislation was the subject matter of critical analysis, and a closing document was drafted under the name of "Basis for cooperative legislation of Latin American Countries," which was later widely circulated in order to receive the opinion of decision-makers and scholars. Subsequently, a new technical meeting was held, where a draft of the "Project for a Framework Law for Cooperatives of Latin America" (the "Project") was discussed. This document was also later disseminated for the collection of feedback.

Finally, the coordinators of the group of experts updated the document using the opinions they had received and submitted it before OCA General Assembly held in Bogotá in November 1988, where it was formally passed. By then, already three congresses on Cooperative Law had been held, which exerted remarkable influence on the preliminary works on the Project.

[22] We should mention, among others, Torres y Torres Lara (1990); Esteller Ortega (1986), Corbella (1985) and Pastorino (1993).

The Project is formally structured as a law, in chapters and sections, each of them including a brief rationale.[23] However, as specified in the introduction, it is not to be considered a "model law" or a text to be replicated, but rather a guide for the modernization and improvement of cooperative legislation, taking into account the most successful experiences and the most appropriate harmonization between the operational requirements of cooperatives and the fundamental principles characterizing them.

The Project starts by characterizing cooperatives and deals with their establishment, members, financial provisions, organs, cooperative integration, dissolution, and liquidation. It also sets forth some provisions regarding State supervision, and the creation of a mixed entity formed by representatives of the State and of cooperatives in order to deal with public policies involving the latter. A significant inclusion is that of the cooperative act, which is defined therein as such act performed between cooperatives and their members, or between cooperatives, in fulfillment of their purpose and subject to Cooperative Law.

The influence the Project exerted on continental cooperative legislation was evident almost immediately with the enactment of the Colombian law of 1988 and later in Honduras, Paraguay, Puerto Rico, Mexico, Panama, Nicaragua, Venezuela, Bolivia, Uruguay, etc. Moreover, it strongly encouraged the furtherance of studies on Cooperative Law.[24]

Changes such as the approval of the Statement on the Cooperative Identity at the International Cooperative Alliance Congress in 1995; UNO Resolution 56/114 on the creation of a favorable environment for Cooperatives; ILO Recommendation 193/2002 on the promotion of cooperatives and the significant developments in comparative Cooperative Law, all occurring during the two subsequent decades, led ICA Americas to resolve an update of the Project in 2007, which was accomplished with the collaboration of ILO.[25]

The updating process was conducted following the same guidelines used for the original drafting of the document, that is, the meeting of a technical team in order to draw up a preliminary document, followed by an extensive process of expert feedback collection. This resulted in a revised version of the Project, which was passed by ICA Americas in 2008.[26] It was later submitted before the Latin American Parliament, which, following broad discussion within different committees thereof, adopted it in 2012, with some adjustments in formalities.[27]

---

[23] The full text was published by the Organización de las Cooperativas de América (1988) in Spanish and Portuguese.

[24] Montolío (1990), p. 232 conducts an extensive research on the background and contents of the Framework Law.

[25] Cracogna (2009), p. 183.

[26] The revised version was published by ACI Americas (2009) in Spanish, Portuguese, and English.

[27] The Latin American Parliament, headquartered in Panama, is formed by members of the different countries of the region. Even though it lacks legislative powers, it can formulate recommendations to national parliaments.

As was the case with the previous Project, the revised version significantly influenced the cooperative laws enacted in the countries of the region as well as the scholarly works on that matter.

7 The Statute of Mercosur Cooperatives

In 2001, the Common Market Group, the executive body of Mercosur, resolved the creation of a Specialized Meeting of Cooperatives of Mercosur (*RECM*), which had, among others, the purpose of developing projects for the promotion of freedom of circulation and establishment of cooperatives in the region. This organ, formed by government officials and representatives of national cooperative organizations of the States Parties, recommended that each country should adopt such measures that would enable and encourage the establishment of cross-border cooperatives and facilitate the legal acknowledgement of cooperatives of the other Mercosur countries.

In order to move in that direction, in 2006, a technical committee was created, which carried out an analysis of the existing background—such as the Statute for a European Cooperative Society[28]—and of the possibilities afforded by both the legal structure and the legislative powers of Mercosur.[29]

On these terms, and following a lengthy internal procedure, the Statute of Mercosur Cooperatives came to be adopted at the Plenary Session of Mercosur Parliament in April 2009.[30] However, only Uruguay has incorporated the Statute into its national legislation through Law 18723, and, taking into account the current relative standstill in Mercosur activity, it does not seem foreseeable that the rest of the countries will take the same action in the short term.

Pursuant to the Statute, Mercosur cooperatives accept members domiciled in more than one State Party and afford them the same status as regards their rights and obligations; they must also provide in their by-laws for the participation of all such members. The members of the incorporating country must represent more than 50% of the total number of members and capital of the cooperatives. Cooperatives named Mercosur Cooperatives may be originally established as such or become so from already incorporated national cooperatives, following a resolution adopted by a supermajority of members at an assembly. The same regulatory system is applied to second-degree cooperatives.[31]

---

[28] Approved as EC Regulation 1453/03.

[29] Different from what is the case in the EU, Mercosur organs do not have their own legislative powers; they are intergovernmental and not supranational. Therefore, regulations originating in Mercosur need to be later passed by each national Parliament and incorporated into national legislation, following the specific procedure thereto, in order to become effective. See Fajardo and Cracogna (2007), p. 479.

[30] It should be pointed out that, even though it is called Mercosur Parliament, this organ also lacks legislative powers, since the projects arising therefrom need to be sent to each national parliament for discussion (Sect. 4, paragraph 14 of the Montevideo Protocol).

[31] Cracogna (2013), p. 165.

8 Conclusion

Half a century after the First Congress on Continental Cooperative Law, during which time this matter has evolved considerably, we should ask ourselves whether it is legitimate to consider that Cooperative Law has achieved its own personality, that is to say, if it is, by now, what we could call scientifically autonomous. As regards legislative autonomy, there is no question that it has already acquired it, even before the aforementioned congress, since cooperative legislation exists set apart from civil, commercial, or corporate statutory provisions—in all the countries of the region. Autonomy in education is perceived in the different universities in which cooperatives are the subject matter of specialized studies, even though academic insertion is still minor,[32]

The existence of a true Cooperative Law entails not only specific laws and regulations on such matter as well as courses for the study thereof. It is also required for it to have its own principles, allowing for the solution to arising problems to be found within a systematic set of rules joined by the same rationale, without having to resort to principles of other branches of the law.[33] In that same sense, Waldirio Bulgarelli concludes that it is from the correspondence between a phenomenon (a group of relationships) and a rule (specific technique) that rules derive their nature and, consequently, the classification into the specific branch of the law to which they belong. He finishes by stating: "This is what happens with Cooperative Law, which is made up of a set of rules ordered and systematized as a whole, with its own technique, and belonging to a certain class of specific relationships, which give it a unique nature, different from the rest."[34]

References

AAVV (1987) Derecho Cooperativo. Anales del III Congreso Continental de Derecho Cooperativo. Rosario, julio de 1986, Idelcoop - Intercoop, Rosario

ACI Américas (2009) Ley Marco para las Cooperativas de América Latina, San José de Costa Rica

Administración de Fomento Cooperativo (1976) Carta Jurídica de San Juan, San Juan de Puerto Rico

Althaus AA (1993) Enseñanza del Derecho Cooperativo. In: Derecho Cooperativo. Tendencias Actuales en Latinoamérica y la Comunidad Económica Europea, Antropos, Bogotá

Bulgarelli W (1967) Elaboraçao do Direito Cooperativo, Ed. Atlas, Sao Paulo

Bulgarelli W (1998) As sociedades cooperativas e sua disciplina juridica. Renovar, Rio de Janeiro

Cooperativas de las Américas (2014) Congreso Continental de Derecho Cooperativo. Guarujá, San Pablo, Brasil. 8, 9 y 10 de octubre de 2013, Intercoop, Buenos Aires

---

[32] Althaus (1993), p. 455.

[33] García Müller (2009), p. 33 mentions different existing opinions regarding the autonomy of Cooperative Law and states that in Latin America the prevailing one is that of acknowledging it as an autonomous discipline.

[34] Bulgarelli (1998), p. 104.

Cooperativas de las Américas (2018) Congreso Continental de Derecho Cooperativo Montevideo 16–18 de noviembre de 2016, Intercoop, Buenos Aires
Corbella C J (1985) Los actos cooperativos, Intercoop, Buenos Aires
Cracogna D (1986) Estudios de Derecho Cooperativo, Intercoop, Buenos Aires
Cracogna D (1992) Problemas actuales del Derecho Cooperativo, Intercoop, Buenos Aires
Cracogna D (2004) O ato cooperativo na América Latina In: en Krueger G, Coordenador, Ato Cooperativo e seu adequado tratamento tributário, Mandamentos Editora, Belo Horizonte
Cracogna D (2009) Nueva versión de la Ley Marco para las Cooperativas de América Latina, Revista Jurídica de Economía Social y Cooperativa, Nº 20, CIRIEC-España, Valencia
Cracogna D (2013) The statute of Mercosur cooperatives In: Cracogna D, Fici A, Henrÿ H (eds) International handbook of cooperative law. Springer, Heidelberg
Daly Guevara J (1967) Derecho Cooperativo. Facultad de Derecho, Universidad Central de Venezuela, Caracas
Esteller Ortega D (1986) El acto cooperativo. Consejo de Profesores Universitarios Jubilados U.C.V., Caracas
Fajardo G, Cracogna D (2007), El derecho cooperativo en la Unión Europea y en el Mercosur. In: Vítolo DR, Embid Irujo JM (eds) El derecho de sociedades en un marco supranacional. Unión Europea y Mercosur. III Congreso Argentino - Español de Derecho Mercantil, Comares, Granada
Franke W (1973) Direito das Sociedades Cooperativas, Ed. Saraiva, Sao Paulo
García Müller A (2009) Instituciones de Derecho Cooperativo, Mutual y Solidario, T. I, Universidad Cooperativa de Colombia, Bogotá
Krueger G (2004) Introduçao. In: Krueger G (coordenador) Ato cooperativo e seu adequado tratamento tributario, Mandamentos, Belo Horizonte
Lopes Becho R (2002) Elementos de Direito Cooperativo, Dialéctica, Sao Paulo
Montolío J M (1990) Legislación Cooperativa en América Latina. Situación, Derecho comparado y Proceso de armonización, Ministerio de Trabajo y Seguridad Social, Madrid
Organización de las Cooperativas de América (1988) América Cooperativa, Documento Especial Nº 3, América Cooperativa, Bogotá
Organización de las Cooperativas de América (1993) Derecho Cooperativo. Tendencias actuales en Latinoamérica y la Comunidad Económica Europea, Antropos, Bogotá
Pastorino R J (1993) Teoría General de Acto Cooperativo, Intercoop, Buenos Aires
Pastorino RJ (1998) Orígenes del Derecho Cooperativo argentino, Intercoop, Buenos Aires
Salinas Puente A (1954) Derecho Cooperativo, Cooperativismo, México
Torres y Torres Lara C (1990) Derecho Cooperativo. La teoría del Acto Cooperativo, INESLA, Lima
Universidad de Los Andes (1971) Primer Congreso Continental de Derecho Cooperativo. Universidad de Los Andes, Mérida (Venezuela)

The Evolution of Cooperative Law: An Appraisal of the Nigerian Situation

Ajibola Anthony Akanji

1 Introduction

The ideal of working together is as old as the indigenous communities within the Nigerian state. Pre-1861, before the advent of British colonialization, there were variants of economics, social, and political structures and various types of economic solidarities among the people of Nigeria. Some of these economic solidarities were called *ajo*, *esusu*, *aaro*, *gayya*, *adashe*, *isisie ego*, *utu*, and *oha*[1] and they were employed for diverse purposes such as agricultural, housing, commerce, and health. These models were reflections of the beliefs, cultures, and norms of the various peoples which were adopted and adapted to the challenges of their time. However, the models of cooperatives were governed by an admixture of group conventions and community codes of conducts, which were products of ethnic and religious ethos.[2] Formal documentations such as writing were alien in the Nigeria of those days, and there was no legislation or forms of written laws.[3] The British took control of the geographical area later named Nigeria from 1861 till 1960, and put in place structures for the ease of administration. The political and economic structures of the various peoples of Nigeria were gradually integrated through the mechanism of the socio-cultural structures of the people, which the British met on ground. The importation and subsequent localization of British and other foreign administrative models played central and regulatory roles in the integration of foreign and local variants of cooperative models. According to

[1] Yebisi (2014).

[2] These were the governing codes for the regulation of conduct within African traditional societies.

[3] Formal documentations and legislations were introduced by the British colonialist.

A. A. Akanji: He is an advocate and solicitor of the Supreme Court of Nigeria.

A. A. Akanji (✉)
Faculty of Law, Lead City University, Ibadan, Nigeria
e-mail: akanjiajibola16@yahoo.com

W. Tadjudje and I. Douvitsa (eds.), *Perspectives on Cooperative Law*
https://doi.org/10.1007/978-981-19-1991-6_4

Awojuyigbe (2007)[4], modern cooperatives were introduced into Nigeria during the colonial period through the effort of the British colonialist who had commissioned cooperative expert C.F Strickland to embark on a feasibility study of cooperatives in Nigeria. The Strickland Report of 1934[5] had reported that Nigeria is a good ground for the introduction of modern cooperatives. This was followed by the establishment of the cooperative department and the appointment of E.F.G Haig as the first Registrar (Director) of cooperatives in Nigeria. Haig encouraged the spread of cooperative ideas as practiced in India, then known as British India. Thereafter, cooperatives were utilized by the colonial government for rural and urban development.[6] The Nigerian Cooperative Societies Ordinance was enacted in 1935,[7] it was modeled after the Indian Cooperative Societies Act of 1904. All ordinances ceased to have the force of law from the 1October 1, 1960 when Nigeria got her independence from the British. Independence came with the sovereignty to make laws, which includes cooperative legislations, without recourse to external power. The above narratives briefly capture the development of the administration and legislation on Nigeria cooperative societies. The author agrees that the evolution of cooperative principles has been instrumental to the development of cooperative law. Hence, an attempt is made to identify intersections between the evolution of cooperative principles and the development of cooperative law in Nigeria.

2 An Assessment of the Evolution of Cooperative Principles

Cooperative principles serve as the guidelines for the administration and management of cooperative societies, and as foundation for the development of the regulatory frameworks on cooperatives. The first known set of cooperative principles where made by the Rochdale Pioneers of 1844.[8] The following were the objects of Rochdale Pioneers as gleaned from their 1844 charter:

The objects and plans of this society are to form arrangements for the pecuniary benefits, and improvement of the social and domestic condition of its members, by raising a sufficient amount of capital in shares of one pound each, to bring into operation the following plans and arrangement:

1. The establishment of a store for the sale of provisions, clothing, etc.

---

[4] See Awojuyigbe (2007).

[5] See Strickland (1938).

[6] Awojuyigbe S.O (supra).

[7] The original text of this legislation is unavailable. However, Yebisi (2014) supra posits that a substantial part of the legislation is reproduced in some subsisting Nigerian cooperative legislations, such as (a) Cooperative Societies Law CAP.35 of Oyo State; (b) Cooperative Societies Law CAP 13, Laws of Ekiti State.

[8] The Rochdale Principles of Co-operation. International Cooperative Alliance, October 29, 2019.

2. The building purchasing or erecting, of a number of houses in which those members, desiring to assist each other in improving their domestic and social condition may reside.
3. To commence the manufacturing of such articles as the Society may determine upon for the employment of such members as may be without employment, or who may be suffering in consequence of repeated reductions in their wages.
4. As a matter of security to the members of this Society, the Society shall purchase or rent an estate or estates of land, which shall be cultivated by the members who may be out of employment, or whose labor may be badly remunerated.
5. That as soon as practicable this Society shall proceed to arrange the powers of production, distribution, education, and government, or in other words to establish a self-supporting home colony of united interests, or assist other societies in establishing such colonies.
6. That, for the promotion of society, a temperance hotel be opened in one of the society's houses as soon as convenient.

Brett Fairbairn (1994)[9] identified some values from the above objects and plans:

a. The Rochdale Pioneers was established for the financial and social well-being of members, as there was a balanced socio-economic guideline.
b. The Rochdale Pioneers envisioned their society as multi-purpose cooperative.
c. They had in mind the location of a Utopian society, as self-supporting home colony devoid of exploitative activities.

Fairbairn (supra) reproduced 14 rules (by-laws) from the charter of the Rochdale Pioneers:

1. That the government of this society shall be vested in its President, Treasurer, and Secretary, three trustees and five directors to be elected at the general meeting.
2. That two auditors be appointed each to remain in office 6 months, and retire alternately.
3. That the officers and board of directors shall meet every Thursday evening at eight o'clock in the Committee Room Weaver's Arms.
4. That general meeting of the members shall be held on the first Monday in the months of January, April, July, and October.
5. That an annual general meeting be held on the "First Market Tuesday" on which occasion a dinner shall be provided at a charge of one shilling each person.
6. Any person willing to become a member of this society shall be proposed and scrutinized and approved of by a majority shall be eligible for election at the next weekly meeting.
7. That should any member wish to withdraw from this society such member shall give 1 month's notice.

[9] Brett Fairbairn (1994).

8. That the officers of this society shall not in any case, nor on any pretense purchase any articles except with ready money, neither shall they be allowed to sell any article except with ready money.
9. That at each quarterly general meeting the officers in their financial statement shall publish the amount of profits realized by the society during the preceding quarter, which shall be divided thus interest at the rate of three and half percent per annum shall be paid upon all shares paid up previous to the quarter's commencement, the remaining profits shall be paid to each member in proportion to the amount of money expended at the store.
10. That the store be opened to the public on the evenings of Mondays and Saturdays, on Mondays from 7 to 9, on Saturdays from 6 till 11.
11. That a cashier and salesman be appointed to conduct the business of store each to serve 6 months alternately, and eligible for re-election.
12. The salesman shall weigh and measure before sale, but shall not receive payment for any articles or goods sold.
13. The cashier shall receive payment for all goods purchased at the store, and he shall give a receipt to each purchaser for the amount received, and he shall pay over to the secretary at each weekly meeting the money drawn at the store.
14. That the store be opened at the proper time by the president.

The Rochdale Pioneers maintained a constant review of their by-laws, particularly in 1854, 1860, and 1879. The establishment in 1895 of the International Cooperative Alliance (ICA) gave impetus to the discussions and development of the Rochdale principles from a more international perspective. The Rochdale principles were appraised at the London congress of 1895 and at the Paris congress of 1896 where it was agreed that ICA would not concern itself with politics or religion. This rule was captured in the statement, "co-operation is a neutral ground on which people holding the most varied opinions may meet and act in common, it is self-sufficient and must not serves as the instrument of any party." The formation of the ICA and resulting activities brought into a single-fold variants of cooperative models and as a result "competing" ideologies.[10] This went side by side with further development of the Rochdale principles on the one hand and discussions about having cooperative principles on a common ground on the other. The trend continued until the codification of the first set of cooperative principles by the ICA in 1937.

Several factors influenced the build-up to this landmark event, which according to Watkins, W.P[11] "where the efforts to codify an official list of cooperative principles in the 1930s derived from several forces, this includes pressures to water down the principles of the cooperative movement due to the temptation to sacrifice considerations of principles to the need to address competitors who employ elements of cooperative principles against the cooperative societies." In view of the foregoing, a special committee of the ICA reconciled the competing interests, and reproduced seven principles from the 1844 Rochdale Charter and its various developments into the ICA cooperative principles of 1937, which contains the following:

[10] Brett Fairbairn (supra).

[11] Williams Pascoe Watkins (1986).

a. Open membership.
b. Democratic control.
c. Distribution of the surplus to the members in proportion to their members in proportion to their transactions.
d. Limited interest on capital.
e. Political and religious neutrality.
f. Cash trading.
g. Promotion of education.

The International Cooperative Alliance (ICA) cooperative principles of 1937 gained widespread acceptance, but became subject to diverse appraisals which were buttressed with the resilient and transient discussions built around the Rochdale Principles that had become characteristics of the cooperative movement. The phenomenon continued into the 1960s, with many brilliant contributions. One of the more outstanding perspectives were those of Paul Lambert, a Professor at the University of Liege, Belgium.[12] In Paul Lambert's work (supra) on the social philosophy of cooperatives, which was first published in French 1959 and in English 1963, he undertook an extensive analysis of cooperative thoughts and Rochdale positions across times and divides to arrive at his version of Rochdale principles. He arrived at the following:

The Rochdale Principles (Lambert 1959)

1. Democratic control.
2. Rules governing the accumulation and distribution of the surplus and the treatment of the net assets.
3. Distribution of surplus among the members in proportion to their purchases.
4. Payment of limited interest on capital.
5. Sale at market prices.
6. Dispersal of the net assets without profit to the members in the event of dissolution of the society.
7. Spirit of service (promotion of the member's interests only in so far as the latter are consistent with the general interest of the community).
8. Freedom for new members to join (principle of the open door).
9. Voluntary membership.
10. Cash purchase and sale.
11. Political and religious neutrality.
12. Education of the members.
13. Determination to take over the world economic and social system and to reorganize it on cooperative lines (i.e., to achieve the cooperative commonwealth).

A striking feature of Lambert's work was his emphasis on democracy. He argued cogently that democracy is the foundation of co-operation, which he further noted is perhaps the sole cooperative principle that is universally applicable to all cooperatives with minimal requirement for modifications and the most distinctive feature

---

[12] Lambert (1963).

of cooperatives in comparison to capitalist business. Lambert continued his works through the 1930s to the 1960s, this produced further construction of the Rochdale Principles and the evolution of cooperative principles. These were in response to changes around the world with radical implications on the cooperative movement. Within this was World War II, which widened the gap between the capitalist and non-capitalist ideologies and promoted the decolonization of many countries in Asia, South America, and Africa. This lead to the emergence of modern cooperatives in developing countries and brought non-European and non-North American members into the ICA and the International Labour Organization (ILO). According to Fairbairn (supra), "there were more new types of cooperatives, and with them more questions about structures and about philosophy and principles."

These challenges were at the center of the 1963 Bournemouth congress of the ICA, a congress which based on the standard of its time had the widest representation of cooperative interests in history. The Bournemouth congress had put in place a commission which had a representative each, from the British movement, India, Western Europe, Eastern Europe, and the United States of America (Watkins 1970)[13] The commission produced the 1966 ICA cooperative principles which are as follows:

The Rochdale Principles (ICA 1966)

1. Membership of a cooperative society should be voluntary and available without artificial restriction or any social, political, religious, or racial discrimination to all persons who can make use of its services and are willing to accept the responsibilities of membership.
2. Cooperative societies are democratic organizations. Their affairs should be administered by persons elected or appointed in a manner agreed by the members and accountable to them. Members of the primary societies should enjoy equal rights of voting (one member, one vote) and participation in decisions affecting their societies. In other than primary societies, the administration should be conducted on a democratic basis in a suitable form.
3. Share capital should only receive a strictly limited rate of interest, if any.
4. Surplus or savings, if any, arising out of the operation of a society belongs to the members of that society and should be distributed in such manner as would avoid one member gaining at the expense of others. This may be done by decision of the members as follows:

    a. by provision for development of the business of the cooperative;
    b. by provision of common services; or
    c. by distribution among the members in proportion to their transaction within the society.

5. All cooperative societies should make provision for the education of their members, officers, and employees, and the general public on the principles and techniques of co-operation, both economic and democratic.

[13] Williams Pascoe Watkins (1970).

6. All cooperative organizations, in order to best serve the interest of their members and their communities, should actively co-operate in every practical way with other cooperatives at local, national, and international levels.

The ICA cooperative principles of 1966 succeeded at the reconciliation of conflicting interests. There was respite in the years after 1966 as there were much less of activities on the subject of deconstructing or reconstructing of either Rochdale or ICA cooperative principles, save for the 1986 work of Watkins on cooperative principles. Watkins, 1986 (supra) identified the following cooperative principles:

a. Association (or Unity).
b. Economy.
c. Democracy.
d. Equity.
e. Liberty.
f. Responsibility.
g. Education.

Thereafter, Sven Ake Böök[14] produced some of his attempts at reconstructing the Rochdale and cooperative principles, which served as the groundwork for the next review of ICA cooperative principles. In his presentation title "Cooperative Values in A Changing world" which he presented at the ICA congress in Tokyo, 1992, Böök argued that cooperatives agree on the following variables:

a. **Basic Values**: Equality (democracy) and equality (social justice), voluntary and mutual self-help (solidarity and self-reliance), social and economic emancipation.
b. **Basic Ethics**: Honesty, caring (humanity), pluralism (democratic approach), constructiveness (faith in the cooperative way).
c. **Basic principles**: Association of persons, efficient member's promotion, democratic management and member participation, autonomy and independence, identify and unity, education, fair distribution of benefits, co-operation nations, and internationally.

Böök identified a fourth variable:

d. **Basic Global Values**: Economic activities for meeting ends, participatory democracy, human resources development, social responsibility, national and international co-operation.

Böök had positioned the fourth variable will provide more concrete actions and oriented expression of the other variables. This he believed is with a view that global values will be incorporated into the next set of cooperative principles. Böök's presentation was a development on previous works.

In the same vain Professor Ian Macpherson of the University of Victory, Canada gave further impetus to Böök's works through his conceptualization of what he called

[14] Böök (1992).

"The Cooperative Identity" which was considered at the ICA congress, Manchester, 1995. The intersection of Böök's and Macpherson's works laid substantial foundation for the current ICA Cooperative Principles of 1995.[15]

3 The Evolution and Development of Cooperative Law in Nigeria

Nigeria got her independence on October 1, 1960 and became a Republic on October 1, 1963. The independence came with the sovereignty to make its laws, including cooperative laws without recourse to external powers. However, the country's first legislation came earlier. The Nigerian Cooperative Societies Ordinance Cap. 39, 1935[16] is Nigeria's first legislation on cooperatives. It was modeled after the Indian Cooperative Societies Act of 1904.[17] It is one of the products of the Strickland Report of 1934. The 1935 Ordinance was a master-to-servant instrument as its provisions conferred enormous discretional powers on the Registrar, an appointed official of the government.[18] Despite the successes of the Strickland Report, the colonial government still nursed reservations about the capacity of Nigeria to successfully manage modern cooperatives. Therefore, strong control of cooperatives was adopted by the central government. The country was regionalized in 1950, with each of the three regions: West, East, North, and West gaining the powers to run their legislature, and the powers to make cooperative legislations. Thereafter, each of the three regions made its cooperative legislation to regulate societies within its territory and held the power to appoint a Registrar for cooperatives. By 1935, the only noticeable international framework on cooperative practice was the Charter of the Rochdale pioneers. Interestingly, the Charter was made in England the home of the then Nigerian colonial government, but the provisions of the 1935 Ordinance as currently reflected in some Nigerian legislations did not reflect the Charter of the Rochdale pioneers.

The first set of ICA principles were made in 1937,[19] 2 years after the coming into the force of the Nigerian Cooperative Ordinance of 1935. Same as it was with the charter of the Rochdale pioneers, there are no evidential links between the 1935

[15] (a) Voluntary and open membership; (b) Democratic member control; (c) Member economic participation; (d) Autonomy and independence; (e) Education, training, and information; (f) Cooperation among cooperatives; and (g) Concern for community.

[16] Supra.

[17] A good number of British legislation were first put to use in the then British Indian, (now India) where they were localized. The localized component which they thereafter carried made them more applicable for use in other parts of the then British commonwealth.

[18] This could have been an extension of the attempts to check the spread of the acceptability of the ideology of the Rochdale pioneers by other cooperative societies in England and within the British commonwealth.

[19] According to Williams Pascoe Watkins (1970), (supra), a special committee of the International Cooperative Alliance identified and reconciled various interests to reproduce seven principles from the 1844 Charter of the Rochdale pioneers.

Ordinance and the seven cooperative principles made by the ICA in 1937. The landmark contributions of Paul Lambert to the development of cooperative principles between 1930 and 1960 lead to his conceptualization in 1959 of the Rochdale principles (Lambert 1959) supra. This period was particularly productive for the Nigerian cooperative movement with the productive trend enduring till the 1980s. The cooperative movement of the defunct Western region of Nigeria was a shining light in this regard as it played significant roles in the socio-economic development of the region. These achievements were well harnessed by the government of the defunct Western region. While the period marked an improvement in the fortunes of the cooperative movement, the results were largely products of administrative ingenuity. First, on the part of the non-governmental actors such as cooperative managers, and secondly on the part of some government departments and their officials who must have adopted some of the evolving trends in the international scene into the administration and management of Nigerian cooperatives. On the other hand, there were no evidential links between the development of cooperative principles by the ICA and the development of cooperative legislation in Nigeria between 1930 and 1960. From the 1950s till date, cooperatives and allied legislations have constitutionally been on the concurrent legislative list.[20] It became obvious that the legislatures of the component governments have been reluctant to improve on the core provisions of the Ordinance of 1935. This is presumably to avoid the consequences of inconsistency with the provisions of a federal legislation on the same subject.[21] Nigeria's first national post-independence legislation was the Cooperative Societies Degree of 1974.[22] The degree made provisions for the administrative powers of the Federal Registrar and support staff, as well as the establishment functions and composition of bodies to oversee cooperative development. Due to the transformation of Nigeria from military to civil rule, the Cooperative Societies Decree, 1974, was enacted into an Act of the National Assembly. It is now known as the Cooperative Development Act.[23]

In its current form, it contains amendments to some of the provisions of the 1974 decree. The hereto provisions for the administrative duties of the Federal Registrar and the support staff for his office have been expunged. These expunged provisions now form part of the Nigerian Cooperative Societies Act.[24] The Nigerian Cooperative Societies Act is a product of the J.T Caxton-Idowu-led 12-member panel set up by the federal government of Nigeria in 1977 to review the existing legal framework on Nigerian cooperatives and to make appropriate recommendations.[25] The panel

[20] Constitution of the Federal Republic of Nigeria 1999, 2nd Schedule pt. 2.

[21] This is the position of Yebisi (2014) (supra). This author agrees with him.

[22] Nigeria has had a history of military rule. Firstly, from 1966 to 1979, and secondly from 1984 to 1999. The military regimes suspend the legislature and make decrees as a substitute for legislature made statutes. Some constant features of Nigerian decrees are: (a) the supremacy of the military; (b) the suspension of the legislature; and (c) in exceptional circumstances, an ouster clause against the judiciary.

[23] Chapter C27 Laws of the Federation of Nigeria, 2004.

[24] Chapter N98, Laws of the federation of Nigeria, 2004.

[25] Yebisi (2014) (supra).

submitted its report in 1978, and in 1993 some of the recommendations of the report were reconciled with among others some expunged provisions of the Cooperative Societies Degree of 1974 (supra) to enact the Nigerian Cooperatives Societies Decree N. 90 of 1993, which is re-enacted into the Nigerian Cooperative Societies Act (supra), herein referred to as the Act.

The Act came into force as a military decree 2 years before the presentation of Sven Ake Böök's presentation of "The Cooperative Identity" in 1995. It became an Act of the Nigerian national assembly and the legislation of a democratic government in 2004, 9 years after Böök's presentation. An appraisal of the provisions of the Act shows significant contradictions with the ICA cooperative principles of 1995.[26] One of the salient features of the Act is the unfettered discretional powers it confers on the Director. Section one of the Act: Appointment of a Federal Director of Cooperatives provides that the President may: (a) appoint a person to be Federal Director of Cooperatives; (b) appoint persons to assist him; and (c) by notice in the Gazette confer all or any of the powers of a Director under this Act on any such person. The Act confers equivalent powers on the Governor of a State[27] in respect of societies registered with the State.

ICA cooperative principles, 1995, prescribe that cooperatives are to be privately owned and controlled autonomous associations, the provisions of Section 1 of the Act[28] impose on Nigerian societies a Director who is a public servant, and whose emergence and occupation of the position is the sole reserve of the President or Governor. The Director exercises discretional powers on the registration of societies and allied matters.[29] This also applies to the powers of a registered society to make and amend its by-laws.[30] The Director's discretion also applies to the qualification for membership of a primary society.[31] The Act confers further discretional powers on the Director on the cancellation of the registration of a society and other auxiliary matters. This discretion covers the effect of the cancellation of the registration of a society; appointment of liquidator after cancellation of registration of a society; and the enforcement of corresponding orders made by the liquidator, an arbitrator or the Director.[32] The Act also provides for the discretional powers of the Director to surcharge and attaches the property of a registered cooperative society.[33] According to Section 48 of the Act, these powers may be appealed through formal complaints to

[26] The provisions of the Act share significant resemblance with the 1935 Ordinance. Particularly with regards the government control of cooperative societies. The author shall explain this shortly.

[27] States are subnational units within the Nigerian federation. State legislatures share concurrent legislative power with the national assembly on cooperative and allied matters. However, when conflict arises between the provision of an Act of the national assembly and the provision of a State law, the principle of covering the field is employed. Therefore, the provision of the Law becomes null and void to the extent of its inconsistence with the provision of the Act.

[28] See Section 1 of the Act.

[29] See Sections 2, 3, 4, 5, and 7 of the Act.

[30] See Sections 11 and 12 of the Act.

[31] See Section 22 (2) of the Act.

[32] See Sections 38, 39, 40, 41, 42, and 43 of the Act.

[33] See Sections 46 and 47 of the Act.

the office of the Minister (Federal) or Commissioner (state) as the case may be, within 30 days from the date the order was made, and the decision of the Minister or the Commissioner shall be conclusive. The Act also confers on the Director discretional powers on the settlement of disputes touching on the businesses of a registered society, cases to be stated on question of law, division of a registered society, amalgamation of registered societies, and prohibition of the use of the word "cooperative."[34]

Further, the Act provides[35] "The Minister or the Commissioner responsible for matters relating to cooperative societies may make all such regulations as may be necessary for the purpose of carrying out or giving effect to the provisions of this Act." The above provisions of the Act bring to the fore some of the disparities between Nigerian cooperative legislation and the recent cooperative principles. Cooperative principles dictate that cooperative societies are privately owned and privately controlled autonomous associations. The Act on its part confines societies to privately owned, but government-controlled, non-autonomous associations. The current position of the Nigerian government as it reflects through the Act is for all practical purposes the same as the 1935 position of the then-colonial government of Nigeria. In comparison, Nigerian societies do not share any of the values identified by Brett Fairbairn (supra). Although they are established for the economic and social well-being of their members, there are no balanced socio-economic guidelines.[36] Also, most primary societies are established for single or at most dual socio-economic enterprises.[37] The Nigerian cooperative movement has not shown traces of viable political nor ideological orientations, it does not assert significant influence on the political and legal structures of the country.[38] Their recessive ideological posture constitutes a drawback to the development of cooperative law in the country and has adverse implications on the quality of their internal organization.

4 Conclusion and Recommendations

Cooperative principles have evolved over the years in response to various factors. The dynamic development of cooperative principles laid the foundation for cooperative laws at all tiers. These landmark achievements are the result of pivotal roles played by the ICA and the ILO. Aside the cooperative principles, the various recommendations

[34] See Sections 49, 50, 51, 52, 53, and 54.

[35] See Section 56 of the Act.

[36] Firstly, on account of the identified deficient statutory framework, and secondly on account of the weak by-laws that draw their validity from the deficient statutory provisions.

[37] This is the conclusion of several authors such as (Awojuyigbe 2007) supra.
Nwankwo et al. (2012).
Rafiu and Kamila (2019).

[38] This position is a product of the author's research findings, particularly from his recent review of the Cooperative Societies Bill (Lagos State), a task he undertook on behalf of the Cooperative Federation of Nigeria. The bill seeks to amend the Cooperative Societies Law Chapter C14, 2015 of Lagos State.

of the ILO Promotion of Cooperatives Recommendation, 2002 (No. 193) are meant to guide government at the national and sub-national levels in the development of their cooperative legislation. ICA cooperative principles and ILO recommendations have not been properly domesticated in Nigeria. This is the primary reason for the inchoate state of cooperative law in the country.

Given the foregoing which does not exhaust the discussion, the following are hereby identified as necessary causes for action:

a. The implementation of the provisions of the Cooperatives Development Act.[39]
b. Improved participation in the activities of the ICA that involves significant undertaking with the Committee on Cooperatives Research (CCR) and the Cooperative Law Committee (CLC).
c. Adoption of the various ILO recommendations on the supervision and development of cooperatives.
d. Establishment of the Nigerian Society for Cooperatives Studies as a research arm of the Cooperative Federation of Nigeria.

References

Awojuyigbe SO (2007) Co-operative administration and fieldwork in Nigeria. Samlolly Publishers Ibadan, Nigeria

Böök SA (1992) Cooperative values in a changing world: report to the ICA congress, Tokyo, October 1992, ed. Margret Pricket and Mary Treacy, Geneva: International Co-operative Alliance. Pg. 35

Fairbairn B (1994) The meaning of rochdale: the rochdale pioneers and the cooperative principles. University of Saskatchwan, Centre for the Study of Cooperatives

Co-operative Development Act CAP. C27 (2004) Laws of the Federation of Nigeria

Co-operative Societies Law CAP. 13, Laws of Ekiti State

Co-operative Societies Law CAP. 35 Laws of Oyo State

Cooperative societies law of chapter C14 of 2015 of Lagos State

Lambert P (1963) Studies in the social philosophy of co-operation, Joseph Letargez, Manchester: Co-operative Union (Originally Published as La Doctrine Cooperative, Brussels and Paris (1959)

Nigerian co-operative societies act chapter N98 (2004) Laws of the federation of Nigeria

Nwankwo F et al (2012) Role of co-operatives in small and medium scale enterprises (SMEs) development in Nigeria: challenges and the way forward. African Res Rev 6(4):140–156

Rafiu AO, Kamila OO (2019) Examination of the roles of cooperatives societies on the promotion of small scale enterprises in Osun State, Nigeria. Int J Res Innovat Soc Sci (IJRISS) 3(4)

Strickland CF (1938) The Cooperative Society as an Instrument of Economic and Social Construction. Int Labour Rev 37(1938):729–753

The 1999 Constitution of the Federal Republic of Nigeria (as amended)

The Rochdale Principles of Co-operation (2019) International Co-operative Alliance, 29th October, 2019.

Williams Pascoe Watkins (1970) The International co-operative Alliance, 1895–1970. London pp 326–327

[39] Section 1 of the Cooperative Development Act provides for the establishment of the Cooperative Development Division in the Federal Ministry of Employment, Labour and Productivity, to establish a National Advisory Council to advise the Minister on matters relating to Cooperative Development. Thereafter, Section 2 provides for the Duties of the Division.

Williams Pascoe Watkins (1986) Co-operative principles today and tomorrow. Holyoake Books, Manchester

Yebisi ET (2014) Nigerian co-operatives societies act, 2004: a bridge still far. Asian J Human Soc Sci 2(2)

Asian Cooperatives and Public Policy Approach, Process, and Prospect

Robby Tulus

1 Introduction

This paper seeks to examine the challenges encountered by Asian cooperatives in the realm of public policy approaches, processes, and prospects. In the first place, public policy approaches cannot be oversimplified owing to the fact that the Asia region is so widespread and diverse (Kurimoto 2020). The cooperative movements in the region are, as a consequence, widespread and vastly heterogeneous as well,[1] so that approaches in public policy must remain relevant to each specific movement. Therefore, public policy must be approached through a well-diversified and coherent fashion. Secondly, in terms of the public policy process itself, the long-drawn-out colonial legacy in the region made it quite arduous and complex for newly independent governments to navigate the progression in a proper and prudent manner.

Despite all these challenges, however, the prospect of public policymaking has seen gradual improvements thanks to the lessons learned of, and concerted efforts made by, the International Cooperative Alliance over the past 30 years.

The defining characteristic of a healthy public policy is active participation of people and representative governments, in a democratic space, that is aimed at achieving fairness and equality. Therefore, active participation becomes an important ingredient for the success of any development process, making opportunities more widely shared in order to achieve more equitable growth and development. The same

[1] Cooperatives in Asia are widespread and varied as discussed in the aforementioned book "*Waking the Asian Pacific Cooperative Potential*, Chap. 4 on *Emerging Asian Pacific cooperative models from a global history perspective.*

This chapter is a reprint from "Waking the Asian Pacific Cooperative Potential", Volume 1, Chapter 5 *Asian Cooperatives and Public Policy*, pp. 47–58, Copyright © 2020 Elsevier Inc., with permission from Elsevier.

R. Tulus (✉)
International Cooperative Alliance, Cooperatives in the Asia Pacific Region, New Delhi, India

W. Tadjudje and I. Douvitsa (eds.), *Perspectives on Cooperative Law*,
https://doi.org/10.1007/978-981-19-1991-6_5

requirement applies to public policy on cooperative development. In order to frame an effective cooperative legislative agenda, governments must engage cooperative representatives to participate actively during all its proceedings, so in the final analysis it will be the cooperative members that will obtain fair and equal benefits from the social and economic gains of the cooperative.

Historical evidence has shown that public policymaking in the Asian Cooperative context is essentially quite distant from being healthy. Control of the state had remained dominant even after countries became independent, curbing any form of proper public policy participation and debates of cooperative representatives in the process. During the pre-independence period of most colonized countries in Asia, cooperative laws were designed by colonial governments without any involvement of the native cooperative representatives themselves. The main consideration of framing cooperative laws at that time had been "*what is good considered by the rulers and not by cooperative members or the people*" (Sharma 1997).

Subsequent amendments of the Cooperative Laws by post-independent governments also failed to incorporate Asian cultural values and local wisdom of the people, so the gist of most cooperative laws was more attuned to political expediencies of those present-day governments.

This paper is thus an endeavor to illustrate how State control over the cooperative movement was so dominant, which prompted the leadership of the International Cooperative Alliance to initiate a process of good public policy discussion forum. The public policy endeavor was primarily focused on reviewing and improving the regulatory framework for cooperatives in the Asia Pacific region. The program methodology utilized by the ICA Regional Office for Asia and the Pacific (ICA ROAP)[2] was to conduct biennial Regional Consultations, followed by Asia Pacific Cooperative Ministers' Conferences (APCMC).[3] The very first APCMC was held in Sydney, Australia, in the year 1990 and the most recent one (at the writing of this paper) was the 10th APCMC held in Hanoi, Vietnam, in 2017. This bold and thoughtful initiative of the ICA AP was relevant as well as prospective, as evidenced by the results of four successive critical studies[4] that preceded the APCMC proper. This paper tries to encapsulate common public policy issues faced by countries in South and South-East Asia,[5] involving three case studies in Bangladesh, Indonesia, and the Philippines.

Although top-down approaches vary among different countries in Asia and are not necessarily as pervasive as depicted by the three case studies, the phenomena

---

[2] ICA ROAP stands for *International Cooperative Alliance, Regional Office for Asia and the Pacific*, a popular abbreviation used before it changed into ICA AP (Asia Pacific) more recently, which change put more emphasis more on the region than the office.

[3] APCMC used throughout this Paper depicts the successive *Asia Pacific Cooperative Ministers' Conferences* being conducted by the International Cooperative Alliance for Asia Pacific (ICA AP) over all these years.

[4] First Critical Study was undertaken in 1996 to furnish the Fourth APCMC held in Chiangmai, Thailand.

[5] Three developing countries in South and South East Asia were selected for the Case Studies pertaining to a 'top-down' approach in cooperative development.

seem quite omnipresent in the region on account of the feudalistic and patriarchal values inherent in the Asian culture.[6] This paper also focused more on countries in the Asian rather than Pacific Region, without any disregard to the latter, inasmuch as existing studies on public policy were more obtainable in Asian countries.

2 Colonial Legacy and Cooperative Legislation in Asia

Cooperative laws and regulations in post-colonial countries in Asia were by and large created by their foregoing rulers. Despite the richness of cultures and traditions in Asia, which ought to be taken into consideration when drafting and enacting cooperative laws and regulations, most post-colonial governments simply adopt the cooperative law left behind by their colonizers. The first cooperative law in India was enacted in 1904 based on the model of the United Kingdom, and in the Philippines, while ruled under the United States of America, its initial cooperative legislation was based on the corporation law of 1906, patterned after the legislative frameworks of European countries (Sharma 1997).

In India, cooperative societies were established based on the Raiffeisen model in 1892 to supply rural credit.[7] Thereafter, the 1901 Famine Commission under British rule recommended that farm credit should be continued to improve agriculture and to prevent famine. By 1904, the Cooperative Society Act was passed. Pakistan was part of India until 1947. Cooperatives in Pakistan originally applied the Bombay/Sindh cooperative Societies Act of India in 1925. Cooperatives in Bangladesh were subjected to the cooperative legislation of Pakistan until it became independent from Pakistan in 1972, but were originally subjected to the provincial Cooperative Societies act of 1912 of India as it was then an Indian State of Bengal. The first cooperative law in Sri Lanka was enacted in 1911, meant primarily for credit cooperatives, and modeled after the Indian Cooperative Law of 1904. The above examples of cooperative legislation in South Asia signify the influence and intensity of foreign rulers in framing the initial cooperative legislation in that region.

Colonial legacy applies to the early cooperative legal frameworks in South-East Asian region as well. In Indonesia, the first Cooperative legislation was enacted by the Dutch government in 1915 based on the Dutch Law (Staatsblad) on Cooperatives of 1876. In Malaysia, the first Cooperative Societies Act was enacted in 1922 and patterned after the Indian Cooperative Societies Act of 1912. In Burma (now called Myanmar) the primary Credit Societies were regulated by the (Burma) Provincial Registrar of Cooperative Societies under the Indian Cooperative Societies Act 1904, and amended in 1912 and 1927, to fight the "Chettiars" or moneylender communities.

---

[6] Pervasiveness of Asian values in the public policy context was emphasized in a paper by Robby Tulus on *"Cooperative Legislation", Legislative and Regulatory trends—with special reference to cooperatives in Asia and the Pacific*, a presentation at the National Congress of the Canadian Cooperative Association, Winnipeg, Manitoba, June 23–26, 1998.

[7] The Raiffeisen model was linked to rural indebtedness as a product of the land revenue system enforced by the Colonial powers to gain revenues from Indian peasants.

Thailand, being a country that has never been colonized, developed its first Cooperative Law called the "Amended Associations Act" in 1916, focused on farm-based cooperatives to provide loans to rice growers, but patterned after the Indian and Burmese cooperative laws.[8]

The European Colonial powers have left a lasting impact on the social economic landscape in Asia. India, Sri Lanka, Malaysia were under British rule, Indonesia under the Dutch, Philippines under the Spanish, East Timor under the Portuguese, and Vietnam under French colonial domination. The British, Spanish, Portuguese, and Dutch colonial powers had different approaches and objectives of colonization. The Dutch and French were interested in accumulating wealth as well as ensuring hegemony. Apart from wealth accumulation, the Spanish and Portuguese were also interested in spiritual conversion. The English imperial power, by contrast, was interested exclusively in the wealth of the colonies. The latter has a more flexible and non-interventionalist approach and thus outlasted all other colonial powers (Hasan and Onyx 2008). It may help to explain why the Indian Cooperative Law of 1904—drafted by the British rulers—continued to render a formidable influence and impact on many other cooperative laws in Asia.

The creation of cooperative laws in many Asian countries, wherein European model laws were embedded at the outset, was further enforced by the establishment of an institution that had colonial underpinnings. The institution of the registrar was established as the sole authority to guide, develop and preserve the cooperative enterprise, with unmitigated absence of members' participation in any decision-making process. This was rationalized by the notion that peasant farmers, who were not well-educated to understand and to form a cooperative enterprise in the rural areas, were in need of an authority—called the "Registrar"—that will be recruited and selected by the colonial authorities themselves. Such control over the cooperative enterprise also meant that colonial governments could maintain their domination over the massive rural jurisdiction under the guise of well-developed cooperative legal framework.

Upon independence, at the beginning of the second half of the twentieth century, the residual legal framework of colonial powers continued to prevail in Asian countries, prompting governments in Asia to practice top-down domination of cooperatives for political expediencies. Cooperatives became mere handmaidens of the government to serve their prevailing policies without much space for self-governance and autonomy. Governments maintained full authority by enacting legal and policy frameworks for cooperatives that suit their political needs. The "registrar" syndrome predominated, leaving little space for public policy debates to ensue. Residues of the European cooperative development model remained uninterrupted whereas opportunities to enshrine Asian values that are based on religion and tradition were missed. These top-down policies led to the failures of cooperatives in many Asian countries the 1960s–1980s, as will be described in the subsequent chapter.

---

[8] Summarized and excerpted from country presentations and background papers from first to third APCMCs (1990–1994).

3 Failed Government Top-Down Approaches in Cooperative Development: *Three Case Studies*

Post-colonial governments in Asia were quite inflexible to allow cooperatives to self-govern in the post-independence period up until the 1980s.

The preponderance of the agricultural sector to meet food sufficiency in many Asian countries has led governments to set up cooperatives that will increase agriculture and food production, and simultaneously raise farmers' income. This well-intentioned yet controversial approach continued to preserve state control over cooperatives, leaving cooperative members to become objects rather than subjects of their own development. Government intervention and assistance had been very noticeable in rural areas, where agricultural cooperatives were vigorously created within the realm of existing national development policies.

In Indonesia, the government approach in cooperative development during the early 1970s was the promotion of the Village Unit Cooperatives, popularly known as KUDs. The legal basis for these government-initiated KUDs was a series of Presidential Instructions, starting from PI 4/1973, to which the Ministry of Cooperatives and Small and Medium Enterprises became the implementing agency. KUD is essentially a multi-purpose Agri-based cooperative which provided multiple services to member-farmers such as agricultural credit via the Peoples' Bank of Indonesia (BRI), field extension services, supply of agricultural inputs, and the processing and marketing of agricultural products. Under PI 4/1973, the idea was to have KUDs promote agricultural productivity, especially in the food sub-sector, increase small farmers' income, sustain the growth of agriculture and attain self-sufficiency in staple products for food security. (Soedjono/Cordero 1997). However, subsequent Presidential Instructions such as PI 4/1984 transformed the KUD into an expanded multi-sectoral cooperative to play a dominant role in all other economic activities at the sub-district (Kecamatan) level, be they agricultural or non-agri-based activities.

The KUD concept was further bolstered by the launching of the KUD Mandiri (Self-Reliant KUD) Program in 1989, which allowed membership of KUD to include non-farmers at the sub-district level (Soedjono/Cordero 1997). The dominance of these KUDs was further demonstrated by business tie-ups with the private sector, to the extent that KUDs owned the monopoly for the procurement of cloves as a lucrative agricultural product that time. In addition to the KUDs, the government promoted cooperatives in urban areas among professional workers, military, and police. The establishment of these professional and employment-based cooperatives was considered a form of political intervention by the government over these professional and agricultural entities, causing the downward drift of cooperatives in both the rural and urban areas in Indonesia (Baswir 2000).

In Bangladesh, the Comilla Model precedes the KUD model of Indonesia, with the same visionary concept of a rural development program, founded by Akhter Hameed Khan. The Comilla Model was Khan's reply to the failure of Village Agricultural and Industrial Development (V-AID) program, launched in 1953 in East and West

Pakistan with technical assistance from the US government (Yousaf 2003). The technical assistance was a governmental level attempt to promote citizens' participation in rural development. Khan argued that for Comilla to develop rapidly, the farmers in its villages must be able to rapidly expand their production and sales, and local infrastructure must be built. However, even if the government had the resources to build this infrastructure, Khan argued, the problem would not be solved. Once constructed, infrastructure must be regularly maintained.

In Khan's view it was essential to develop "vigorous local institutions" capable of performing this type of local maintenance and management of the infrastructure. After independence of Bangladesh, while the First Five-Year Plan gave general endorsement, both theoretical criticisms and practical difficulties became more severe.

There are similarities between the Comilla model and the KUD model since both were researched and initiated by academicians, in Bangladesh by Akhter Hameed Khan who was the founder of the Bangladesh Academy for Rural Development, whereas in Indonesia by Mubyarto who was a well-known researcher and lecturer on agricultural and village economics at the Gajah Mada University in Indonesia. Both academicians started with pilot projects on rural development based on two goals: first, to provide a real-life learning situation for rural development, and second, to devise pilot programs with a basic institutional framework (pre-cooperatives) which could serve as models capable of replication. The basic institutional framework was called BUUD in Indonesia, a precursor of the KUD. However, both their well-intentioned initiatives were usurped by the government, and replication of the Comilla and BUUD programs suffered from distortion, mismanagement, corruption, and subversion (Quddus 1993).

In the Philippines, during the same period in the 1970s, a similar top-down approach of cooperative development could be witnessed. Philippines was under martial law, and a Presidential Decree (PD) No. 175 was issued with the aim to strengthen the cooperative movement.

Moreover, PD No. 175[9] was tied up to the Marcos land-reform program (PD No. 27) which made it compulsory for a tenant-farmer to join a cooperative called Samahang Nayon, which is a pre-cooperative farmers' organization. The Samahang Nayons were encouraged to form Area Marketing Cooperatives on a municipality-wide basis, and also to form Cooperative Rural Banks on a province-wide basis. Farmers benefit would include the right to borrow funds from government banks through the Co-op Rural Banks (CRBs) or local rural banks, with the assurance of being supplied with farm inputs such as seed, fertilizers, pesticides, etc. However, since the formation of Samahang Nayons was haphazard, the resulting AMCs and CRBs formed were only few and weak. The Samahang Nayons peaked at 200,000

[9] Presidential Decree No. 175, April 14, 1973, *"Strengthening the Cooperative Movement"* repealed all past cooperative laws. Portions or parts of any other laws inconsistent with PD 175 are likewise repealed. This Presidential Decree thus overruled laws enacted by the Congress as the legislative arm in the Philippines.

involving at least 3 million farmers. Only 3% survived. The 14-year program reportedly utilized billions of dollars in loans and grants from the World Bank and other international financial institutions, thus being wasted by the government for quick fixes through weak and haphazardly created cooperative institutions.

All the above three cases of the KUD in Indonesia, the Comilla in Bangladesh, and the Samahang Nayon in the Philippines bore evidence of the fact that government-initiated cooperatives from the top-down are doomed to fail. From a public policy point of view, there seem to be inadequate legislative processes to seek a balance between government's desire to initiate and control cooperatives for the public good on the one hand, and the desire of the cooperative institutions themselves to have the flexibility to respond to the challenges in the marketplace and hence adjust their strategies based on members' needs. Failures of these top-down approaches are attributed to a misconception of the cooperative basic identity. Instead of promoting self-help, self-governance, and self-responsibility of the cooperatives for long-term transformation, governments were instead using cooperatives as means for political expediencies, for quick and technical fixes that were mired with fraud and corruption in the process.

Several case studies mentioned earlier focused primarily in post-colonial countries in South and South-East Asia where excessive state control predominated, and which caught the attention of the International Cooperative Alliance as will be described in the following chapter. Whereas case studies on public policy issues are quite palpable in the foregoing three countries, this chapter is by no means trying to neglect policy anomalies which also exist in other more developed countries in East Asia such as Japan, Korea, and China, including Singapore in South-East Asia. Other case studies written in this book bring to light the extent to which governments in more developed countries also continued to carry the day.

The revelation of government control over cooperatives in the preceding case studies could be the subject of further in-depth studies in the public policy domain insofar as cooperative laws are concerned. Cooperative laws corresponding to the three case studies were omnibus ones, which encompassed all cooperative types and sectors. The omnibus law seems prevalent in most Asian countries, and presumably drafted for the most part by governments that could well perpetuate their interest to exercise ongoing control over cooperatives. Two countries in Asia, namely, Japan and South Korea, are the only ones adopting sectoral cooperative laws, to the extent that there exist different laws for different cooperative sectors, and regulated by different Ministries as well. The presumption that cooperatives could be better supervised and be more autonomous and independent to foster growth under the sectoral laws, is subject to another study. While vertically well regulated and supervised, one could argue if horizontal coordination among so many Ministries involved in cooperative regulation and supervision is conducive for the overall growth, development, and independence of cooperatives.

The choice of one omnibus cooperative law vis-à-vis sectoral laws has an "*effect on the legislative procedure, for example on the designation of the lead ministry in charge of the formulation of the law or the amendments to the law. Worldwide one finds any thinkable combination, from many laws to no law. The trend is towards having one single general law covering all types of cooperatives*".[10]

4 Public Policy Initiatives of the ICA

The disproportionate roles and relationship between the government and the cooperative movement in a number of ICA member countries in Asia have caught the attention of the ICA, notably its Regional Office for Asia and the Pacific (ROAP). This challenging reality led the ICA ROAP (currently called ICA AP) to initiate a Consultation in Singapore in the year 1987 to bring together permanent secretaries and top cooperative leaders from Asian countries to begin an honest dialogue. Professor Hans-H Münkner, an advocate of this dialogue, stated that "*Cooperatives must be allowed to play their role as self-help organizations, representing and defending the interests of their members and to work according to their own fundamental ethic ideals expressed in the cooperative principles*". The consultative process in Singapore produced a relationship-promoting element as it did raise the awareness among regulators and cooperative leaders regarding current impediments obstructing cooperative growth, chiefly among ICA members in developing countries at that time. On account of this awareness, the initial public policy dialogue began in earnest.

Following the Singapore dialogue, and with support of head-office, ICA AP, as the ICA regional office was later called, formulated a public policy forum by instituting two successive events, firstly a dialogue between the cooperative movement and high-ranking officials in charge of cooperatives to assess current cooperative policies and legislation, followed by a policy endorsement by a Ministerial level delegation. Both events were more popularly known as an Asia Pacific "*Regional Consultation*" followed by an Asia Pacific "*Cooperative Ministers' Conference*" (APCMC), organized mostly on a biennial basis from 1990 up until 2012, and conducted more sparingly of late.

This well-received public policy initiative set forth fresh debates about the role of the state and how such role should be transformed from a predominantly top-down mechanism into that of a partnership approach. Up until now (2018), ten consecutive APCMCs had been successfully organized in Sydney (1990), Jakarta (1992), Colombo (1994), Chiangmai (1997), Beijing (1999), Nepal (2002), India (2004), Kuala Lumpur (2007), Bangkok (2012), and Hanoi (2017). While applauding the successful organizational labors of the ICA Asia Pacific in staging all ten APCMCs, ICA AP was determined to put more emphasis on substantiating the results of the APCMS, particularly the impact on government policies to create a more enabling environment for cooperatives to self-regulate and thus achieve their self-reliant

[10] Extensive assessment of one versus several cooperative laws, or no cooperative law whatsoever was revealed in the Third Revised edition of the *"Guidelines for Cooperative Legislation"* by Henrÿ (2012).

growth and development. A significant instrument used by ICA AP was a series of in-depth Critical Studies, enriched with field investigations, which had been conducted since 1996 prior to the Co-op Ministers' Conference in Chiangmai, Thailand, in 1997.

Reflecting on all ten APCMCs, it is safe to conclude that governments and cooperative movements are becoming more aware of the imperatives of good policies and legislation that is predisposed to enhancing the competitive strength of cooperatives in an ever-changing environment. It also enabled the ICA AP and its members to embark on relevant public policy issues pertaining to cooperatives, all aimed at cooperative development and the well-being of its members. One big challenge was to defeat the stigma within the public at large in that cooperatives were by and large government-led and hence destined to fail. The combination of Regional Consultations, Critical Studies and subsequent discussions at all nine APCMCs constituted tangible settings to debate of the right prerequisites for developing genuine cooperatives. The prevalence of genuine cooperatives would be the only means to defeat the lingering stigma. Thus, it would be incumbent on part of the government to create an enabling policy and legal environment that are conducive to the development of genuine cooperatives.

The arduous process of policy debates toward building a consensus on what constitutes a genuine cooperative was buoyed up with the promulgation of ILO Recommendation 193 in 2002,[11] stating that "*Governments should provide a supportive policy and legal framework consistent with the nature and function of cooperatives and guided by the cooperative values and principles*". The ILO Recommendation 193, which applies to all types and forms of cooperatives, re-enforces some of the key and contextual declaration of all preceding APCMCs.

Critical lessons drawn from the initial five APCMCs could be summarized as follows[12]:

1. *The need to maintain regional-national-local links, to ensure that inputs at the Regional Conference reflect the needs and concerns of members at the primary level. Legislative issues must first be addressed at the grassroots level, and subsequently at the national and regional levels by linking local responses with different higher-level stakeholders, including governments, universities, and civil society organizations;*
2. *Current sponsorship of the Co-op Ministers' Conferences could be defined as equal funding from ICA sponsors (Swedish Cooperative Center/SCC, Canadian Cooperative Association/CCA, Développement International Desjardins/DID, as well as ICA Members) for the preparation of the "content" on the one hand, and from host governments for the preparations and implementation of the actual execution of the conference itself on the other. ICA must acquire the skill to craft a strategy that increases member financing, matched by co-op sponsors*

[11] *ILO Recommendation 193*, Recommendation concerning Promotion of Cooperatives, Adoption: Geneva, 90th ILC session (20 June 2002).

[12] Lessons learned from Technical Paper "*The ICA Asia Pacific Cooperative Ministers' Conferences and Regional Consultations*", Robby Tulus, p. 26.

and government funds, so as to avoid shifting the ownership of the Conference from members (i.e., ICA ROAP) to that of external agencies.

3. *There is a significant time gap between the execution of the Regional Consultation and the actual Minister' Conference itself. Such a gap tends to diminish the momentum created by the Consultation that needs to be picked up and confirmed by the high-level Ministers' Meeting. It seems plausible to link the Regional Meetings of Co-op Chief Executives and Government Bureaucracy directly to a high-level Conference among Co-op Ministers and elected co-op leaders in a quick succession. Such a mechanism will not only keep the momentum active but also the overall cost down.*
4. *Most governments and members of ICA in Asia Pacific have been used to making statements at the Ministers' Conference, which are frequently unrelated to the issues being addressed by the respective Ministers' Conference. Member-countries of ICA in Asia–Pacific should be motivated to take greater interests and self-initiatives in legislative reforms. Through this experience cooperatives could document processes that show how an independent enterprise is critical to making "self-regulation" work: Encouraging a healthy movement and at the same time public accountability of state institutions. Statements reflecting these experiences would be relevant and useful for others.*

5 Sustaining the Momentum of Public Policy Debates on Cooperatives

The initiative of ICA AP to launch policy debates by means of Regional Consultations and APCMCs is worth sustaining in view of the varying degrees of government dictates that are still in existence across the growing cooperative movements in Asian countries. There continued to be changed in the political landscapes that prompted cooperative ministers or corresponding ministries to be subjected to unavoidable socio-political and structural changes. The predicament is the changed or different outlook of cooperative ministers operating under such new political settings, which is often different from their predecessors, and worst still when positive outlooks are being annulled for their political conveniences.

With the realization that the cooperative ministry, or the ministry in charge of cooperatives, is only a subcategory of the government system, reforms in cooperative legislation and policies could take some time to materialize. Critical Studies and Regional Consultations would be inclined to reprocess old themes to keep new cooperative ministers/officials abreast with fundamental issues that were still unresolved. In other words, tools and standards were missing that would allow both old and new players to undertake a joint assessment in a consistent manner. The only constant is the dedicated pursuit of ICA AP to convene APCMCs so as to keep the wheels of good government-cooperative relations running smoothly (Shankar/Cronan 2001).

A new milestone arose following the UN International Year of Cooperatives in 2012 when governments, international development actors, and UN agencies credibly recognized the significant contribution of cooperatives in achieving a socially just, economically equitable, and culturally inclusive society. This augurs well with the newly promulgated Sustainable Development Goals (SDGs) by the United Nations, to which the International Cooperative Alliance has pledged its contribution by way of concrete actions of its members, and in close partnership with the government and its stakeholders, as well as within the context of its "Blueprint for a Cooperative Decade".[13]

Realizing that limitations still exist where APCMCs are concerned, the ICA AP took a progressive step in 2016 to include and engage parliamentarians during its Regional Consultation in Nepal. This allowed member of the legislative body who are knowledgeable about cooperatives to take part in the policy debates, apart from government officials and Ministers in charge of cooperatives. Furthermore, in addition to addressing and concentrating on legal issues like in the past, the Consultation was a first attempt to address other specific issues affecting cooperative development in the region. This new initiative was a breakthrough in terms of getting ICA AP member cooperatives to deliberate issues such as: (a) Food Sovereignty (and security), (b) New Cooperative Approaches (Innovation), (c) Cooperatives and the Transition from the Informal into the Formal economy, (d) Regional and Global engagement of Cooperatives, and (e) Enabling Environment (Legislative and Regulatory Frameworks)[14] both at the Regional Consultation and the APCMC agendas. Such a holistic discussion within the 10th APCMC framework has allowed the ICA AP not only to keep, but to sustain, the momentum of its public policy advocacy, so much so that it will (a) enrich the partnership of the cooperative Movement and their respective governments as well as key stakeholders to bring about sustained economic democracy, (b) comprehend the substantive progress made by the Co-op Movement in Asia Pacific, (c) Capture and outline well-defined key elements of the SDGs which Cooperatives could contribute to the attainment of the Sustainable Development Goals of the United Nations.[15]

6 Conclusion

The far-reaching influence of European colonial powers, that has left an enduring imprint on cooperative development in Asian countries, cannot be undermined. Asian norms and values, driven by rich cultural traditions and religion are critical elements to enhance the workings of cooperatives in most Asian countries. Values such as

---

[13] "*Blueprint for a Cooperative Decade*", Paper written under the guidance of the Planning Work Group of the International Cooperative Alliance by Cliff Mills and Will Davies, Center for Mutual and Employee-Owned Business, University of Oxford, originally published in January 2013.

[14] Concept Note, 10th Asia Pacific cooperative Ministers' Conference, April 18 to 21, 2017, Hanoi, Vietnam.

[15] Excerpts from "*HANOI 10th APCMC RESOLUTION ON Multi-Stakeholder Partnerships in Realizing the SDGs*", April 2017, and Critical Appraisal of "*Strengthening Cooperative Multi-stakeholders' Partnerships in Asia Pacific*", by Robby Tulus.

Gotong Royong in Indonesia and Bayanihan in the Philippines, for example, are derived from longstanding community traditions in these countries to readily help each other in time of need, hence values that are conducive to cooperative development. However, it is also imperative to carefully heed the interpretation of Asian values by political figures and authorities in Asia which often serves their own political interest.[16]

Therefore, in the context of a promoting a healthy public policy on cooperative development, it is important to refer to those time-tested Asian values which are in conformity with community traditions and basic human rights. The latter has been historically ignored for the sake of satisfying political interests of post-colonial as well as current political leaders. The preponderance of government control over cooperatives after independence only helped to create a lingering dependency on government support. Cooperative leaders, instead of promoting the cooperative values and creating benefits for members, opted to please the government for their rent-seeking purposes. Examples of the KUD in Indonesia, Samahang Nayon in the Philippines, and Comilla in Bangladesh, all served to show that cooperatives were by and large run by the government rather than by the people. Cooperatives were stigmatized as being government organs, and as a result the public lost interest in joining cooperatives in most of the developing nations in Asia over the post-independence period. Evidence-based data has shown that the credit union movement in Asia[17] seems to be the only perceptible cooperative sector that is an independent and member-driven one that is not government controlled.

The unhealthy environment for cooperative development in the Asia region until the late 1980s had urged the ICA, notably its leadership in Asia and the Pacific, to initiate a public policy forum to overcome the stigma attached to cooperatives. In the late 1980s and the early 1990s ICA AP began to open up a set of policy debates to rebuild the image of cooperative as genuine people-centered and member-based cooperatives.

The historical milestone of the ICA Centennial Congress in 1995[18] afforded co-operators all over the world a keen understanding of the Cooperative Identity Statement, thus creating a new space to empower the ICA AP to advocate the cooperative identity in various public policy domains, most notably during the Asia Pacific Regional Consultations and Asia Pacific Cooperative Ministers Conferences.

Slow as the case may be, governments have begun to see cooperatives more as a partner for creating peoples' welfare, rather than viewing them as mere instruments to expedite their national policy agendas, or worst still to cater to their narrow political needs and interests. The Promotion of Cooperatives Recommendation (No. 193) of the ILO, provided a parallel empowerment tool to advocate and create autonomous

---

[16] More explicit description of this cautionary theme on Asian Values could be found in the earlier chapter of this book by Akira Kurimoto's 'Why Waking Asian Pacific Cooperative Potential?'

[17] Data on Credit Union Network Strength 2017 in Asia published in the Annual Report 2017–2018 of the Asian Confederation of Credit Unions, p. 5.

[18] The ICA Centennial Congress held in Manchester in September 1995 adopted new Cooperative Principles that is contained within a "*Statement on the Cooperative Identity*", including an official Definition and Basic Cooperative Values.

and self-reliant cooperatives in many developing as well as developed countries due to the realization of a more enabling environment that is favorable for cooperative development.

The adoption of the Blueprint for a Cooperative Decade by the ICA in 2012 was another milestone which has showcased a dramatic improvement of the visibility and the understanding of the Cooperative model. The Blueprint came as the UN declared its International year of Cooperatives, so its adoption is a repositioning of cooperatives as a democratic enterprise where members have a voice and must actively take part in bringing about socio-economic as well as environmental sustainability.

This is a far cry from when governments tend to dictate cooperatives from the top-down in the past, toward a more favorable conduct as partners that work together with cooperatives in meeting the sustainable development goals of the UN. The fact that the UN recognized cooperatives in its core documents as playing a central role in meeting the Sustainable Development Goals, certainly helped in obliterating the old stigma of cooperatives as being mere handmaidens of governments.

It became apparent that the potential of cooperative development in Asia has now been gradually awakened and must be further sustained, and doing so by integrating the inherent and time-tested Asian values, by responding to members' start-ups among the young entrepreneurs, and by incorporating the wisdom and strength of women members from the ground up.

References

Baswir R (2000) Cooperatives and the new order authority, Jakarta, Kompas Newspaper

Hasan S, Onyx J (eds) (2008) Comparative third sector governance in Asia, structure, process, and political economy. Springer, UAE & Sydney

Henrÿ H (2012) Guidelines for cooperative legislation, 3rd edn. International Labour Office, Geneva

Kurimoto A (2020) Why Asian Pacific cooperative models matter?. In: Waking the Asian Pacific cooperative potential. Elsevier

Kurimoto A, Dongre Y (2020) Emerging Asian Pacific cooperative models from a global history perspective. In: Waking the Asian Pacific cooperative potential. Elsevier

Münkner HH (1989) Cooperative ideas, principles and practices. Marburg/Lahn.

Münkner HH (ed) (2005) 100 years Indian cooperative credit societies act, India 1904—a worldwide applied model of cooperative legislation, ICA ROAP, New Delhi

Münkner HH (2015) Cooperative principles and cooperative law. Lit Verlag/Wien

Quddus MA (1993) Rural development in Bangladesh: strategies and experiences. Book/Working Paper, Bangladesh Academy for Rural Development

Shankar R, Cronan G (2001) 2nd critical study on cooperative policy and legislation, International Cooperative Alliance

Sharma GK (1997) Cooperative laws in Asia and the Pacific. Bonow Memorial Trust, The COOP Times, New Delhi, India

Soedjono I, Cordero M (1997) Critical study on cooperative legislation and competitive strength. Document Press International Cooperative Alliance, Regional Office for Asia and the Pacific, India

Tulus R (2017) Strengthening cooperative multi-stakeholders' partnerships in Asia Pacific. A critical appraisal of past, present and future APCMCs. Presentation at the 10th Asia Pacific Cooperative Ministers' conference, Hanoi, Vietnam

Turnell S (2013) History of Burma's financial system. Nordic Institute of Asian Studies Press, Australia

Yousaf N (2003) Allama Mashriqi & Dr. Akhtar Hameed Khan: two legends of Pakistan. New York. Allama Mashriqi is one of the founding fathers of Pakistan and Akhtar Hameed Khan, a world-renowned social scientist

National Constitutions and Cooperatives: An Overview

Ifigeneia Douvitsa

To Hagen,
the Rockstar of our field!

1 Introduction

The de jure or "big c" constitutions are the legal documents that are self-defined as the fundamental or the supreme laws of countries, regulating the state's structure and powers, as well as its relationship with the public and are usually harder to amend or repeal than other laws (Law 2010). Evidence shows that such legal documents "proclaiming their higher status appear in 90% of the countries" (Elkins et al. 2009, p. 49), making constitutions a global legal phenomenon that exceeds specific legal traditions and families in the current world. Apart from their superiority, the constitutions also tend to bear other features, such as being constitutive of a legal system, written, justiciable, and expressing a common ideology (Raz 1998). However, such features may not appear in all constitutions, due to the variety and pluralism of the constitutional universe. Even if "*constitutions are not textbooks on the governance of a particular country, it does not follow that such textbooks should, or even can – without peril – ignore the constitution of that country*" (Finer et al. 1995, p. 2). In many cases, they are still at the center of the political debate and considered to shed some light to the political scene and the country's historic, economic, and social

This chapter is a reprint from "National Constitutions and Cooperatives: an Overview" published by the *International Journal of Cooperative Law, 2018, Issue I, pp. 128–147, with permission of IUS COOPERATIVUM Association and the Editors of the International Journal of Cooperative Law.*

I. Douvitsa (✉)
Hellenic Open University, Patra, Greece
e-mail: ifigeneiadouvitsa83@yahoo.gr

W. Tadjudje and I. Douvitsa (eds.), *Perspectives on Cooperative Law*,
https://doi.org/10.1007/978-981-19-1991-6_6

particularities (Finer et al. 1995; Breslin 2009). Furthermore, research findings indicate that majority of constitutions not only claim to limit government power, but are reasonably or fully operative in practice (Breslin 2009, p. 29).

The current article focuses on a specific institution protected by the constitutions, that of cooperatives. A broadly accepted definition of cooperatives is the one included in the historic Statement on the Cooperative Identity in 1995, established by the International Cooperative Alliance (ICA), which is the representative organ of cooperatives worldwide (ICA 1995). According to the latter, the cooperative is an autonomous association of persons united voluntarily to meet their common economic, social, and cultural needs and aspirations through a jointly owned and democratically controlled enterprise (ICA 1995). The ICA also prescribed a set of cooperative values (self-help, self-responsibility, democracy, equality, equity, and solidarity) and cooperative principles (voluntary and open membership, democratic member control, member economic participation, autonomy and independence, cooperation among cooperatives, concern for community) for all the cooperatives to follow (ICA 1995).

Such cooperative values and principles have been incorporated in the 193/2002 "Promotion of Cooperatives" Recommendation of the International Labour Organization (ILO R. 193), which calls upon legislators to create an adequate legal environment "*consistent with the nature and function of cooperatives and guided by the cooperative values and principles*" (ILO R. 193, para 6). The latter is considered to be the "*first and only instrument of universal applicability on cooperative law adopted by an international governmental organization*" (Henrÿ 2013, p. 66). There has been a growing agreement in literature and case law that the ILO R. 193 is legally binding, constituting the nucleus of public international cooperative (Henrÿ 2013).

The growing literature on cooperatives has focused mainly on ordinary law, whereas there has been little investigation of where the national constitutions stand toward cooperatives. Therefore, the present study aspires to address that gap, undertaking an investigation of the national constitutions on a worldwide scale.

2 Research Methodology

In this research context, the legal texts that have been examined are the ones that are self-defined as constitutions and the supreme laws of the country, an approach that has been widely used in large-scale inquiries (Law 2010). According to previous research, the vast majority of countries have such texts (Elkins et al. 2009, p. 49). The inquiry has been based on available databases and a previous study of the ICA Legislative Working Group which took place in 2009 (ICA 2009). Its findings have been updated and the number of constitutions that were studied has been broadened.

3 Main Findings

(i) *Constitutions with cooperative-related articles: An increased tendency*

For the period from 1900 to 2016, in which new constitutions have emerged from new and old polities, the introduction of the term "*cooperative*" in the constitutional texts has increased (Fig. 1). This highlights a growing interest in the cooperative institution by the national legislator who has been willing to introduce relevant articles to regulate it. The highest percentage of such constitutions is noted during the first half of the twentieth century and the lowest in the 1990s, after which the total number of such constitutions reaches to a plateau (Fig. 1). Based on the above, the cooperative-related articles were introduced in the early constitutions of the century, especially during the post-war era, whereas it is rare for such inclusion to take place in the newest and recent contemporary constitutions of the late twentieth and twenty-first centuries.

The earliest introduction of such provision took place in Mexico with the Constitution of 1917, which in ar. 123.30 among other provisions in favor of labor and social welfare; it acknowledged the form of cooperatives. On the other hand, the latest inclusion of cooperatives in a national constitutional text belongs to Morocco. In an attempt to enhance the powers of the parliament and limit those of the King, the Moroccan constitution of 1996 was amended in 2011 and in its ar. 71 it includes cooperatives to the list of subjects under the legislative powers of the Parliament.

(ii) *The current Constitutions*

The study found that the countries that have introduced cooperative articles in their constitutions are in Africa: *Angola, Central Africa, Congo, Egypt,*

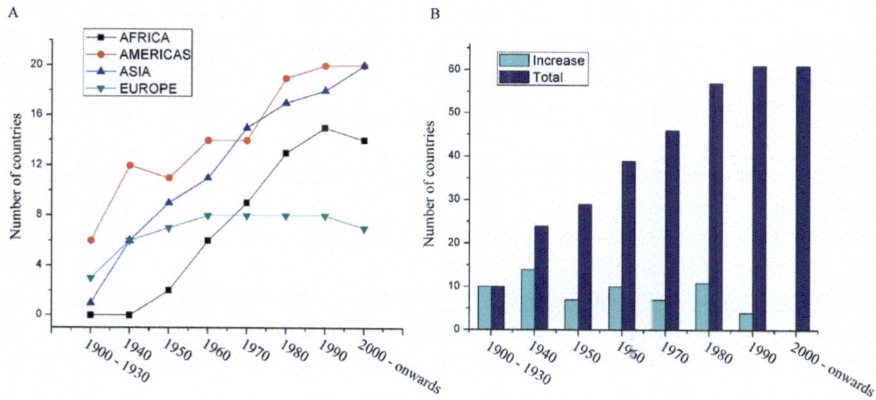

Fig. 1 Increase of constitutions with cooperative provisions from 1900 to 2016. **a** Number of countries with cooperative provisions in their constitutions in each region for 1900–2016. **b** Increase and total number of countries with cooperative provisions for 1900–2016 Permission from Douvitsa (2018)

Equatorial Guinea, Ethiopia, Guinea-Bissau, Kenya, Morocco, Mozambique, Namibia, Nigeria, Sao Tome and Principe, Swaziland; in Asia: *Bangladesh, China, Cyprus, India, Iran, Korea (DPR), Kuwait, Malaysia, Myanmar, Nepal, Pakistan, Philippines, Sri Lanka, Taiwan, Tajikistan, Timor-Leste, Thailand, Turkey, Uzbekistan, Yemen*; in the Americas: *Bolivia, Brazil, Colombia, Costa Rica, Cuba, Dominican Republic, Ecuador, El Salvador, Guatemala, Guyana, Haiti, Honduras, Mexico, Nicaragua, Panama, Paraguay, Peru, Suriname, Uruguay, Venezuela;* and in Europe: *Belarus, Bulgaria, Greece, Italy, Malta, Portugal, Serbia, Spain.* Compared to Africa (14/54, 26%) and Asia (20/48, 41%), South America has the highest rate (20/35, 57%), whereas Europe the lowest (8/43, 19%).

(iii) *Latin America: a region with an abundance of constitutions with cooperative provisions*

Latin America is found to possess the highest percentage of countries with cooperative provisions at constitutional level, compared to the regions of Africa, Asia, and Europe. Due to the particularity that the former presents, a further examination is needed.

Historically, the idea of the Rochdalean cooperativism was brought to Latin America by European immigrants, in the late nineteenth and early twentieth centuries. Since then, cooperativism has been acknowledged by cooperative laws and constitutional provisions. Specifically, the first constitution of the Latin American region that recognized the status of cooperatives was the Mexican Constitution of 1917, as a result of the 1910 revolution. Its content was radical for its time, due to the social and economic rights that it prescribed, which later constituted the essence of modern labor law (Gargarella 2014). Its main influence was the Spanish Constitution of Cadiz (Mirow 2015), which however did not have any references to cooperatives. From the study's research, it was noted that the Mexican Constitution was also the first constitution of the world that acknowledged modern cooperativism. Under the domino effect most of the Mexican constitutional provisions influenced the rest of the countries that promulgated new constitutions at the time, such as Peru (1919), Honduras (1924), Brazil (1937), Bolivia (1938), El Salvador (1939) (Carozza 2003; Figueroa 2011).

To better understand the constitutional history of the region, its division into three distinctive periods, which are the period of liberal-conservative constitutions (1850–1910), of social constitutionalism (1910–1950), and of multiculturalism and human rights (1950–2010), has proved useful (Gargarella 2014). The first wave of the introduction of cooperative articles in Latin American constitutions took place during the period of social constitutionalism, "*in which they expressed, through the use of legal language, the main social change that had taken place in the region during the first half of the twentieth century- namely the incorporation of the working class as a decisive political and economic actor*" (Gargarela 2014, pp. 12–13). In the cooperatives' case, it even took the active form of participation in constitutional drafting, as in the case of the Brazilian constitution of 1988 (Cracogna 2016).

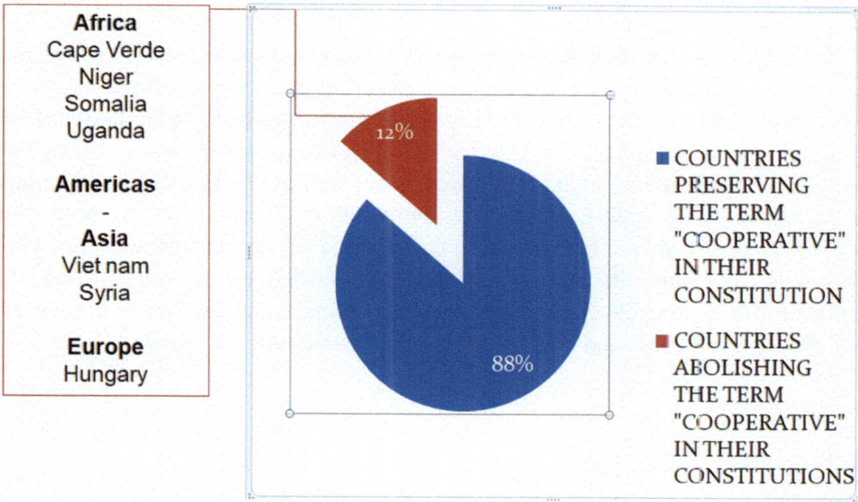

Fig. 2 The vast majority of countries preserve the term "cooperative" in their current national constitutions. Percentage of countries that preserved the term "cooperative" in their constitutions (blue color) and countries that abolished it (red color) Permission from Douvitsa (2018)

A particular trait of the Latin American constitutionalism is constant reform or replacement of the constitution, arising the issue of their entrenchment (Eustace 2014). Nevertheless, the constitutional protection of cooperatives does not seem to be affected by the phenomenon of fluid constitutionalism. In fact, unlike those in other regions, none of the Latin American constitutions currently in force have abolished the constitutional protection of cooperatives (Fig. 2).

4 Conclusions

The present study focuses on the domestic constitutions of the world that introduce specific provisions about cooperatives, offering in that matter a general overview. This topic presents an interesting area for research in the field of cooperative law due to the constitutions' supremacy over ordinary laws, their potential to enforce supranational norms, as well as their embedding of political considerations, morals, and ethics. Despite that, the topic has not attracted sufficient scientific interest. Thus, this study aspires to contribute to the gap in research by undertaking a study on constitutions and cooperatives in a worldwide scale.

Our findings show that one out of three constitutions in the world introduces cooperative-specific articles in their texts and the number of such constitutions increased from 1900 to 2016. The content of the cooperative-related provisions in the constitutional text varies from country to country, covering different chapters of the constitution from articles on governmental powers to the allocation of power and the protection of human rights.

The largest number of such supreme laws appears in the countries of Latin America and their promulgation may be traced to the period of social constitutionalism, in which the working class started to have a significant presence in the political and economic sphere. Despite Latin America's fluid constitutionalism, the acknowledgement of cooperatives has not been removed by any of the contemporary constitutions of the region. Latin America's strong commitment to the constitutional protection of cooperatives is also indicated by the fact that the Mexican Constitution of 1917 was the first constitutional text in the world to acknowledge cooperatives. Thus, the constitutional protection of cooperatives was a Latin American innovation, a fact that shows the richness and particularity of their constitutional history.

References

Breslin B (2009) From words to Worlds: exploring constitutional functionality. The John Hopkins University Press, Baltimore

Carozza PG (2003) From conquest to constitutions: retrieving a Latin American tradition of the idea of human rights. Scholarly works, paper 581

Cracogna D (2016) Las cooperativas en las constituciones nacionales. In: 1st International forum on cooperative law and IInd continental congress on co-operative law, Montevideo, 16th–18th Nov

Elkins Z, Ginsburg T, Melton J (2009) The endurance of national constitutions. Cambridge University Press, Cambridge

Eustace R (2014) Fluid constitutions: a Latin American phenomenon. In: COHA, 3th July

Figueroa D (2011) Current constitutional developments in Latin America. International legal research informer, summer issue, pp 8–18

Finer SE, Bogdanor V, Rudden B (1995) Comparing constitutions. Clarendon Press, Oxford

Gargarella R (2014) Latin American constitutionalism: social rights and the "engine room" of the constitution. Notre Dame J Int Comp Law 4(1):9–18. Available at: http://scholarship.law.nd.edu/ndjicl/vol4/iss1/3

Henrÿ H (2013) Public international cooperative law. In: Cracogna D, Fici A, Henrÿ H (eds) International handbook of cooperative law. Springer, Berlin, pp 65–88

ICA (1995) Statement on co-operative identity. General Assembly of the International Co-operative Alliance. Available at http://www.gdrc.org/icm/coop-principles.html

ICA Legislative Working Group (2009) References to cooperatives in national constitutions. Centre International de Conférences Genève-CICG, 18 Nov

Law D (2010) Constitutions. In: Cane P, Kritzer HM (eds) The Oxford handbook of empirical legal research. Oxford University Press, Oxford, pp 376–398

Mirow MC (2015) Latin American constitutions: the constitution of Cádiz and its legacy in Spanish America. Florida International University College of Law

Permission from Douvitsa I (2018) National constitutions and cooperatives. An overview. Int J Coop Law (1):128–147

Raz J (1998) On the authority and interpretation of constitutions: some preliminaries. In: Alexander L (ed) Constitutionalism: philosophical foundations. Cambridge University Press, Cambridge, p 152 ff

The Legal Regulation of the Cuban Cooperative Sector: Analysis of Its Current State with a View to the Unification of the Sector

Orestes Rodríguez Musa and Orisel Hernandez Aguilar

1 Introduction

On April 10, 2019, the new Constitution of the Republic of Cuba was published, which formulated a general recognition of the cooperative, breaking with the previous limitation of this to the agricultural sphere. In that same year, new norms were promulgated that ordered, separately, the two manifestations of the national cooperativism: agriculture (Decree-Law No. 365 "On Agricultural Cooperatives" and Decree No. 354 "Regulation of the Decree-Law of the Agricultural Cooperatives", of May 24, 2019) and the non-agricultural one (Decree-Law No. 366 "Of Non-Agricultural Cooperatives" and Decree No. 356 "Regulations of Non-Agricultural Cooperatives", of August 30, 2019).

Despite the fact that none of these regulations was presented with the intention of advancing the rapprochement between the two existing modalities, as they are under the protection of the unifying precept of the Charter, it is valid to question to what extent between them it was possible give an approximation. In this task, the election parameters to be considered must be those that delineate the identity of these figures, that is, "the principles of cooperativism" (Constitution of the Republic of Cuba, 2019: Article 22 b.).

The full understanding of the cooperative identity can only be achieved by studying the guidelines that govern the internal and external functioning of the entity. These guidelines are contained in a set of rules resulting from the fluctuations

"Some excerpts in this document come from «Unification of the cooperative sector Cuban. Critical notes in the light of cooperative principles», with permission from CIRIEC-Spain, Legal Review of Social and Cooperative Economy".

O. R. Musa (✉) · O. H. Aguilar
Legal Sciences, Law Department of the University of Pinar del Río, Pinar del Río, Cuba
e-mail: musa@upr.edu.cu

O. H. Aguilar
e-mail: oriselha@upr.edu.cu

W. Tadjudje and I. Douvitsa (eds.), *Perspectives on Cooperative Law*,
https://doi.org/10.1007/978-981-19-1991-6_7

of prevailing economic and political interests in different historical contexts, from which the International Cooperative Alliance (ICA) offers its own catalog according to the needs of cooperatives to world level, decisively contributing to their "universal reach, by making them applicable to all types, times and places"(Llobregat Hurtado 1990, p. 16).

Consequently, the objective of this work has a double implication, since it aims to assess the current regulations of the Cuban cooperative sector, emphasizing the degree of unification that can be evidenced in them, in accordance with the constitutional guideline, taking as reference the principles of the movement raised by the ICA.

2 Constitutional Regulation of Cooperatives: Analysis of Its Current State

As has been explained on other occasions (Rodríguez Musa 2017), historically the legal regulation of the cooperative has not been consistent with its identity, since its classification has been forced into other figures that do not include its double economic and social content, or it was defined from reductionist conceptions that have not favored its development in accordance with the satisfaction of popular needs. Despite this, the cooperative is currently expanding into other spheres of the national economy, based on an experimental legislative framework. In this process, difficulties have arisen that distorted the associative nature of the institution and its purpose of serving its members and the community.

The Charter of April 10, 2019, after a widely participatory popular process, in Article 22, subsection d), recognizes "private property: that which is exercised over certain means of production by Cuban or foreign natural or legal persons ...". Thus, comes the appropriate basis to authorize the creation of private companies under legal forms of a lucrative nature. In this way, the need for those who have used cooperatives to cover up this type of economic activity would disappear.

In addition, Article 22 of the new Constitution, in its subsection b), recognizes "cooperative property" as "sustained by the collective work of its proprietary partners and in the effective exercise of the principles of cooperativism." The letter of this precept has some aspects that signify an evolution with respect to the old Constitution of 1976, as well as other elements that generate uncertainty and various absences that could result in inertia, namely:

Inertia: The reduction of its legal nature to "Form of property", neglecting the associative bond that it implies, the corresponding service purpose, the values that are inherent to it and the institutional environment in which—according to its identity—it must be articulated. In addition, the emphatic formulation regarding the "collective work of its proprietary partners" as a support for cooperatives, could appear as a limitation to establish other types of cooperatives different from work cooperatives, such as consumer or credit cooperatives (nonexistent until now in the country), which are also inspired by popular socio-economic needs.

Evolution: In another sense, the agrarian perspective of the old Constitution disappears. Now cooperatives, regardless of the sector of the economy where they develop, will have constitutional protection. Furthermore, the relevance of some "principles" that should mark the functioning of these institutions is recognized, as they are part of a movement that overcomes and strengthens them.

Uncertainty: However, it is worth asking what "Principles of cooperativism" refers to the Constituent Assembly, since in Cuba those raised by the International Cooperative Alliance have never been mentioned, nor has a uniform criterion been used to define them. Therefore, there may be different interpretations of the Constitution that—in this case—made by the legislator.

Against this background, the will of the legislator and the enforcement authority are decisive to enhance the articulation of a national cooperative movement.

3 Legal Regulations of Cuban Cooperativism: A View Regarding the Unification

As anticipated in the introduction, below is an assessment of the level of rapprochement that can be seen between the new Cuban regulations of the two fundamental forms of existing cooperatives, taking as reference points to guide said examination the principles that the ICA has systematized, inasmuch as they synthesize the essential aspects of the identity of said figures.

- *Voluntary and open association*

  Due to its content, regarding the form of integration into the cooperative, this principle occupies the first place in the ICA catalog. Its name indicates that it combines two elements: the autonomous decision and consent to assume the associative commitment and the accessible nature of the incorporation, given by minimal conditioning factors.

  Following this logic, in the enumeration of the operating rules made by the regulations of the Agricultural Cooperatives (CAs) and the Non-Agricultural Cooperatives (CNAs), the first aspect that is pointed out is that of the voluntary nature of admission and permanence. The dictates in both cases are almost identical and lack a statement regarding the way in which access is ordered, a question that can only be clarified with a complete reading of the two Decree-Laws.

  Among the requirements for entry to cooperatives, in the first order, it is established that the minimum age is 18 years. This contrasts with the minimum working age, hindering access to membership status for people who, according to Law 116 of 2014, Labor Code, have the capacity to enter into employment contracts, which is acquired at 17 years of age, and even, exceptionally from the age of 15.

  To belong to both the CAs and to the CNAs, the condition of permanent resident in Cuba is required, being able to carry out the tasks that the corporate purpose in question deals with and making contributions to the goods and work cooperative.

The number of possible partners for the CAs is not determined for any moment of their development. For CNAs, the situation is different. Initially, its constitution requires the will of at least three interested parties and the setting of the minimum and maximum number of partners is reserved to their statutes. In addition, the Special Provisions of Decree-Law No. 366 introduce a set of legal limits to the possibilities of variation of the number of members in the CNAs before and after the entry into force of the aforementioned Decree-Law, cooperatives of national scope and construction cooperatives. These measures can be attributed to the experimental nature of these associative forms, the anomalies detected in their development and the economic policy of the country.

The prohibition of conflict of interest is a common condition in both cases, although it is configured differently according to the terms of the activity in question.

Complying with the previously related requirements, the access process during the establishment of the cooperative is presented in similar terms, while the subsequent incorporation procedure varies subtly. CAs forcefully demand a trial period and CNAs can do the same or directly allow their incorporation. Other disparities are observed in the term of the test, which in the CAs does not exceed ninety business days and in the CNAs it has a limit of nine months.

The loss of consensuality, which implies access, gives rise to two types of situations, foreseen in the two cooperative forms: some, in which it is no longer in the interest of the member to remain in the entity, and others, in which the corporate group decides to do without one of its members. Only for CNAs the loss of the requirements to be a member is contemplated for such purposes. In the case of the CA, a cause is specified relating to non-compliance with the production plan or the deviation of it repeatedly. Another issue to take into consideration is that the CNA reserves the possibility that the statutes establish other assumptions that generate such consequences.

Regarding guarantees, in any case, cooperative members are assured the right to collect the advances pending payment, the debts for the goods contributed, the profits that correspond to them until the day they leave and other rights recognized in law.

- *Democratic control by members*

Perhaps the identifying element par excellence of this principle is its expression in the form of «one associate, one vote», as it provides an important pillar to distinguish the cooperative association from capitalist societies (Rodríguez Musa 2017, p. 47). However, its implications go beyond the equal recognition of the rights of all members to transcend the scope of effective participation in decision-making through the role assigned to the General Assembly as the guiding center of cooperative work.

In both sectors of national cooperativism, recognition of this guideline has been formulated in the form of «collective decision and equal rights of cooperative members/partners». As a consequence of this, the powers to attend the general assemblies with voice and vote are established; elect and be elected for management positions and administrative functions; know the status of the management of the cooperative; be informed and approve the annual economic plans, financial statements and internal checks; and voluntarily associate or join the corresponding union and trade union organizations.

This democratic potential, inherent in being a member, is complemented by the weight of the General Assembly in the decisions of the cooperative. Its designation as a superior body is supported by the control it exercises over the rest of the entity's fabric since the main positions are chosen from within it, are accountable to it and can be revoked by it.

These attributions are correlated with the approval of the fundamental internal regulations, regardless of their name in each case (Hernández Aguilar 2020, p. 105–106); that of constituting the assembly body as the last instance in cooperative processes; and that of issuing pronouncements aimed at directing the merger, division, or dissolution of the organization.

- *Economic participation of associates*

The purpose of this principle is to provide guidance on how members should invest in their cooperatives and manage their financial results. The uniqueness of this involvement regime highlights the *sui generis* character of this form of company, since it functions in a way that capital serves the organization and does not dominate it.

The first thing that is noticed when reading the articles that in Decree-Law No. 365 and Decree-Law No. 366 deal with the general rules of Cuban cooperatives is the absence of a provision clearly focused on harmonizing the extremes that understands the idea of economic participation of the associates. The closest thing to the content of interest here is the declaration of economic self-sustainability of the CAs and of the economic sustainability of the CNAs. However, throughout the regulations contained in the legal bodies examined, the cross-sectional presence of the elements that make up this principle is appreciated, with some dispersion, asymmetry and inaccuracies.

The term social capital does not appear in the regulations relating to the CAs and the mention of the contributions of the members is interspersed with the explanation of their duties and with the assets of the cooperatives (Campos Pérez 2018, p.197). To this must be added the complexity of its form of integration, given the significant variations that operate depending on whether it is Basic Units of Cooperative Production (UBPC), Agricultural Production Cooperatives (CPA) or Cooperatives of Credit and Services (CCS) due to the type of economic activity that each cooperative form is called upon to carry out.

The systematic use of the aforementioned categories is different in the case of CNAs. Even when the interrelation between such elements is perceptible, it is possible to appreciate the delimitation between the cooperative patrimony, the initial working capital and the monetary and non-monetary contributions of the partners.

Regarding the use and distribution of the surpluses of the cooperatives, it is known that it is regularity that the deduction of certain amounts that are assigned to funds and reserves must be attended first (García Müller 2006, p. 88), or other requirements of the general and/or internal rules. Thus, in the entire sector in the country, it is necessary to previously comply with financial and tax commitments and with the amounts of the amounts allocated to the funds and corresponding reserves.

Regarding the fundamental forms and moments in which the distribution of surpluses is carried out, both in the CAs and in the CNAs, there are different advances, the benefits of another type that the partners receive throughout the year and the distribution that is performed at the end of this.

However, it should be noted that in terms of advances and benefits there is no exact unity regarding their conception. In Decree-Law No. 365, it is understood that the former are limited to "all the income that the cooperative member obtains before closing the economic cycle" with which any non-monetary remuneration would be a benefit. For its part, Decree-Law No. 366 assumes that advances can be in "cash, goods or services", leaving out of these only benefits associated with cooperative funds or other forms defined by the Assemblies.

Finally, it should be noted that in all cases the principle is enshrined that the distribution will be based on the final results of the production and the quantity and quality of the work performed, with the exception that in the CNA 'in no case the amount of the highest profit that corresponds to a partner can exceed three times the lowest."

- *Autonomy and independence*

  Autonomy must be an element that cuts across all legal provisions relating to the cooperative. Its spirit must overcome the cold legal definitions and inform, from start to finish, the legal instrumentation of the figure through concrete elements. However, the express recognition of the principle, in addition to being valuable to typify the cooperative phenomenon, endows autonomy with the legality that its effective protection requires, operating as an essential prerequisite for its inherent effects to be deployed.

  On other occasions, it has been argued that, when regulating the legal relations between the State and agricultural cooperatives in Cuba, a model was assumed that has substantially limited the autonomy that should characterize them (Rodríguez Musa 2017).

  This perspective is maintained in the new Decree-Law No. 365, where the principle of autonomy is not established among its guiding principles and it is provided that the Minister of Agriculture authorizes the constitution of agricultural cooperatives; that state control over them is exercised by the organs, agencies, and entities of the State empowered to do so; that the cooperatives contract and sell to the state entities the agricultural and forestry productions that are demanded to cover the needs foreseen in the plan of the national economy for the destinations of state interest; that their relations with the state companies to which they are linked are manifested through contracts in order to develop their fundamental line of production, reconcile and agree on their development program, their annual production plan, volumes, assortments, and destinations of the productions for the state commission, or other different purposes that pay tribute to the economy plan; and that the dissolution of the agricultural cooperatives is approved by the Resolution of the Minister of Agriculture.

Regarding the CNAs, among the principles that govern them according to the new Decree-Law No. 366, 2019, is "economic autonomy and sustainability", according to which the cooperative has economic independence, freely disposing of its assets within the limits established by law.

However, these associative forms retain an experimental character from their origin, in keeping with the rigorous administrative process for their approval and dissolution. Likewise, section 1 of article 17 of Decree No. 356, 2019, regulates 21 aspects that the Statutes must contain, which can contribute (as has happened up to now with the previous regulations), so that said Statutes are overloaded with contents, procedures and detailed rules. This regulatory tone of the legislator is enhanced when article 6 of Decree No. 356, 2019 itself requires the intervention of the competent public authority in the approval of various transcendental contents for the operation of the cooperative, as the organ or body of the State who is responsible for authorizing the constitution of the cooperative, in the same act it approves its national or territorial scope, corporate purpose and secondary, eventual or support activities that are authorized; the name of the applicants; the property and other assets to be transferred, as well as the conditions under which this transfer will take place. It also approves the goods or services that constitute the state commission; the main inputs to be supplied by the state supplier; the prices of goods and services that will remain centrally established; and the results that are expected to be obtained with the new form of management, both in quantity and quality of productions or services, if applicable, as well as the conditions under which this assignment will be made. It also approves the goods or services that constitute the state commission; the main inputs to be supplied by the state supplier; the prices of goods and services that will remain centrally established; and the results that are expected to be obtained with the new form of management, both in quantity and quality of productions or services, if applicable, as well as the conditions under which this assignment will be made. It also approves the goods or services that constitute the state commission; the main inputs to be supplied by the state supplier; the prices of goods and services that will remain centrally established; and the results that are expected to be obtained with the new form of management, both in quantity and quality of productions or services, if applicable.

- *Education, training and information*

The complexity and scope of this principle make it "the golden rule of cooperativism." The actions that give it its name show its breadth: education, understood as a constant process in life through which knowledge, skills, beliefs, values, or habits are acquired by different methods and in varying degrees of depth; training, as an educational modality aimed particularly at creating technical, theoretical, and practical knowledge in individuals for the performance of a certain activity; and information, as a form of access to an organized group of data, related to an entity or phenomenon, that make up a message and allow the necessary level of knowledge to be acquired for decision-making.

The regulations of the two Cuban cooperative sectors require, in relatively similar terms, that these organizational forms promote cooperative education. However, from the articles referring to this topic, the absence of allusions to the information stands out, in contrast to the reiteration of dictations on training and education actions. In addition, it should be noted that the subjects involved in such activities in the case of the CAs are restricted to the cooperative members, their families and the contracted workers, while in the CNAs it is planned, in principle, that they be the members, although there is room for to their families and the community, if the link between education and the cooperative culture that the latter deals with is understood. In any case, of the aforementioned norms, it is necessary to praise the success of attributing responsibilities to state entities whose collaboration is essential in achieving the intended purpose. Accordingly, Decree-Law No. 365, entrusted the State with the promotion of Agricultural Cooperatives with «the allocation of places in the study continuity plans for the training of the qualified mid-level workforce, skills in education level programs short-cycle higher education and careers at universities, as well as promoting and managing the requalification and postgraduate improvement of its technicians." Regarding Non-Agricultural Cooperatives, Decree No. 356, entrusted the Ministry of Higher Education with the preparation of "the preparation and training program on the principles of operation of cooperatives.

As this task of overcoming must be assumed by the finances of the cooperatives, it has been foreseen that it will be paid in the CAs by the Development Fund, as one more of its functions, and in the CNAs by a fund specifically destined to the education and training of members."

- *Cooperation between cooperatives*

  Since its inception, cooperatives have practiced collaboration with each other as a favorable formula for their success. "External solidarity as an extension of internal solidarity shows that it is a question of finishing a process … to achieve the shared goals of cooperativism" (Martínez Charterina 2012, p. 141). However, in the Cuban socialist legal system, by recognizing this principle, it has permeated a lucrative nature that is alien to inter-cooperation.

  To illustrate this, it is worth mentioning that the new Decree-Law No. 365 for CA establishes that "collaboration between cooperatives and other entities" is materialized by "providing goods or services, providing information and exchanging experiences and other activities for the benefit of production. and the fulfillment of their corporate purposes, according to the approved corporate purpose, for which they sign contracts in the appropriate cases or another document that is agreed upon, when the collaboration does not have a commercial purpose."

  In a similar sense, under the principle of "collaboration and cooperation between cooperatives and other entities," Decree-Law No. 366 for CNA establishes that "cooperatives are related to each other and with other entities, state or not, through contracts, collaboration agreements, exchange of experiences and other legal activities."

  Consequently, this supposed collaboration and cooperation has been materialized—as a rule—through compensation and contracts, not giving way to date to the sustained institutionalization of higher forms of organization of the movement, such as second-degree cooperatives, which do not even they are mentioned in the most recent legislative changes.

- *Commitment to the community*

Regarding the commitment of Cuban cooperatives with the community, the formulation in the legislation of the CAs and that of the CNAs has come closer in their formulation.

To illustrate this, it is worth mentioning that Decree-Law No. 365 conceives "social responsibility and contribution to the development of the national economy" among the principles that govern them in agriculture. In this regard, it warns that "the plans and programs of agricultural cooperatives have the fundamental objective of contributing to the sustainable economic and social development of the communities in which they are located, the municipality and the country in general, in harmony with the environment, paying special attention to the latter and enforcing in its demarcation the provisions of the Cuban and international environmental legislation signed by the Cuban State, as well as the other legal provisions in force related to the activities they carry out".

For its part, Decree-Law No. 366 establishes among the principles that govern the operation of CNAs the "social responsibility, contribution to the planned development of the economy and the well-being of the partners and their families," whose content warns that «The cooperative's plans aim to contribute to the sustainable economic and social development of the nation from the territorial scope where it carries out its activities, to protect the environment, to develop its corporate purpose without speculative intent, and to guarantee disciplined compliance with fiscal obligations and others …».

As can be seen, in both cases the planned nature of the economy, the harmonization between local and national interests, and the protection of the environment are weighted. However, when referring to the social responsibility of Cuban cooperatives on other occasions, it has been argued the relevance of the national legal system approaching a "Direct Cooperative Social Responsibility Management Model," different from the one carried out through of State intermediation (Alfonso 2008, p. 48).

In Cuba, the practical application and institutional articulation of this principle, to date has not led this way, but to the same extent that the scenario of coincidence between popular interest and cooperative interest is consolidated, as well as the conscious practice of direct social responsibility, the intermediation of the State would lose meaning to preserve the general interest through formulas such as authorization of the corporate purpose, the price caps, the state commission and the collection of taxes.

4 Conclusions

From the foregoing, it can be summarized that:

- The constitutional regulation of cooperatives, in addition to repeating the idea that these are a form of ownership focused on collaboration only in the field of work of the partners, offers a favorable outlook for the differentiation of it with respect to associations with a purpose lucrative private sector and leaves useful bases for provisions of the authorities and the legislator that would allow, through the principles of cooperativism, to articulate the development of this figure, from its unification, with the social aspirations that define its identity.
- The ordering norms of the two Cuban cooperative typologies show, from their new legal formulations of 2019, a remarkable approximation in terms of the fundamental rules that back them up. However, this progress, insofar as it supposes an advance towards the legal unification of the sector, is marred by noticeable insufficiencies in terms of the level of assimilation by the own principles that have been given, of the contents systematized in the principles of the ACI and, on which depends, to a large extent, the improvement of national cooperatives in order to validate their particular identity and social projection.

Bibliography

Alianza Cooperativa Internacional Para Las Américas (2009) Ley Marco para las cooperativas de América Latina. Alianza Cooperativa Internacional para las Américas, San José

Alfonso AL (2008) Modelo de gestión de la responsabilidad social cooperativa directa. Estudio de caso: cooperativa de producción agropecuaria Camilo Cienfuegos. Tesis presentada en opción al grado científico de Doctor en Ciencias Económicas, Centro de Estudios de Desarrollo Cooperativo y Comunitario. Facultad de Ciencias Económicas, Universidad de Pinar del Río, Pinar del Río

Campos Pérez Y (2018) El capital social cooperativo como manifestación del principio de participación económica. Análisis teórico-legal en Cuba. En Boletín de la Asociación Internacional de Derecho Cooperativo, No. 53, Universidad de Deusto, Bilbao, pp 173–206

Cracogna D (2001) La legislación cooperativa en el mundo de hoy. Presentado en el Seminario de legislación cooperativa en Uruguay, el 22 de noviembre de 2001. Consultado en http://www.neticoop.org.uy/article118.html, el 13 de mayo de 2010

Fajardo García IG, Cruz MM (coord.) (2018). El cooperativismo en Cuba. Situación actual y propuestas para su regulación y fomento. CIRIEC-España, Valencia

García Müller A (2006) Instituciones de Derecho Cooperativo, Social, Solidario o de Participación. Mérida

Hernández Aguilar O (2020) La actividad registral relativa a las cooperativas en Cuba. Perspectivas para su desarrollo. En Deusto Estudios Cooperativos, No. 15, Universidad de Deusto, Bilbao, pp 87–117

Llobregat Hurtado ML (1990) In: Bosch JM (ed) Mutualidad y empresa cooperativa. Barcelona

Martínez Charterina A (2012) Sobre el principio de cooperación entre cooperativas en la actualidad. En Boletín de la Asociación Internacional de Derecho Cooperativo, No. 46, Universidad de Deusto, Bilbao, pp 133–146

Rodríguez Musa O (2017) La constitucionalización de la cooperativa. Una propuesta para su redimensionamiento en Cuba. Editorial Vincere Asociados, Brasilia-DF

Legislation

Constitución de la República de Cuba. Gaceta Oficial de la República de Cuba, Edición Extraordinaria Nº 5, La Habana, 10/4/2019
Decreto-Ley No. 365 (2019a) «De las Cooperativas Agropecuarias». Gaceta Oficial No. 37 Ordinaria de 24 de mayo de 2019
Decreto-Ley No. 366 (2019b) «De las Cooperativas no Agropecuarias», Gaceta Oficial No. 63 Ordinaria, de 30 de agosto de 2019b
Decreto No. 354 (2019) «Reglamento del Decreto-Ley De las Cooperativas Agropecuarias». Gaceta Oficial No. 37 Ordinaria de 24 de mayo de 2019
Decreto No. 356 (2019) «Reglamento de las Cooperativas no Agropecuarias», Gaceta Oficial No. 63 Ordinaria, de 30 de agosto de 2019

Cooperative Law and Social and Solidarity Economy Law

Social Enterprises and Social Cooperatives in the New Italian Legal Framework for Third Sector Organizations

Antonio Fici

1 Introduction

According to the Italian National Institute of Statistics ("ISTAT"), there were almost 360,000 active non-profit organizations ("NPOs") in Italy at 31 December 2018. Their number has been constantly increasing over the last decades. Indeed, the ISTAT reported only 235,000 active NPOs at the end of 2001.

Of these 360,000 NPOs, 85% are recognized or non-recognized associations, 4.4% social cooperatives, 2.2.% foundations, 8.4% NPOs established in another legal form (social enterprises, mutuals, etc.).

The Italian legislator has always shown great interest in NPOs, especially those devoted to social utility purposes, such as assistance to persons in need. This has led to a large-scale production of special laws on the subject, which started immediately after the unification of Italy.

Law 3 August 1862 no. 753 meticulously regulated "*opere pie*", namely, charitable institutions and other legal entities having the purpose of helping disadvantaged

[1] Cf. Zamagni (2000).

A long relationship of esteem and friendship, I hope mutual, unites me to Hagen. With him and other generous colleagues we have contributed, I believe, to revive the fortunes of cooperative law, often neglected even by the cooperative movement itself. The result is that the current situation is no longer that of ten years ago, when Dante Cracogna, Hagen Henrÿ and I conceived the "International Handbook of Cooperative Law", later published by Springer in 2013. The function that Hagen has continued to perform in recent years as the chairperson of the ICA Cooperative Law Committee, where I also have the honour of sitting, has further strengthened the role of cooperative law. Also for this we have to thank professor Henrÿ. And these notes of mine, which I am happy and honoured to be able to dedicate to him, will certainly not be sufficient for this purpose.

A. Fici (✉)
Private Law, University of Tor Vergata, Roma, Italy
e-mail: antonio.fici@uniroma2.it

W. Tadjudje and I. Douvitsa (eds.), *Perspectives on Cooperative Law*,
https://doi.org/10.1007/978-981-19-1991-6_8

persons, assisting them, providing education to them, initiating them into professions, arts or crafts.[1]

Law 15 April 1886, no. 3818, introduced "mutual aid societies", whose main purpose was to offer their members a subsidy in cases of illness or inability to work or old age, as well as to help the families of deceased members.

Along similar lines, in the 1990s, there was a new wave of special laws on individual NPOs, such as "voluntary organizations" (Law no. 266/1991), "social cooperatives" (Law no. 381/1991) and "associations of social promotion" (Law no. 383/2000), among others.[2] Of particular importance in that period is Legislative Decree no. 460/1997, which introduced specific tax measures in favour of "non-profit organizations of social utility", known as "ONLUS" from the Italian acronym. Legislative decree no. 155/2006 on "social enterprises" further enriched the already broad and complex Italian legal framework.

Some of these special laws, like those on social cooperatives of 1991 and on social enterprises of 2006, became models for foreign legislators since many countries followed Italy in introducing similar laws on these subjects.[3]

The myriad of special laws was certainly not able to help the development of what was already known at the time as the "third sector", which was the main reason why, in 2017, a legislative decree (no. 117/2017) introduced the "Code of the third sector" ("CTS"),[4] which, by repealing preceding laws, reorganized the entire area on new and different bases, without, however, breaking the connections with the past.

On the other hand, the Italian Civil Code of 1942 overlooked and still overlooks NPOs, providing a very bare regulation of the two general legal forms of NPOs in Italy, which are the association and the foundation.

2 From Non-profit Organizations to Third Sector Organizations: The Code of 2017

The regulation of associations and foundations is found in Articles 14–42 *bis* of the Italian Civil Code ("CC"). Presidential Decree no. 361/2000 lays down the procedure by which they acquire the legal personality.

While foundations must have legal personality to exist as such, associations may ("recognized associations") or may not ("non-recognized associations") have legal personality. The majority of Italian associations are associations without legal personality. This is due to the fact that non-recognized associations have the same legal capacity as recognized ones and, moreover, enjoy more organizational autonomy than recognized associations, being directly subject only to a few provisions of the

[2] Cf. Vaccario and Barbetta (2017), p. 445 ff.

[3] See, for references, Fici (2017) and Fici (2020b).

[4] Available at https://www.normattiva.it/uri-res/N2Ls?urn:nir:stato:decreto.legislativo:2017-07-03;117.

CC (Articles 36–38), one of which stipulates that they are regulated by their members' agreements.

On the other hand, the persons who act in the name and on behalf of the non-recognized association are also personally and jointly liable for the association's obligations (Article 38 CC). The legal personality of associations and foundations is therefore necessary only for excluding the liability of their directors and legal representatives for the entity's debts (so called "perfect patrimonial autonomy"). However, the procedure for obtaining the legal personality is lengthy and the requirements for its concession are stringent (associations must have minimum assets of around 40,000 EUR, while foundations' assets vary from 60,000 to 120,000 EUR approximately), so that most Italian associations prefer to act without legal personality (foundations do not have any alternative, since the legal personality is necessary for their very existence). As we shall see, this situation is different for third sector organizations, which may acquire the legal personality in a different manner and with lower minimum assets.

Less than 30 articles of law are dedicated by the CC to associations and foundations, which are not even defined therein. In contrast, greater attention is given to NPOs acting for the social utility, for which a specific optional status has been recently introduced by an ad hoc legislation, the status of "third sector organizations" ("TSO").[5]

Pursuant to the Code of the third sector (Article 4), the status of TSOs may be acquired only by organizations that:

- are incorporated as recognized or non-recognized associations or as foundations;
- are independent from the "excluded entities", i.e. they are not directed or controlled by those entities that may never acquire the status of TSO, namely, public entities, political parties, trade unions, professional associations, associations representing economic categories and representative organizations of employers;
- exclusively or mainly carry out one or more activities of general interest;
- have a non-profit purpose and exclusively pursue civic, solidaristic and social utility purposes;
- are registered in the single national register of the third sector ("RUNTS").

The law identifies the activities of general interest that an organization has to perform in order to obtain the status of TSO. It provides a long list of activities that, for that purpose, are deemed to own this nature (Article 5 Legislative decree no. 117/2017). This list includes the following activities:

(a) social services;
(b) health services;
(c) socio-health services;
(d) education, instruction and professional training;

[5] Cf. Fici (ed.) (2018).

(e) services aimed at safeguarding and improving the conditions of the environment and the prudent and rational use of natural resources, as well as the protection of animals and prevention of stray animals;
(f) services for the protection and enhancement of the cultural heritage and the landscape;
(g) university and post-university training;
(h) scientific research of particular social interest;
(i) organization and management of cultural, artistic or recreational activities of social interest, including activities, also editorial, for the promotion and dissemination of the culture and the practice of voluntary work and of activities of general interest;
(j) radio broadcasting of a community nature;
(k) organization and management of tourist activities of social, cultural or religious interest;
(l) extra-curricular training aimed at the prevention of early school leaving and academic and educational success, at preventing bullying and at combating educational poverty;
(m) instrumental services to third sector entities rendered by entities composed of not less than 70% of third sector entities;
(n) development cooperation;
(o) fair trade;
(p) services aimed at the insertion or reintegration into the labour market of disadvantaged workers and persons;
(q) social housing, as well as any other temporary residential activity aimed at satisfying social, health, cultural, training or working needs;
(r) humanitarian reception and social integration of migrants;
(s) social agriculture;
(t) organization and management of amateur sports activities;
(u) charity, distance support, free sale of food or products or provision of money, goods or services in support of disadvantaged people or of activities of general interest;
(v) promotion of the culture of legality, peace between peoples, nonviolence and unarmed defence;
(w) promotion and protection of human, civil, social and political rights, as well as the rights of consumers and users of activities of general interest, promotion of equal opportunities and mutual aid initiatives, including time banks and joint purchasing groups;
(x) handling of international adoption procedures;
(y) civil protection;
(z) requalification of unused public assets or assets confiscated from organized crime.

TSOs are also allowed to perform activities "other" than those of general interest (which, as said, must be carried out exclusively or at least prevalently), but only on the condition that they are provided for by their statutes, and are secondary and instrumental (Article 6 Legislative decree no. 117/2017).

The status of TSO is acquired from the day of the registration in the RUNTS. Applications are examined by the (national and regional) public offices of the RUNTS, which authorize the registration in the presence of the requirements for an organization's eligibility as a TSO. The status is maintained as long as registration persists. Deregistration may depend either on an organization's free choice or on the authority's decision after having ascertained that the organization has lost the necessary requirements for qualification or has violated the various rules regarding the organization and management of a TSO contained in the same Code.

By registering in the RUNTS, third sector organizations may also acquire the legal personality. To that end, they must be incorporated by a notarial deed and have minimum assets at the time of registration of 15,000 EUR, if associations, or 30,000 EUR, if foundations. When assets decrease by more than 1/3, the aforementioned minimum shall be reconstituted.

The Code of the third sector recognizes seven sub-types (or sub-statuses) of third sector organizations, which are:

(1) voluntary organizations;
(2) associations of social promotion;
(3) philanthropic entities;
(4) social enterprises, including social cooperatives;
(5) associative networks;
(6) mutual aid societies;
(7) other entities of the third sector.

Each sub-type of TSO has its own characteristics.[6] The RUNTS is divided into seven sections: one for each sub-type (or particular status) of TSO. An organization wishing to acquire the status of TSO must indicate, while applying for registration, the section of the RUNTS in which it wants to be registered (it is possible to be registered in only one section, except for the associative networks, which may be registered in two sections).

3 Social Enterprises and Social Cooperatives as a Particular Type of Third Sector Organizations

Among the sub-types of Italian TSOs, the social enterprise warrants and requires special attention, because it has particular characteristics relative to all other types of TSOs.[7]

---

[6] Differences among sub-types mainly regard the activities performed and the way in which they are performed: cf. Fici (ed.) (2018), p. 91 ff.; Fici (2020a), p. 31 ff.

[7] Cf. Fici (2020a), p. 43 ff.

Social enterprises find their particular regulation in a formally separate act, namely Legislative decree no. 112/2017 which is, however, to be considered a substantial part of the Code of the third sector, notwithstanding the formal separation.[8] Compared to the other sub-types (or sub-statuses) of TSO it is a *sui generis* sub-type (or sub-status) mainly because:

- SEs acquire the status by registering in a specific section of the Register of enterprises (rather than in the RUNTS);
- SEs perform the activities of general interest in an entrepreneurial way, i.e., they sell the services rather than provide them for free; in addition, SEs may be characterized, rather than by the performance of a general interest activity, by the working integration of disadvantaged persons and workers, who shall be at least 30% of an SE's total workforce;
- not only associations and foundations but also companies of whatever type (including cooperatives[9]) may acquire the status of social enterprises; the status is also available to companies composed of only one shareholder, provided that the single shareholder is not an individual, a public entity or a for-profit organization, which are the "excluded entities" in the specific field of the social enterprise (they may not acquire this status);
- companies (with the status of) SEs may remunerate members' shares within certain limits;
- SEs are subject to specific governance requirements and a specific form of public control.

Social cooperatives of Law no. 381/1991 are now recognized as *ex lege* social enterprises (Article 1, para 4, Legislative decree no. 112/2017), of which they constitute the most diffuse typology. Like SEs, social cooperatives must either perform an activity of general interest ("social cooperatives of type A") or provide the working integration of disadvantaged persons ("social cooperatives of type B"). Social cooperatives are SEs with a democratic structure given that cooperative law imposes the rule "one member, one vote" in the members' general meeting.

Social enterprises in the company form, and social cooperatives as *ex lege* social enterprises, are third sector entities, and as such they must therefore be kept separate from "benefit companies", another new creature of Italian law.

Law no. 208/2015 introduced into the Italian legal system the status of "benefit company", which may be assumed by a company (including a cooperative) that, in carrying out its economic activities, pursues, in addition to the aim of distributing profits, one or more aims of common benefit and operates in a responsible, sustainable and transparent manner vis-à-vis individuals, communities, territories and the environment, cultural and social heritage, entities and associations as well as other

---

[8] As regards the regulation of social enterprises, Legislative decree no. 112/2017 replaced Legislative decree no. 155/2006.

[9] Indeed, under Italian law, cooperatives are formally a particular type of companies.

stakeholders. "Common benefit" means the pursuit of one or more positive effects, or the reduction of negative effects, for the company's benefited stakeholders.[10]

4 A New Approach in the Regulation of the Non-profit Purpose

The CC does not define associations and foundations, still less their institutional purpose. However, the prevailing opinion is that both associations and foundations may have any lawful purpose other than profit sharing. This follows from the fact that companies are assigned a specific purpose by Article 2247 CC, which is the distribution to members of profits generated by an economic activity. Therefore, having to be kept distinct from companies, associations and foundations could not have the same purpose as companies, and so they are considered NPCs, in the limited sense that they are not allowed to distribute profits to their founders and members.[11]

Therefore, since their purpose is not positively defined by law, and provided that no distribution of profits take place, associations and foundations may, in principle, pursue either the public or the private benefit.

The legislator's approach to TSOs is completely different.

Not only have TSOs to act for a non-profit purpose but they must also exclusively pursue civic, solidaristic and social utility purposes by undertaking, at least prevalently, one or more general interest activities.

In order to ensure and safeguard their purpose, the law prescribes that the assets of a third sector organization, including any profits, income, proceeds, revenues however denominated, must be used to carry out the statutory activity for the exclusive pursuit of civic, solidarity and social utility purposes (Article 8, para 1, CTS).

For that purpose, a non-profit organization is barred from distributing, directly or indirectly, profits and operating surpluses, funds and reserves, however denominated, to founders, associates, workers and collaborators, directors and other members of the corporate bodies, also in the case of withdrawal or any other hypothesis of individual dissolution of the associative relationship (Article 8, para 2, CTS).

The law goes on to identify some situations that are deemed to integrate, under any circumstances, an indirect distribution of profits and assets by an NPO (Article 8, para 3, CTS). These hypotheses are:

(a) the payment to directors, auditors and all those who hold an organizational role, of an individual remuneration not proportionate to the activity carried out, to the responsibilities borne and to the specific competences, or in any case higher than that provided in entities operating in the same or similar sectors and conditions;

---

[10] Cf. https://www.societabenefit.net/wp-content/uploads/2017/03/Italian-benefit-corporation-legislation-courtesy-translation-final.pdf.

[11] Cf. Hansmann (1980) and Verrucoli (1985).

(b) the payment to dependent or self-employed workers of wages or payments 40% higher than those established, for the same qualifications, by the collective agreements referred to in Article 51 of Legislative Decree 15 June 2015, no. 81, except for proven necessities relating to the need to acquire specific skills for the purpose of carrying out certain activities of general interest (those referred to in Article 5, para 1, letters (b), (g) and (h), CTS);
(c) the purchase of goods or services for considerations that, without valid economic reasons, are higher than their normal value;
(d) the sale of goods and the provision of services, under more favourable conditions than those of the market, to shareholders, associates or participants, to founders, to the members of the administrative and control bodies, to those who in any capacity work for the organization or are part of it, to persons who provide gifts to the organization, to their relatives within the third degree and to their relatives in law within the second degree, as well as to the companies directly or indirectly controlled or connected by them, exclusively by reason of their quality, unless such sales or provisions constitute the object of the activity of general interest performed by the TSO;
(e) the payment to persons other than banks and authorized financial intermediaries, of interest rates, due on loans of all kinds, four points higher than the annual reference rate.

The same non-profit purpose characterizes social enterprises which are, however, allowed, albeit only if established in the company form (including the cooperative form), to remunerate the members' paid-up shares up to a certain extent. Companies recognized as social enterprises may allocate a share of less than 50% of their annual profits, after deduction of the losses accrued in previous years, to the distribution, also as free shares or free financial instruments, of dividends to shareholders, not exceeding in any event the maximum interest of postal bonds, increased by 2.5 points relative to the paid-up capital (Article 3, para 3, lit. a), Legislative decree no. 112/2017).[12]

An asset-lock also operates upon a TSO's dissolution, in which case its residual assets must be devolved to other TSOs, subject to the positive opinion of the competent office of the RUNTS. The acts of devolution of residual assets concluded in the absence or in contrast with the office's opinion are null and void (Article 9 CTS).

The same happens when an entity is cancelled from the RUNTS and thus loses the status of TSO, although in this event the assets to be devolved are only those accumulated during the time of its presence on the RUNTS (Article 50, para 2, CTS). However, a stricter rule applies to SEs: if they are de-registered and lose their status, they must devolve all their assets disinterestedly, following the deduction, in the case of social enterprises in the company form, of the members' paid-up shares (Article 12, para 5, Legislative decree no. 112/2017).

[12] Only this subjective restriction (and not also that regarding the limit of 50%) applies to social cooperatives of Law no. 381/1991.

5 Activities and Taxation

Associations and foundations, notwithstanding their functional characterization, may, in principle, perform any kind of activity, including commercial activities that generate profits (i.e. profit-making activities). Given the non-distribution constraint, if profits are generated by the commercial activity, they may not be distributed to founders and members.

TSOs are bound by the requirement to undertake, at least prevalently, activities of general interest. The performance of other activities is restricted. However, no restrictions in general exist with regard to the manner in which the activities of general interest are to be conducted. Thus, these activities might also be commercial, and even exclusively or predominantly so. Yet, some TSOs, such as voluntary organizations, may perform only secondary commercial activities. The exact opposite is true of SEs: they are identified by the very performance of commercial activities of general interest.

In any event, the volume of commercial activities in comparison to non-commercial activities affects the tax regime of NPOs and TSOs.

Legal entities other than companies (such as associations and foundations) are, in principle, subject to corporate income tax. They receive specific consideration in Presidential Decree no. 917/1986,[13] which in its Article 73, para 1, makes a distinction between.

(a) Those that have (lit. b) ("commercial entities") and
(b) Those that do not have as their main or exclusive object the carrying out of commercial activities (lit. c) ("non-commercial entities").[14]

While "commercial entities" are treated as companies, "non-commercial entities", although not being tax-exempt in any event, are recipients of specific provisions that may fully or partially lead to this result.

Some activities performed by non-commercial entities, although substantially commercial in their nature, are, however, considered "non-commercial" under tax law so that profits generated by these "non-commercial activities" are not taxed.

"Non-commercial" is "the supply of services not falling under article 2195 of the Civil Code provided in compliance with the institutional purposes of the entity, without specific organization, and in exchange of considerations that do not exceed the directly attributable costs" (Article 143, para 1, Presidential decree no. 917/1986).

"Non-commercial" is also the activity carried out, in conformity with its institutional purposes, by an association with its associated members, if the activity is not provided in exchange for a specific consideration (Article 148, paras 1 and 2, Presidential decree no. 917/1986). However, for some associations (including those of

[13] Available at https://www.normattiva.it/uri-res/N2Ls?urn:nir:stato:decreto.del.presidente.della.repubblica:1986-12-22;917.

[14] According to Article 73, para 4, Presidential decree no. 917/1986, "main object means the activity essential to directly achieve the primary purposes indicated by the law, by the act of incorporation or by the statute".

social promotion and of amateur sport), even activities performed with their members in exchange for a specific consideration are considered "non-commercial" (Article 148, para 3, Presidential decree no. 917/1986), but these associations must meet some specific requirements (Article 148, para 8, Presidential decree no. 917/1986), including the prohibition to distribute, even indirectly, profits or surpluses as well as funds, reserves or capital during the life of the association, unless the distribution is required by law, and the obligation to allocate the assets of the entity, in the event of its dissolution, to another association with a similar purpose.

In addition, there are some revenues that are, in any event, tax-exempt, namely:

(a) sums from public fundraising carried out by a non-commercial entity occasionally, including through the provision of goods of modest value or services to the sponsors, during celebrations, anniversaries or awareness campaigns (Article 143, para 3, Presidential decree no. 917/1986);
(b) contributions paid by public administrations to a non-commercial entity under certain agreements or accreditation schemes for social purpose activities exercised in conformity with the institutional purposes (Article 143, para 3, Presidential decree no. 917/1986);
(c) contributions paid by the members, if they are not provided in exchange for the provision of a service (Article 148, para 1, Presidential decree no. 917/1986).

Any commercial activity of non-commercial entities is subject to taxation, in which case non-commercial entities may enjoy a particular flat tax regime provided for by Article 145 of Presidential decree no. 917/1986.

In order to demonstrate their nature as non-commercial entities and to pay the taxes on commercial activities (but also to obtain the deduction of VAT paid on purchases[15]), non-commercial entities are required to keep separate accounts for any commercial activity exercised (Article 144, para 2, Presidential decree no. 917/1986).

Regardless of any provision in their statutes, non-commercial entities lose this fiscal status if they mainly carry out commercial activity for an entire tax period (Article 149, para 1, Presidential decree no. 917/1986). There are some parameters that may be employed to conduct this evaluation, namely:

(a) the prevalence of fixed assets relating to the commercial activity, net of amortization, over those relating to other activities;
(b) the prevalence of revenues from commercial activities over the normal value of the sales or services relating to the institutional activities;
(c) the prevalence of income from commercial activities over those from institutional activities (i.e., contributions, subsidies, gifts and membership fees);
(d) the prevalence of the negative components concerning the commercial activity over the remaining expenses.

In conclusion, associations and foundations may be classified, under tax law, either as commercial entities or as non-commercial entities, depending on the volume of commercial activities in relation to non-commercial ones. As non-commercial

[15] See Article 19 *ter* of Presidential decree no. 633/1972.

entities they may be fully tax-exempt (if they do not carry out commercial activities or carry out activities qualified as "non-commercial") or only partially tax-exempt (they are subject to corporate tax only with regard to their commercial activities).

For associations and foundations with the status of ONLUS pursuant to Legislative decree no. 460/1997, the carrying out of the institutional activities for the pursuit of the solidarity purposes is not considered to be a commercial activity, so that corporate tax does not apply. Moreover, the income from related activities (to institutional ones) does not fall within the taxable profit (Article 150 Presidential decree no. 917/1986).

The dichotomy between "commercial entities" and "non-commercial entities", which is a peculiarity of Italian tax law, is also employed by the CTS to determine the taxation of TSOs. Indeed, third sector organizations (other than social enterprises) may be "commercial" or "non-commercial" depending on the relationship between the volume of non-commercial activities and that of commercial activities (Article 79 CTS). Non-commercial TSOs may opt for a specific tax treatment regarding the income from their commercial activities. This fiscal regime is not yet in force, since it is currently subject to the authorization of the European Commission.[16]

Social enterprises are "commercial entities" by definition, even when they have the legal form of associations or foundations. However, their particular law provides that the profits re-invested by them in the activity do not constitute taxable income (Article 18 Legislative decree no. 112/2017). This measure is still not in force since it is subject to the authorization of the European Commission. However, the same rule already applies to social cooperatives of Law no. 381/1991.

VAT does not apply to non-commercial activities of non-commercial entities (Article 4, para 3, Presidential decree no. 633/1972[17]).

There are some services (such as socio-health services or home assistance of disabled persons and other disadvantaged people) that, if provided by an ONLUS, are VAT-exempt (Article 10, para 1, n. 27 *ter*, Presidential decree no. 633/1972). This provision will in future apply to non-commercial TSOs rather than to the entities with the ONLUS status.[18]

A reduced VAT rate (5% rather than 22%) applies to social cooperatives of Law no. 381/1991 that provide specific health, socio-health, assistance and educational services (Table A), Part II *bis*, no. 1, Presidential decree no. 633/1972).

Furthermore, there are some services, usually provided by NPOs or TSOs, such as, for example, those pertaining to kindergartens or retirement homes for the elderly, whose provision is exempt from VAT (Article 10, para 1, n. 21, Presidential decree no. 633/1972).

---

[16] Still to be requested by the Italian Government. Cf. Fici (ed.) (2018), p. 155 ff.

[17] Available at https://www.normattiva.it/uri-res/N2Ls?urn:nir:stato:decreto.del.presidente.della.repubblica:1972-10-26;633%21vig=.

[18] Pursuant to Article 89, para 7, lit. b), CTS, which will enter into force beginning from the fiscal year following that in which the authorization of the European Commission for the new tax regime of TSOs is granted.

References

Fici A (2017) A European statute for social and solidarity-based enterprise. European Union, Brussels. https://www.europarl.europa.eu/RegData/etudes/STUD/2017/583123/IPOL_STU%282017%29583123_EN.pdf
Fici A (ed) (2018), La riforma del terzo settore e dell'impresa sociale. Una introduzione. Editoriale scientifica, Napoli
Fici A (2020a) Un diritto per il terzo settore. Studi sulla riforma. Editoriale scientifica, Napoli
Fici A (2020b) Social enterprise laws in Europe after the 2011 "Social Business Initiative". A Comparative Analysis from the Perspective of Worker and Social Cooperatives. CECOP, Brussels. https://cecop.coop/uploads/file/bzuQI79nF5yrrwoDvUNUg47Ro7iaHA6wAxsvK9yo.pdf
Hansmann HB (1980) The role of nonprofit enterprise. Yale Law J 89/5:835 ff
Sepio G (2020) Italy. Country profile. In: Legal environment for philanthropy in Europe. https://www.philanthropyadvocacy.eu/legal-environment-for-philanthropy-in-europe/
Vaccario C, Barbetta G P (2017) Legal aspects of civil society organizations and their relation with government: Italy. In: van der Ploeg TJ et al (eds) Civil society in Europe. Minimum norms and optimum conditions of its regulation. CUP, Cambridge, p 445 ff
Verrucoli P (1985) Non-profit organizations. A comparative approach. Giuffrè, Milano
Zamagni V (ed) (2000) Povertà e innovazioni istituzionali in Italia. Dal Medioevo a oggi. Il Mulino, Bologna

Taxation of Agricultural Processing Companies: A Special Type of Social Economy Entities in Spain

Marina Aguilar-Rubio

To Professor Hagen Henrÿ,
for whom the world has become too small.

1 Introduction

The importance reached by certain agricultural processing companies (hereinafter APCs) within the Spanish agri-food sector, contrasts with the little historical interest that has risen. In 2020, 12,221 entities of this kind were accounted for, which cluster 304,839 memberships, figures far from negligible.[1] On the other hand, most of the biggest Spanish vegetable sales companies are APCs and the total annual billing gives very important figures.

According to Spanish law, APCs are civil companies with an economic and social purpose, established for the production, processing and marketing of agricultural, livestock or forestry products, the improvement of the rural environment, the promotion and development of agriculture and the provision of common services that serve this purpose. However, despite this conceptualization, as we will see, it has been concluded from its legal status and its functioning that it is a hybrid

[1] Spanish Ministry of Agriculture, Fisheries and Foodstuff Annual Report 2020 https://www.mapa.gob.es/es/alimentacion/temas/integracion-asociativa/informeanualsatano2020_tcm30-380032.pdf.
[2] Vargas-Vasserot (2012), p. 22.

Study carried out in the framework of the RDI project for the generation of "frontier" knowledge of the Andalusian Plan for Research, Development and Innovation (PAIDI 2020): "The reformulation of cooperative principles and their statutory adaptation to meet current social, economic and environmental demands" (P20_01278).

M. Aguilar-Rubio (✉)
Tax Law, Law School, Social Economy and Cooperative Law Research Center (CIDES), University of Almeria, Almeria, Spain
e-mail: magui@ual.es

W. Tadjudje and I. Douvitsa (eds.), *Perspectives on Cooperative Law*,
https://doi.org/10.1007/978-981-19-1991-6_9

entity between civil societies, agricultural cooperatives and commercial companies.[2] Thanks to public policies to support the concentration of companies in the primary sector, APCs are becoming the main productive companies of reference in the field of Spanish agri-foodstuffs. Although they have differences with agri-food cooperatives, they are serving as legal entities for the economic development of rural areas, thanks to their essentially participatory, community and mutualist nature and have also been classified as social economy entities by Law 5/2011 on Social Economy.

APCs precedent are the so-called Trade Union Groups of Colonization, which were set up after the Spanish Civil War as an intermediary between farmers and the State.[3] The necessity of having to adapt the legal system of this partnership cooperation to the new political, legal and economical reality of the country triggered their reform and conversion process into another social type which could perform easier challenges of a more competitive agriculture. Thus, APCs were born by the end of the 1970s as a particular formula of agricultural associationism to promote development through societies which could adapt well to rural environments.

The Royal Decree 1776/1981, which endorsed the statute that regulates the Agricultural Processing Companies (hereinafter the APC Regulation), only has 14 articles and has not been altered since its enactment. It was only developed in 1982 by the brief Order of the Ministry of Agriculture to specify requirements for incorporation and registration.

The APC Regulation has systematically been left out of all modernization process which has been developing for decades in our Corporate Law, thanks to the shield, many times fictional, of the civil nature of these societies. Basic questions such as minority rights, protection of third parties, management responsibilities, right to rebuttal agreements or general meeting call, are not even mentioned in its regulation, refers as subsidiary law to the Civil Code (Art. 1.3), without taking into account that a large part of these societies work internally and externally as capital companies, limiting member's responsibilities to their contribution. The reason why an absolutely outdated rule, with severe omissions and carried out with an awful legal technique is lasting so long has to be found within the great flexibility of these companies, contrasting with what happens with their competitor by functional resemblance, namely agricultural cooperatives.[4] Furthermore, their regulation is State-run,[5] not like cooperatives, whose regulation is regional.[6]

---

[3] Carbonell and Paniagua-Gil (1974), pp. 19–32.

[4] Mauleón-Méndez (2015), p. 461. Its legal framework grants willingness of members a broad margin in the bylaws.

[5] Until now, apart from an excessive APC autonomous Registry Regulations, only Aragon and Catalonia have regulated APC. See Decree 15/2011 of the Regional Government of Aragon and Decree 1999/2013, in Catalonia.

According to article 149.3 of the Spanish Constitution, state rule should prevail, in case of conflict rose, over that of the Autonomous Region in all that is not ascribed to the exclusive competence of them, as this is the case. Due to this, it has been claimed that these autonomous rules are declared unconstitutional and have no practical effect since they have invaded competences which are state-exclusive in regulating this social type.

[6] A cooperative law by Autonomous Region (except Canary Islands that has a Bill) and the Spanish Law 27/1999 of Cooperative with state character give us the number of 17, to which many special

Nevertheless, for years, the tax regime for APCs was in a deplorable state of confusion and legal uncertainty, fully opposed to the necessary transparency and simplicity tax rules require for its appropriate implementation.[7] This situation improved, to a certain extent, with the Spanish Law 20/1990 on Cooperative Tax System within the common territory.[8] In this act, it is envisaged to ensure these entities within the general tax system, without prejudice of the establishment of certain special rules enforceable in the Corporate Tax and the recognition of some benefits in other taxes, therefore a break rises with the traditional assimilation of APCs to agricultural cooperatives since the enactment of cooperative tax system regulations.

The purpose of this study, after the explanation of this special social type, is to analyse its tax legal system within the common state. This question has had scarce doctrinal treatment, but its interest is justified because the quantitative and qualitative relevance of this kind of company in the legal system's traffic, its flexibility and indeterminacy and its special tax system.

2 Agricultural Processing Companies' Legal System Approach

The longevity of the APC Regulation is surprising, both because its important legal amendments *undergone* by the corporation legislation and, particularly, to that on cooperatives, and because of the unusual legal technique used: the regulatory rule is the result of a delegation authorized by a pre-constitutional Royal Decree-Law 31/1977 but carried out almost 3 years after the Spanish Constitution enforcement. This has generated confronting positions within the authors on its constitutionality, ranging from the unreserved acceptance[9] to rejection.[10]

The scarce control these companies undergo and their very much deficient legal system of publicity, protection to members and third parties or responsibility of administrators, to give some examples, makes their integration within the agri-food cooperative or within a profound reform of their legal framework indispensable.[11] This has been attempted unsuccessfully.[12]

---

laws have to be added (for credit cooperatives, for small size cooperatives, to update the sector, etc.).

[7] Juliá-Igual and Server-Izquierdo (1992), p. 113, Luque-Mateo (2000), p. 13.

[8] Regarding to taxation, in Spain, we have common regime and regional (*foral*) regime. The latter is that for Basque Country and Navarra Regions. The rest of Spain is considered common territory. Basque Country and Navarra have enacted similar laws to the State Law 20/1990, and they are left out from this paper since its treatment is quite the same. About this, Aguilar-Rubio (2018).

[9] Barberena-Belzunce (1994), pp. 304–308.

[10] Rosembuj (1991), pp. 7601–7602.

[11] Argudo-Périz (2007), p. 30.

[12] In December 2015, the Ministry of Justice set up a Paper of the General Codification in order to elaborate a draft bill on APCs, whose work ended up in June 2017. Because of the lack of political support, this legal proposal was not even discussed in the proper section of the General

Actually, there are no elements which allow to rigorously speak about a distinctive social type to those already existing, but about a hybrid form among civil societies, agricultural cooperatives and capital companies whose use in the traffic was due to the legislator intention to promote agricultural development thanks to some societies which would adapt better to rural areas than any other reason. Article 1.1 defines APCs as "civil companies with a social-economic purpose regarding production, processing and commercialization of agricultural, livestock or forest product, implementing improvements in the rural area, agrarian promotion and development and giving common services that help that purpose". This legal concept only involves three essential features of these societies: its civil character that, as we will state later, is arguable; its social-economic and mutualistic purpose, which refers that the obligation to participate in activities means member's main duty[13]; and its compulsory relationship with the agrarian sector, which is excessively undefined.[14]

The civil nature of APCs is controversial and has significant implications in the legal sources scheme (subsidiarity of the Civil Code against Corporate Law) and in the judicial settlement of disputes (Courts of First Instance or Commercial Court). Clearly, if we literally consider the APC Regulation, these companies have a civil character. Nevertheless, this does not match with many APCs' business reality. A great number of big agri-food companies in Spain are APCs. This has motivated that some authors defend that it is the social purpose and how to achieve it what must be taken into account in order to classify APCs as a civil or commercial company.[15]

Along with these characteristics it has been understood that, in the recognition of the APCs' social-economic purpose, its mutualist character is implicit. Due to this, they are systematically included in the social economy.[16] Nevertheless, we cannot obviate that, although APCs are participative entities, many aspects of its legal system do not match with the social economy ideal.

Codification Commission, although in November 2018 it was published in the Ministry of Justice's web page for information purposes only. https://www.mjusticia.gob.es/cs/Satellite/Portal/1292428955676?blobheader=application%2Fpdf&blobheadername1=Content-Disposition&blobheadername2=Grupo&blobheadervalue1=attachment%3B+filename%3DPropuesta_de_la_Ponencia_para_la_elaboracion_del_borrador_de_Anteproyecto_de_Ley_de_Sociedades_agra.PDF&blobheadervalue2=Docs_CGC_Propuestas.

[13] According to the Supreme Court Decision dated March 11, 1996, the non-compliance to this duty is a reason for APCs forced exclusion. As it is logical, being forced to participate in APCs mutualistic activities will only affect those kinds of members that, because of their status, are in conditions to do it (as is the case of owners of agricultural holding).

[14] In this regard, it is remarkable that any activity related to agriculture, livestock or forestry, even if this relationship is indirect, could have an APC social object: well extraction, setting up a factory, opening a retail business or any agricultural complementary industry, processing companies and production commercialization by members or third parties, etc. For López-de Medrano (1995), p. 234, due to the broad social purpose scope, APCs could be the cover of economic realities which have little to do with their designation.

[15] Vargas-Vasserot (2012), p. 162, López-de Medrano (1995), p. 244. On the other hand, Corral-Dueñas (1989), p. 438 or Cuenca-Anaya (1983), p. 389 defend them as civil character.

[16] As it has been said above, Law 5/2011 of Social Economy includes APCs among entities which play part in it (Art. 5.1).

Beyond its definition, from the remaining APC Regulation, other characteristics are obtained to complete its legal system regarding different aspects:

- Asset liability (Art. 12): members are personally responsible for social debts, unless otherwise agreed in the bylaws, therefore they tend to answer partially with the capital share contributed.
- Members (Arts. 5 and 7.2.a)): mainly associate with natural persons owning agrarian holdings or agricultural workers who should directly participate in the mutualist activity.
- Leave (Art. 6.3): members are entitled to liquidate their participation in the social equity with real value.
- Profit participation (Art. 7.1.d)): members should obtain earnings or benefits according to their participation in the mutualist activity or in the capital share.
- Capital share (Art. 8): it is divided into nominative slips which represent aliquot parts and could vary because of the eventual ins and outs of members.
- Corporative structure (Arts. 10 and 11.2): the APCs' basic bodies are the General Meeting which, as a matter of principle, works in a democratic way since, generally, each member has a vote, and the Governing Board, which is the administrative body.
- Acquiring personality (Art. 12): APCs acquires personality and full capacity to function as from the date of their registration.

In view of these legal characteristics, together with the economic reality and usual content of their bylaws, APCs have been defined as companies with own legal personality acquired upon registration, mainly founded by agrarian holding owners and agrarian workers, which associate in order to actively participate in carrying out economic and social activities related to agriculture, livestock and forestry, benefiting all members. With a corporative and democratic structure, their members are entitled to a voluntary separation and, through the provisions of the bylaws, may limit liability for social debts and share the profits according to their participation in the company.[17]

3 Precedents to Agricultural Processing Company's Tax System: The Controversial Assimilation to Cooperatives

Trade Union Groups of Colonization's legal system (the APCs' forefathers), are framed within what was called "associative and team agriculture taxation", which traditionally had tax benefits.[18] Their origin was related to rural cooperatives, although lately they drifted apart in their private legal system. Both figures were linked together in the tax part, which continued after the appearance of the APCs, whose legal system was based on a constant reference to Decree 888/1969, on Cooperative Tax Statute until the enactment of the Law 20/1990.

[17] Vargas-Vasserot (2010), p. 164, (2018), p. 55.

[18] Corral-Dueñas (1985), p. 1477.

The APC Regulation only addressed taxation through these very inaccurate terms: "APCs will continue enjoying tax exemption and tax credit presently recognised, without prejudice that, as societies of common Law, they could be applicable" (second final provision). This wording did not clarify questions already raisen before its enactment: as no specific tax benefit existed for the APCs—since those they enjoyed were because of cooperatives—the dichotomy continued between the likeliness of applying to APCs the *protected* cooperative tax system, with preferential tax treatment in case of meeting requisites, or subdue them into a tax system with no particularities.

Most authors agreed to defend the first position, that is assimilating the APC tax regime to that applicable to cooperatives with preferential tax treatment.[19] Despite the fact that this position was preponderant, this assimilation was controversial. Thus, first Central Economic Administrative Court resolutions[20] and the Directorate-General for State Litigations matters' report of 1983 refused this assimilation, based on these points:

- The derogating provisions of the previous regulation were included both in the Corporate Taxation and the Tax of Property Transmission rules.
- The lack of explicit mention of the system continuity regarding APCs, which did happen to cooperatives.
- The necessity of an explicit referral regulation in order to understand that APCs should enjoy an equivalent legal system, which does not happen.[21]

In any case, Law 20/1990 enforcement eliminated the legal assimilation regarding taxation effects among APCs and agri-food cooperatives with preferential tax treatment, establishing a specific system for APCs based on the absence of some characteristic cooperativist principles.

[19] Along with some judicial pronouncements (Supreme Court Decisions of 24 September 1983; 14 May 1984; 27 April 1988; 16 January 1989; 22 October 1989) and administrative practice (Central Administrative-Economic Court Decisions after a criterion change in the resolution of 6 July 1988, this position is maintained after 20 September 1989 and 29 October 1990).

The Economic-Administrative Courts resolve economic-administrative claims, which for more than 100 years have constituted a special appeal in Spain to challenge tax acts before the Administration itself. Although there are called "courts", they are not jurisdictional bodies. In fact, despite the functional independence they enjoy, it should be noted that they form a part of the Ministry of Finance.

[20] Referring to those decisions before 6 July 1988, which meant a change in the criteria: 11 November 1987 and 12 May 1988.

[21] Barberena-Belzunce (1994), p. 319.

4 Agricultural Processing Companies' Income Taxation

4.1 Cooperative Tax System

Law 20/1990s first additional provision states their tax system as follows: "Agricultural Processing Companies registered in the General Registry of such entities of the Ministry of Agriculture or, in its case, of the Autonomous Regions, will be applied the general tax system, with the exception foreseen in the following sections, and as a consequence, will be subject to the Corporate Income Tax". Therefore, those entities are subject to the general regulation of Corporation Tax with no preferential tax treatment within this tax, compared to those *protected* or *specially protected* cooperatives, which already enjoy advantages.[22]

Besides, the related-party transactions concept was extended specially to the relationship among members of the APCs. Thus, first additional provision continued stating that: "For the purpose of this Tax, operations carried out by APCs with members will be calculated upon market value. Market value will be the normal price of assets, services and provisions which will be determined between independent parties because of those operations. Nevertheless, with regards to APCs which, according to their bylaws, perform services or provisions to members, the price for the corresponding operations will be counted for the one applied, if it is not lower than the price of said services or provisions, including the corresponding part of the entity's general expenses. Otherwise, the latter will be applied".

The legislator could consider that economic transactions performed by individuals with a dependence relationship (linked) could be not subject to a supply and demand law, therefore fixed process could differ from those applied by independent companies in a free competition market. As a consequence, it involves a comprehensive regulation of those aspects related to these operations, specially, its assessment, which is the main problem related parties operations have in matters of taxation.

Broadly speaking, Law 27/2014 on Corporate Tax makes it compulsory to have to mark all performed operations among linked entities or individual into market price, even those situations in which there is no tax planning strategy. Thus, when prices are different from those of the market are agreed, the tax authority will act by adjusting these prices for the difference between the agreed price and that of the market.

---

[22] In Spain, the tax protection which cooperatives obtain is linked directly with the common intrinsic element to those entities. On the one hand, to maintain the condition of a cooperative with preferential tax treatment it is necessary not to exceed 50% of the total volume of cooperative operations with third parties not members; on the other hand, only those results considered cooperative have a reduced tax rate on the Corporate Tax and, finally, other allowances because of the legal requirement of endowing non distributable funds of cooperatives, so this is an added financial burden.

The existing relationship between the regulation of a special tax system and the limitations because of its economic system justify, *sensu contrario*, that APCs do not have a special system since, i.e. they do not give funds nor have limitations regarding profit sharing.

This is why related operations between members and APCs, when bylaws state it, are allowed to be assessed not by the market price but the cost price, always insofar that the price is not lower than a specific amount. This is one of the unique real specifications APCs enjoy in matters of Corporate Tax regarding other taxpayers. Other advantages are applicable because of referral to other regulations (i.e. small-sized companies). In fact, this exception that benefits APCs regarding other societies has been questioned from a State's aid perspective.

Secondly, in its original version, Art. 9 of Law 20/1990, dedicated to agrarian cooperatives, which can be *specially protected*, allows APCs to be members of these cooperatives, provided that they are established in fulfilment of the APC Regulation. This reference disappeared in the last amendment, made by Law 3/2013 on promoting the integration of cooperatives and other associative agri-food entities. Nevertheless, this does not mean that these entities cannot be partners of first-grade cooperatives and even those of second degree, as cooperative laws normally recognize.

And, finally, Law 20/1990 first final provision explicitly derogated Decree 1515/1970, by which it was declared the implementation of the tax system established for group cooperatives to Trade Union Groups of Colonization and APC Regulation second final provision.

The consequence of the above is "the rupture of tax treatment APC enjoyed until that moment, in other words, its alignment or assimilation with agrarian cooperatives, with the same tax advantages as the last ones".[23]

Such evolution cracked the doctrine reaffirmed by the Spanish Economic-Administrative Courts and the case-law from the Supreme Court as well as the predominant opinion within the authors, which until that moment defended tax equalization between APCs and agrarian cooperatives. Besides, since then, disappeared the difference between tax *protected* and not *protected* APCs, as a consequence the tax system in this law was imposed on any APC.

4.2 Corporate Taxation

In current Law 27/2014, on Corporate Tax the principle unification of the special tax systems in one whole legal text subsists, with the only exception being the regimes of cooperatives and public utility associations and foundations. In fact, it included APCs in the list of taxpayers (Art. 7.1.b)) improving the lack of systematicity of previous laws, and that were treated as a case of exclusion of the income allocation system.

The fact that APCs are subject to Corporate Tax general system does not prevent them from being subject to any other special tax regimes, insofar as application conditions are met.

They will be more likely to be applied to APCs:

---

[23] Luque-Mateo (2000), p. 64.

4.2.1 Tax Consolidation Regime

It implies that the different companies that form this group are considered as a single taxable person, paying taxes for the sum of basic taxable charges of all companies within the group, allowing the automatic compensation of profits and losses achieved by the different companies in the group. It is an optional regime whose application means the lack of taxation in the individual regime of Corporate Tax of the entities within the group.[24]

The main advantages of applying this regime are as follows: companies will pay taxes as a whole, compensating one's losses with another's profits, thus fostering a significant financial saving; future losses of certain companies will be compensated automatically with other companies' profits, and the immediate tax payment will be lower; it is not compulsory to have to record operations among companies which are part of the group; the financial burden of companies is reduced against the group's result or eliminating the intragroup operation results; finally, the obligation to document-related operations disappears.

4.2.2 Tax Regime for Small-Sized Entities

An APC will be a compact-size entity, for the purpose of this regime, when the net amount of last year's turnover has been lower than ten million euros. This companies could benefit from certain elements in a special regime of redemption:

- Freedom of amortization and accelerated amortization according to some conditions and terms (Arts. 102 and 103).
- Impairment losses to cover the risk exposure of possible insolvency could also be deducted up to a limit of 1% over the existing debtors to the end of the tax period in which this special tax regime is applicable (Art. 104).
- Set as a tax incentive, the levelling reserve of the taxable base of Art. 105 Law 27/2014 allows to lower the taxable base obtained up to 10% of the amount, with an annual limit of up to 1,000,000 euros. This allows to reduce taxation for a specific tax period in order to establish the possibility of moving those negative tax base offset towards tax periods previous to the one generated in some conditions.
- Regarding assets purchased under the special regime of financial lease, those taxes due belonging to the depreciable asset's cost recovery are considered as deductible expense, with a limit of three times lineal amortization according to the official amortization scale approved (Art. 106).

Being a micro-, small or medium enterprise means being able to implement, at the same time, the following tax benefits.

[24] On March 7, 1997 the Directorate-General for Taxation claimed that, insomuch as APCs have legal entity and are subject to and not exempt from Corporate Tax, they will bear the condition of dominant societies within a group of societies for the purpose of applying the regime.

4.2.3 Incentives for Priority Associative Exploitation Labelling

Besides, provided that an APC has the label of priority associative holding according to Law 19/1995, of Agricultural Holding Upgrading (Art. 6.a) enables priority associative holding becoming an APC) it has amortization freedom of tangible and intangible fixed assets during the first 5 years since its recognition, according to Art. 12.3.d).

4.2.4 Other Tax Incentives for APCs

State-wide, it is also applicable a reduced rate of taxation of 15% for recently set-up entities (Art. 29.1).

APCs could also get, provided that legal requirements are met, tax incentives because of research, development and tech innovation (Art. 35). In fact, in the current regulation, it the development of these activities is being promoted among small and medium enterprises too, with the purpose of entering the market and achieving a competitive product or service and not having an outdated one.

Finally, APCs creating employment could benefit from deduction for employment contract for indefinite duration under Art. 37, although only those companies which have less than 50 workers could make use of it. The company will be entitled to deduct three thousand euros from the whole tax due when the first employee with employment contract of indefinite duration supporting entrepreneurs or if younger than 30 years is recruited. Also, Art. 38 keeps a deduction in the whole tax due to an average increased in the disabled staff recruited, performed during the tax period, regarding the average disabled staff in the immediately prior period. A new contract is a requirement since it means an increase in the number of employment positions and disabled employees recruited by the entity and must appear in the disabled employee registry demanding employment in the Employment Offices.

5 Other Taxes on Agricultural Processing Companies

Even though the main characteristic of the APC tax system after the enforcement of Law 20/1990 was the implementation of general corporate taxation system, this regulation foresaw some tax benefits in other taxes. Thus, the regulation determined in section third of first additional provision that: "Agricultural Processing Companies set-up for the fulfilling of aims recognised in Royal Decree 1776/1981 and registered in the General Registry of Agricultural Processing Companies of the Ministry of Agriculture, Fisheries and Foodstuff or, in this case, in the Autonomous Regions, will enjoy some of the following tax benefits:

(a) In the Capital Transfer Tax and Stamp Duty, total exemption for company incorporation and capital increase.

(b) In the local Tax on Business Capital, they will enjoy a 95% bonus of the tax due and charges corresponding to the activities performed".

And also stated that: "Enjoying these benefits, without prejudice to implementation, in any case, of what is established in sections one and two of this provision will be subject to not having a substantial modification of own characters of APCs, to keep necessary requirements for the registration in the mentioned Registry and not violating existing regulations". The concurrence of circumstances which the regulation typifies as disqualifying to enjoy a special tax regime determines the loss of benefits enjoyed in the fiscal year done, without prejudice to what is envisaged in the Law 58/2003, on General Taxation about surcharge and interest on delay and about offences and penalties, especially those about obtaining undue tax benefits or deductions.

In terms of implementation and verification of the tax benefits mentioned above, Law 20/1990 will be applied to APCs, whereby no prior administrative statement will be required. Tax Inspection is competent to verify concurrent circumstances to enjoy those benefits. Therefore, APCs are subject and pay taxes in the general type of Capital Transfer Tax and Stamp Duty in Spain and have some exemptions given by the cooperative tax system's regulatory laws.

Total exemption because of company creation and capital increase in corporate operations, in that moment, meant an advantage when choosing the form of the company type to implement since it involved saving, that it is later maintained regarding capital share variability. Nevertheless, this exemption was broader for agrifood cooperatives according to the "special tax treatment" they enjoyed and does not protect APCs. In any case, the before-mentioned tax benefit lack importance since in Art. 3 of Royal Decree-Law 13/2010, modified Art. 45.I.B)11 Royal Legislative Decree 1/1993, on Capital Transfer Tax and Stamp Duty generalizing the exemption of company creation and capital increase to all companies.[25]

Together with this bonus, and to the purpose of this tax, it is necessary to highlight that when APCs qualify as priority associative holdings, they will enjoy other exemptions, according to Law 19/1995, of Agricultural Holding Upgrading.

Municipal Tax on Business Capital subject to APCs since the moment they perform any business activity but, thanks to the exemption regulatory rules of cooperatives tax regime for APCs, 95% of the tax due and corresponding surpluses to activities performed, with no limitation according to activity type, will be bonified.[26] Municipalities have the obligation to annually report the list of APCs which have effectively enjoyed these bonifications and tax expenses incurred to the Directorate-General of Coordination of Local Finances of the Ministry of Finance. In this sense,

[25] According to the current wording of this provision, it will exempt from company creation, capital increase, contributions by members which do not mean a capital increase and the transfer to Spain of the effective management headquarters or registered office of the company when neither of them are previously located in a State member of the European Union, under some circumstances.

[26] Thus, Art. 88 Royal Legislative Decree 2/2004, of Regulatory Law of Local Finances states that: "about the tax instalment, the following bonuses will be applied: a) Cooperatives, unions, federations and confederations and agricultural processing companies will enjoy a bonus envisaged in Law 20/1990, December 19th, about Cooperatives Tax System".

for example, APCs who perform agrarian activities themselves will not have to pay any tax due to develop their activities, import raw materials which take part of its productive process, sell wholesale or retail sales or export product of their activities nor own warehouses and deposits for the previously mentioned operations.

We cannot leave out other exemptions included in Royal Legislative Decree 2/2004, of Regulatory Law of Local Finances (hereinafter RLLF) which could also favour APCs: the one for taxable person who starts activity in the Spanish territory during the first two tax periods of this tax (Art. 82.1.b) RLLF); and another for taxable person of Corporate Tax who have a business net amount lower than one million euros (Art. 82.1.c) RLLF).

6 Conclusion

APCs' tax regime in Spain does not include special benefits in big taxes that charge income and consumption. In other words, they do not have a subjective exemption, since they are APCs, in the main tax which charges its income, Corporate Tax, nor VAT, tax of direct character, which charges economic transactions done. But this do not impede them from accessing both special regime and objective exemptions which are regulated for these taxes as much as they meet appropriate requirements.

In the Capital Transfer Tax and Stamp Duty and local Corporate Tax, which are not very important taxes within the whole system, is where bonuses are regulated expressly for this social type.

The foregone conclusion is that APCs do not enjoy a specific tax system which promotes their establishment and operation. Inasmuch as, on the one hand, it is considered that these entities have a mutualist character when recognizing its economic-social purpose and, on the other hand, due to this they are included among those entities of the so-called Social Economy, it will be advisable that the legislator provide them with their own tax incentives, in compliance with the promotion and dissemination of social economy stated in Art. 8 of Law 5/2011, of Social Economy.

References

Aguilar-Rubio M (2018) La tributación de las Sociedades Agrarias de Transformación en el régimen común y en los regímenes forales de Euskadi. Forum Fiscal 239:1–19

Argudo-Périz JL (2007) La multifuncionalidad de las instituciones jurídicas asociativas agrarias en las políticas de desarrollo rural y regional. REVESCO-Rev Estud Coop 92:11–40

Barberena-Belzunce I (1994) Sociedades Cooperativas, Sociedades Agrarias de Transformación y Sociedades Anónimas Laborales: Régimen fiscal. Aranzadi, Pamplona

Carbonell R, Paniagua-Gil J (1974) Grupos Sindicales de Colonización. Estud Coop 32:19–32

Corral-Dueñas F (1985) Régimen fiscal de las Sociedades Agrarias de Transformación. Rev Crít Derecho Inmobiliario 571:1471–1497

Corral-Dueñas F (1989) Sociedades Agrarias de Transformación: su regulación vigente. Rev Crít Derecho Inmobiliario 591:437–458

Cuenca-Anaya F (1983) Sociedades Agrarias de Transformación: constitución, representación y régimen fiscal. Rev Derecho Notarial 124:49–64

Juliá-Igual JF, Server-Izquierdo RJ (1992) Fiscalidad de cooperativas. Teoría y Práctica. Pirámide, Madrid

López-de Medrano F (1995) Notas críticas al Estatuto Jurídico Privado de las Sociedades Agrarias de Transformación. CIRIEC-Esp Rev Jurídica Econ Soc Coop 7 233–268

Luque-Mateo MA (2000) Régimen fiscal de la Sociedad agraria de Transformación. Universidad de Almería-Instituto de Estudios Almerienses, Almería

Mauleón-Méndez E (2015) La sociedad agraria de transformación a la luz de los principios cooperativos de la ACI y de la ley de economía social. CIRIEC-Esp Rev Jurídica Econ Soc Coop 27:459–494

Rosembuj T (1991) Régimen fiscal de las Cooperativas. PPU, Barcelona

Vargas-Vasserot C (2010) Las Sociedades Agrarias de Transformación. Aproximación crítica a su régimen legal. Rev Derecho Soc 35:159–180

Vargas-Vasserot C (2012) Sociedades Agrarias de Transformación. Empresas agroalimentarias entre la economía social y la del mercado. Dykinson, Madrid

Vargas-Vasserot C (2018) «Las Sociedades Agrarias de Transformación». In: Integración y concentración de empresas agroalimentarias. Dykinson, Madrid

Are Cooperatives Part of Social and Solidarity Economy?

David Hiez

After some others in the past, Hagen Henrÿ is nowadays the most prominent cooperative lawyer worldwide. I have had the chance to meet him, as a colleague and as a friend. By his kindness, his calmness, but also his energy, I am still impressed by his perpetual but quiet movement. But our relationships were centred around our common and professional interest for cooperative law. In that field, thanks to him, I have learned a lot and achieved a little. These modest pages are the witness of this, as well as a try to express my gratitude.

The topic of the incorporation of cooperatives into social economy has already been scrutinized.[1] However, this work was mainly focused on Latin world and targeted to a spanophone audience. We would like to try a more comparative study, which presents the advantage to extend the spectrum.

But the choice of the topic is also dictated by the dedicatee. As such, Prof. Henrÿ did not study in depth the incorporation of cooperatives into social economy, but he tackled explicitly that tricky question.[2] Based on the opposition between the political concept of social economy and the legal form of the actors, Prof. Henrÿ concentrates on the second aspect to highlight similitudes and differences between cooperatives and other legal forms usually attached to social economy. Moreover, he analyses precisely the ILO recommendation R193 of 2002 on the promotion of cooperatives and conclude «that there cannot be any doubt as to the fact that this instrument, {…} does not allow for cooperatives to be considered as an indistinguishable element of a type called "social economy enterprise"».[3] The insistence on the impossibility to

[1] Cooperativismo y Desarollo, 2019, Volume 27, num. 114.

[2] Henrÿ 2012, p. 31–37.

[3] Henrÿ 2012, p. 37.

D. Hiez (✉)
University of Luxembourg, Esch-sur-Alzette, Luxembourg
e-mail: david.hiez@uni.lu

W. Tadjudje and I. Douvitsa (eds.), *Perspectives on Cooperative Law*,
https://doi.org/10.1007/978-981-19-1991-6_10

confuse cooperatives and social economy is at least the proof of their proximity, in contrast with stock companies.

Whereas we fully share that assessment, we would like to question it radically. Indeed, even if cooperatives are generally included into social economy (1), it appears that some legislations consider them differently (2). Based on that uncertainty, we will plead for that connexion (3).

1 A General Inclusion of Cooperatives into Social Economy

It is very common to make a connexion between cooperatives and social and solidarity economy (SSE). This is true if one considers both the origin of social economy and the legislations that regulate that sector.

1.1 Cooperatives as Motor of the Elaboration of SSE

The datation of birth of social economy is debated, but whatever is the selected date, no one contests that cooperatives were an important player in the game. We will distinguish four important dates along the development of social economy: half of the nineteenth century, end of the nineteenth century, and two conflicting evolutions of the 1970s. These different dates are important and equally true in a certain way; we will not try to elucidate their articulation, we only want to prove that, during any of these periods, cooperatives were connected involved into the development of SSE.

Mid-nineteenth century can be considered like the mythological birth of social economy. It is presented in most discourses on social economy as the golden age.[4] The period is usually presented as a critic and an attempt to find an alternative way to capitalism, with two sides: on the one hand, the concrete achievements through cooperatives and mutual, on the other hand, authors like Robert Oen or Charles Fourier. It is interesting that the promotors of solidarity economy (a more recent and critical version of social economy) keeps the same references for its origin.[5] Into these experiences, the cooperatives have the first place, notably the Rochdale pioneers. Therefore, cooperatives are at the root of social economy, even if cooperatives of the nineteenth century cannot be fully assimilated to the most frequent model of contemporary cooperatives. At their first stage, the activities of cooperatives were far wider, mixing the core activity with education, mutual aid, professional organization... Legally speaking, the situation was far scrambled. Indeed, no legislation regulated cooperatives or any other legal form nowadays related to social economy;

---

[4] Draperi 2007, p. 75; Ciriec 2017, p. 6; Grigore 2013, p. 111.

[5] Laville 2010, p. 36. The same observation can be made from the presentation made on the spanish version of wikipedia: https://es.wikipedia.org/wiki/Econom%C3%ADa_solidaria.

this allowed the diversity of experiences and activities that the posterior development of legislation fixed.

The second period comes with the end of the nineteenth century and the beginning of the twentieth. Here are the first real usages of the expression social economy. Its paternity is debated, but the authors agree that it appeared into the French school. If some authors mention Charles Dunoyer or Frédéric Le Play,[6] the most elaborated concept comes from Charles Gide. He defines it «the study of contractual, quasi-contractual or legal voluntary relationships {…}. It does not rely on the free game of natural laws to ensure human happiness, nor on the inspirations of a devotion or a vague philanthropy, but it believes in the necessity and efficiency of a rational, deliberate and voluntary organisation».[7] It is not a hazard if Charles Gide is also the most prominent cooperative thinker and one of the most important actor of its development. But that emergence of social economy remained at that time purely conceptual with no institutional achievement.

The third phase of social economy occurs during the 1970s, starting with an institutional initiative and then conceptually precised.[8] In the 1970s, cooperative and mutual federations, joined by associations pursuing an economic activity, decided to establish a common connecting committee, of mutualist, cooperative and associative activities (CLAMCA).[9] The conceptualization is made notably by Henri Desroche, firstly in 1977 in the closing discourse of the conference of CLAMCA.[10] Nonetheless the cooperative movement was one of the founder of CLAMCA, but Desroche is himself also a specialist of cooperation and he builds his conception of social economy on cooperative thinking.

The fourth phase of the contemporary social economy arises with the emergence of solidarity economy in the 1980s in France and at the end of the twentieth century in South America. At a first glance, cooperatives are less present in that new trend, very critical about social economy, accused to have given up its first claims and to have adopted many practice of capitalist enterprises with which it competes. This is particularly true in the French side, where solidarity economy is at first connected with the emergent WISEs, that usually adopt the legal form of association and sometimes companies but rarely cooperatives. This is less true in South America, even if the critics are very strong as well against ancient cooperatives which have sometimes collaborated with dictatorial regimes. However, the new solidarity economy enterprises are thereby very community centred and generally use the legal form of cooperatives.[11] By the way, we have seen that promoters of solidarity economy

---

[6] Poirier 2014, p. 5.

[7] *«L'étude des rapports volontaires, contractuels, quasi-contractuels ou légaux. {…} Elle ne se fie pas au libre jeu des lois naturelles pour assurer le bonheur des hommes, ni d'ailleurs aux inspirations du dévouement ou d'une vague philanthropie, mais elle croit à la nécessité et à l'efficacité de l'organisation voulue, réfléchie, rationnelle.»* Gide 1913, L'économie sociale; cité par Draperi 2007, p. 10.

[8] Ciriec 2017, p. 6.

[9] Duverger 2014, p. 30–43.

[10] Desroche 1977, p. 33–59.

[11] Reyes and Guerra 2011, p. 29.

don't hesitate to search some roots in the nineteenth century. The opposition between social economy and solidarity economy has tended to fade. Even if it remains partly lively, it is exclusively among actors and has no legal consequences.

1.2 *The Legal Inclusion of Cooperatives into SSE*

Since twenty years, the laws on social economy have flourished,[12] and most of them explicitly mention cooperatives. The most systematic scientific study on social economy legislations[13] observe that nearly all these legislations refer to cooperatives and that this legal form is generally the most important one. They give two explanations for that pre-eminence: on the one hand, cooperatives may run their activities in any domain of human life; on the other hand, it is the single legal form that can rely on internationally recognized principles and definition.[14]

As the SSE legislations are umbrella legislations, they do not regulate the functioning of cooperatives nor their creation or liquidation. However, the definition and principles established by these legislations apply to cooperatives, which have to comply with them. More, the principles stated in these umbrella legislations are often strongly inspired by the cooperatives regulation.[15] If the general presence of cooperatives into the SSE acts, their substantial pre-eminence can be only explained by its relatively more ancient and solid regulation.

That double anchorage of cooperatives into SSE is a worthy feature. Indeed, cooperatives occupy the core of the two competing and complementary approaches of SSE. When the SSE legislations (the most frequent solution) provide a list of legal forms of related enterprises (statutory approach), cooperative is the first of them. When it defines social economy by common principles (normative approach),[16] these principles are mainly inspired again by cooperative law. And this observation is true also for legislations that provide with a more reformative conception, including notably some requirements about labour organization or ownership, these provisions are also present in the national cooperative legislation. We can take the example of Colombian law, in which the reference to a fair distribution of ownership is both present into the solidarity economy law[17] and into the cooperative law.[18]

[12] We do not consider the nuances between social economy, solidarity economy, social and solidarity economy, which does not impact the relationship with cooperatives.

[13] Cairre and Tadjudje 2019, p. 74–88: These authors adopt a large conception of such legislations, including the legislations that do not refer explicitly to social economy, provided that their scope contains several legal forms usually related to social economy; that choice is discussable.

[14] Cairre and Tadjudje 2019, p. 81.

[15] For the French example, see: Hiez 2019.

[16] Most legislations combine the two approaches.

[17] Colombia 1998, art. 3, p. 1.

[18] Colombia 1989, art. 2.

Nevertheless, that strong connexion between cooperatives and social economy is not universal, and it is necessary to inquire into the countries where it is absent.

2 The Temptation to Exclude Cooperatives from SSE

There are two categories of countries for which the question of relationship between cooperatives and SSE is more meaningful. This is the case, first, where the country is not culturally familiar with SSE. The question arises also where the legislation does not list the legal forms included into social economy.

2.1 The Situation of Cooperatives in Countries Ignoring SSE

If cooperatives are present in all countries, even if they are not always regulated by special legislation, social economy is less universal. The tendency is the extension of SSE, but 20 years ago all the Anglo-Saxon area ignored it totally, as well as Germany and eastern Europe, as well as Asia. As our previous examples show, the situation has changed and everywhere the notion starts to be more familiar, even if not usual. In these countries, the most popular flag around which non-conventional enterprises are grouped is non-profit organizations. It is interesting to sum up how cooperatives can be considered when compared, either to companies, or to non-profit organizations. The five core structural characteristics of the business corporation are: (1) legal personality, (2) limited liability, (3) transferable shares, (4) centralized management under a board structure and (5) shared ownership by contributors of equity capital.[19] «Cooperatives derogate to some of these features: like non-profit corporations, municipal corporations, or other types of incorporated entities, they are «jointly owned enterprises»[20]; their shares are usually not transferable[21]; they «allocate voting power and shares in profits proportionally to acts of patronage, which may be the amount of inputs supplied to the firm (in the case of a producer cooperative), or the amount of the firm's products purchased from the firm (in the case of a consumer cooperative).[22]

These differences are not only legal, technical, but are related to the key purpose of the enterprise as well as its functioning. As the question of its object is usually pointed out, we can say a word about its management.

On the one hand, the agency problems into companies is sum up as «conflicts between managers and shareholders, conflicts between controlling and non-controlling shareholders, and conflicts between shareholders and the corporation's

[19] Armour et al. 2017, p. 5.

[20] Armour et al. 2017, p. 15.

[21] Armour et al. 2017, p. 10.

[22] Armour et al. 2017, p. 13.

other contractual counterparties, including particularly creditors and employees».[23] On the other hand, we can refer for cooperatives to the cooperative quadrilateral designed by Henri Desroche. Its starting point is the isolation of four fundamental groups: members (who defined and initiated the project), board members (elected to define orientations in compliance with the project), the managers (designed by board members to implement the project) and employees (subordinated to managers).[24] These four groups constitute the four angles of the cooperative quadrilateral: lower right the members, upper right board members, upper left managers and lower left employees. Equilibrium is reached when there is a good communication and convergences between these four groups. Pathologies may occur by horizontal or vertical conflicts: either the chairman and the manager block the functioning, or there is a clash between the political and the economic sides. We will not develop further this model,[25] but it is not only utilized for cooperatives, but more generally for the groupings of SSE. It shows perfectly the opposition to companies.

2.2 *The Cooperatives in the Countries Where SSE Legislation Gives no List of SSE Enterprises*

Social economy legislations that do not refer to cooperatives are few. Caire and Tadjudje mention Italy, that would include only social cooperatives,[26] but more interestingly four countries without any reference to the legal form of enterprises: Bolivia, Venezuela, Nicaragua and Luxembourg.[27] The example of Nicaragua is less convincing for our purpose, since we focus on cooperatives and cooperativism is one of the key attribution of the competent ministry[28]; the three other examples are more interesting since they explicitly reject any reference to a legal form. In America, they consider either socio-productive community organizations,[29] or farmer's economic organizations, indigene of origins, based on the concept of buen vivir[30]; in these two countries however, most cooperatives are included into the new arrangement, which mitigates their originality regarding our questioning.

The situation is very different in Luxembourg since, nonetheless there is no reference to the legal form, but moreover, most cooperatives are out of SSE. It is

[23] Armour et al. 2017, p. 3.

[24] Draperi 2007, p. 51.

[25] Koulytchizky 1999, p. 77–84.

[26] Cairre and Tadjudje 2019, p. 74–88: The consideration of Italy is itself discussable, since Italian law does not refer to social economy but to third sector, and the exclusion of cooperatives other than social ones is related to the definition of this third sector.

[27] Cairre and Tadjudje 2019, p. 74–88.

[28] Venezuela 2012, art. 3.

[29] Organisaciones socio-productivas communitarias 2008.

[30] Bolivi 2013.

defined and regulated through a dedicated act in 2016.[31] The act refers to legal persons governed by private law who have four cumulative characteristics: continuous production, distribution or exchange of goods or services (article 1, line 2); support through their activity for fragile individuals or a contribution to the realization of a goal (article 1, lines 3 and 4); autonomous management (article 1, line 5); and the reinvestment of at least half of profits in the company's activity (article 1, line 6).[32] The act contains no other precision about the SSE-based enterprises and, therefore, any legal form is allowed. Cooperatives are regulated by the law of 10 August 1915 on commercial companies, which was a copy paste of Belgian law. Legally, they are defined as organizations whose shareholders and/or subscribed capital are variable, and whose shares are non-transferable to third parties (article 811–1). This definition is purely formal, no specific cooperative principle is integrated into Luxembourgish cooperative law. Only a few default provisions such as equal voting rights may apply if no alternative provision has been stated in the cooperative's by-laws (article 811–5 4°). The cooperative are not targeted to its members' needs. In addition, no legal indication exists that identifies a cooperative as a legitimate SSE-based enterprise. Some cooperatives refer to International Cooperative Alliance (ICA) principles in their by-laws, but this is only optional.

The majority of Luxembourgish cooperatives have adopted market-based business models and rely on their commercial activity for most if not all of their resources. Although an entrepreneurial dimension is a rule rather than an exception for these cooperatives, their commercial activity creates an issue in relation to their compliance with social dimension and governance criteria. We can identify four cooperative types in the country: Cooperatives operating like commercial companies and mainly serving their shareholders' interests; Cooperatives primarily serving mutual interest; Cooperatives combining mutual interest and general interest; and cooperatives operating in the work integration sector, especially with disabled people. Cooperatives, associations and mutual never collaborated, and nor cooperatives neither the other organizations consider that they share the same values. The enterprises included nowadays into SSE remain strongly influenced by philanthropy and only few cooperatives that have adopted the same values are included. A new trend has emerged, coming from the ecological concerns (organic agriculture of producers and consumers, renewable energy production, co-housing); these cooperatives are more inspired by international recognized cooperative principles and this could impulse a new development but, so far, the remain few. Two consequences derive from that situation: on one hand, cooperatives remain weak and rather unknown into the society, on the other hand, SSE meets difficulties to develop beyond social aid and work integration. This is a very good example to emphasize the opportunity to get closer cooperatives and social economy.

---

[31] Loi du 12 décembre 2016 portant création des sociétés d'impact sociétal, mémorial A255, Luxembourg.

[32] Hiez 2017, p. 110–117.

3 Rationale for the Inclusion of Cooperatives into SSE

The benefit of the connexion between cooperatives and SSE are numerous: economic, legal, social, political... Naturally, we will deal with the legal aspects, and we will try to demonstrate that these benefits are both for SSE and for cooperatives.

3.1 The Benefits for Social Economy

Apart from cooperatives, social economy is generally composed mainly of associations, mutual and foundations. A special mention must be made about traditional communities, which join the sector in many countries and notably in Latin America.[33] We confess that we don't know enough these communities so that our observations do not concern them and we assume that they are likely to provide theoretical and practical resources. But if we limit the look to associations, mutual and foundations, we think that they are weak for the establishment of a legal regulation for SSE.

The weakness of associations is double. Firstly, their focus is not economic. The activities of associations are oriented to sport, culture, religion, politics... Economics play an increasing role in their functioning because of the general marketization of our society, but that evolution has been progressive and their recent experience into these activities do not provide them with many resources to face these new and specific questions: how to include economic constraints, how to get capital, competition with capitalist enterprises... Secondly, associations are very different around the world and their relations ships with the state are so various that it is difficult to find common features; in Europe, it is meaningful that, into the process to establish a European statute for the enterprises of SSE[34] was very quickly stopped for associations[35] and did not profit of the short involvement of the Commission for these legal statutes.

The situation is very different for mutuals, which can rely on a long experience. Their light influence on the general framework of SSE is more related to the narrow spectrum of their activities, usually limited to health sector.

As for foundations, they occupy a special place into SSE. They are recognized only in six European social economy legislations and in Cabo Verde,[36] which legislation is mainly inspired by the Portuguese act. Their inclusion into SSE is discussed, because they are not a member-based organization. Actually, they consist in a capital targeted at the pursuit of a philanthropic purpose, which management is disconnected from

[33] They are probably lively as well in other continents where traditional societies remain, but they have been covered by European institutions through colonization.

[34] See for associations: Proposition de règlement (CEE) du Conseil portant statut de l'association européenne (92/C 99/01). Proposition modifiée de règlement (CEE) du Conseil portant statut de l'association européenne (93/C 236/01).

[35] Communication from the Commission to the Council and the European Parliament—Outcome of the screening of legislative proposals pending before the Legislator /COM/2005/0462 final.

[36] Caire and Tadjudje 2019, p. 74–88.

any group of members. They are the legally closest organization from charities in common law. That could be a reason to deepen its connexion with other SSE-based enterprises, but this work has not been accomplished so far.

By contrast, cooperatives rely on a solid legal history and provides to SSE with a fruitful model. This does not mean that cooperative law proposes solutions to all the challenges of SSE, but it is at least a good toolbox. The reasoning of the European court of justice about cooperative taxation,[37] confronted to the state aid regulation, is a good example.

The next step is the elaboration of a conceptually more consistent framework for SSE. Indeed, its legislation states so far only some principles and objectives but do not establish a full set of rules. Surely SSE does not need a homogeneous legal statute; it will remain a general umbrella under which various legal forms will develop. However, the elaboration of a solid pattern would be useful in order to reinforce its identity alternative to the capitalist one.

3.2 *The Benefits for Cooperatives*

We must not divinize cooperatives and they are not the do-gooder of SSE. Their relationship is mutually beneficial. The first reason of the emergence of SSE is the awareness of cooperatives of their weakness; it is noticeable that in many countries the turn-over of cooperatives is far lower of the association's one. Here are the reasons why cooperatives and other SSE organizations have already collaborated in many parts of the word, but there are other reasons to go further.

The point is not quantitative and cooperative law is also itself fruitfully inspired by other legal statutes. Cooperatives are not a static fixed model. The example of the so successful social cooperatives in Italy, and more generally of general interest cooperatives, is a very good example. Cooperatives are defined by the satisfaction of their members' needs, and this is historically intricated into a very broad notion of these interest. If one refers to the mythic Rochdale pioneers, they were very far from the consumer cooperatives that we know nowadays. This change derives from the specialization of any legal status; in that sense, this shrinkage is the price to pay for the legal recognition and regulation of cooperatives. But it creates also the risk to impoverish cooperativism to a selfish tradition, related to the conception of mankind through the prism of homo economicus.

Other SSE organizations, less dedicated to economic activities, are less likely to be influenced by this bias on the humankind conception. Therefore, they restitute to human being its fullness and indirectly stimulates the revival of a more complex and more diverse thinking of cooperativism. The cooperative principles established in 1995 by the ICA are not the final truth, if ever they are a truth, of cooperative history. They are only a moment, and should be seen as an open door towards the future more

[37] ECJ 2011, Joined Cases C-78/08 to C-80/08, Ministero dell'Economia e delle Finanze and Others v. Paint Graphos Soc. coop. arl and Others.

than the succession of the past. In that sense, the statement about the concern for community, may be considered as the way to reintroduce, through community, all that was previously included through a non-economic conception of each member. He increasing number of general cooperatives all over the world could be a confirmation.

Another crucial point could be the distinction between non-profit and for-profit organizations. Indeed, cooperatives meet some difficulties to enter into this classification and it is not effectless. This impacts at least the establishment of statistics and, more directly for law, the tax treatment, maybe the question of competition law.

Let's take the first random quotation found on Internet through a google search: «Contrary to popular belief coops are not non-profits, and do aim earn profits.».[38] But, of course, the same presentation precise immediately that, nevertheless, they differ from companies, because of cooperative principles. We have already touched that question and stop here, referring only to a classical debate among cooperative lawyers to decide if cooperatives should be qualified as companies or not. Hagen Henrÿ put it so clearly as simply: cooperatives «are not-for-profit enterprises "not-for-profit" to be distinguished from "non-profit"».[39] However, some other authors claim for the qualification of non-profit organizations.[40] And the point seems to be actually undecidable, since related to the definition given to not-for-profit and non-profit. When Hagen Henrÿ claims a clear distinction to these two notions, he highlights that cooperatives are business organizations, requiring to make profits in order to make its business sustainable, whereas its purpose is not to distribute profits to its members. Nevertheless, that does not fit perfectly with the most common definition of non-profit: a non-profit organization is one prohibited by law or irrevocable internal decisions from distributing profits to those in control of the organization.[41] Meanwhile, some authors do not oppose non-profit and not-for-profit.[42]

To elucidate these hesitations or contradictions, a new category arises: hybrid organizations. Surely this fits with the development of organizations sharing some features with the two major categories of organizations, but hybridity may also appear as an easy and light solution to a difficult question. To tackle the core question of profitability, it is proposed to establish the notion of limited profitability.[43] We will not close that discussion hereby but we want only to show how the inclusion of cooperatives into SSE may help to clarify their definition and classification.

This short article claims for no conclusion, since it is an invitation to further research on cooperative law and its alike. But we would like to draft one last idea around that invitation. It appears that cooperative law is going out of the shadow in which it stood during several decades. In the beginning of the nineteenth century,

---

[38] University of Alasca Anchorage: https://www.uaa.alaska.edu/academics/business-enterprise-institute/coop-development/what-are-cooperatives.cshtml.

[39] Henrÿ 2012, p. 37.

[40] Finfrock and Talley 2014.

[41] Hansmann 1980; Salamon and Anheier 1992.

[42] O'Connell 2018, p. 388.

[43] Driquez 2017.

lawyers studied cooperatives, since it was new and questioned the traditional categories into a developing capitalism. After the Second World War, apart from international cooperation and the new states post-colonization, cooperative law vanished from the scene. Since the 1990s, the evolution is reversed, first through the interest of international organizations, and then of academic thinking. But the focus and purpose have changed since the first round of cooperative law. Whereas it aimed mainly into the first wave at the recognition and establishment of cooperative legislations, i.e. the legal translation of the best practice revealed by the diverse concrete experiences. In the present wave, the major point is to find the right place for cooperatives into the legal system, both among other organizations and in coordination with key questions for business law. When it is increasingly common to recognize that capitalism is in crisis, cooperative law is not anymore a problem for lawyers costumed with traditional concepts but a possible solution for concerned lawyers. Hagen Henrÿ has felt that evolution and has been the most eminent actor of that revival. A new page is to be written on that basis.

References

Armour J, Hansmann H, Kraakman R, Pargendler M (2017) What is corporate law? In: Kraakman R et al (eds) The anatomy of corporate law a comparative and functional approach, 3rd edn. Oxford University Press

Bolivia (2013) Ley No 338—Ley de organizaciones económicas campesinas, indígenas originarias y de organizaciones económicas comunitarias para la integración de la agricultura familiar sustentable y la soberanía alimentaria

Caire G, Tadjudje W (2019) Vers une culture juridique mondiale de l'entreprise d'ESS ? Une approche comparative internationale des législations ESS, RECMA, pp°353

Ciriec (2017) Recent evolutions of the social economy in the European Union. European Economic and Social Committee

Colombia (1989) Ley 79 De 1988, Diario Oficial No 38.648 de 10 de enero de 1989 Por la cual se actualiza la legislación cooperativa.

Colombia (1998) Ley 454 De 1998, Por la cual se determina el marco conceptual que regula la economía´a solidaria, Diario Oficial. Ano CXXXIV, n.43357.6, Agosto

Desroche H (1977) Rapport de synthèse ou quelques hypothèses pour une entreprise d'économie sociale, CLAMCA, 20.000.000 de sociétaires, 800.000 emplois: actes du colloque du CLAMCA des 20 et 21 janvier 1977. SIEM publishing, Paris

Draperi J-F (2007) Comprendre l'économie sociale. Dunod publisher, Paris

Driquez L (2017) Le but non-lucratif en droit de l'union européenne ou de la nécessité d'adopter une notion nouvelle de lucrativité limitée. MGEN publisher, Paris

Duverger T (2014) La Réinvention de l'économie sociale: une histoire du CNLAMCA, RECMA, pp°334

ECJ (2011) Joined Cases C-78/08 to C-80/08, Ministero dell'Economia e delle Finanze and Others v. Paint Graphos Soc. coop. arl and Others

Finfrock J, Talley EL (2014) Social Entrepreneurship and Uncorporations. Illinois Law Review 18674

Gide C (1913) L'économie sociale

Grigore AA (2013) Social economy entities: a worldwide overview. Rev Appl Econo Res 6(2)

Hansmann HB (1980) The role of non-profit enterprise, Yale Law J 89:835.2

Henrÿ H (2012) Guidelines for cooperative legislation, 3rd revised edn. International labour organization publisher
Hiez D (2017) Sociétés d'impact societal: première reconnaissance législative de l'économie sociale et solidaire—loi du 12 décembre 2016 portant création des sociétés d'impact sociétal». Journal des tribunaux Luxembourg
Hiez D (2019) Le droit coopératif et l'économie sociale et solidaire en France. Cooperativismo & Desarrollo 27(1):1–30. https://doi.org/10.16925/2382-4220.2019.01.13
Koulytchizky S (1999) Le quadrilatère d'Henri Desroche revisité, RECMA, pp°272
Laville J-L (2010) Politique de l'association. Seuil publisher, Paris
O'Connell A (2018) Taxation and the not-for-profit sector globally: common issues, different solutions. In: Harding M (ed) Research handbook on not-for-profit law. Edward Edgar Publishing
Organizaciones socio-productivas comunitarias (2008) Decreto con rango, Valor y fuerza de ley para el fomento y desarrollo de la economía popular, agosto
Poirier Y (2014) Economie sociale et solidaire et concepts apparentés: Les origines et les définitions: une perspective internationale
Reyes S, Guerra P (2011) Economia solidaria, cooperativismo y relaciones laborales. Fundacion de Cultura Universitaria
Salamon L, Anheier HK (1992) In search of the nonprofit sector: the question of definitions. Voluntas 3:125
Venezuela (2012), Ley no.290, ley de organización, competencia y procedimientos del poder ejecutivo, art. 29 ter ; added by ley n°804, la gaceta—diario oficial 10–07–12

Legal Specificities and Essence of Cooperatives

Japanese Cooperative Legislation Impacting the Cooperative Structure and Culture

Akira Kurimoto

1 Introduction

Japanese cooperatives have grown to sheer size organizations in some aspects. Agricultural cooperatives are ranked among the largest for agriculture, insurance and banking sectors in the World Cooperative Monitor, while the membership of consumer cooperatives accounts for more than 70% of aggregated membership of European counterparts affiliated with the EUROCOOP. However, they are institutionally and organizationally divided in Japan's political economy, lacking the sense of identity as a cooperative sector. This phenomenon can be explained from the prevailing socio-economic environment while it is partly due to the peculiar legal framework, that has given impacts in the path-dependent evolution of cooperatives. I described the evolution of the cooperative legislation in Japan from the Industrial Cooperative Act of 1900 to the separate legislations based on industrial policies after WWII. Herewith, an overview of Japan's cooperative legislation and its characteristics is presented. Then, the question on how it has impacted in forming the cooperative structure and culture will be analysed. Finally, this paper concludes with some suggestions to enhance the cooperative status in the political economy and its contribution to the sustainable and resilient development.

2 Overview of the Japanese Cooperative Legislation

(1) Fragmented cooperative legislation

The most striking feature of the Japanese cooperative legislation is a lack of the general law. Most of countries have a unified cooperative law or a basic law in addition

A. Kurimoto (✉)
Japan Co-operative Alliance, 3-8-6, Ohanajaya, Katsushika-ku 1240003, Tokyo, Japan
e-mail: akurimotojp@gmail.com

W. Tadjudje and I. Douvitsa (eds.), *Perspectives on Cooperative Law*,
https://doi.org/10.1007/978-981-19-1991-6_11

to the specific laws (Kurimoto, 2013). South Korea was in the same situation until the Framework Act of Cooperatives was enacted in 2011. The Industrial Cooperative Act of 1900 had regulated all types of cooperatives and allowed them to run multiple functions (supply, marketing, credit, production or services) but separate cooperative laws were enacted after World War II and now there exist more than ten laws serving specific needs of different types of cooperatives (See below). The administrative agencies with jurisdiction are also divided into the Ministry of Agriculture, Forestry and Fisheries (MAFF), the Small and Medium Enterprise Agency (SMEA) and the Financial Services Agency (FSA). The Consumer Cooperatives Act, an exception to the legislation by industrial policy, is under the jurisdiction of the Ministry of Health, Labor and Welfare (MHLW), but consumer cooperatives are also divided from other cooperatives by a vertically divided legal and administrative system. In addition, since there was no law on the basis of which workers cooperatives were established in Japan, those who want to establish such cooperatives were forced to use other legal entities such as NPOs (NPO Act), limited companies (Companies Act) or joint enterprise cooperatives (SMEs Cooperatives Act). The Workers Cooperatives Act was enacted in 2020 under the jurisdiction of the MHLW.

- Agricultural Cooperatives Act (referred as ACA, No. 132 of November 19, 1947)
- Consumer Cooperatives Act (referred as CCA, No. 200 of July 30, 1948)
- Fisheries Cooperatives Act (referred as FCA, No. 242 of December 15, 1948)
- Small and Medium-Sized Enterprise Cooperatives Act (No. 181 of June 1, 1949)[1]
- Act on Cooperative Banking (No. 183 of June 1, 1949)
- Shinkin Bank Act (No. 238 of June 15, 1951)[2]
- Labor Bank Act (No. 227 of August 17, 1953)
- Tobacco Growers Cooperatives Act (No. 135 of April 1, 1958)
- Forest-owner Cooperatives Act (No. 36 of May 1, 1978)
- Norinchukin Bank Act (No. 93 of June 29, 2001)[3]
- Worker Cooperatives Act (referred as WCA, No. 78 of December 4, 2020)

In addition to these cooperative laws, the Act on Prohibition of Private Monopolization and Maintenance of Fair Trade (No. 54, April 14, 1947, hereafter referred as Anti-Monopoly Act) and the Corporation Tax Act (No. 34, March 31, 1965, hereafter referred as CTA) apply to all types of cooperatives. Article 22 of Anti-Monopoly Act exempted from its application such acts of a cooperative (including a federation) which conforms to the requirements and which has been formed pursuant to the provisions of law, except for the cases where unfair trade practices are employed, or

---

[1] SME Cooperatives Law has several categories of cooperatives; (i) A business cooperative, (i)-2 A minor business cooperative, (i)-3 A fire mutual aid cooperative, (ii) A credit cooperative, (iii) A federation of cooperatives and (iv) A joint enterprise cooperative.

[2] Shinkin literally means credit bank, that is owned by members, mainly SMEs operating in urban communities.

[3] Norinchukin literally means "agricultural and forestry central bank", serving agricultural, fishery and forest-owners cooperatives. It was originally founded as the Industrial Cooperative Central Bank in 1923.

where competition in any particular field of trade is substantially restrained, resulting in unjust increases of prices, following the example of Capper-Volstead Act of 1922. These requirements are; (a) aiming at mutual benefits among small producers or consumers, (b) voluntary and open membership, (c) equal voting right for each member and (d) limited compensation when distributing surplus.[4] Thus, the Anti-monopoly Act defined the criteria for *Ideal-typus* of cooperatives to be applied to all kinds of co-ops.

The tax law applies different tax rates based on corporate status rather than the judgement based on functions. The CTA provides for different rates for public institutions (Annex 1, no tax), non-profit institutions (Annex 2, no tax) and cooperatives and related entities (Annex 3, reduced rate). Cooperatives are applied the favourable tax treatment, but the differential in tax rate between conventional companies and cooperatives has been dwindling from from 12.3 to 4.4% during 1984–2016.

(2) Elements of organizational law mingled with those of business laws

In the Japanese juridical system, there are many cases where the legal elements of organization concerning the establishment and operation of corporations and the legal elements of business that restrict the freedom of business in certain industries for the sake of public welfare are mixed. This is a common characteristic of for-profit corporations, non-profit organizations, and cooperatives, which have arisen as a result of the successive creation of corporate statuses in accordance with policy objectives since there was no General Corporation Law as an organizational law.[5]

This legal and administrative system of "public policy-business regulation-corporate status" in the Japanese private law is extremely convenient for the supervisory authorities, but it hinders cross-sectional thinking about the relationships among businesses/services, and creates gaps between systems and waste due to overlapping administration. In the cooperative law, not only the organizational law elements such as the establishment, organization, accounting and supervision of cooperatives are provided but also the regulations on financial businesses (Banking Act, Insurance Business Act, Financial Instruments and Exchange Act, etc.) are largely applied mutatis mutandis to the credit and insurance businesses of cooperatives, resulting in the proliferation of branch numbers and making the structure of the cooperative law extremely complicated (e.g., Article 11-5-2 ACA). Furthermore, the credit business of agricultural cooperatives is regulated by the MAFF and the FSA, while the business of labour banks is regulated by the MHLW and the FSA.

---

[4] These requirements draws on the ICA Cooperative Principles adopted in 1937.

[5] The "Report of the Study Group on Organizational Forms and the Law" describes the choice of organizational form as follows (Bank of Japan Institute for Monetary and Economic Studies 2003).

"However, in certain industries, it is not legally possible to choose an organizational form other than a specific one, or the choice may be limited to a certain range. For example, the need to establish a medical corporation to conduct medical treatment and a social welfare corporation to conduct social welfare activities is an example of the former, and the limitation of the organizational form of a stock exchange to a securities membership corporation or a stock company, and the limitation of the organizational form of an insurance company to a mutual company or a stock company, respectively, is an example of the latter.".

(3) Strong control and promotion by ministries in line with industrial policies

The specific cooperatives laws are characterized by the principle of approval by the competent government agencies and strong regulation/supervision.[6] The establishment of a cooperative, amendment of the bylaws and insurance/loan business rules, merger and dissolution of a cooperative require the approval of the administrative agency. In addition, the administrative agency has the authority to grant permission for non-member use and to supervise the collection of reports, inspections, orders for improvement and dissolution. In case of the agricultural cooperatives, there were special laws to promote their reorganization through policy and tax measures.[7]

(4) Hindering the free establishment of cooperatives to meet new needs

The current provisions on membership and business in the specific cooperative laws make it difficult to establish new types of cooperatives whose activities are designed to meet new needs caused by socio-economic changes. For example, due to the limitation of membership, it is not possible to establish "mixed production and consumption type cooperatives" (Kono, Naofumi 1998) in which farmers and consumers participate, or "multi-stakeholder cooperatives" in which volunteers and others participate. In addition, it is not possible to establish cooperatives that meet the needs of production and distribution of renewable energy and businesses that address social inclusion of the disabled persons. In addition, a variety of corporate systems, such as non-profit organizations (NPOs), approved local associations, general incorporated associations, joint stock companies and limited liability companies, are being used as local management organizations to revitalize depopulated areas, but cooperatives are not included. As shown in the case studies of Italy, the United Kingdom and Canada, community cooperatives can be powerful receptacles for regional revitalization.

(5) Delay in modernization of cooperative legislation

In the twenty-first century, Japan has been modernizing its legal system in order to respond to the globalization of the economy and society. The new Companies Act, which came into effect in 2006, was reorganized by integrating the Limited Company Act and the Special Act of the Commercial Code, and became a general law on companies. It stipulates the establishment, organization, operation and management of joint stock companies and equity companies (general partnership companies, limited partnership companies and limited liability companies), and allows for a great deal of autonomy in the design of the articles of incorporation to accommodate various types of companies, from very small companies to large publicly traded companies.

On the other hand, the Act for the Promotion of Specified Non-Profit Activities (NPO Act) was enacted in 1998, and three laws related to the reform of the public

---

[6] The ccompetent government agencies are prefectures and ministries.

[7] For example, the Agricultural, Forestry and Fishery Co-ops' Reconstruction and Readjustment Act of 1951 and 1953 aiming to rescue ailing cooperatives in the first industries, the Act for Promoting Mergers among Agricultural Co-ops of 1961 aiming to accelerate the mergers and the JA Bank Act of 2001 aiming to reorganize and streamline credit business of agricultural co-ops.

interest corporation system were enacted in 2008. The revision of articles related to public interest corporations, including Article 34 of the Civil Code, indicates that the era of the state's monopoly on interpretation of public interest has undergone a major transformation. The General Incorporated Association and General Incorporated Foundation Act was intended to be a general law for non-profit corporations and incorporated the Intermediate Corporation Act, but the NPO Act was retained, so there is a juxtaposition of legal entities with similar characteristics. In addition, non-profit corporations under special laws (medical corporations and social welfare corporations) have been reformed in line with the Companies Act.

In contrast, the cooperative legislation lacks the momentum to move to the general laws. Since 2000, some important amendments were made to the CCA in 2007, the ACA in 2015, and the FCA in 2017, while the WCA was enacted in 2020 after campaigning of more than 20 years. These are amendments and addition of specific laws, and have not yet led to a fundamental review of cooperative legislation including the enactment of a general law reflecting socio-economic changes.

3 Some Characteristic Aspects of the Japanese Cooperative Legislation

(1) Establishment

Cooperatives are established upon government's approval while they need to acquire the license for banking business from the FSA Commissioner. They can conduct *Kyosai* insurance business under individual cooperative laws. The provisions of the Banking Act and the Insurance Business Act apply mutatis mutandis to cooperatives. Only the WCA allowed to establish worker cooperatives without government's approval.

Cooperatives can set up subsidiary companies except for banking and insurance businesses based on the Companies Act but those companies are subject to regulations put by cooperative laws and ministry ordnances/guidelines for supervision. In addition, the Agricultural Land Act provides for the types of corporations qualified to ownership and utilization of farm land, and add to the complicated nexus of regulations on cooperatives.

(2) Membership

Membership is strictly defined; farmers for agricultural co-ops, fishermen for fishery co-ops, SMEs for SME co-ops, workers for workers co-ops, etc., except for consumer co-ops that accept anyone as members. It is not possible to set up multi-stakeholder co-ops or community co-ops that have different classes of membership.

ACA has two categories of membership; farmers as full members and non-farmers as associate members "who have their domicile in the district of the said agricultural cooperative, or those who have been continuously receiving supplies or services related to their business from the latter, and who reasonably use the facilities of the latter". The fact the associated members outnumbers the full members is questioned and the government expressed the intension to set a cap to their use. A farmers-group corporation engaging in farm management (including production or processing undertaken using farm crops and livestock products as raw materials, and other activities laid down by the Ministerial Ordinance, and forestry that is carried out side by side with agriculture) is also qualified to a full member.

(3) Activities

Each cooperative laws enumerate the types of business to be conducted, while CCA has not allowed to engage in credit business. ACA, FCA and CCA allowed cooperatives to operate multiple functions as multi-purpose cooperatives but such legal arrangement has been exceptional while the Banking Act and the Insurance Business Act prohibit banks and insurance companies to operate other businesses. This is why multi-purpose cooperatives have been criticized by these industries. In the CCA amended in 2007, a clause was introduced to separate insurance business from other businesses.

As for non-member use, the ACA and other laws regulate non-member use to 20–25% of the amount of business used by members, but the CCA completely prohibits non-member use and imposes strict regulations, including penalties, that are unparalleled in the world. In addition, this law has imposed an area restriction to consumer cooperatives operating in communities to go beyond the prefectural area. This was extended to neighbouring prefectures by the amendment of the law in 2007, but the insurance business continues to be confined within prefectures. This is an issue that needs to be reviewed in comparison with the Companies Act, which has been deregulated in tandem with the international trend of deregulation.

4 Cooperative Legislation's Impact to the Cooperative Structure and Culture

The lack of a general or basic law on cooperatives is one of the reasons why the identity as a cooperative sector has not been nurtured. In terms of the political and economic system, the division of institutions based on industrial policies has created industry triangles of trade associations, bureaucrats and legislature. It is comparable with revolving door system in the United States, but the Japanese system was much fortified under ministries' commanding heights associated with the long-term government of the Liberal Democratic Party (LDP). It is said that this has led to the polarization of the political economy through the pursuit of specific interest of industries (*Compartmentalized Pluralism* as Masahiko Aoki put it). Once such a government-led system was praised in Chalmers Johnson's *MITI and the Japanese Miracle: the Growth of Industrial Policy, 1925–1975* but it has lost its currency since the 1990s when the Japanese industries lost their competitive edge in the world economy through the revolutionary changes brought by globalization and information technology.

The industry-specific cooperative legal system gave an enduring impact to the structure of cooperatives. Agricultural cooperatives have developed a pyramidal integrated structure in line with the government's administrative system. First of all, they operate multiple functions such as supply, marketing, credit, insurance, health care and other businesses (Kurimoto, 2004). These multi-purpose cooperatives play a dominant role in the rural economy throughout the country and provide the indispensable infrastructure of rural life from cradle to grave, while specialist cooperatives also operate in dairy, livestock and flower sectors in some limited geographic areas. Secondly, they organize the three-tier *keitou* system from national federations, prefectural federations and primary co-ops in parallel with the administrative system of central government, prefectures and municipalities (cities, towns and villages). The multiple functions are also vertically integrated in *keitou* system. The amended Agricultural Cooperatives Act in 1954 introduced provisions on the central unions such as JA Zenchu (national) and JA Kenchu (prefectural) as coordinating bodies of those functions.[8] They have been exclusively designated by central and prefectural governments and have compulsory membership of JAs and federations. JA Zenchu could publish model bylaws that bound outsiders as well. It could make propositions on co-op-related matters to the government. Zenchu's National Audit Organization could conduct compulsory auditing of JAs. Kenchu could make territorial coordination within a prefecture when new co-ops were established. Such special functions were abandoned when the Act was amended in 2015 that transformed JA Zenchu to a general incorporated association without changing organization names, and the *keitou* system remained intact.

To cope with intensified competition, the vertical integration from three tiers to two tiers has been carried out since the 1990s with mixed speeds. Zenkyoren (National Mutual Insurance Federation of Agricultural Co-ops) integrated all prefectural federations in 2000. Zen-noh (National Federation of Agricultural Co-ops) integrated 32 Keizairen (prefectural supply and marketing cooperative federations) out of 47, while Norinchukin Bank (Central Bank for Agriculture and Forestry) integrated 19 Shinren (prefectural credit cooperative federations). The supply, marketing and insurance businesses have been declining while credit business is still maintaining a bulk of deposits and loans. The losses generated in supply and marketing businesses have been offset by profits earned by banking and insurance businesses but such a cross-subsidization is becoming more difficult because of the Bank of Japan's zero-interest policy that curtails bank's earning capacity and intensified competition while rapidly shrinking rural population results in the eroding base of insurance business (Fig. 1).

In contrast, consumer cooperatives have grown from grass-root consumer groups and federated from the bottom (Kurimoto, 1992, 2005, 2010, 2017). This is why there exist some national federations with different strategies. The mainstream cooperatives seek to organize a majority of consumers in each prefecture to exercise a market power and buy CO-OP brand products from the Japanese Consumer Cooperative Union (JCCU), while Seikatsu Club/Green Co-op groups aim to promote a social movement pushing a radical ecologist stance. The PAL System group locates itself

[8] JA stands for Japan Agricultural cooperative.

Level/Function	Coordination	Supply/ marketing	Credit	Insurance	Healthcare	Tourism
National level	JA Zenchu	Zen-noh	Norinchukin	Zenkyoren	Zenkoren	JA Tourist
Prefectural level	JA Kenchu	Keizairen	Shinren	(integrated)	Koseiren	
Municipal level	JAs (multi-purpose, specialized)					
Membership	Full members/associate members					

Fig. 1 JA group's organizational structure based on Keitou

in between, often collaborating with the latter group. These cooperatives belonging to different groups compete each other to earn consumers' support and patronage. In addition, there are national federations of insurance, housing, health and university cooperatives. At prefectural level, prefectural unions are organized to coordinate joint actions among these cooperatives and promote public relations with local governments and other entities. All federations and unions are affiliated with the JCCU that is recognized as a national centre.

One of characteristics of consumer co-op structure is the regional consortiums that were created to obtain economy of scale among cooperatives since 1990 to avoid the legal constraint that prohibited mergers beyond prefectural borders. This constraint was partially eased in 2007 when the amended Consumer Cooperatives Act allowed the mergers of cooperatives in neighbouring prefectures. Since then, Co-op Kobe and Osaka Kita Co-op were amalgamated in 2011. Likewise, Co-op Mirai was set up through the merger of Co-op Tokyo, Saitama Co-op and Chiba Co-op, while U Co-op was founded by merging Co-op Kanagawa, Co-op Shizuoka and Co-op Yamanashi in 2013. Today, these mega co-ops and regional consortiums accounts for 90% of aggregated turnover (Fig. 2).

Different types of cooperatives have developed heterogeneous organizational cultures and political orientations that have been intensified in the course of organizational evolution due to the historical path dependency. Cooperatives have strengthened their identities in their respective industries, and this situation has hindered the establishment of a cross-sectoral cooperative identity, combined with the lack of general cooperative policies and contact points on the part of the government. The JA group, the largest entity in terms of business turnover and political influence to the government, has been institutionalized as an agent for implementing agricultural policy pursued by the MAFF that has heavily supported JAs with public policy measures and subsidies. It has established itself as a strongest pressure group of protectionists against trade liberalization and rendered votes for the LDP. Thus, so-called agricultural policy triangle was formed by JA Zenchu, LDP's agricultural lobby and the MAFF. When the government imposed the structural reform by amending the Agricultural Cooperatives Acts in 2015, this coalition was partially marred but looks like survived. In contrast, consumer cooperatives have been "contained" by the protectionist commercial policy backed by the anti-cooperative campaigns of small retailers. They have been often seen as anti-government organizations because of

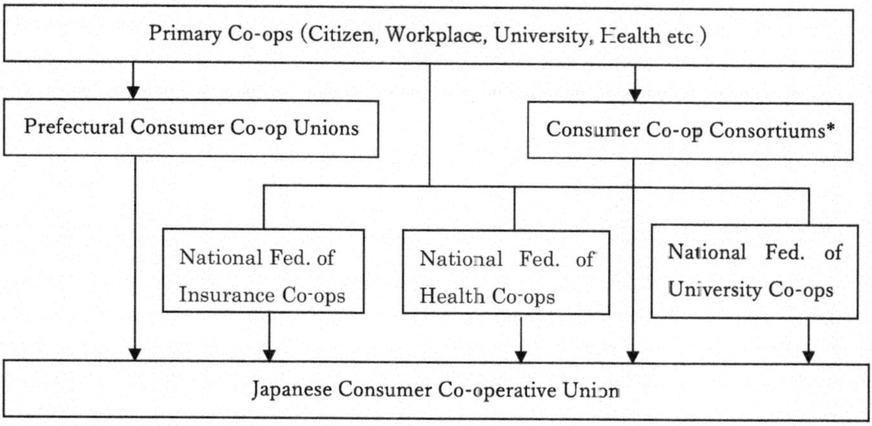

*Consortiums are joint organization of primary co-ops for joint buying and development of private brands and IT system. They include regional federations, Seikatsu Club/Green Co-operative Federations and Pal System Co-operative Federation.

Fig. 2 JCCU group's organizational structure

consumerist, ecologist and pacifist campaigns. They have little political influence to the government although they have exercised some influence in enacting pro-consumer legislation such as the Product Liabilities Act (1994) and the Food Safety Basic Act (2003).

On the occasion of the International Year of Cooperatives (IYC), the Japanese cooperative camp launched the IYC Commemorative National Executive Committee ahead of the rest of the world in 2010 and reaffirmed the need to establish a cooperative identity. The Executive Committee submitted a "Draft Cooperative Charter" to the government, including "Guidelines for Action in Government's Cooperative Policy", but there was no response from the government, and the contact point in the government was not determined until the end, so it failed to make an impact on the Japanese political economy.

5 Conclusion

There are two events that can lead to the improvement in the cooperative legislation. Firstly, the Japan Cooperative Alliance (JCA) was established in 2018 inheriting the activities of the Japan Joint Committee of Cooperatives (JJC) as a coordinating body of the ICA members' international relations and the IYC Memorial National Council as a coalition to promote joint action among cooperatives. It is expected to become a driving force for promoting collaboration among cooperatives and establishing the cooperative identity in Japan. The JCA should play a vital role in facilitating collaboration among the established cooperatives and between older and new cooperatives.

Secondly, the Worker Cooperatives Act unanimously passed the Diet in December 2020 after campaigning for two decades. There are some features that can help to set up cooperatives more easily; establishment with smaller minimum membership (5 members), incorporation without government permission, any kind of activities allowed except for financial businesses, simpler governance structure, etc. This Act has a potential to give impact to the existing cooperative laws.

It seems to be unrealistic to think about the general cooperative law uniting the existing laws given the fact the current legislation has continued around seven decades and cooperatives have evolved in quite different structure and culture as mentioned above. Therefore, it is advisable to enact the Framework Act of Cooperatives (FAC) consisting of the framework law and the general cooperative law that enables to set up the general cooperatives without linkage to industrial policies (Kurimoto 2020). It will coexist with existing laws but it provides for the common principles on cooperative laws that set the legal norm for enacting or amending cooperative laws. FAC in South Korea has contributed to the explosion of cooperatives since 2012. In addition, it is advisable to set up the facilities to promote the cooperative development financed by donation from larger cooperatives and the transfer from the indivisible reserves. The Italian cooperative mutual funds set up in accordance with the 1992 Act have contributed to cooperative start-ups and restructuring through channelling 3% of net surplus and transferring the residual assets of existing cooperatives. In these regards, the experiences in South Korea and Italy are of great relevance to reforming the Japanese cooperative legislation.

References

Kurimoto A (1992) Japan's consumer co-operative movement: a comparative review. In: Tzuzuki C (ed) Robert Owen and the World of Co-operation, Hokusen-sha

Kurimoto A (2004) Agricultural co-operative in Japan: an institutional approach. J Rural Cooperation 32(2)

Kurimoto A (2005) The institutional change and consumer co-operation: Japanese vs European Models. Consumerism versus Capitalism? Amsab-Institute of Social History

Kurimoto A (2010) Evolution and characteristics of Japanese-style consumer co-ops. Toward Contemporary Co-operative Studies: Perspectives from Japan's Consumer Co-ops, Consumer Co-operative Institute of Japan

Kurimoto A (2013) Chapter 23: Japan. In: International handbook of cooperative law. Springer

Kurimoto A (2017) Building consumer democracy: the Trajectory of consumer Co-operation in Japan, 1950–2010. Global History of Consumer Co-operation since 1850, Brill

Kurimoto A (2020) Proposal on the framework act of co-operatives. Seikyo Soken Report, No. 92 (Japanese)

Kono, Naofumi (1998) Sansho Kongogata Kyodokumiai (Farmer-Consumer Mixed Cooperatives)

Legal Regulation of Cooperatives' Activity in Russia: Current State and Development Trends

Yu. M. Goryachkovskaya, G. A. Semenenko, and V. V. Kutko

1 Introduction

Cooperation is a broad social phenomenon that clearly demonstrates a person's need for cooperation, mutual assistance, and equality in the main spheres of social life. The ideas and practice of the cooperative movement have been successfully used earlier and are being used nowadays both to mitigate social contradictions and mobilize forces that can revive and strengthen economy, stimulate self-initiated activity, unleash everyone's creative potential, which is crucial for foundations of any civil society.

The world cooperative movement is the largest socio-economic movement of modern time. It brings together about 700 million cooperators. Its center, the International Cooperative Alliance (ICA), unites 317 organizations (274 fully entitled and 43 associated) from 112 countries. Among ICA members, there are international and national cooperative organizations from all economic sectors: industry, agriculture, banking, health care, housing construction, insurance, consumer market, tertiary industry, and others.

Thus, a significant part of the world's population, to any extent, uses services of cooperative enterprises, which are economic, information, and advertising or cultural and educational institutions.

Yu. M. Goryachkovskaya (✉) · G. A. Semenenko · V. V. Kutko
Belgorod University of Cooperation, Economics and Law, 308023, 116a, Sadovaya str., Belgorod, Russia
e-mail: kaf-tigp-zav@bukep.ru

W. Tadjudje and I. Douvitsa (eds.), *Perspectives on Cooperative Law*,
https://doi.org/10.1007/978-981-19-1991-6_12

2 Regulatory Framework of Cooperatives' Functioning in Russia

All over the world, including in Russia, the basis for the legal regulation of the of cooperative organizations' activities is the Statement on the Cooperative Identity, promulgated at the XXXI ICA Congress in 1995. It enshrines universal cooperative values and principles that are fundamental to the essence, social purpose, and operation of all types of cooperatives. These are the principles of voluntary and open membership; cooperation and democratic control on the part of members (which, as a rule, is set forth in the formulation of the principle "one member—one vote"); member's participation in the cooperative's economic functioning, etc. The implementation of cooperative principles in the cooperatives' socio-economic activity contributes to the preservation of cooperative identity, which will be discussed in more detail at the XXXIII ICA Congress.

As a follow-up to the Statement, every country adopts its national cooperative laws.

The Constitution of the Russian Federation enshrines the general principles and provisions that establish the legislative basis for the Russian cooperative organizations' activities. Everyone shall have the right to a free use of his abilities and property for entrepreneurial and economic activities not prohibited by law (Article 34); the right (either individually or jointly with others) to freely own, use and dispose of their property if this does not harm the environment and does not violate the rights and legitimate interests of other persons (Articles 35, 36); the right to make free use of one's abilities for work, choose a type of activity and profession (Article 37).[1]

These principles and rights are detailed and specified in particular in general and special regulatory legal acts. Thus, general rules relating to creation, state registration, and reorganization of cooperatives are enshrined in the Civil Code of the Russian Federation[2]. The activities of housing and housing-construction cooperatives are regulated by the Housing Code of the Russian Federation.[3]

Special cooperative laws regulate the procedure for the creation, liquidation, and operation of certain types of cooperatives. These include:

- On Consumer Cooperation (consumer societies, their unions) in the Russian Federation: Law of the Russian Federation of June 19, 1992, No. 3085-1 (as amended on 2.07. 2013)[4];

---

[1] Constitution of the Russian Federation: adopted by a popular vote on 12.12.1993 with amendments approved during a nationwide vote on 01.07.2020.

[2] Civil Code of the Russian Federation (part two) of January 26, 1996, No. 14-FL (as amended on December 27, 2019).

[3] Housing Code of the Russian Federation of December 29, 2004, No. 188-FL (as amended on December 30, 2020).

[4] On Consumer Cooperation (consumer societies, their unions) in the Russian Federation: Law of the Russian Federation of June 19, 1992, No. 3085-1 (as amended on 2.07. 2013).

– On Production Cooperatives: Federal Law of May 08, 1995, No. 41-FL (as amended on 31.07. 2020)[5];
– On Agricultural Cooperation: Federal Law of December 08, 1995, No. 193-FL (as amended on July 31, 2020 as amended and restated entered into force on 12.10.2020)[6];
– On housing Savings Cooperatives: Federal Law of December 30, 2004, No. 215-FL (as amended on June 27, 2019);
– On Credit Cooperation: Federal Law No. 190-FL of July 18, 2009 (as amended on July 13, 2020)[7];
– On Horticulture Production and Home Garden Management for Citizens' Own Needs and on Amending Certain Legislative Acts of the Russian Federation: Federal Law No. 217-FL dated July 29, 2017 (as amended on 9.11. 2020)[8], and other federal laws.

Thus, the Constitution of the Russian Federation outlines the economic activity principles for all legal entities. The Civil Code of the Russian Federation defines cooperatives' legal status as one of the legal entities' forms; specifies the rules for creation, state registration, and reorganization of cooperatives. And special laws on certain types of cooperatives (consumer, industrial, agricultural, credit, etc.) reflect their legal status peculiarities.

However, we should note that the main problem concerning the legal regulation of cooperatives in Russia is the lack of a general framework law on cooperatives, which would enshrine the general legal framework for cooperatives, their legal status, the procedure for creation, reorganization, and dissolution. Undoubtedly, the positive moment is the existence of laws regulating activity of certain types of cooperatives, for example, credit, agricultural, housing since, on the one hand, successful experience can be useful for drafting texts of similar laws in other countries (successful formulations, practically tested means of legal regulation, effective tax regimes, incentives, benefits, etc.). On the other hand, the cooperative legislation shortcomings of one country may serve as a warning for another.

Nevertheless, activity of other types of cooperative (insurance, housing construction, garage, cottage building) has not received sufficient legal regulation. So, a problematic point requiring special attention is the statutory regulation of inheritance in housing cooperatives.

At the same time, cooperative legislation is constantly evolving: in recent years in Russia, both at the federal and regional levels, a number of targeted programs have been developed to support and cultivate certain types of cooperation. Federal

[5] On Production Cooperatives: Federal Law of May 08, 1996, No. 41-FL (as amended on 31.07. 2020).

[6] On Agricultural Cooperation: Federal Law of December 08, 1995 No. 193-FL (as amended on July 31, 2020 as amended and restated entered into force on 12.10.2020).

[7] On Credit Cooperation: Federal Law No. 190-FL of July 18, 2009 (as amended on July 13, 2020).

[8] On Horticulture Production and Home Garden Management for Citizens' Own Needs and on Amending Certain Legislative Acts of the Russian Federation: Federal Law No. 217-FL dated July 29, 2017 (as amended on 9.11. 2020).

incentive programs can be adopted in order to support certain economic sectors, and regional ones can be valuable for stimulating cooperatives' development in different regions of the Russian Federation. For example, in recent years, state authorities of the Russian Federation have provided very significant attention and support to agricultural cooperatives.

For example, the following program acts, forming conceptual foundations and development goals of cooperative organizations functioning in certain economic sectors, have been adopted:

Food Security Doctrine of the Russian Federation,
Concept for Sustainable Development of Rural Territories until 2020,
Strategy of Sustainable Development of Rural Areas of the Russian Federation for the Period up to 2030,
State program on Agricultural Development and Regulation of Agricultural Products, Commodities and Food Markets, 2013–2020,
Concept of Rural Cooperation Development for the period up to 2020,
Departmental special-purpose program on Rural Cooperation Development in the Russian Federation for the period up to 2025, etc.

3 On Concept of Cooperatives in Russian Legislation and Their Purposes

A general legislative definition, universal for all types of cooperatives, is not enshrined in Russian legislation due to the absence of a general framework law On Cooperatives. The Civil Code of the Russian Federation contains two separate definitions concerning a consumer cooperative (Article 123.2) and a production cooperative (Article 106.1).

However, special laws on certain types of cooperation/cooperatives contain corresponding definitions.

So, in the Russian Federation Law On Consumer Cooperation (on consumer societies, their unions) in the Russian Federation, instead of the term "cooperative" they use the term "consumer society", which means a voluntary association of citizens and (or) legal entities, created, as a rule, on a territorial and membership basis by combining members' property shares for conducting trade, procurement, production, and other activities in order to meet material and other needs of the cooperative members.[9]

A production cooperative is a voluntary association of citizens on a membership basis for joint production and other economic activities based on their personal labor

[9] On Consumer Cooperation (consumer societies, their unions) in the Russian Federation: Law of the Russian Federation of June 19, 1992, No. 3085-1 (as amended on 2.07. 2013).

and other participation as well as pooling of the members' (participants') property shares.[10]

A credit consumer cooperative is a membership-based voluntary association of individuals and (or) legal entities on territorial, professional, and (or) social principles in order to meet the financial needs of the credit cooperative's members (stockholders).[11]

An agricultural cooperative is an organization created by agricultural producers and (or) citizens engaged in private subsidiary farming on the basis of voluntary membership for joint production or other economic activities based on pooling of their property share contributions in order to meet the material and other needs of cooperative members.[12] They are subdivided into production and consumer.

A housing or housing-construction cooperative is a voluntary association of citizens and legal entities (in cases specified by law) on the basis of membership for meeting citizens' housing requirements, as well as for managing multi-family dwellings.

Housing saving cooperative is a consumer cooperative created as a voluntary association of citizens on the membership basis in order to meet its members' needs in residential premises by combining cooperative members' shares. In fact, all housing cooperatives are consumer cooperatives.

It should be noted that the Civil Code of the Russian Federation (article 50) prescribes the division of all legal entities, operating in Russia (organizations, enterprises, institutions, partnerships, cooperatives, etc.), into two separate groups: commercial and non-commercial organizations. Such a division occurs according to the legal entity's purpose of establishing and functioning. Commercial organizations are focused on profit earning as the main objective of their operation (including profit distribution among participants), and non-profit organizations do not have such a goal. In this sense, cooperative organizations, depending on the type and purpose of their activity, can be both commercial (production cooperatives—Part 2, Article 50 of the Civil Code of the Russian Federation) and non-commercial (consumer, housing, house-building, horticultural, garage, agricultural, consumer, credit, mutual insurance association, etc.—clause 1, part 3, Article 50, and Article 123.1 of the Civil Code of the Russian Federation).

The core characteristic of consumer cooperatives' legal status, that emphasizes their special role in society, is the direct indication of the Federal Law On Non-Commercial Organizations to the fact that it does not extend its action (force) to consumer cooperatives (part 2, Article 1). The commercial (i.e. production) cooperatives' status and rules of procedure are regulated by a number of special laws on certain types of commercial organizations mentioned above.

---

[10] On Production Cooperatives: Federal Law of May 08, 1996, No. 41-FL (as amended on 31.07.2020).

[11] On Credit Cooperation: Federal Law No. 190-FL of July 18, 2009 (as amended on July 13, 2020).

[12] On Agricultural Cooperation: Federal Law of December 08, 1995, No. 193-FL (as amended on July 31, 2020).

In general terms, the intention of establishing cooperatives in the Russian Federation is to satisfy various kinds of cooperative members' needs. As a rule, such needs are material, housing, financial, social, and others. However, the list of shareholder's needs cannot be interpreted too broadly: not all needs of a shareholder are subject to satisfaction, but only the ones defined while establishing a cooperative or for which he/she joined the organization.

It should be noted that purposes of different cooperative types are directly specified in the corresponding special laws.

For the most effective implementation of their goals (coordinating same-type cooperatives, representing and protecting their interests, providing them with information, legal and other services, organizing employees' training and retraining, carrying out scientific research, and other activities), all types of cooperatives have the right to form unions, associations, and other structures on a voluntary basis. Such a structure can be formed on a territorial (regional, interregional, federal, international), sectoral or other principle. Cooperative unions are self-adjusting organizations.[13]

For example, the following largest national cooperative structures (unions, associations) are represented at the federal level, uniting agricultural cooperatives of different types:

Russian Association of Rural and Farm Enterprises and Agricultural Cooperatives (AKKOR), founded in 1990;
Agro-Industrial Union of Russia (Rosagropromsoyuz), founded in 1997;
Fund for Rural Credit Cooperation Development of (FRCCD), founded in 1997.
Rural Cooperatives Credit Union, formed in 1997;
Union of Russian Gardeners, formed in 1998;
Union of Fishing Collective Farms of Russia (Rosrybkolkhozsoyuz), formed in 1985;
Federal Union of Agricultural Consumer Cooperatives, formed in 2002;
Russian Selfregulating Organization of Audit Unions of Agricultural Cooperatives "Agrocontrol Union", formed in 2003.
Self-regulating Organization of Audit Unions of Agricultural Cooperatives "Russian Union of Chayanov", formed in 2000.

4 Conclusion

Summing up, we would like to draw the following conclusions.

First, in order to further improve cooperatives' performance, it is necessary to eliminate the legal regulation fragmentation of certain cooperatives' activity. One special law On Cooperatives, common to all cooperatives, should be adopted. This

[13] Simon Gächter, Benedikt Herrmann and Christian Thöni (2010) Culture and cooperation. Int J Account: https://doi.org/10.1098/rstb.2010.0135.

law shall inshrine the definition of a cooperative, its essential features, enumeration of cooperatives' types, the rules and procedure for its creation, state registration, transformation, and liquidation, as well as other provisions common to all cooperatives.

Secondly, it is necessary to provide more detailed cooperative regulation, especially concerning activity of certain cooperative types—housing-construction, insurance, garage, and others—through the adoption of special laws. This is due to the fact that nowadays their activities are not regulated by the Civil Code of the Russian Federation (there are no separate articles referred to them), and the Federal Law On Consumer Cooperation (Consumer Societies, Their Unions) in the Russian Federation does not govern agricultural consumer cooperatives and other specialized consumer cooperatives (Article 2). As a result, these cooperatives (garage, housing-construction, etc.) are deprived of legal basis.

Thirdly, to improve the legal framework of Russia, as noted earlier, it is necessary to develop a general framework law on cooperatives, which shall consolidate the general definition of the concept of "cooperative", basic principles of functioning and a number of other general issues.

Fourthly, it is necessary to clearly define the limits of state bodies' supervisory powers concerning cooperative organizations in order to avoid excessive state interference in cooperatives' operation and ensure their independence.

Fifthly, such types of cooperative organizations as housing, gardening, dacha condominiums require additional changes and further legal regulation.

Sixthly, it is necessary to pay more attention to legislative stimulation and interests harmonization of numerous cooperative structures (unions and associations).

In general, it should be said that improving Russian cooperatives' performance is a laborious and lengthy process; the legal framework of cooperatives should change as a result of both joint efforts of PR agents and cooperatives' democratic participation in lawmaking.

References

Civil Code of the Russian Federation (part two) of January 26, 1996, No. 14-FL (as amended on 27 Dec 2019)

Constitution of the Russian Federation: adopted by a popular vote on 12 Dec 1993 with amendments approved during a nationwide vote on 01 July 2020)

Gächter S, Herrmann B, Thöni C (2010) Culture and cooperation. Int J Account. https://doi.org/10.1098/rstb.2010.0135

Housing Code of the Russian Federation of December 29, 2004, No. 188-FL (as amended on 30 Dec 2020)

On Agricultural Cooperation: Federal Law of December 08, 1995, No. 193-FL (as amended on 31 July 2020)

On Credit Cooperation: Federal Law of July 18, 2009, No. 190-FL (as amended on 13 July 2020)

On Consumer Cooperation (consumer societies, their unions) in the Russian Federation: Law of the Russian Federation of June 19, 1992, No. 3085-1 (as amended on 2 July 2013)

On Horticulture Production and Home Garden Management for Citizens' Own Needs and on Amending Certain Legislative Acts of the Russian Federation: Federal Law No. 217-FL dated July 29, 2017 (as amended on 9 Nov 2020)
On Non-commercial Organizations: Federal Law of 12.01.1996, No. 7-FL (as amended on 30 Dec 2020)
On Production Cooperatives: Federal Law of May 08, 1996, No. 41-FL (as amended on 31 July 2020)

Regulating and Managing the Cooperative Difference

Hans-H. Münkner

1 What is a Cooperative Society?

A cooperative society is one of the legal forms by which a private firm can operate on the market.[1] Beuthien defines cooperatives as a special form of economic association, using excess earnings as much as possible for member-promotion.[2] Cooperatives have a particular object: To promote their members.

Cooperative societies have their own way to grow by joining vertically integrated systems. They are a special type of private enterprise in which personal participation is more important than capital contribution (Fici 2013a, p 7).

Cooperatives and similar member-owned businesses are extremely flexible forms that can be adapted to solve a variety of economic problems. However, members must be involved in ownership of their democratically controlled economic organization (Birchall 2003, p. 30). The identity of cooperatives is multi-facetted, comprising several aspects: purpose, objects pursued, organizational and financial structure.[3]

In the cooperative law of the United Kingdom (UK), cooperative societies are not expressly defined. Instead of underlining the special object of member promotion, reference is made to a 'bona fide cooperative' (section 1 Industrial and Provident Societies Act IPSA (1965). Section 1 (3) IPSA excludes organizations with the purpose 'to carry on … business with the object of making profit mainly for the payment of interest, dividends or bonusses on money invested or deposited with or lent to the society or any other person'). Criteria to define a 'bona fide cooperative'

[1] Fici (2013a), p. 5.

[2] Beuthien (2018), German Cooperative Societies Act (GenG), Randziffer (RZ) 19.

[3] Fici (2013a), p. 19.

H.-H. Münkner (✉)
University of Marburg, Marburg, Germany
e-mail: muenkner@mailer.uni-marburg.de

W. Tadjudje and I. Douvitsa (eds.), *Perspectives on Cooperative Law*,
https://doi.org/10.1007/978-981-19-1991-6_13

resemble those contained in the ICA Statement of the cooperative identity, values and principles.[4]

Cooperative societies should be genuine, member-owned businesses, driven by the needs and priorities of their members, who have joined voluntarily and made real commitment. They should be seen by other agencies as self-reliant, autonomous organizations, mobilizing local resources, rather than relying on grants or subsidies from outside. They should:

- provide a forum for discussion,
- pool local resources,
- build bargaining power and claim-making power,
- widen the option for income-generating activities and
- enhance local control over factors of production.[5]

Cooperatives are based on cooperative values and principles to put these values into practice: Self-help, equity, democracy, equality among members and solidarity. Co-operation among cooperatives in vertically integrated systems is a source of strength of cooperatives.[6]

Cooperative societies are enterprises, not charities (Birchall 2003, p. 3).

This means that in their operations on the market, cooperatives societies have to earn more than they spend.

Type-specific methods of audit have to be designed, allowing to measure success not only in terms of economic efficiency but also success in member promotion. Instruments developed for this purpose are Promotion Plan and Promotion Report.[7]

2 How to Define the Cooperative Difference?

Henrÿ points to the fact that at global level, ILO R 193, especially para 7 (2) centers on the distinction of cooperative societies from other types of enterprises (Henrÿ 2012, pp. 5, 6). Cooperative societies have a dual nature, consisting of two elements: the cooperative group and the cooperative enterprise, having as its purpose to promote the members of the cooperative group.

It is agreed that transactions of cooperative societies with their members are of a special nature, referred to in Spain and the Latin American countries as '*actos cooperativos*'. In Germany, '*Zweckgeschäfte*' (purpose transactions), are transactions with members for which the cooperative society was formed and '*Gegengeschäfte*' (counter transactions) are usually carried out with non-members, to make purpose transactions possible. In German Cooperative Law this rule is contained in § 8 (1) No. 5 GenG, but this section was amended so that a cooperative society may allow

[4] Snaith (2013), p. 742; Snaith (2017), CR UK, pp. 700, 701.

[5] Birchall (2003), p. 13.

[6] Birchall (2003), pp. 3, 4.

[7] (Blümle 1994; Weber and Brazda 1994, pp. 736–745).

transactions with non-members in its by-laws. For the distinction of cooperative societies from stock companies, see Henrÿ (2012).[8]

2.1 Books on the Cooperative Difference

Many books have been published on how to protect the cooperative difference, e.g.:

- Parnell E (1955): Re-inventing the cooperative enterprise for the twenty-first century, Plunkett Foundation.
- Davis P (1999): Managing the Cooperative Difference, a survey of the application of modern management practices in the cooperative context, ILO, Cooperative Branch, Geneva.
- Birchall J (2003): Rediscovering the Cooperative Advantage, ILO, Cooperative Branch, Geneva.
- Münkner H and Ringle G (Hrsg.) (2008): *Alleinstellungsmerkmale genossenschaftlicher Kooperation—der Unterschied zählt* (Unique features of the cooperative form of organization – it is the difference that counts), Marburger Schriften zum Genossenschaftswesen 107, Göttingen.
- Ringle G and Münkner H (Hrsg.) (2012): *Wirtschaftliche Kooperation – anders wirtschaften!* (Economic co-operation—doing business differently!) *Marburger Schriften zur genossenschaftlichen Kooperation 111*, Baden-Baden.

2.2 Books on Cooperative Law

There are relatively few books on cooperative law.

The two leading commentaries on German cooperative law are kept up to date by many editions:

- Lang-Weidmüller (2011): Commentary on the Cooperative Societies Act 2011, 37th revised edition, De Gruyter, Berlin, Boston.
- Beuthien V (ed) (2018): Beck's short commentaries, Vol. 11, Cooperative Societies Act and the law on transformation and combines as well as the Statute of the European Cooperative Society, 16th revised edition. C. H. Beck, München.

On international level, two new books have been published:

- Cracogna D et al. (eds) (2013): International Handbook on Cooperative Law and
- Fajardo G et al. (2017): Principles of European Cooperative Law – Principles, Commentaries and National Reports, interesentia, Cambridge–Antwerp–Portland.

Other books on cooperative law published in new edition are:

[8] Henrÿ (2012), pp. 37–39.

- Henrÿ H (2012): Guidelines for Cooperative Legislation, 3rd revised edition, ILO Geneva.
- Münkner H (2015): Cooperative Principles and Cooperative Law, 2nd revised edition, LIT, Wien Zürich and
- Münkner H (2016): Ten Lectures on cooperative Law, 2nd revised edition, LIT, Wien, Zürich.

3 How Can Cooperative Law Reflect, Regulate and Protect the Cooperative Difference?

Cooperative societies need a special legal framework that adequately reflects their particular nature and function.[9] Such cooperative law has to contain clear rules on the definition (purpose, objectives pursued), formation, organizational and financial structure, relations among cooperatives, dissolution, merger and conversion etc.[10]

In many countries, new sections were introduced into cooperative laws, which deviate from the cooperative principles of the ICA and align cooperative law increasingly to company law. The intention of the legislators may have been to make cooperative societies stronger, but in fact they are weakened by blurring the cooperative difference (see infra, 4.2).

4 Development Trends

4.1 Size of Cooperative Societies and of Cooperative Groups

Originally, the usual size of cooperative groups was that of face-to-face groups, living and working in one community or district, having interests in common, described by credit unions with the term 'common bond', allowing solid group relations and facilitating member-relations management. Another special feature of cooperative groups is that membership must be open and variable and not closed. The cooperative group must be large enough to have economic weight and to allow effective member-promotion but is must also not be too large to allow stable member relations.

4.1.1 Large Cooperatives

Successful cooperatives have a tendency to grow. In Germany, large cooperatives having more than 1,500 members may introduce a meeting of delegates to replace or supplement the general meeting (§ 43a GenG). In such large cooperative societies,

[9] Fici (2013a), pp. 7, 19.

[10] Fici (2013a), p. 9.

special provisions were introduced to guarantee basic rights of individual members. Even among members of large cooperative societies, there may be a strong common bond.

4.1.2 Small Cooperatives

By allowing the formation of very small cooperatives, reducing the minimum number of founder members to three (Germany, Finland) or to five (SCE). There is a need to make special rules for them.[11]

Small and even 'micro cooperatives' may have good reasons to exist, e.g. cooperatives of medical doctors, lawyers or tax consultants working in one city, organizing a joint office or other joint services. In other countries, e.g. in Austria, there are no regulations regarding a minimum number of members (Beuthien 2018, § 4 GenG, RZ 1). In Germany, small cooperatives are allowed to work without a supervisory committee, i.e. only with a board of directors and general meeting (§ 9 (1) GenG) and are subject to audit only every second year (§ 53 (1) GenG) to reduce legal cost.

4.1.3 The Cooperative Way to Grow

Different from commercial enterprises, which usually grow by merger and acquisition, cooperatives have a special way to grow by vertical integration into a cooperative system, in which the principle of subsidiarity is applied.[12] In Germany, newly formed cooperative societies are obliged by law to join a vertically integrated cooperative system (Verbund).[13]

4.2 Trends to Deviate from Cooperative Principles

During the last decades, several trends can be observed to deviate in cooperative laws from the cooperative principles, agreed upon by the ICA and its member organizations, laid down in the ICA's Statement on the Cooperative Identity and turned into international cooperative law.

4.2.1 Plural Voting

Cooperative societies can introduce plural voting, e.g. in Germany: § 43 (3) GenG, where there is a limit of two additional votes for members promoting the business

---

[11] Henrÿ (2013b), p. 382; Henrÿ (2017), p. 147.

[12] Grosskopf et al. (2016), p. 138.

[13] Grosskopf et al. (2016), pp. 138–148.

of the cooperative society in a special way (§ 43 (3) No. 1 GenG). However, more votes per member are allowed in cooperatives in which more than 3/4 of the members are businessmen: plural voting up to maximum 1/10th of the total votes in general meeting (§ 43 (3) No. 2 GenG).

Where the clear and simple rule: 'one member—one vote' is replaced by plural voting, special provisions are required to record:

- Who is attending the general meeting,
- with how many votes,
- on which type of decision the votes are cast and
- whether additional votes count or not.

Similar problems with plural voting occur in the supervisory committee. The German cooperative law contains rules to avoid, that regular members are outvoted by investing members (§ 8 (2) GenG). Explanations in Beuthien's Commentary of 2018 on § 8 GenG cover seven pages of small print. The section on the meeting of delegates (§ 43a GenG) has seven subsections with explanations on 19 pages of Beuthien's Commentary of 2018 (pp. 595–614).

4.2.2 Allowing 'Purpose Transactions' with Non-members

This means that transactions for which the cooperative was formed, are not only carried out with members but are also allowed with non-members (§ 8 (1) No. 5 GenG). According to art. 1 par. 4 SCER, also in European Cooperative Societies, benefits can be extended to non-members.[14]

4.2.3 Different Categories of Members

A new trend is to introduce different categories of members: regular members and investing members or promoting members, not using the facilities of the cooperative enterprise but contributing share capital and/or social power. Such multi-stakeholder cooperatives with plural voting need special legal provisions to avoid that one category of members dominates the other (e.g. in Germany (§§ 43a (1); 8 (2) GenG).

According to § 8 (2) GenG, the by-laws of a cooperative society may stipulate that persons who are not using the goods from or producing goods for the cooperative, or are not using the services from or rendering services for it, may qualify as investing members. This new rule opens the way to multi-stakeholder cooperatives (MSC).

[14] Fici (2013b), p. 143.

4.2.4 Companization, i.e. Adjustments in Cooperative Law to Company Law

Are cooperative societies allowed to work with fixed share capital? In Germany, a new rule to this effect was introduced as a reaction to the requirements of international accounting standards, which would require variable share capital to be booked not as equity capital but as debt. According to International Accounting Standards (IAS-VO and International Financial Reporting Standards (IFRS), capital contributions that can be withdrawn by the member are classified as debt and not as equity.[15]

In countries where variable capital is a distinctive feature for cooperative societies, like in France *'société à capital variable'*, to allow cooperatives to work with fixed capital is surprising. The Finnish cooperative law (Chap. 5, Sect. 2) even allows 'stock-exchange cooperatives'.[16]

Under German cooperative law, cooperative societies may pay not only patronage refund but also dividend on share capital, if this is decided by the members.[17]

Another trend that can be observed is approximation of cooperative audit to company audit, prescribing only financial audit.

4.2.5 General Interest Cooperatives

General interest cooperatives are a new category of cooperatives, introduced for example in Italy where such general interest cooperatives are regulated in a special law and distinction is made between prevalent mutual cooperatives and other cooperatives.[18]

In the UK, there is a clear separation of cooperative societies serving mainly their members and societies formed to serve the interests of the community (BenComs). This is in line with the 7th Cooperative Principle of the ICA, leaving it to the members to decide, whether they want to serve the interests of others.[19]

Other important trends in cooperative law are Internationalization and Globalization, see infra Henrÿ's message.

5 Henrÿ's Message

In his contribution to the International Handbook on Cooperative Law (2013), Henrÿ points to the fact that there is International Public Cooperative Law, which influences national legislators (Henrÿ 2013c, Chapter 38, pp. 803–823). Henrÿ emphasizes that

[15] Lang-Weidmüller (2011), § 8a GenG, RZ 3.

[16] Henrÿ (2017), p. 148.

[17] § 19 (2) GenG, see also Beuthien (2018), GenG § 1, RZ 10 and § 19 GenG RZ 7.

[18] Fici (2013c), pp. 484, 485; Fici (2017a, b), pp. 351, 352.

[19] Snaith (2017), pp. 629–636: Cooperative and Community Benefit Societies Act (CCBSA 2014).

this distinction is restricted to Law on Cooperatives and does not apply to Cooperative Law, which is much broader (Henrÿ 2013c, p. 803).

The main international instruments concerning cooperative societies are:

- The ICA statement on the cooperative identity 1995,
- UN Guidelines (2001) aimed at creating a supportive environment for the development of cooperatives and
- ILO R 193 (2002): Promotion of Cooperatives (Henrÿ 2012, p. 1).

The full text of these instruments is quoted in form of annexes in the third edition of Henry's Guidelines for Cooperative Legislation. The motto of the third revised edition of these Guidelines for Cooperative Legislation (2012), setting the spirit of this edition, is: 'Cooperative enterprises build a better world, but cooperatives cannot save the world'.[20]

Henrÿ identifies three major trends:

- Renaissance of cooperative law, renewed interest in the subject, which may lead to a cooperative legal science.
- Supra-nationalization and
- Internationalization.

By integrating the definition of 'cooperative society' by the ICA, including cooperative values and principles, into ILO R 193 of (2002), para 2 and Annex, i.e.:

- An autonomous association of persons united voluntarily,
- who satisfy their needs through an enterprise,
- which they own jointly and which they control democratically,[21]

the cooperative principles of the ICA became a legally binding instrument as far as cooperative law is concerned, calling upon legislators to establish or maintain the cooperative identity.[22]

As a result, Henrÿ observes that there is

- more respect for public international cooperative law, with its obligation to maintain cooperatives as distinct legal entities and to keep away from the trend to 'isomorphism', giving all business organizations the same form and approximating cooperatives to companies.[23]
- But there is also a trend to align cooperatives to stock company law through economization and growth (Henrÿ 2013a, pp. 808, 809, FN 30).

Legislators have to find a rationale for a cooperative law that distinguishes cooperative societies from other types of enterprises. They have to find consensus on

[20] Henrÿ (2012), p. 1.

[21] Henrÿ (2013c), p. 807.

[22] Henrÿ (2013c), p. 808.

[23] Henrÿ (2012), pp. 9, 11.

what constitutes the identity of cooperatives and how cooperative identity can be translated into effective cooperative law.

Big cooperatives, growing by merger and acquisition, require paid, professional managers. With such managers, often trained outside the cooperative system, the information gap between managers and members is growing. Such professional managers usually seek to put competitiveness, growth and financial stability before the interests of the members. The cooperative-specific 'member-centrism' is at stake. According to Henrÿ, alignment of cooperatives to stock companies also risks reducing the cooperatives' capacity to contribute to sustainable development.[24]

Introduction of the multi-stakeholder cooperative (MSC) paved the way for development of new forms of cooperatives: social cooperatives, general interest cooperatives and liberal profession cooperatives (Henrÿ 2013c, p. 817). The problem for the legislators is not to align the special features of cooperatives to stock companies but to adjust them to modern requirements—taking account of the competitive advantage of cooperatives.

Due to modern technology and because space and time are losing importance, national, regional and international legislations are becoming ineffective. Henrÿ underlines that in times of global production and consumption, the unity of economic spaces and jurisdictions is dissolved. With lessened effectiveness of state law and a rising number of informal actors, he sees a trend to bring cooperatives in a state of extra-legality – (not illegality). He identifies an 'internormativity' moving from law to non-legal norms and vice-versa (Henrÿ 2013c, p. 818, FN 67), moving from multi-layered national, regional and international systems to a global system of laws, where geographic boundaries of jurisdiction dissolve into boundaries by subject-matter and transnational or even global laws substitute national laws.

Cooperative laws appear to be national, where in fact their substance is derived from regional or international law, and other cooperative laws are in the process of being harmonized, by reforms, by model laws or by guidelines, some of which are presented by Cracogna et al. in the International Handbook of Cooperative Law (2013).

ILO rejected the idea of presenting a model law (Henrÿ 2012, p. 5) and rather opted for adoption of an international and supranational instruments like ILO R 193 on Promotion of Cooperatives. The same trend is shown by the Regulation of the European Cooperative Society (SCE R 2003) and the Statute of Mercosur Cooperatives 2009.[25]

But there are also model laws, e.g. in case of the Credit Union National Association (CUNA) Inc.: The Model Credit Union Act, 1987, Washington D.-C., first published in 1945, revised eight times up to 1994.[26]

Henry sees an unavoidable trend to globalization. The question and challenge for the lawmakers is: How can the peculiarities of cooperatives be safeguarded within this trend?

---

[24] Henrÿ (2012), p 19.

[25] Cracogna (2013a), pp. 158–162.

[26] Münkner (1994), pp. 543–550; Baker (1994), pp. 186–189.

With his writings on international cooperative law and in particular with the third revised edition of his Guidelines for Cooperative Legislation, published by the ILO in 2012, and in his contributions to the International Handbook of Cooperative Law,[27] Henrÿ gives a detailed description of the cooperative form of organization mainly from the legislators' point of view.

Henrÿ recommends:

- to avoid competitive disadvantages for cooperative societies as compared to other forms of business organizations,
- to enlarge the scope of cooperatives by adjusting them to changing conditions,
- to avoid problems for the special image of cooperatives and
- to see the cooperative identity not as a weakness but as a strength of cooperatives, which exists to ensure just co-operation on the market for all. As people-centered enterprises, cooperatives have not only a competitive disadvantage but also an advantage when they move from single purpose to multi-purpose, from homogeneous membership to multi-stakeholder cooperatives, serving either their members or also non-members, i.e. operating as social cooperatives (Henrÿ 2012, p. 18).

With his writings on cooperative law, his advocacy for International Public Cooperative Law, setting guidelines for national legislators, Henrÿ has left his footprint in the Cooperative Law Scene and in literature on cooperative law usually perceived and described as the domain of national lawmakers and seen mainly from their perspective. He has no doubt that cooperative societies will be a suitable form for performing in a changed business world as 'children of necessity' and 'children of preference' (Henrÿ 2012, p. 2).

6 Challenge for the Legislator

The challenge for the legislator is how to ensure the effectiveness of a global system of laws on specific matters that escape the sovereignty of the states, a process accelerated by harmonization. Such process is already on the way at all levels and many cooperative laws have already been harmonized with the laws of stock companies.

Growing cooperatives need professional management. However, ways have to be found 'to avoid to managerize cooperatives but rather to cooperatize managers' (Davis 1999, p. 129).

[27] Cracogna et al. (2013), Chaps. 2 and 38.

6.1 How Should the National Legislator Perceive the Specificities of Cooperatives and Regulate the Cooperative Difference?

Interpretation of cooperative values and principles should be done by taking account of different economic, historical, social and political parameters.

This advice is not always followed by national legislators. E.g. in case of cooperative legislation in Italy: With its peculiar distinction between mainly mutual cooperatives, meeting all aspects of cooperative identity and other cooperatives, the law authorizes organizations to work under the name 'cooperative society' while lacking full cooperative identity: allowing business with non-members, dividend on paid-up capital and distribution of assets in case of dissolution. This is creating problems for the global image of cooperatives.[28] The task is to define what is the essence of cooperatives under several prisms.

As already mentioned above, these problems have been dealt with from the economic and social point of view in many books for many years, with titles like 'Re-inventing the Cooperative Enterprise for the 21st Century' (Parnell 1995), 'Managing the Cooperative Difference' (Davis 1999), 'Rediscovering the Cooperative Advantage, poverty reduction through self-help' (Birchall 2003).

6.2 How to Reduce Cooperative Disadvantages Without Blurring the Cooperative Difference?

The challenge is how to reduce competitive disadvantages of cooperatives without blurring their distinct features, which constitute the comparative advantages of cooperatives as reflected in the ICA Statement on the Cooperative Identity, taken over by the UN Guidelines (2001) and ILO Recommendation 193 (2002).[29] According to Henrÿ's view, there is International Public Cooperative Law, which influences national law-makers and economic actors.

What can the national legislator do? Birchall,[30] proposes three measures to improve the performance of cooperative enterprises:

- to improve the performance of such enterprises from within,
- to offer positive framework condition and
- to strengthen promotional institutions through training.

[28] Fici (2013a), p. 59.

[29] Henrÿ (2013a), p. 84.

[30] Birchall (2003), p. 66.

Such recommendations are also contained in the UN Guidelines aimed at creating a supportive environment for cooperatives (2001), ILO Recommendation 193 concerning the promotion of cooperatives and in the EU Commission's Communication on the Promotion of Cooperative Societies in Europe of 2004.

7 Conclusion

In its Blueprint for a Cooperative Decade (2011–2020), the ICA gives cooperatives an important role in sustainable development. This Blueprint was subject to a critical analysis by a colloquium of experts held in Marburg in 2015.[31]

We are witnessing the globalization of production and the abolition of barriers to the movement of means of production—especially capital and labor—while lacking global lawmakers and global law enforcement mechanisms (Henrÿ 2012, p. 17). The question is not whether cooperative legislation should follow and support integration, but how peculiarities of cooperatives can be safeguarded within this trend (Henrÿ 2012, p. 5). There is a need to center on the distinction of cooperatives from other types of enterprises.[32]

Experience with inter-state and international laws is reported in the third revised edition of Henrÿ's Guidelines for Cooperative Legislation (pp. 46–55), where he offers short summaries of the new texts.

Some of these texts are presented and discussed in detail in Part II of the International Handbook of Cooperative Law[33] which Henrÿ edited together with Dante Cracogna and Antonio Fici (2013a, b, c):

- the European Cooperative Societies Regulation (2003),
- the Framework Law for Cooperatives in Latin America (2008),
- the Statute of Mercosur Cooperatives (2009) and
- the OHADA Cooperative Regulation (2011).

In the foreword to his book 'Rediscovering the Cooperative Advantage' (2003), Birchall complains about 'cooperative blindness' of development agencies engaged in promoting cooperative-type organizations without realizing that they are in fact promoting cooperatives and fail to draw on the rich cooperative experience. The potential of cooperatives for reducing poverty and to contribute to sustainable development is often overlooked (Birchall 2013, p. iv).

Henrÿ, quoting a Regional Director of the ICA, confirms this impression:

'It is strange that it is easy to obtain funds for projects and programs dealing with human rights, democracy and the rule of law in abstract terms, whereas no money is made available for the development of genuine cooperatives, which are practical realization of these aims' (Henrÿ 2005, p. 181).

[31] Lehnhoff (2015), pp. 11–13.

[32] Henrÿ (2012), pp. 5, 6, 46–55.

[33] Cracogna et al. (2013), pp. 65–186.

To end, attention should be drawn to an important point made by Beuthien:

'A certain reluctance to deal with cooperatives as a legal form is not only based on economic and legal grounds. It is also caused by the fact that the merits of cooperatives in social history have been forgotten by the general public. ... What is needed is a future oriented memory of cooperative traditions' (Beuthien 2018, p. 24).

References

Baker C (1994) Credit unions, world council of in. Dülfer (ed) International handbook of co-operative organizations. Vandenhoeck & Ruprecht, pp 186–189

Beuthien V (2018) Beck'sche Kurzkommentare, Band 11, Genossenschaftsgesetz mit Umwandlungs- und Kartellrecht sowie Statut der Europäischen Genossenschaft

Blümle E (1994) Probleme der Effizienzmessung bei Genossenschaften (Problems of measuring efficiency of co-operative societies). In: Vorträge B, Bd. 5, Schriften zur Kooperationsforschung, Tübingen 1976

Birchall J (2003) Rediscovering the co-operative advantage, poverty reduction through self-help. ILO Co-operative Branch, Geneva

Cracogna et al (2013) International handbook of co-operative law. Springer, Heidelberg, New York, Dordrecht, London

Cracogna D (2013a) The statute of Mercosur co-operatives. In: Cracogna et al (eds) International handbook of co-operative law. Springer, Heidelberg, New York, Dordrecht, London, pp 153–164

Cracogna D (2013b) Framework law for co-operatives in Latin America. In: Cracogna et al (eds) International handbook of co-operative law. Springer, Heidelberg, New York, Dordrecht, London, pp 165–186

Davis P (1999) Managing the co-operative difference—a survey of the application of modern management practices in the co-operative context. ILO Co-operative Branch, Geneva

European Commission (2004) Communication on the promotion of co-operative societies in Europe, COM (2004) 18 final of 23 February 2004

European Co-operative Societies Regulations (SCER). Council Regulation n. 1435/2003 of 22 July 2003

Fici A (2013a) An introduction to co-operative law. In: Cracogna et al (eds) International handbook of co-operative law. Heidelberg, New York, Dordrecht, London, pp 3–62.

Fici A (2013b) The European co-operative society regulation. In Cracogna et al (eds) International handbook of co-operative law. Heidelberg, New York, Dordrecht, London, pp 115–151

Fici A (2013c) CR Italy. In: Cracogna et al (eds) International handbook of co-operative law. Heidelberg, New York, Dordrecht, London, pp 479–501

Fici A (2017a) Definition and objectives of co-operatives. In: Fajardo et al (eds) Principles of European co-operative law—principles, commentaries and national reports, intersentia, Cambridge, pp 19–45

Fici A (2017b) CR Italy. In: Fajardo et al (eds) Principles of European co-operative law—principles, commentaries and national reports, intersentia, Cambridge, pp 347–408.

Grosskopf W et al (2016) Our co-operative, idea–Mission–achievements, 2nd revised edition LIT, Wien, Zürich, Münster

Henrÿ H (2005) Co-operative credit societies act, India 1904 – a model for development lawyers? In: Münkner H (ed) 100 Years of co-operative credit societies act, India 1904—a world-wide applied model of co-operative legislation. In: International Co-operative Alliance (ICA), Asia Pacific, New Delhi, pp 164–200

Henrÿ H (2012) Guidelines for co-operative legislation, 3rd revised. ILO, Geneva

Henrÿ H (2013a) Public international co-operative law. In: Cracogna et al (eds) International handbook of cooperative law. Springer, Heidelberg, pp 65–88

Henrÿ H (2013b) CR Finland. In: Cracogna et al (eds) International handbook of cooperative law. Springer, Heidelberg, pp 373–392
Henrÿ H (2013c) Trends and prospects of co-operative law. In: Cracogna et al (eds) International handbook of cooperative law. Springer, Heidelberg, pp 803–823
Henrÿ H (2017) CR Finland. In: Fajardo et al (eds) Principles of European co-operative law—principles, commentaries and national reports, Intersentia, pp 141–162
International Co-operative Alliance (ICA) Asia-Pacific: recent trends in co-operative legislation in Asia-Pacific, (no year, 2006), New Delhi
Lang-Weidmüller (2011) Genossenschaftsgesetz, Kommentar (Commentary on the co-operative societies act 2011), 37th revised edition, De Gruyter, Berlin, Boston
Lehnhoff D (2015) Introductory remarks. In: Mölls S, Münkner H (eds) (2015) pp 9–19
Mölls S, Münkner H (eds) (2015) ICA blueprint for a co-operative decade 2011–2020, a critical analysis. In: Marburg Colloquium 2013, Marburger Schriften zur genossenschaftlichen Kooperation 117, Nomos, Baden-Baden
Münkner H (1994) Law, international co-operative. In: Dülfer (ed) pp 543–550
Münkner H (2017a) Cooperative audit. In: Fajardo et al (eds) Principles of European co-operative law–principles, commentaries and national reports, intersentia, pp 97–118
Münkner H (2017b) Chapter 8, CR Germany. In: Fajardo et al (eds) Principles of European co-operative law–principles, commentaries and national reports, intersentia, pp 253–345
Parnell E (1995) Reinventing the co-operative enterprise for the 21st century. Plunkett Foundation, Long Hanborough/Oxford
Snaith I (2013) CR United Kingdom. In: Cracogna et al (eds) International handbook of cooperative law. Springer, Heidelberg, pp 735–757
Snaith I (2017) CR United Kingdom. In: Fajardo et al (eds) Principles of European co-operative law–principles, commentaries and national reports, intersentia, pp 625–717
UN Guidelines (2001) aimed at creating a supportive environment for the development of co-operatives, A/56/73, E/2001/68, adopted at 88th plenary session, 19 December 2001, A.RES.56.114
Weber W, Brazda J (1994) Promotion balance sheet, promotion report, promotion system. In: Dülfer E (ed) International handbook of co-operative organizations. Vandenhoeck & Ruprecht, Göttingen, pp 736–745

Evidence of Companization in Brazilian Cooperative Law

Leonardo Rafael de Souza

1 Introduction

In Brazil's legislative reality, legal reflections on cooperative societies have been going on for nearly 130 years. "Rochdalean Cooperativism", under the premise of the International Cooperative Alliance, has been recognized in Brazilian law since 1932, and since 1971, the Brazilian cooperative law has accepted cooperative principles as valid norms. However, all this time seems not to have been sufficient for the development of a consistent legal doctrine that includes the practical and human aspects of the cooperative movement.

Consequently, what is taking place in Brazil since the Federal Constitution of 1988 is a process of overlapping norms and jurisprudential interpretations that do not take into account the proper aspects of cooperative societies, weakening the cooperative identity in the perception of the population, despite the efforts of some jurists and researchers.

Under the pressure of competition, the current development of Brazilian cooperativism involves introducing law projects, updates, and regulations that ignore cooperative identity in favor of corporate structures and remove the social and cultural objectives of the jointly owned and democratically controlled enterprise. In practice, we are facing an evident process of *companization* in Brazilian cooperative law, confirming the perceptions of Professor Hagen Henrÿ.

Therefore, the objective of this contribution is to demonstrate the evolution of this process, highlighting laws, projects, and regulations that raise doubts about the future of Cooperativism and Cooperative Law in Brazil. We want to give voice to Hagen Henrÿ in defense of a cooperative law that understands and protects cooperativism around the world.

L. R. de Souza (✉)
Pontifical Catholic University of Paraná, Curitiba, Brazil
e-mail: leonardo.rafael@pucpr.edu.br

W. Tadjudje and I. Douvitsa (eds.), *Perspectives on Cooperative Law*,
https://doi.org/10.1007/978-981-19-1991-6_14

2 Overview of Brazilian Cooperative Law

As was the case for the Rochdale Pioneers, the creation of cooperatives in Brazil occurred before the law itself. The first Brazilian society to have in its name the term "Cooperative" was probably the Ouro Preto Public Employees Economic Cooperative Society, founded on October 27, 1889, in the State of Minas Gerais.[1] Apparently without an exact perception of what this conceptual novelty represented, the first law to allow the formation of a cooperative society was published 1 year later by Decree No. 796 of 1890.[2]

As shown above, Brazilian Cooperative Law is not new. Its legal reflections are 130 years old, more than necessary time for the development of a legal framework and a strong legal doctrine on the practical and human aspects of cooperativism. In fact, during this period, important laws were created, such as Decree No. 22.239 of 1932, which recognizes the Rochdalean assumptions even before the first revision of the principles at the ICA Congress in Paris (1937), and the still binding Act No. 5,764 of 1971, also known as the *General Law of Cooperative Societies.*[3]

However, the authoritarianism of the Brazilian governments established in this same period (military dictatorships) imposed, in practice, strong intervention and control on cooperative societies, as happened with the regimes of 1937–1945 (President Getúlio Vargas) and 1964–1985 (Military Presidents). Pinho (1973), for example, criticizes the continuity of the strong interference of the government on cooperative societies, noting that the text of the law did not stem from the free development of Cooperativism in Brazil, but from the knowledge of some idealists who gave a technical vision to the law, without popular participation or inspiration. The consequence was not a law that represented popular feelings or the cooperative movement, but a casuistic form of control of collective action historically practiced by cooperative societies.

This changed only with the 1988 Federal Constitution, conceived to build a just society through respect for human dignity, the valorization of human labor and free initiative.[4] For cooperatives, the constitutional text ensured State protection (article 174, §2º), support for cooperative business (article 146, III, "c") and freedom of association and democratic control (article 5, XVIII), among other guarantees.[5] In practice, the Constitution brought the expressed option for the consolidation of Cooperativism as one of the alternatives to compensate the socioeconomic distortions and inequalities of the country.

Even with the new Federal Constitution, the fundamental aspects of cooperative societies remained in force with Law No. 5764 of 1971. The difference is that the constitutional text guaranteed the cooperatives themselves, by their statutes,

---

[1] Pinheiro (2008).

[2] Cracogna et al. (2013).

[3] Perius (2001).

[4] Nascimento (1989).

[5] Brasil (1988).

autonomy to establish their own management rules. Decisions finally belonged to the members and no longer to public policy.

Moreover, the law was limited to presenting basic requirements such as the indication of possible governing bodies, the mode of election of their board members, their responsibility in managing the cooperative society and the creation of supervisory bodies. Article 38 establishes that the General Assembly is the supreme body of the cooperative, responsible for deciding the business related to its object and making the appropriate resolutions for the development and defense of its identity.

With the establishment of these freedoms, the growth of the Brazilian cooperative movement was exponential. Today, according to data from the Organization of Brazilian Cooperatives, there are 6887 cooperatives in operation in Brazil, with over 14 million members and 400,000 employees.[6] In addition, the development of specific models of cooperatives justified the creation of complementary legislation, such as Act No. 9864 of 1999 (social cooperatives), Complementary Act No. 130 of 2009 (credit cooperatives), and Act No. 12.690 of 2012 (labor cooperatives). Also, the Civil Code of 2002 granted the cooperatives recognition as companies.[7]

Despite that legal development, some cooperatives continued to suffer from strong State intervention in their operations, especially credit cooperatives and health cooperatives.[8] In these cases, under the pretense of overseeing cooperative activity, State agencies have imposed on cooperative societies the establishment of corporate governance rules that ignore the cooperative identity, such as credit cooperatives and their strong supervision by the Central Bank of Brazil.[9] On the other hand, other cooperative models, like labor cooperatives, have been viewed with suspicion by courts and governments, demanding legal alternatives that ignore the essence of cooperative activity to enforce typical employee protections.[10]

All these demands already have repercussions in the Brazilian National Congress, in the form of law projects for cooperative societies that observe essentially the economic development and the establishment of governance policies typical of capital societies, sometimes disregarding their own aspects.

3 Some Brazilian State Interferences in the Structures of Cooperative Societies

Since the recent democratization of Brazil, one of the great examples of interference in the functioning of cooperative societies has been practiced by labor courts

---

[6] OCB (2019).

[7] Cracogna et al. (2013)

[8] This term is used for a type of medical work cooperative that is also a health insurance operator. In Brazil, these cooperatives are regulated and supervised by the *National Supplementary Health Agency* (Agência Nacional de Saúde Complementar—ANS).

[9] SOUZA (2017).

[10] Assumpção (2015).

and by the Ministry of Labor against labor cooperatives. On the pretext that labor cooperatives defraud worker's rights because they supposedly created alternatives to the legal employment protection guaranteed by Brazilian Labor Law, many of them were inspected and sentenced to pay compensation and penalties (Martins 2003). In other words, while the General Law of Cooperative Societies (Act No. 5764) and the Brazilian Labor Law (CLT, article 442) guaranteed cooperative workers their autonomy as a member, many cooperatives were forced to close down because they were not able to pay the imposed penalties.

It is true that many "fake cooperatives" were created in Brazil. However, the combat did not take place against the false members and their false representatives, but against the cooperative model. As a result, of the 2,024 existing labor cooperatives in Brazil in 2003 with 311,856 members, only 943 cooperatives (with 98,713 members) remained in 2017.[11] This reduction, said Assumpção still in 2015, was the result of an organized inspection by the Brazilian authorities against the misuse of the purpose of labor cooperatives.[12]

To prevent the disappearance of labor cooperatives, the cooperative movement agreed to relativize aspects of Act No. 5764 to introduce a new law where labor cooperatives were transformed into an instrument to combat labor precariousness, by mean of admitting the insertion of typical rules of employment relations in the regulation of work cooperatives. In practice, Act No. 12,690 of 2012 ignored the dual character of the member (worker and owner) to guarantee typical rights of employees of other corporate models. While advocates argue that workers' rights are constitutional rather than typical of employees, what is seen is a current difficulty for labor cooperatives in managing social funds that guarantee these mandatory minimum rights.[13]

By treating cooperative workers as employees, what the state imposed was a typical labor management of capital companies, forcing cooperatives in their management to consider legal requirements that affect the identity of labor cooperatives, that is, to guarantee members alternative ways of managing work. Once again, the assumed understanding is that the sacrifice was imposed on cooperative societies in general, not on false members and their false representatives.

Another example of State interference over Brazilian cooperative activity occurred with credit cooperatives. This has happened since 2006, when the National Monetary Council (CMN)[14] sought specific regulations for credit cooperatives in view of their growth in Brazil, and the Central Bank initiated a project called "Cooperative Governance", whose objective was to encourage Brazilian credit cooperatives to adopt good governance practices.[15]

---

[11] OCB (2019).

[12] Assumpção (2015).

[13] Miranda (2013).

[14] Under Brazilian law (Act No. 4,565/1964), it is the responsibility of the National Monetary Council to regulate the Brazilian financial system, where credit cooperatives are located. The Central Bank of Brazil has the competence to supervise and guide the operation of these financial institutions.

[15] Ventura et al. (2009).

In addition, the Central Bank of Brazil discusses with the credit cooperatives the management system proposed by article 47 of Act No. 5764, suggesting to clearly establish the segregation between the Board of Directors and Administrative Council. Through a law project initiated in 2004 and approved in 2009 (Complementary Act No. 130), the Directors sitting on the board did not only have to be members, but also market professionals appointed by the Administrative Council (Article 5).

At the same time, the Central Bank of Brazil launched a book called *Cooperative Governance: Guidelines and Mechanisms for Strengthening Governance in Credit Cooperatives*, authored by Ventura et al. (2009). In this book, professionals from the Central Bank apply concepts of governance to credit cooperatives from the productions of the Brazilian Institute of Corporate Governance (IBGC). The following year, these same conclusions are transformed into regulations for credit cooperatives through CMN Resolution 3859 (2010) and CMN Resolution 4434 (2015).

In practice, the Central Bank of Brazil began to demand from credit cooperatives changes in their bylaws/statutes to create a bipartite management model, explained by Neto et al. (2018) as a two-level management system: strategy and control. The Board of Directors (generally non-members and market professionals) is responsible for contracting rights and obligations, while the Administrative Council[16] represents the interests of members in the strategic direction of the cooperative.

More recently, this same governance structure from capital societies to cooperative societies has also been imposed on health cooperatives. Without any distinction between the models of societies authorized as health operators, the National Health Agency (ANS), through Resolution 443/2019, mandated for the cooperative societies the adoption of the same two-level management system. In other words, ignoring the social and cultural aspects that also involve cooperatives, the new resolution imposes minimum governance practices with an emphasis on internal control and risk management, all with strictly economic objectives.

As seen, the governance structures proposed on their theoretical basis for addressing the agency conflicts and informational asymmetries inherent in capital societies were simply copied into the cooperative reality. To control the operational risks of these cooperatives, the Brazilian State ignored the legal frameworks proposed by the International Cooperative Alliance. As a consequence, the lack of full understanding of cooperative identity is focusing once again on the economic aspects typical of profit-seeking companies.

---

[16] Here, the author makes an alert justified in the typical problems of translations. In studies dealing with the representation of members in executive bodies, such as Hagen (2012a) and Münker and Mateus (2011), they are called merely Board of Directors, defined as Hagen (2012a, p. 86) "As the executive organ/body of the cooperative, the board of directors must function according to precise legal rules." In Brazil, however, the present study will show that the Board of Directors is divided into manuals and the law into two specific bodies. The first is the representative body of the members, elected at a general meeting between them, responsible for the strategic direction of the Cooperative, which the author will call Administrative Council. The second body is the Board of Directors, who deals directly with the management of the cooperative. Here, the author will refer Board of Directors or simply Directors. In any case, the reading of this article will make clear this division, whose nomenclature is used by the author as a methodological approach.

It is important to note that the idea of social bodies in a stock company, as thought by the Brazilian legislator (Act No. 6404 of 1976), is based on the adequacy and understanding of the company as an institutional society in which capital, not its owner's person, has importance and accentuation.[17] In addition, Bensoussan and Boiteux (2018) pointed out that the governance model of stock societies in Brazil has, as a rule, a large and anonymous collective with little personal interest. It ignores that cooperative relations are guided not only by the logic of price but also by collective desires in the face of reality.[18]

Although the Brazilian State justifies this governance model by the idea of preservation of the public interest of credit cooperatives and health cooperatives, it is troublesome that draft bills in the National Congress intend to extend these governance rules to other types of cooperatives. Draft Law 6692 (2013), for example, argues that governance structures are suitable for cooperatives because, like companies, they have a strong economic performance that requires the professionalization of management.

Obviously, it is not intended here to deny the existence of cooperatives that require professional and close market management. Similarly, this reflection accepts the need to develop governance mechanisms for cooperative societies. However, what is being discussed is the solutions proposed by the Brazilian State, especially in the cases of credit cooperatives and health cooperatives, which ignore the social and cultural reality of cooperative societies.

What was proposed in all cases were foreign solutions to cooperative action, adopting without reflection typical alternatives of corporations and ignoring their own aspects such as solidarity, self-help, cooperation between cooperatives and social responsibility, among others. It is at this moment that the collaboration alerted by Hagen Henrÿ regarding the "companization" of cooperative societies becomes evident in the Brazilian reality.

4 State Interference as an Expression of the *Companization* of Cooperatives

The term "companization" is presented by Henrÿ (2012a), p. 10, as "those processes in legislation through which the features of cooperatives are being approximated with the features of stock companies[19]", a phenomenon inserted in a process of "uniformization" of all the forms of business organizations and widely in legislative processes around the world.

---

[17] Mamede (2004).

[18] Souza (2017).

[19] To understand its terms, Henrÿ (2012a, p. 10) also explains the concept of stock company: "The term 'stock company' is used as a generic term designating those enterprise types which centre on invested capital."

Within the legal and business reality, this "companization" refers to the attempt to approximate cooperative law with the law applicable to stock companies through various initiatives that, together, ignore the proper aspects of the cooperative model. In this sense, Henrÿ (2012a), p. 12, states that one of the ways to enforce this alignment is to approximate laws that address "highly interconnected issues of capital structure, management, and control mechanisms".

In a previous reflection, Henrÿ (2012), p. 4, argues that this "companization" attempts to justify itself as the "necessary means to ensure equal treatment of all enterprise types in view of competitiveness." However, this argument is doubtful for Henrÿ because it reduces competitiveness precisely where capitalist companies are better qualified: in their financial goals.

Despite this concise concept, the "companization" phenomenon is a consequence of a series of historical trends summarized by Henrÿ (2018), p. 9, in the article *Trends in Cooperative Legislation: What needs harmonizing?*[20]:

> Since then, three trends have marked cooperative law, namely, a pronounced distinction of the cooperative form of enterprise from other organizational forms over a period of ca. 120 years, roughly from 1850 to 1970; an approximation of the legal structural features of cooperatives with those of capital-centered enterprises ("companization"), starting at the beginning of the 1970ies; and a mutual approximation of enterprise forms as of the 1990ies, while the center of cooperative law-making has been shifting since then from the national to the regional and international levels.

As seen, the "companization" of cooperative societies has been going on since the 1970s. As an initial result, the cooperative movement faced a serious identity crisis. Pressured by competitiveness, cooperative societies have relegated non-economic goals to a secondary role, sometimes accepting an approach that harmonizes them with corporations, with purely economic objectives.[21]

In the early 1990s, the ICA proposed to work on rescuing the identity aspects of cooperativism, recovering the characteristics and fundamental objectives of cooperative societies. Under the coordination of Sven Ake Böök, the cooperative movement was concerned with identifying the nature and values that underlie modern cooperation. It is from this rescue that ICA presented its "Statement on the Cooperative Identity" in 1995. However, this ICA's effort to affirm the cooperative identity has brought a contradictory evolution, also discussed by Henrÿ (2012), p. 4:

> On the one hand, legislators have been approximating the features of cooperatives with those of capitalistic companies over the past four decades, especially as concerns capital structure, management and control mechanisms ("companization"). On the other hand, the respect for the public international cooperative law with its obligation put on legislators to maintain the cooperative identity is growing. Further companization will soon clash with the principle of the economy of legislation. Separate laws with similar contents on cooperatives and on stock companies makes one of them redundant.

This contradiction has already been identified and received specific criticism. Meira and Ramos (2015), for example, discussed "companization" when analyzing

---

[20] Henrÿ (2018).

[21] Miranda (2017)

the Portuguese Cooperative Code reform, as did Pönkä (2019) with the Finnish Cooperatives Act. In the same vein, Münker (2014) criticizes this general trend of "companization" because it devaluates membership and encourages free-riders.

It is in this historical and doctrinal context that the recent Brazilian legislation reveals itself as evidence of a "companization" process of cooperative societies. These laws and/or regulations forget that, before being able to understand managerial, accounting, and financial aspects, as well as understanding the cooperative's risk profile, the member of the cooperative must also understand the aspirations of his/her community, understand that the cooperative is also a political body with its own expectations and conflicts.[22]

5 Concluding Remarks

The International Cooperative Alliance (ICA) recognizes in its various publications (ICA 2013; ICA 2015) that cooperatives today face the challenge of complying with regulations that are imposed on this type of society without proper understanding of their nature. As already mentioned by Henrÿ (2012a), there are aspects of the identity of cooperatives that are not taught in business schools and on which legal and economic texts are concentrated.

In the same way, unfortunately, in current Brazilian Cooperative Law, there is no real understanding of the nature and essence of the cooperative enterprise. Even recognizing the intention of the Brazilian Federal Constitution to foster cooperativism, what is perceived is the disregard for the cooperative spirit that surrounds the cooperative enterprise. Thus, other laws and principles are imposed on cooperatives, weakening the real objective of cooperative principles and the autonomy of Cooperative Law as pillars of collective and incidental action for the common good.

Also in Brazil, Cooperative Law is placed in the background, confirming the "companization" process. Regulations, tax and corporate laws, among others, ignore the cooperative identity. This not only destroys cooperative law but also removes the cause-effect sense of existence from the entities constituted under the cooperative idea expressed in the ICA Cooperative Identity Statement.

As Hagen Henrÿ (2012a) teaches, it is necessary (also in Brazil) that cooperative law leaves its current crossroads between deepening the process of "companization", back to a cooperative law, which translates the cooperative identity or towards a new cooperative law. In the name of cooperative identity, we think it is necessary to defend the proper aspects of cooperativism, otherwise, we will enter into a new identity crisis, as well studied by Böök (1992).

---

[22] Miranda (2017).

References

Act No. 5764, December 16, 1971. Defines the national cooperative policy, establishes the legal regime of cooperative societies, and makes other arrangements. Recovered from http://www.planalto.gov.br/ccivil_03/LEIS/L5764.htm

Assumpção LFMD (2015) A terceirização precarizante e a (in) capacidade emancipatória das cooperativas de trabalho Revista Do TST 81(3):165–191

Bensoussan FG, Boiteux FN (2018) Manual de direito empresarial. Podivm, Salvador

Böök SA (1992) Valores cooperativos para un mundo en cambio: informe para el Congreso de la ACI. ACI, Tokio

Brazilian Federal Constitution (1988) Recovered from http://www.planalto.gov br/ccivil_03/constituicao/constituicao.htm

Complementary Act No. 130 (April 17, 2009) Provides for the national cooperative credit system and repeals provisions of Act No. 4595 of December 31, 1964 and Act No. 5764 of December 16, 1971. Recovered from http://www.planalto.gov.br/CCIVIL_03/leis/LCP/Lcp130.htm

Cracogna D, Henry H, Fici A (eds) 2013 International handbook of cooperative law. Springer. Berlin

Gonçalvez Neto AA et al (2018) Sociedades cooperativas. Lex, São Paulo

Henrÿ H (2012) Sustainable development and cooperative law: corporate social responsibility or cooperative social responsibility? University of Oslo faculty of law research paper (2012–23)

Henrÿ H (2012a) Guidelines for cooperative legislation, vol 3. ILO. Genebra

Henrÿ H (2018) Trends in cooperative legislation: what needs harmonizing? J Res Trade, Manage Econom Dev 5(1) (9)

International Co-operative Alliance (2013) Blueprint for a co-operative decade. Recovered from https://www.ica.coop/sites/default/files/publication-files/blueprint-for-a-co-operative-decade

International Co-operative Alliance (2015) Guidance notes to the co-operative principles. Recovered from https://www.ica.coop/en/guidance-notes

Mamede G (2004) Direito Societário: sociedades simples e empresárias, vol 2, Atlas, São Paulo

Martins SP (2003) Cooperativas de Trabalho. Atlas, São Paulo

Meira DA, Ramos ME (2015) Os princípios cooperativos no contexto da reforma do Código Cooperativo português. CIRIEC Revista Jurídica De Economía Social y Cooperativa 27:401–427

Miranda JE (2013) A dissonância axiológica na plêiade da Lei 12.690/2012. Conteudo Juridico, Brasíça

Miranda JE (2017) Filosofía cooperativa. Curitiba: Juruá

Münkner HH (2014) Ensuring supportive legal frameworks for co-operative growth. ICA 11th Regional Assembly, Nairobi

Nascimento TMC (1989) A ordem econômica e financeira e a nova constituição: arts. 170 a 192. Aide, Rio de Janeiro

Organization of Cooperatives of Brazil (ed) (2019) Agenda Institucional do Cooperativismo. OCB, Brasília

Pinho DB (1977) Economia e cooperativismo. Saraiva, São Paulo

Pinheiro MAH (2008) Cooperativas de crédito: História da evolução normativa no Brasil. 6. ed. Brasília: BCB

Pönkä V (2019) Are cooperative societies transforming into cooperative companies? Reflections on the finnish cooperatives act. Eur Bus Law Rev 30(1):77–99

Souza LR (2017) Cooperativas de Crédito: resoluções do CMN e os valores cooperativos. Juruá, Curitiba

Ventura EVC et al (2009) Governança Cooperativa: diretrizes e mecanismos para fortalecimento da governança em cooperativas de crédito. BCB, Brasília

The Hybridization of Cooperatives and Cooperative Law. Insights from the Netherlands

G. J. H. van der Sangen

1 Introduction

In this chapter, I address the legal objective and identity of the cooperative against the background of developments of hybridization of cooperatives in the Netherlands. Forms of hybridization[1] of cooperatives include amongst others: transactions with non-members, federated models and holding structures, equity raising by non-members, listing of cooperatives on stock markets, patronage based on market conform prices, the initiation of unrelated diversified business activities and the election and composition of boards by non-members. The way the legislator in the Netherlands approached these different types of hybridization of cooperatives has been viewed as facilitating cooperatives, providing room for innovations in organizing cooperatives.[2] A key question is whether types of hybridization themselves are at odds with the objective and identity of the cooperative. This results in the subsequent question whether hybridization of cooperatives has also led to the hybridization or—in the wording of Hagen Henrÿ—companization of cooperative law itself. The chapter demonstrates the companization of cooperatives themselves in particular since the Second World War. In reaction to the companization of cooperatives, the

[1] Hybridization is also called deformation: van Diepenbeek (1990), p. 78 referring to Emelianoff (1942), p. 225. Also, the terminology denaturation is used: Bartman and van der Meijden (1992), pp. 13–35.

[2] van der Sangen (2013), p. 558 and Bier (2017).

This chapter builds on the author's presentation at the 2018 ICA Research Conference *Cooperatives in a rapidly changing world: innovation in enterprise and community*, in the legal session on 'Hybrid cooperative organizations', Wageningen, 4–6 July 2018. He would like to express his gratitude to all the participants during this session for sharing their insights and discussions, in particular to Hagen Henrÿ.

G. J. H. van der Sangen (✉)
Department Private, Business and Labour Law, Tilburg Law School, Tilburg, Netherlands
e-mail: g.j.h.vdrsangen@tilburguniversity.edu

W. Tadjudje and I. Douvitsa (eds.), *Perspectives on Cooperative Law*,
https://doi.org/10.1007/978-981-19-1991-6_15

Netherlands' legislator repeatedly facilitated the companization of cooperatives by changing cooperative law as the legislative history of Netherlands' cooperative law will show.

At the same time, legislators have some leeway in designing special policy instruments to promote cooperatives based on the acceptance of the ICA-principles vis-à-vis investor-owned firms, in which cooperatives operate according to the principles of solidarity and mutuality as the embodiment of the specific identity of cooperatives.[3] However, in this respect, the Netherlands' legislator has not produced a legal framework that facilitates small cooperatives or social economy cooperatives. If the Netherlands' legislator does want to promote the enhancement of cooperatives vis-à-vis investor-owned firms actively, the question arises of the demarcation of the cooperative legal form distinct from the investor-owned firm, a demarcation we find in business organizational law, tax law and competition law.[4]

The main objective of this chapter is to clarify types of hybridization of cooperatives as indicators of the companization of cooperatives as well as to clarify how cooperative law has an impact on the phenomenon of hybridization of cooperatives as the demarcation of the cooperative legal form distinct from investor-owned firms. In this respect, the chapter may provide answers to the question Hagen Henrÿ so eloquently raised: '*The legal challenge consists in dealing with the fading distinctiveness of cooperatives caused by rather contradictory and unbalanced legislative processes: on the one hand, we observe a growing respect for public international cooperative law, with its obligation on law-makers to restore and/or maintain the distinctiveness of cooperatives. On the other hand, we observe a dominant process of companization of cooperatives. Globalisation adds to the complexity of this imbroglio-like legislative situation in the cooperative arena.*'[5]

2 The Legal Objective and Identity of the Netherlands' Cooperative

According to the International Cooperative Alliance,[6] the International Labour Organization[7] and the United Nations,[8] a cooperative is an autonomous association of persons united voluntarily to meet their common economic, social and cultural needs

[3] Joint cases ECJ EU 8 September 2011, C-78/08, 79/08 and 80/8.

[4] On this theme from a business organizational point of view Fici (2014), pp. 147–158 and Fici (2017), pp. 539–549.

[5] Henrÿ (2012a, b), pp. 197–233.

[6] https://www.ica.coop/en/cooperatives/cooperative-identity. Accessed 14 July 2021.

[7] ILO R193—Promotion of cooperatives recommendation, 2002 (No. 193). https://www.ilo.org/dyn/normlex/en/f?p=NORMLEXPUB:12100:0::NO::P12100_ILO_code:R193. Accessed 14 July 2021.

[8] Resolution adapted by the General Assembly of the 88th plenary meeting of the United Nations, 19 December 2001 (A/RES/56/114).

and aspirations through a jointly owned and democratically controlled enterprise. Member States to the International Labour Organization have the obligation—by means of cooperative law legislation—to ensure that cooperatives adhere to the ICA Principles of voluntary and open membership, democratic control, member participation, autonomy and independence, education, training and information of (potential) members, co-operation amongst cooperatives and concern for communities.[9] While doing so, a cooperative—ideally—is based on the value of self-help, self-responsibility, democracy, equality, equity and solidarity. In the tradition of their founders, cooperative members believe in the ethical values of honesty, openness, social responsibility and caring for others. These principles and values pinpoint the cooperative objective and identity of the cooperative which combines an economic aspect (the jointly owned enterprise) with social and solidarity aspects.

However, looking at the historical legal development of cooperative law in the Netherlands, the legal objective and identity of the cooperative has always been defined in strictly economic terms ever since the first Act on Cooperative Associations of 1876.[10] According to the current article 53, section 1, Second Book, Netherlands Civil Code (hereinafter: 2:53.1 NCC), a cooperative is:

> an association established as a cooperative by virtue of a notarial deed. Under its articles of association, its statutory objective must be to provide for certain material needs of its members under contracts, other than insurance contracts, concluded with them in the business its conducts or causes to be conducted to that end for the benefit of its members.

Notice that the legal definition provides a description of the mandatory economic activity of the cooperative vis-à-vis its members and that there is no reference whatsoever to any of the cooperative principles or values of international public cooperative law. This has been a deliberate choice of the Netherlands' legislator to set the cooperative apart from the association of article 2:26 NCC.[11] Although the preamble of the SCE Regulation refers to international public cooperative law,[12] this did not trigger the Netherlands' legislator—while implementing the SCE Regulation into Netherlands law—to meet its international public cooperative law obligation in this respect.[13]

As well as in business organizational law as well as in tax law, the Netherlands legislator regulated the economic activity of the cooperative as an ancillary organization vis-à-vis its members in the way Emelianoff[14] described the cooperative:

---

[9] ILO R193, article 7.

[10] An overview of the legislative history of cooperative law is provided in Chap. 3 of van der Sangen (1999) and in the English summary.

[11] van der Sangen (1999), pp. 86–93.

[12] Council Regulation No. 1435/2003 of 22 July 2003 on the Statute for a European Cooperative Society (SCE), *OJ* L 207/1 of 18 Augustus 2003, preamble under 10.

[13] Law Implementing the SCE Regulation of 14 September 2006, *Staatsblad* 2006, 425.

[14] Emelianoff (1942), pp. 248 and 249.

> cooperative organizations represent the aggregates of economic units. (…) The true nature of such an agency can be thoroughly understood only if we clearly keep in mind that the cooperative represents the associated economic units in their functioning and not their association as a separate economic entity.

Emelianoff described the cooperative as a form of incomplete vertical integration. This economic approach is also used in the current Corporate Income Tax Law 1969 that applies to cooperatives as well as.[15] Only in case and to the extent a cooperative operates as a fully ancillary organization in the patronage operations with its members and distributes the net proceeds as refunds to the volume of the patronage, the net proceeds are deductible from the Corporate Income Tax and, insofar, it prevents double taxation.[16]

So, while the legal objective and identity according to Netherlands' cooperative law has been described only in economic terms, the regulation of the cooperative in business organizational law in the Second Book of the NCC does not only lack a reference to the internationally accepted cooperative principles and values but also fails to facilitate them. Cooperative law in the Netherlands does not mandate open membership, membership participation is not mandatory from the perspective of the members, does not impose rules on cooperatives to organize education and training, and information to (potential) members, nor mandates in any way cooperatives to cooperate amongst themselves nor imposes rules of concern for communities other than corporate social responsibility norms that apply to all business forms.[17] What remains is that current cooperative law in the Netherlands adheres to the principle of 'one member, one vote' (as a default rule),[18] that the board is appointed by and composed with its members (as a default rule)[19] and that member economic participation is an obligation for the cooperative towards its members but not necessarily vice versa.

Making things worse in this respect, the Netherlands' legislator facilitated different forms of hybridization to prevent that these 'hybridizing' cooperatives—notably large producer cooperatives and cooperative banks—had to dissolve the cooperative,[20] safeguarding that these cooperatives remained formally established as a cooperative. Over the years, the scope of the legal objective and identity of the cooperative in the Netherlands has been broadened to an extent that Timmerman proclaimed '*Anything goes*'.[21] At one point, even a 'one member'-cooperative has been accepted under Netherlands' cooperatives law to facilitate

---

[15] van der Sangen (1999), pp. 47–50.

[16] van der Sangen (2013), pp. 557–558 with further references.

[17] See for further analysis van der Sangen (2019b), pp. 48–55.

[18] Article 2:38.1 NCC.

[19] Article 2:37 NCC.

[20] Until 1989, a cooperative that did not meet the legal definition of the cooperative in article 2:53.1 NCC was deemed to be null and void. Since 1989, article 2:21 NCC stipulates that a cooperative that does not meet the legal definition of the cooperative, can be dissolved by the court on request of the public prosecutor or any other interested party. van der Sangen (1999), Chap. 3, para 5.

[21] Timmerman (2000), passim.

private equity constructions in which the cooperative functions as a sub-holding legal entity to circumvent Dividend Withholding Taxation, a tax that does not apply to cooperatives.[22]

At the same time, we need to consider that the Netherlands' legislator has a liberal attitude towards company law law-making in general. The objective of business organizational law—which includes cooperative law—is primarily to facilitate entrepreneurs by providing off the rack legal business forms in order to lower transaction costs in setting up and maintaining the legal business form, to lower costs of solving potential agency problems, to offer default rules in case end-users are not in the position ex ante contract for optimal provisions and to safeguard the rule of law: to protect minority members and other stakeholders and to prevent the abuse of the cooperative form.[23] Until to date, in the parliamentary proceedings to the subsequent cooperative law statutes, the question whether cooperative law should mandate to encapsulate other interests than the economic interests of the existing members, has never been properly addressed and, accordingly, has been left to decide upon to the initial incorporators and later members of the cooperative through amendments of the articles of association. Netherlands' cooperative law gives little guidance in this respect. On the contrary, the legal definition of the cooperative has been broadened to facilitate the hybridization of cooperatives. So, what are these forms of hybridization of cooperatives that have been facilitated in Netherlands' cooperative law historically?

3 A Short Historical Overview of Netherlands' Cooperative Law Statutes

The first cooperative law statute came into force in 1876.[24] Before this act, cooperative organizations had to use either the public company (*naamloze vennootschap*) or the association (*vereniging*) to obtain legal personality. However, to become an 'cooperative association' required prior formal approval of the Crown, which was rejected generically in 1874 in cases the articles of association of the cooperative provided for the distribution of profits to its members, which was prohibited for associations. This triggered the legislator to introduce a separate act on cooperatives in 1876.

In the first statute on cooperatives of 1876, cooperatives were viewed both as an association and as a business with the possibility to distribute profits to its members. The cooperative was still a non-complex organization. After the First World War,

[22] van der Bijl (2010), pp. 130–136 and Asser-Rensen 2-III (2017), para 216. With critisism: Dortmond (2007), p. 5.

[23] Summarizing common insights from law and economics in Kraakman et al. (2017), passim and Vermeulen (2003).

[24] This historical overview of the subsequent cooperative law statute is based on van der Sangen (1999), Chap. 3, Asser-Rensen 2-III (2017), para 210 and Dijk/van der Ploeg (2019), para 1.2.3.

a substantial number of cooperatives under the Act of 1876 became bankrupt. In this period, members had an incentive to claim that they were not a member of the cooperative in order to avoid the statutory payment of their share in the deficit of the cooperative upon liquidation. The mandatory member registration system failed to provide the necessary evidence and certainty in this respect. Also, cooperatives—notably agricultural producer cooperatives—became more complex because of an increase of the number of members, the expansion of their territory and mergers.

These developments were addressed in the second statute on cooperatives in 1925, introducing not only more stringent rules on members' liability in case of liquidation of the cooperative but also the possibility of delegated decision-making and federated models to cope with the increasing growth and complexity of cooperatives.[25] The 1925 Act on Cooperative Associations worked well for decades and has been an important impetus for future statutes on the cooperative as well as on the association. However, the 1925 statute on cooperatives, has been withdrawn as of 1976, the year in which a revision of the complete Netherlands' Civil Code entered into force.

During the revision of the Civil Code in 1976, cooperative law has been incorporated in the Second Book of the Civil Code on *Legal Persons*. In fact, this has been the first development that has led to the companization of cooperative law, because general rules for all legal persons and some specific rules for private companies limited by shares were applied to cooperatives as well, for example, the rules on legal mergers,[26] the rules for group law[27] and the rules for annual accountants for companies, without providing specific provisions for cooperatives.[28]

But more importantly, the scope of the definition of the cooperative has been broadened in 1976 in several ways. Firstly, cooperatives have been allowed to operate as a holding cooperative provided that one of its subsidiaries entered into the contracts with the members to fulfil its mandatory statutory objective.[29] Secondly, cooperatives were allowed to enter into contracts on the same footing as with its members with non-members. The acceptance of non-member transactions is at odds with the principle of open membership.[30] The only requirement for transactions with non-members is that the article of associations allow these transactions.[31] These two new features combined also has led to the creation of cooperatives with subsidiaries that engaged in diversified business activities that have no or little economic connections with the membership transaction of the members and their business. In this case, members of the cooperative are also investors through the holding cooperative in non-related and diversified business activities of its subsidiaries, some of which are active abroad.

---

[25] Meerburg et al. (1925), passim. Delegated decision-making and federated models are regulated in the current articles 2:39 and 41 NCC, which articles go back to the Act of 1925.

[26] Article 2:308 NCC.

[27] Articles 2:24a, 24b en 24c, 2:403 and 406 NCC.

[28] Article 2:360.1 NCC.

[29] This followed from the definition of the cooperative in art. 2:53.1 NCC.

[30] There is no provision in Netherlands cooperative law that mandates the cooperate to offer using non-members a membership.

[31] Article 2:53.3 and 4 NCC.

Between 1976 and 1989, in which a second but smaller revision of the Second Book of the Civil Code took place, a cooperative that did not adhere to the material definition and features of the cooperative in article 2:53.1 NCC, was null and void as a legal person. Although in practice, this has not led to major issues—since the definition was broad enough—in 1989 the legislator chose to refrain from giving a material definition of the cooperative and instead introduced the current formal definition of the cooperative by which a cooperative is required to incorporate in the articles of association the mandatory objective and identity of the cooperative as defined in article 2:53.1 NCC. Since 1989, a cooperative is only null and void as a legal person in case the cooperative has been established without a notarial deed.[32] In case of non-compliance to the formal definition, the cooperative may by dissolved by the court on request of the Public Prosecutor's Office or any interested party, like the members.[33] However, in practice, no cooperatives have been dissolved based on the provision of article 2:21 NCC.

4 Underdeveloped Specificity of the Cooperative in Netherlands Law

While the legal objective and identity of the cooperative in the legal definition of the cooperative in article 2:53.1 NCC is not very pronounced, the Netherlands' legislator has made an effort to take into account the specific nature of the cooperative vis-à-vis the private companies limited by shares (*naamloze vennootschap* and *besloten vennootschap*) to some extent. Large cooperatives with 100 or more employees and equity of 16 million euros and a mandatory works council, are mandated by law to create in a supervisory body—like large private companies limited by shares—to which important mandatory decision rights are attributed.[34] In case this so-called *structuurregime* applied to private companies limited by shares, the management board is not appointed by the general meeting of shareholders but by the independent supervisory board. One third of the supervisory board is recommended by the works council.[35] In order to safeguard that members of a cooperative remain in democratic control over their cooperative, this provision of the *structuurregime* does not apply to cooperatives: the members of the management board in a cooperative in all instances are appointed by the general assembly of the cooperative.[36]

As indicated above, in tax law the specific nature of the cooperative is taken into account in the Corporate Income Tax to avoid double taxation of the net proceeds but

---

[32] Article 2:4 NCC.

[33] Article 2:21 NCC.

[34] Article 2:63b-63j NCC. Most important is the provision of article 2:63j NCC that requires prior approval of the supervisory board to major decisions of the board as listed in that article.

[35] Art. 2:162 and 272 NCC.

[36] On the Netherlands *structuurregime* for cooperatives: Dortmond (1991) and Schreurs-Engelaar (1995), Chap. 5.

under (too) strict requirements.[37] Also, the Dividend Withholding Tax does not apply to cooperatives, provided the cooperative economically benefits the businesses of its members through their membership with the cooperative.[38] Apart from a regulation of business-to-business credit cooperatives[39] and a ministerial decree for subsidizing community renewable energy cooperatives,[40] there are no special facilities for other types of cooperatives, like worker cooperatives.

5 How the Netherlands' Legislator Dealt with Forms of Hybridization

After the overview of the history of cooperative law and highlighting the lack of the legislator's initiative to pinpoint the specific legal objective and identity of the cooperative in accordance with international public cooperative law, I tried to illustrate how cooperative law itself facilitated the hybridization of cooperatives and their activities. In the section, I will briefly address how current cooperative law deals with specific forms of hybridizations we encounter in practice.

According to generally accepted definitions of the cooperative, a cooperative is for member benefit.[41] However, it depends on the national cooperative law how the principle of member benefit is regulated. In this respect, Netherlands' cooperative law refrained from promulgating basic default rules in this respect. The law only stipulates that a cooperative is allowed to distribute profits amongst its members, not that members as a default rule are entitled to it.[42] Unless the articles of the cooperative provide otherwise, a member is not entitled to be paid a refund or a share in the net proceeds.[43] In practice, several cooperatives pay market conform prices to their members in the transactions with the cooperative. In fact, this technique leads to the creation a profit of the cooperative similar to the profit of an investor-owned firms. If provided in the articles of association, a cooperative is also allowed to enter into transactions with non-members on the same footing as with the members. In

[37] For example, the profit of the cooperative is only deductible from the corporate income tax if the profit is paid-out to the members after closing of the book year in proportion to the volume of the transactions of the members. Any reservation of the profit of the cooperative leads to double taxation. van der Sangen (2013), para 25.11.

[38] Beudeker and Kastrop (2018), para 4.

[39] Article 2:54o Act on Financial Supervision (*Wet Financieel Toezicht*). Act of 3 July 2015, *Staatsblad* 2015, 304 on Supervision of Credit Unions (*Wet Toezicht kredietunies*) leading to changes in the Act on Financial Supervision as of 1 January 2016.

[40] Ministerial decree of 27 Februari 2021 Subsidieregeling coöperatieve energieopwekking, *Staatscourant* 3 March 2021.

[41] Dunn (1988).

[42] Article 2:26.3 NCC read in conjunction with article 2:53a NCC.

[43] van der Sangen (1999), p. 249.

both cases, the question arises if and to what extend the cooperative is still for the benefit of its members.[44]

We concluded that federated models and delegated decision-making and holding structures can be used according to Netherlands' cooperative law with no restrictions. The use of subsidiaries while the cooperative itself operates as a holding company is widespread under producer cooperatives in the Netherlands. It also opens the possibility for the holding cooperative to set up or acquire subsidiaries with unrelated diversified business activities. Netherlands' cooperative law allows this without restrictions, provided the patronage with its members is also covered as well through one or more designated subsidiaries to that end.[45] In particular, producer cooperatives have divided the cooperative organization in a cooperative member organization that acts as controlling shareholder on the one hand and a sub-holding company on the other hand that leads the corporate group of the cooperative businesses and their subsidiaries. This raises serious questions whether members via the cooperative are still in effective control[46] of the cooperative organization.[47]

Combining all these forms of hybridization together, it results in a cooperative that settles the transactions with its members on the basis of market conform prices, that generates a non-distributable profit to members, that is allowed the reinvest the profit in diversified business opportunities. Note that according to current corporate law paradigm in the Netherlands—that also applies to cooperatives—the decision on the corporate strategy is an exclusive authority of the board of the holding company which also includes the financing of the cooperate group as a whole.[48] Finally, it gives the cooperative the possibility to raise equity from non-members, provided that the voting rights of non-members is restricted to 1/3 of the total amount of votes actually cast at the general meeting.[49] Also, non-members are allowed to appoint less than half of the total number of members of the management board.[50] These features, combined, allow cooperatives the raise equity on the stock market, for it provides the possibility to safeguard the specific interests of non-member investors in the cooperative.[51] The case of Rabobank[52] and its stock listing provides an example for equity raising of non-members as well as ForFarmers[53] and, in the past, the

---

[44] This is the case with cooperative banks. On this issue van Diepenbeek (1990), pp. 110–112.

[45] van der Sangen (1999), p. 251.

[46] Terminology used by Hansmann (1996), p. 11.

[47] On this issue Bijman et al. (2014), pp. 641–661.

[48] High Court 10 January 1990, NJ 1990/465 and 466 (*OGEM*), High Court 13 July 2007, NJ 2007/434 (*ABN AMRO*) and High Court 4 April 2014, NJ 2014/286 (*Cancun*).

[49] Article 2:38.3 NCC.

[50] Article 2:37 NCC.

[51] See for financial innovations and their legal modalities in equity raising from non-members van der Sangen (1999), Chap. 6.

[52] https://www.rabobank.com/en/investors/funding/certificates/index.html#. Accessed 14 July 2021.

[53] https://www.forfarmersgroup.eu/en/investors/information-for-shareholders.aspx. Accessed 14 July 2021.

cooperative pharmaceutical organization OPG, the first cooperative that was listed on the Amsterdam stock exchange in 1992.[54]

6 An Evaluation of How the Netherlands' Legislator Dealt with Hybridization

Unlike some other countries,[55] the Netherlands' legislator since 1874 choose to design one single statute for all types of cooperatives. This 'one size, fits all'-approach of cooperative legislation has been upheld in the 1976 revision of the Netherlands Civil Code, when cooperative business organizational law has been incorporated in the Second Book of the Civil Code on *Legal Persons*. The focus of the legislator historically has been to facilitate producer and banking cooperatives and their growing complexity and forms of hybridization of their cooperative activities. Yet, specific rules on financing cooperatives with equity are missing as well specific rules on accounting.

While expanding the scope of the legal definition throughout the years, cooperative law in the Netherlands gives little guidance to potential members how a cooperative could operate on the basis of the principles and values set out by international public cooperative law. In the recent past, the cooperative sector itself has tried to define and create more awareness on the specific nature of the cooperative and its objective and identity through voluntary codes, like the 2015 *NCR Code voor Coöperatieve ondernemingen*. However, an evaluation of this code showed a low compliance rate mainly because the code was too detailed, was designed as a legal document and referred to rules of the Netherlands Corporate Governance Code for stock listed companies with regard to compliance, remuneration, the composition of the supervisory board and rules with regard to inside information.[56] The *Nationale Coöperatieve Raad*,[57] the Netherlands' umbrella organization for cooperatives, has revised the code in 2019 fundamentally to make the code more principles-based and in line with the ICA Principles. The *Coöperatie Code 2019* was based on three pillars: cooperative entrepreneurship, collectivity and mutuality, and member involvement. Also, the code avoids using legal terminology as far as possible.[58]

Although there is an increasing awareness of the potential of cooperatives under gras root and civil society initiatives,[59] a quick start for a new wave of the cooperative movement in the Netherlands could benefit from an overhaul of the legal

[54] The latter has been described extensively by van der Sangen (1999), pp. 413–427.

[55] To name a view France—vide Hiez (2013), p. 396—and Japan—vide Kurimoto (2013), p. 506.

[56] Flamman (2019), p. 10.

[57] https://www.cooperatie.nl.

[58] https://www.cooperatie.nl/wp-content/uploads/2019/10/Folder-Co%C3%B6peratie-Code-2019-sept-2019-Platform.pdf.

[59] Bosma and De Jonge (2014) provide an overview of the applications of the cooperative models in practice in the Netherlands.

infrastructure on cooperatives. Under the current rules for cooperatives, there are underdeveloped tax incentives for small cooperatives to adhere to the ICA-principles and the principles of solidarity and mutuality. A separate statute for worker cooperatives is missing while incentives in labour law and social securities law to set up worker cooperatives are too weak. In general, cooperatives in the Netherlands play only a minor role in the social economy sector for this sector itself—to date—is not very well developed. To be sure, the Netherlands' government has presented a draft law on the private company with a social objective and gave it into consultation Spring 2021.[60] The cooperative as a viable option was not mentioned in the draft. It seems that the cooperative is just another business form like any other to the Netherlands' legislator.

7 Conclusion

The development of cooperative law in the Netherlands started with a separate act on cooperatives in 1874. Cooperatives were non-complex organizations. With the growth and the increasing complexity of cooperatives, the legislator in 1925 regulated delegated decision-making and federated models. In 1976, the legislator facilitated several forms of hybridization of cooperatives and their activities, such as transactions with non-members, the use of subsidiaries to organize (unrelated) diversified business activities but did not produce specific financing and accounting rules for cooperatives. Also, from the beginning of cooperative law legislation, the objective of the cooperative was defined in purely economic terms and no reference has been made in the subsequent Netherlands' cooperative laws to the principles and values of international public law, although the Netherlands as a member to the International Labour Organization has an obligation to ensure that cooperatives adhere to the ICA Principles. A cooperative is not just another business form like any other, we learn from the advocacy of Hagen Henrÿ for cooperative law as a distinct field of law separate from investor-owned firms.[61] In the footsteps of Hagen Henrÿ, I take up the advocacy of cooperative law as a genuine and specific discipline in the Netherlands.[62] The Netherlands' legislator may find inspiration in the opus of Hagen Henrÿ[63] when he—the Netherlands' legislator—returns to the initial concept why we regulated the cooperative as a separate legal business form in the first place. In honour of Hagen Henrÿ, I close with a quote of J. H. Boudewijnse from 1899: '*A genuine cooperative is a cooperative that in its endeavors adheres to the same principles once put into practice so brilliantly by the Pioneers of Rochdale. A false cooperative concerns the*

[60] https://www.internetconsultatie.nl/bvm.

[61] Henrÿ (2013), pp. 810–816 and Henrÿ (2017), pp. 39–52.

[62] See van der Sangen (2019a, b), pp. 36–43.

[63] Henrÿ (2012a, b).

type of association that, formally established as a cooperative and acknowledged as such by law, only strives for self-interested objectives.[64]

References

Asser C, Rensen G (2017) Mr. C. Assers Handleiding tot de beoefening van het Nederlands Burgerlijk Recht. 2. Rechtspersonenrecht. Deel III. Overige Rechtspersonen. Vereniging, coöperatie, onderlinge waarborgmaatschappij, stichting, kerkgenootschap en Europese rechtsvormen, Kluwer, Deventer

Bartman S, Van der Meijden E (1992) Holdingcoöperatie, evolutie of denaturatie? Strijdige belangen in evenwicht. Beschouwingen over het Bedrijfsfinancieel recht, Utrecht, pp 13–35

Beudeker M, Kastrop E (2018), Fiscaliteit & de coöperatie. In: Zaman D et al (eds) De coöperatie anno 2017, Ars Notariatus 166, Wolters Kluwer, Deventer, pp 11–27

Bier B (2017) Cooperatives under dutch law, a flexible format not only for framers CIRIEC España. Rev Jurídica Economía Soc Cooperativa 30:161–219

Bijman J, Hanisch M, van der Sangen G (2014) Shifting control? The changes of internal governance in agricultural cooperatives in the EU. Ann Public Coop Econ 85(4):641–661

Bosma M, De Jonge E (2014) Publiek Geheim. De coöperatie in beweging, Frissewind, Amsterdam

Boudewijnse J (1899) Welke zijn de beginselen die aan de toepassing der coöperatieve denkbeelden ten grondslag behooren gelegd te worden, Drukkerij Trio, 's-Gravenhage

Diepenbeek van W (1990) De coöperatieve organisatie. Coöperaties als maatschappelijk en economisch verschijnsel, Eburon, Delft

Dijk/Van der Ploeg (2019) Van vereniging en stichting, coöperatie en onderlinge waarborgmaatschappij, 7th edn. Wolters Kluwer, Deventer

Dortmond P (1991) De coöperatie; van vereniging naar houdstermaatschappij en beursrechtspersoon. Kluwer, Deventer

Dortmond P (2007) De zuivere holdingcoöperatie: een coöperatie? In: van der Sangen GJH et al (eds) De coöperatie: een eigentijdse rechtsvorm. Boom legal publishers, The Hague, pp 1–7

Dunn J (1988) Basic cooperative principles and their relationship to selected practices. J Agric Corporation 3:1998

Emelianoff I (1942) Economic theory of co-operation, Washington

Fici A (2014) The essential role of cooperative law. Dovenschmidt Q 4:147–158. https://doi.org/10.5553/DQ/221199812014002004005

Fici A (2017) The essential role of cooperative law and some related issues. In: Michie J et al (eds) The Oxford handbook of mutual, co-operative and co-owned business. Oxford University Press, Oxford, pp 539–549

Flamman M (2019) De nieuwe coöperatie code 2019. Coöperatie 641(2019–12):9–11

Gezelle Meerburg O et al (1925) Practische handleiding bij de Wet op de Coöperatieve Vereenigingen, N. Samson, Alphen aan den Rijn

Henrÿ H (2012a) Basics and new features of cooperative law—the case of public international cooperative law and the harmonization of cooperative laws'. Uniform Law Rev 2012:197–233

Henrÿ H (2012b) Guidelines for cooperative legislation, 3rd edn. ILO, Geneva

Henrÿ H (2017) Co-operative principles and co-operative law across the globe. In: Michie J et al (eds) The Oxford handbook of mutual, co-operative and co-owned business. Oxford University Press, Oxford, pp 39–52

Hiez D (2013) France. In: Cracogna D et al (eds) International handbook of cooperative law. Springer, Berlin, pp 393–411

[64] Boudewijnse (1899), p. 15.

Kraakman R et al (2017) The anatomy of corporate law: a comparative and functional approach. Oxford University Press, Oxford
Kurimoto A (2013) Japan. In: Cracogna D et al (eds) International handbook of cooperative law. Springer, Berlin, pp 503–523
Schreurs-Engelaar M (1995) Organen van de coöperatie. Kluwer, Deventer
Timmerman L (2000) "Anything goed" in het rechtspersonenrecht. In: Van Dijk G, Faber D (eds) Coöperaties en nv's: fiscale rivalen? Van Gorkum, Assen, pp 21–27
van der Bijl P (2010) De coöperatie als houdstermaatschappij: houdstercoöperatie of concerncoöperatie. Ondernemingsrecht 3:130–136
van der Sangen G (1999) Rechtskarakter en financiering van de coöperatie. W.E.J. Tjeenk Willink, Deventer
van der Sangen G (2010) National report for the Netherlands. In: Cooperatives Europe, Euricse, Ekai (eds) Study on the implementation of the regulation 1435/2003 on the Statute for a European Cooperative Society (SCE), pp 779–801
van der Sangen SG (2013) The Netherlands. In: Cracogna D et al (eds) International handbook of cooperative law. Springer, Berlin, pp 541–561
van der Sangen G (2019a) The principles of European cooperative law and their impact on future law-making on cooperatives. The case of the Netherlands. Int J Coop Law II 2019:39–56
van der Sangen G (2019b) De rol van principles in het coöperatierecht. Tijdschrift Voor Ondernemingsbestuur 2019–2:36–43
Vermeulen E (2003) The evolution of legal business forms in Europe and the United States. Kluwer Law International, Deventer

Homogenization of Enterprises' Models: Waiving the Cooperative Alternative to Capitalism

Yifat Solel

1 Introduction

In Yanis Varoufakis's fictional novel, 'Another Now', he describes a parallel-post-capitalist world that was separated from this world after the 2008 financial crisis. In this 'other now,' there are no banks, no stock exchange markets, and all businesses are owned and controlled by their workers. One of the characters in the book, confronted with this alternate reality, responds by saying: "If democratic corporations, based on a one-person—one-share rule, were better in any sense, they would exist in the here and now".[1]

Though cooperatives are often overlooked by economists and by decision-makers rooted in the capitalist system, it is not out of ignorance that those words were put in this character's mouth. While cooperatives are exactly as described: democratic enterprises, based on one-person—one-vote organizations, they seem to relinquish the position of clearly suggesting a holistic alternative to the capitalist system.

In order to become a viable alternative, cooperatives must be recognized as a clearly distinct form of enterprise, a clarity that seems to be lacking and decreasing, as they are becoming very similar to capital-based[2] companies. The process, which

[1] Varoufakis 2020, p. 95.

[2] I chose to use this term to differentiate between cooperatives and capitalist forms of incorporation because the legal definition of cooperative is not the same in every country—in some, the cooperative model is covered by company laws, in others, there are specific legal form or forms for cooperatives. It is also meant for differentiating between small, local businesses, and stock exchange market-based corporations relating to the second kind. This paper does not discuss the differences within privately owned companies and it acknowledges the fact there are private businesses embedded in a community that achieves social value.

Y. Solel (✉)
Law School, Haifa University, Haifa, Israel
e-mail: yifat.solel@gmail.com

W. Tadjudje and I. Douvitsa (eds.), *Perspectives on Cooperative Law*.
https://doi.org/10.1007/978-981-19-1991-6_16

Henrÿ refers to as 'companization,' (Henrÿ 2012, 2015, 2018(1), 2018(2)) has become the default modus operandi, so that cooperatives lose their uniqueness.

The crisis of trust that surfaced with COVID-19 relates to both the political and the economic spheres, and particularly to the collaboration between governments and corporations. It has a lot to do with the exclusion of democracy from the economic sphere, the lack of transparency and the widespread belief that there is nothing capital-based companies will not do for the sake of maximizing profits. The crisis presents an opportunity to promote cooperatives as vital economic alternatives—not utopian ideas, but long-time operating, clear and distinct forms of people-based democratic organizational and incorporation models, which do not follow the logic and practice of the capital-based company but instead offer a viable economic-democratic option both for enterprises and the political-economic system. This chapter will try to outline the main reasons for companization, to discuss the threats they pose and suggest some ideas for preventing this process.

2 Homogenization Processes of Enterprises

It is safe to assume that, in general, cooperative's founders have at least some idealistic pretenses at the foundation time—it is rarely a default registration choice. While a cooperative must hold both economic and social elements,[3] its location on the spectrum between the social and the economic can be repositioned as time passes, members change, and interests alter. As a viable organization, it is affected by internal processes, financial needs, legal contexts, and economic environment.

Internal reasons for Companization

Companization may creep on a cooperative from inside—with time, changing circumstances, the second generation of members, or as it becomes a mass-membered organization without making the necessary governance adaptions.

Time, in this respect, refers not only to months and years, but to different periods in a cooperative's life and especially to a generational change. Like any business, a cooperative must remain relevant and adapt itself to changing circumstances. A cooperative, more than any other business, has to be flexible and attentive, for unlike capital-based companies, it endorses a variety of goals instead of the unitary profit maximization, and as it aims to serve the varying needs and aspirations of its members over time. The second generation of members, especially of a successful mass-membered cooperative, often takes the cooperative for granted. If it does not make efforts to revitalize the cooperative notion—democratic participation and members' involvement—it is likely to become identity-vague.

Even more than a second generation of members, a change might be brought by a second generation of cooperative's leaders. While the first generation of cooperative's leaders usually grows out of its founders, the second generation is likely to be brought

[3] Pellegrin-Rescia and Levi (2005).

from outside the cooperative and be required to have former business managerial experience. As the market is dominated by capital-based companies, it is hard to find business leaders with a cooperative background eligible to replace the founders. This phenomenon is highly underestimated—in many cases, a cooperative becomes a hybrid enterprise in practice as its leaders do not grasp the distinct rationale, or want to be assessed according to the standards of a business they have been accustomed to—mainly profit maximization.

Legal and regulatory reasons for companization

However, it is not only internal reasons that catalyze companization of cooperatives. Henrÿ attributed the companization of cooperatives mainly to "the ever more pronounced approximation of the legal features of cooperatives with those of capitalistic companies through law in the wide sense".[4] The legal structures that require cooperatives to operate along the same lines as capital-based companies may be transparent—incorporation laws that do not recognize the distinct form of cooperatives or allow the formation of so-called cooperatives without regard for cooperative values and principles—but "the alignment of cooperative law on stock company law, goes beyond introducing stock company characteristics into the cooperative laws proper. It can also be read from the, at times, indiscriminate application of other rules to cooperatives which were designed for stock companies and which contribute to shaping cooperatives as institutions and/or to defining their operations…generally we need to look at labour law, tax law, competition law…"[5] Even when a state recognizes the distinctive nature of cooperatives in an incorporation legislation, it seldom adapts other laws to meet the cooperative special features. Court decisions complete this process by making decisions applying the capital-based company rationale to cooperatives. For that matter, using the legal rationale of capital-based company shares may result in anti-cooperative court decisions, and even de-mutualization of cooperatives.[6] Applying the same rationale of antitrust laws to cooperatives might end up in determining an operation as restrictive agreement due to the assumption that monopolizing a market is bound to violate its clients' interests[7]—ignoring the absurdity of this claim when the clients are all members (or get the same terms as members) of the monopolistic cooperative.[8]

---

[4] Henrÿ (2018a, b) p. 255.

[5] Henrÿ (2012) p. 218.

[6] As the Israeli Supreme Court did in the case of the historic consumers' cooperative, deciding it is within the interests of the members to receive the real value of their historic members' shares—thus forcing the cooperative to de-mutualize. HJC 8047/98 Levit Versus The Labor Minister and others.

[7] RA(Jer) 19,545–04/10 Shovrey Bar Versus The Antitrust Authority Director.

[8] It should be mentioned, that in both cases above, the cooperatives played a dominant role in allowing the non-cooperative decision. In the consumers' cooperative case, the cooperative had distanced itself from all cooperative motives and was not even able to identify most of its current members. In the competition case, a third-layer cooperative was applying for an exclusion, based on the argument that the monopolistic cooperative allows for competition, instead of arguing that the monopolistic cooperative does not violate members and non-members' economic interests, even though there is no competition.

Cooperatives may be required to operate not only according to state laws and regulations but also according to international regulations, "Especially those elaborated by the International Accounting Standards Board (IASB), the Financial Accounting Standards Board (FASB) and the Basel Committee on Banking Supervision…"[9]. The decision to compel cooperative banks to meet the same requirements as capital-based banks after the 2008 crisis—though the 2008 crisis had clearly manifested the resilience of the cooperative model—could be considered a result of ignoring the cooperative model, but also as an informed decision to compromise the cooperative model.[10]

Standardizing the law is not a unique process developed in order to compromise cooperatives. "(t)he stock companisation of cooperatives is part of a wider process of standardising all types of enterprise on stock company criteria, i.e., not only cooperatives. In fact, it is part of a wider process of standardising laws".[11] It is an important presentation of standardizing political conception, shaping all forms to fit the same economic and political logic. The stock company is the form best-serving capitalism, it is the embodiment of the separation between economy and society, and the essence of subordinating people to economic interests; as such, the system is bound to prefer it and try to diminish all other forms of incorporation.

"Where comparative lawyers conceive these processes as standardisation, they join hands with those economists who see in law, especially in the plurality and diversity of laws, costs … to be reduced".[12] These are the same economists who identify with TINA. As there is no alternative to the capitalist system, why would there be various forms of incorporation?

3 Beware of Corporate Social Responsibility

Corporate Social Responsibility has become the new normal, "More and more enterprises are already assuming greater social responsibility".[13] Milton Friedman's saying—"There is one and only one social responsibility of business—to use its resources and engage in activities designed to increase its profits…"[14]—though still the default operation scheme, has lost its charm.

Criticism against CSR suggests its main purpose is public relations,[15] and as far as CSR reports are within the prerogative of a corporation, they can certainly be defined as nothing more than that.[16] Henrÿ suggests "The distinction will be on

[9] Henrÿ (2012) p. 218.
[10] Birchall and Hammond Ketilson (2009) pp.15–26; Cornée et al. (2018) pp. 19–21.
[11] Henrÿ (2012) p. 219.
[12] Henrÿ (2012) p. 219.
[13] Henrÿ (2015) p. 83.
[14] Friedman (1970).
[15] Shamir (2010).
[16] Bebchuk et al. 2020.

the question of whether corporate social…responsibility remains beneath the law mark—so to speak—or whether it can be formulated as legally binding obligatio in solidum and/or be part of social and societal compulsory audit, as is already the case for cooperatives",[17] and indeed CSR is gaining more and more formalist structures, although it is still mainly a self-regulating instrument. However, additional consideration is required for determining whether such a formalization is indeed a positive development, both for its practical implications—whether legal requirements will be sufficient to provide an effective appraisal of a capital-based company's conduct authentically; and from a normative perspective—whether such a formalization will have favorable outcomes.

It would be dismissive to suggest that all CSR activities of all businesses are designed only in order to enhance their public 'likeability,' but it is safe enough to claim it is the dominant motivation of capital-based companies. Motivation aside, the fact is that CSR is always an external operation for a capital-based company, since its goal is to engage a capital-based company in non-capital interests. It is highly questionable whether measuring and auditing of CSR can present an authentic picture of the company performance. It is likely that the orientation of regulations for compliance of CSR reports will be designed so as not to compromise the main interests of the companies. For example, it is safe to assume that transparency will always be subjected to commercial interests and trade secrets. Furthermore, any favorable regulation will be applied by auditing and measuring agencies—that play a major role in designing the way information is presented and decisions are formed. They draw their conclusions according to the information provided by the company and asserts, these conclusions as objective evaluation. The evaluation business is an important component in administering the whole CSR system.

As for the normative dilemma, while legal requirements may—though not necessarily—have marginal positive effects on capital-based companies' operation or on the public's ability to appreciate it, it is likely that they end up only allowing capital-based companies to claim they have met the legal obligation and thus get a seal of approval. It will also allow for the further erosion of distinctive enterprise models.

Capital based-companies—even the most social and environmentally friendly ones—will always consider CSR as external to their operation. Cooperatives, on the other hand, are committed to serving their members 'goals and aspirations' and to operate according to 'concern for the community,' so social and environmental responsibilities are in their operation's core. "…as far as social justice is concerned, cooperatives, by definition, must take into account all their members' needs. To them, social justice is not a matter of CSR or charity, but of solidarity".[18] While profit-maximization companies attempt to bridge that chasm using mechanisms liks CSR, it is inexplicable why some cooperatives decided to embrace this term and use it to describe cooperative operation.[19] When cooperatives choose to use CSR terminology, they reduce their social and environmental commitment from the core of

[17] Henrÿ (2012) p. 215.

[18] Henrÿ (2012) pp. 223–224.

[19] Tadei and Delécolle (2012); Viktoria et al. (2017).

the enterprise to a nice-to-have add-on. For profit-maximization companies to pursue CSR means they have compromised their economic interests in the name of the social or environmental goal they promote, but cooperatives reject the dichotomy and regard social and environmental goals in unison with their economic goals. Terminology matters. As cooperatives start considering their social operation in terms invented to describe non-essential-to-business activities, they are abandoning their identity and contributing to the homogenization process.

4 Globalization and Technology—Once a Threat Becoming Opportunity

Globalization had been described and conceived as a threat to cooperatives as well as to collective and workers' rights. It allowed multinational corporations to engage in market shopping, "possibility for employers to source labor virtually, new forms of labor, and the gradual confusion between capital, labor, and product…make it difficult, if not impossible, to organize labor for participatory, collective, social justice securing action expressing through labor and social protection laws, and it reduces the representativeness of organized labor".[20] I would suggest this does not necessarily need to be the case anymore. At this stage of globalization, not only it is not to be feared, it might even allow for better and closer cooperation between workers and users than ever before.

Globalization was a threat only as long as it was so complicated and expensive that it could only be used and exploited by multinational corporations. The technology developed in the past decade has brought globalization home—online commerce as well as Skype and Zoom meetings, became an easy to use, platform-based, household daily practice . "The online economy has in common many of the dangers identified in the globalization discourse: circumventing states' laws, and venue shopping—lacking proficient international political institutions capable of protecting the public from exploitative conduct. At the same time, the online economy introduces technologies that allow people to connect and promote their mutual goals and interests on the largest scale in human history".[21]

Platforms are a form of infrastructure that serves the sharing economy, as well as capital-based companies.[22] Platform economy has no intrinsic value—platforms are only platforms and as such they can be used for promoting various goals and objectives. The first platforms were created to enable the sharing of resources and connecting people and were then exploited by capital-based companies that for a while were able to introduce themselves as bearing social value only due to their use of platforms. Despite the magnitude in which capital-based companies entered the platform arena, they cannot erase the fact that "clearly self-interest and sharing go

[20] Henrÿ (2015) p. 86.

[21] Solel (2019) pp. 257–260.

[22] Benkler 2011; Belk 2013, Grassmuck 2012.

together ... the promise of the sharing economy isn't about the defeat of self-interest, it's about the alignment of self-interest and the common good".[23]

For cooperatives, platforms have become a way to reconceptualize. Since the platform economy originated in ideas of sharing and collaboration, it was a natural development for initiatives that needed to formalize their operation to choose the cooperative model—which already embeds those notions. Platform cooperativism is about structural change, a change of ownership; it is about solidarity. Platforms can be owned and operated by inventive unions, cities, and various other forms of cooperatives, everything from multi-stakeholder and worker-owned co-ops to producer-owned platform cooperatives.[24]

The term 'sharing economy' is not very different from CSR—both are used by capital-based companies in order to gain sympathy that is translated into profits. It is the democratic component—the ownership and control of users, stakeholders, members—that distinguish the cooperative model from all other forms of enterprises. The capitalist system easily accepts the sharing economy as long as its enterprises and mechanisms are charity-based and do not compromise the current order, the same way it accepts CSR as an annex to companies' main practice. The cooperative model is a game-changer because it allows accumulation of economic power in its members' hands, and encourages members to be active in decision-making processes, awakening dormant democratic capacities.

Platforms create opportunities to enhance users' democratic involvement in different aspects of their economic and social life. The technology allows direct and long-distance participation and thus can help develop—perhaps for the first time in such magnitude and scale—of a democratic economy.[25]

5 The Democratic Trust Crisis—COVID-19 as an Opportunity for Change

COVID-19 has brought to the surface a crisis of trust that has been bubbling for many years.[26] It is a dual crisis: vis à vis the political and the economic systems. More than a dual crisis, it is the public's acute distrust of the collaboration between political leaders and profit-maximization companies.

The political system excluded democracy from the economic system. The twenty-first-century's economic and political regimes were described as growing closer and closer to the nineteenth century in terms of the concentration of wealth and political power.[27] A democratic regime that relates only to the political sphere and withholds democracy from the economic sphere is suffering from a fundamental democratic

[23] Gorenflo (2012).

[24] Scholz (2017) p. 181.

[25] Solel (2019) 262.

[26] Sucher and Gupta (2019); Zuckerman 2021.

[27] Piketty (2014).

deficiency. The distrust developed with the rise of neo-liberalism, since the 1970s, and has reached historical high levels in recent years.[28] Adding to the ongoing trust crisis was the 'fake news' culture embraced by world leaders, blurring the difference between truth and lies.

COVID-19 brought the trust crisis to an extreme. The fact that the major drugs' companies developing and producing COVID-19 vaccinations were to make billions of euros in profits from selling their product,[29] profits that depend mainly on the speed of the development, affirmation, and production—caused many to doubt the reliability of the vaccines. The fact that governments funded to a great extent the research, development, and production process by offering guarantees to purchase the vaccines once they are produced—thus reducing the capital risk of the pharmaceutical companies—did not increase their reliability.[30] It has been estimated that 25% of people in France, Germany, and the USA will refuse the vaccine[31]— a vaccine for a pandemic that has already killed over 6 million people worldwide.

The trust crisis of COVID-19 is dramatically greater than the one following the 2008 crisis and it is costing people's lives. Regulation has not been enough to generate trust. The pharmaceutical companies operate according to strict regulation. It is one of the most regulated industries, companies must comply to different states' legislated rules and go through authorization and approval processes of multiple states and international organizations. All of the above has not been enough to induce trust in millions of people who chose to risk their lives by refusing to get vaccinated.

Measuring, auditing, and even public supervision have proven to be insufficient. It seems there is an urgent need for a different mode of operation. Nationalization of public interest companies will just transfer the power from one untrustful mode to another, the answer can be in cooperativization—make them become stakeholders owned, transparent, democratically controlled enterprises.

6 Could Cooperatives Become the Bearers of Change?

Are cooperative capable—systemically—to become the alternative for capitalist order? The cooperative movement was never a revolutionary one. It did aspire to change society, but usually in an unthreatening way and preferred a very wide spectrum of cooperative enterprises to a distinct organizational form and ideological perspective.

---

[28] Zuckerman 2021.

[29] The financial times, February 2, 2021.

[30] The agreements signed between governments and pharmaceutical companies in connection with the COVID-19 vaccines are puzzling. There were contradicting publications regarding the amounts paid, but it is clearly the pharmaceutical companies were based mostly on public funds and assurances and yet the agreements do not determine the price they will demand, and there are no limitations for the profits the companies will gain from selling this product that was paid by public funds (notwithstanding its public role).

[31] The Guardian, February 4, 2021.

There are many cooperatives that do presume to pave the road for changing the world, but there are many others that settle for finding a reasonable path to make a living or operate in the market within the system. [32]

The companization processes described above pose a great threat for 'the cooperative'—as a specific business model and as a concept, for they blur the differences to a point there are no clear distinctions between cooperatives and capital-based companies. This lack of clear distinction between cooperatives and capital-based companies poses a threat not only to the cooperative model but also to the potential of a viable alternative to the capitalist system.

The double system trust crisis should become the catalyst for a systemic change that will end the ostracization of democracy from the economic system and thus allow for bona fide democracy in the political system. Cooperatives are the embodiment of economic democracy and can become the building blocks of a postcapitalist society. There are cooperatives willing to raise this flag, including parts of the Platform Cooperativism movement that definitely have the aptitude, the skills, and the urge, to generate viable alternative organizational types adding up to a systemic change. The legal forms exist, the values and principles are recognized, what's left is a public will, courage and solidarity. Though it seems that the cooperative movement hasn't got the revolutionary spirit, as David Graeber put it "At times like these, any awakening of the democratic impulse can only be a revolutionary urge".[33]

References

Hansrnann H (1999) Cooperative firms in theory and practice. The Finnish J Business Econ 4:387–403

Henrÿ H (2015) Social justice through enterprises: the end of the 1972/1973 conjuncture? A Legal Persp Int J Soc Qual 5(2):81–96

Solel Y (2019) If uber were a cooperative: a democratically biased analysis of platform economy. Law Ethics Human Rights 13(2):239–262

Taddei J, Delécolle T (2012) The role of cooperatives and CSR: the case of the french agricultural sector. Int Bus Res 5(7):73

Ademilua V (2017) Cooperative societies and corporate social responsibilities (CSR) opportunities for rural developments in Africa. J Culture Soc Develop 30

Bebchuk L, Kastiel K, Tallarita R (2021) For whom corporate leaders bargain. Forthcoming, Southern California Law Rev 93

Birchall J, Hammond Ketilson L (2009) Resilience of the cooperative business model in times of crisis, International Labour Organization

Cornée S, Fattobene L, Migliorelli M (2018) An overview of cooperative banking in Europe. In: New cooperative banking in Europe

Friedman M (1970) "A friedman doctrine—the social responsibility of business is to increase its profits. The new York Times, September 13

[32] Hansmann (1999) pp. 387–403.

[33] Graeber (2014).

Gorenflo N (2012) “Researchers flub conclusions about sharers due to limited zipcar survey. Shareable: work and enterprise, July 24 https://www.shareable.net/blog/researchers-flub-conclusions-about-sharers-due-to-limited-zipcar-survey
Henrÿ H (2012) Basics and new features of cooperative law—the case of public international cooperative law and the harmonisation of cooperative laws, 17 UNIF. L. REV. 197
Henrÿ H (2018a) (1) Who makes the law? Parliaments, Governments, courts or others? social justice through cooperatives at stake. IUS dicere in a globalized World a comparative overview (1) volume one d'Alessandro CA, Marchese C (ed) Studies in law and social sciences, Roma TrePress
Henrÿ H (2018b)(2) Trends in cooperative legislation: what needs harmonizing? J Res Trade Managem Econ Developm 51(9)
Scholz T (2017) In: Uberworked and underpaid, how workers are disrupting the digital economy. vol 181
Shamir R (2010) capitalism, governance, and authority: the case of corporate social responsibility annual review of law and social science 6:531–553

A New Stage of the Macro-economic Development. Attempt to Develop a Realist-Optimist Perspective for the Cooperative Sector in Six Theses

Peter Herrmann

1 Capitalism is not Regenerating Itself, but an Endless Row of Crises with a Decreasing Breathing Space During Interim Phases

The view on capitalism is—in general throughout history and even from left critiques—by and large characterised by the supposition of a fundamental equilibrium, crises being seen as (at most) temporary deviation. One could easily suggest that there is no reason to question this—if the normal is seen in boom or bust, in both cases we find an oscillation. However, in fact, it is essential to define what 'the normal' is—with such definition as point of reference we have also an indication of the direction for moving forward.

2 There is no Capitalism—There are only Different Ways and Forms of Accumulating Capital for Private Profit, Frequently Going Hand in Hand with a Change of the Technological Basis, i.e. a Shift in the Development of the Productive Forces

Simple terms are often used as shorthand to explain more complex concepts. In the context of capitalism, the terms 'neoliberal' and 'austerity' have been used frequently. The usefulness of such terms does however depend significantly on what we seek to achieve. Problems arise through broad and inconsistence use of terms *(see, for*

P. Herrmann (✉)
Human Rights Centre, Law School of Central South University, Changsha, China
e-mail: herrmann@esosc.eu

W. Tadjudje and I. Douvitsa (eds.), *Perspectives on Cooperative Law*,
https://doi.org/10.1007/978-981-19-1991-6_17

instance, in the case of the term neoliberalism Birch, 2017*; for austerity Herrmann*, 2011*)*.

Differences between trade capitalism, industrial capitalism and global-finance capitalism are often overlooked and widely ignored despite each having very distinct societal consequences.[1] The nature of these difference, based on the driving force of the accumulation process and its specific form of defining and generating value, is the most useful for the present context. By referring to defining and generating value, we have to denote the two dimensions of value: exchange value and use value. While exchange value is the only one that is of immediate economic interests, it is dependent on use value. In fact, it is becoming a quasi-parasite of it—a relationship that most obviously is essential for capitalism but impossible under non-capitalist conditions.

We witness a major shift in this respect: while global-finance capitalism is still in full swing, it is energy depleting. It attempts to save itself by searching for new spheres of investment which are opening up in the varied fields of new technology, marked by a move from simple information technology[2] to big data and AI activities. Themselves differentiated, the most important aspect of this new capitalism is the closely linked 'business model', commonly known as sharing economy. More encompassing, we should speak of *network-share-smart service capitalism.*[3] The term 'sharing economy' is misleading because it is in the distributive and organisational sense, as well as being misleading in technical terms. Actually we find—in theory and practice—the opposite of what is at first sight suggested, dividing and distributing, distributing part of an entity. In fact and in a technical sense—as again and again also emphasised by the actors in the field—it is a matter of re-merging, i.e. an original entity that had been split and of which the parts had been violently separated from each other,[4] is now to some extent merged again and from different sides accessible and controllable; in other words, the segments are again brought together by understanding them as elementary forms.[5] This can be understood as quantum–mechanical re-figuration by which the new quality of capitalism is established, however this addresses the fact of socialisation of production in a new way, namely, by effectively acknowledging the need of some form of redistribution. So far we can summarise the 'new economy' as one standing on two pillars:

---

[1] One may consider adding something like service capitalism though this seems to be at this stage too early although it had been proposed already in the 1950s/60s. For the present context, the difference between more or less local finance capitalism remains marginal—so far, services including the coverage of the administration of financial matters—had been more or less tightly annexed to the industrial processes or, in the case of finance capitalism, they had been integral part.

[2] Which had been usually only meaningful if annexed to other activities.

[3] This cumbersome term is due to the fact that we are still witnesses of a work-in-progress model.

[4] Referring to the presentation of the overall process of production in the introduction of Marx' Grundrisse (*Marx (*1857*), pp. 17–48*).

[5] The common models of demand and supply, marginalism, etc. are not in a position to deal with the concept of elementary forms and relationality as it is closely linked.

- The first is surplus capital, the result of over-accumulation, not finding a field for 'reasonable' investment.[6] The alternative option is that of risk and/or joint venture capital investment. Being idle, excess money would mean ceasing to exist as capital—thus any kind of investment, even one that is likely to end with a loss, is chosen.
- The other concerns a technological upsurge or a technological change that has a structural effect—a difficult to decide question: where exactly is the point that allows us to speak of a qualitative leap? It is probably easy to agree upon seeing Gutenberg's printing press as a qualitative leap. But, leaving other functions aside, looking only at the 'type-writing' function, we may well suggest that today's equipment with voice input does basically the same as the person who at some stage prepared the actual printing. Such an extremely reductionist perspective is, of course, not agreeable. However, determining the exact point of a technical turn is difficult. The model which Kondratieff offered is surely of some help, if we understand it as merger and mutual supportive development of changes in four respects: the means of production, the energy source, the life regime and the mode of living. Seeing this in a regulation-theoretical perspective, we may also say that all the political economy of societies is in simple terms concerned with • the development of productive forces and thus the means we use in order to generate material value (machines, organisation of labour and its administration), • the energy source, • the regulative mechanisms, including application and distribution of time within a framework of new mechanisms of governance[7] • finally, conditions of realisation in daily life.

3 Today's Economic and Social Problems Arising from the Most Recent and Still Ongoing Shift in the Development of the Productive Forces are thus not a Matter, Taking Place After the Process of Production; Instead, we are Dealing at the Core with Matters that Need to be Addressed Ex-ante, as Part of Structuring the Productive Process Itself and Even Before that, as Part of Defining What the Productive Process Embodies

'There is only one way to see things, until someone shows us how to look at them with different eyes' (attributed to Picasso). The lack of terminological precision

[6] That is, an area, which is more or less adjunct to the existing 'core business', thus promising a perhaps moderate, though at least reasonable and reasonably secure profit rate; not voting for such conservative investment strategy are complex, encompassing, for instance, market saturation, an unfavourable outlook on the profit rate while the profit itself maybe considered being sufficient or vice versa.

[7] To be considered are the huge numbers of unemployed.

opens of course the door to confuse matters further. A broad definition of capitalism is proposed by Joe Brewer in a short piece titled This Is How Capitalism Actually Works (Brever 2016). He states: 'Here is how capitalism actually works — use a legal framework of private ownership to extract value from the labor of others. The end game is a system that hoards wealth, stifles innovation, and ultimately destroys the value created by cooperation among those who seek to do things that cannot be done alone'. Of course, at first sight such catch-all approach is agreeable—a plausible formula that gives not least also a flair of the contradictory character—and it even allows to smile at our own credulity and inadequacy, be it as customers, consumers or as workers. But agreeing on such broad approach makes us easily overlook that the ways of generating value had been decisively different over time: the classical definition that still stands at the very core today is that of the value of labour power. However, while maintaining this approach, one has to see that the variety of capitalism is surely different to that usually discussed under this title, seen in the widest possible sense as matter of political management *(see Hall and Soskice (eds.)* 2001 *and the debate on this work).* Taking capitalism seriously, we may want to look at this broad outline in order to move on to the concrete economic and legal forms this process takes. A first approach is about locating generating value in a chain of intermediation in space and/or time, linking this to the forms of property.

Thus, we are looking at two forms of appropriation, the first being the metabolism with the rest of nature, the second the appropriation of the product in terms of property. We can also interpret these with reference to four categories—these are proposed by following closely the work by Frigga Haug, who elaborates a four-in-one perspective comprising of employment, reproductive work, cultural development and politics from below *(see Haug* 2008/2009[2]*; see also Herrmann* 2012*).* Taking these four dimensions as indicators, it is suggested that we can draw a line which allows to determine congruence and discord of socialisation of production on the one hand and consumption on the other hand. Marx' wider understanding of production as social process and part of being human *(see Marx* 1857*, pp. 17–48),* not reduced on the socio-individual producer of goods or, even more limited, of commodities, is applied. Commodity production and also the politics and policies on the stages of world and national governments are complemented—seconded or counteracted—by the immediate production of the social, understood as 'an outcome of the interaction between people (constituted as actors) and their constructed and natural environment. Its subject matter refers to people's interrelated productive and reproductive relationships. In other words, the constitutive interdependency between processes of self-realisation and processes governing the formation of collective identities is a condition for the social and its progress or decline' (van der Maesen and Walker (2012), p. 260).

Accepting the validity of the two characterisations of 'man making history'—doing so under given conditions and doing so in small steps without considering or being aware of the wider context and direction—this making of history is a complex process: merging, welding together and separating by activities (action, practice, behaviour, narratives, expectations, projections …) undertaken and omitted by individuals,[8] members of classes, groups, etc. pp liquidation and creation, sublation and supersession.

4 Enhanced Social Inclusion Requires Primarily a Reintegration of Work and Life, not a Balancing Act

The crucial thesis at present is that understanding the human being as social—in the tradition, for instance, of Aristotle and Marx—requires a fundamentally different methodological approach, applying the open concepts of relationality and processuality as an ultimate step towards realising dialectical thinking. It is based on the interpretation of socialisation as process by which exclusion is increasingly overcome. In short, we may say it is about the degree of merging labour, work and action *(referring to the terms used by Hannah Arendt—see Arendt* (1958)*)*. And it is equally about overcoming the institutional drift, attributing different dimensions of activities and behaviour to separate social spaces. Common understanding of digital(isation) suggests that it is a means for establishing general connectedness—while this is a somewhat problematic understanding of the term, as in fact analogue systems are encoding information in non-quantified variables. What remains important here is that digitisation suggests that reality is ordered and presented in a way that allows structured access and establishing algorithmic-logical connections. We may say that digitisation, merged with artificial intelligence, is a paradoxical attempt to unify a segregated reality, namely, the segregation of exchange value from the complex reality of use value. It is also a matter of overcoming the individualist approach underlying the orientation on exchange value and societal orientation of use value.

[8] Even individuation is bound to the social character of human existence.

5 We Conclude that the Capitalist Formation—As an Umbrella for Different Accumulation Regimes[9]—Gained Stability by Accepting its Fundamental Disfunction, Caused by Reducing Wealth on the Production and Availability of Commodities. Economists have Hitherto only Tried to Regain a bit of Society, Extending the System of Commodification in Various Ways; the Point is to Overcome the Commodity System Itself

It is surely tempting to speak of a paradoxical attempt to reunify segments of the reality that had been torn apart. However, this denies the fact that all societal formations and constellations are relational, not least shaped by power, thus being open to permanent change—thus they are also processual. The same is—cum grano salis—true for the understanding of profit and wealth: essential here are questions concerned with determining the overall cost of generating value and the beneficiaries of profit. We may say that we find a parallel in economics and law—as much as we can speak with Rudolf von Jehring of a 'The Struggle for law' (Jhering 1879), we can also speak of a struggle for economics—not only concerning the large questions as outlined in Marx' Capital, but even more so issues on a smaller scale.

It is exactly here that cooperatives (using the term in the broadest sense) come into play—as combat organisation and also as tentative success. We can gain some new understanding by borrowing from quantum theory and its emphasis of relationality.

> *Modern physics now comes to the surprising conclusion: matter is not made up of matter! If we take matter further and further apart, hoping to find the smallest, shapeless, pure matter, there will be nothing left in the end that reminds us of matter. In the end there is no more matter, only form, shape, symmetry, relationship. This realization was and still is very confusing. If matter is not composed of matter, this means: The primacy of matter and form turns around: The primary is relation, the matter the secondary. According to the new physics, matter is a phenomenon that appears only after a certain coarsening. Matter/substance is a coagulated form. Perhaps we could also say: at the end of all the fragmentation of matter, something remains that resembles more the spiritual – holistic, open, vivid: Potentiality, the possibility of realization. Matter is the slag of this spiritual – decomposable, delimitable, determined: Reality*
>
> *(Dürr (2010[3]); translation P.H.)*

If we emphasise that it is important to acknowledge that today commodification is not limited on the production of commodities and the evocation of consumerism but equally characterising production itself, we see the centrality of decommodification as a fundamental and broad approach, emphasising that the wealth of society cannot be reduced on the availability of commodities ('matter'). Instead, the wealth consists in relationships and processes: 'potentialities, possibilities of realisation'. These are

---

[9] Or: the 'use (of) a legal framework of private ownership to extract value from the labor of others' (Brever).

by no means arbitrary. Institutions like firms, enterprises and also cooperatives can be seen as temporary reifications—the different forms, be they economic or legal are supporting or hindering the unfolding of those potentialities.

Cooperatives are forms that, if combined with digitisation and AI, are well positioned to enhance the potentialities, providing a ground on which they can be transformed into real options and realities—in fact coops specifically define what a sufficiently wide and creative understanding of digitisation and AI means and vice versa, digitisation and AI grant a huge potential to elevate the idea of cooperatives on a larger scale. A central point, and with this a major challenge for economics and jurisprudence, is given by the fact of reshuffling the elements of the process of production, namely, production in strictu sensu, consumption as productive process, distribution and exchange.

This is also the foundation for revisiting the theory of value, seeing it in a new light: the question is not anymore to shift from production to exchange as determining factors of value. Instead, we are now dealing with a different perspective, namely, the shift from simple exchange of commodities on distinct markets to a complex relationality of ownership. While the legal dimension of property and the control that is emerging from it remains central, it is suggested to enhance the view taken and develop a perspective on labour (relationships) that is going beyond a simple calculation of the invested specifically (and differently) qualified time of production.

The scope of the process of production is going far beyond the production of goods and entailing the production of living conditions and living (e.g. working conditions and satisfaction gained from work, relation to nature and its sustainability). One of the most criticised aspects of Marx' political economy—the theory of value—has to be seen as well in this light, insofar he limits the analysis apparently simply on the quantifying analysis of time as determinant of value. Furthermore, reference is made to an ideal-typical version of the capitalistic mode, making us easily forget that (a) there is not one capitalist mode only[10] and (b) even within any capitalistic mode there are other factors, essentially part of the generation of value within a society—housework, a factor still mainly on the shoulders of women, being the most pronounced one. This reference and the present formulation are important in another respect: commonly, and with some justification, we speak of housework as burden. However, in this case and in others we should not forget the other side(s), e.g. the deep satisfaction arising from care work, the creative aspect that is part of nearly any activity, the non-commodifiable aspect of social relationships even if veiled by market relationships, etc. And, while it is true that we find processes of disembedding, as outlined by Polanyi and equally 'compensating' mechanisms that provide a kind of ex-post reintegration, it is equally true that we find a double integrity of a specific kind: commodified action maintains some non-commodifiable 'meaning' and will always depend on it. At the very same time, productive economic activities depend on some form of provisions that (today) appear as matter of commodification—there are transfers in both directions without which neither society nor the productive process would exist. However, within a capitalist mode of production the relations

[10] This had been issued earlier in this contribution.

are reversed and/or confused. As much as we are witnessing the disembedding of the economy, we are also witnessing a segregation of the elements of the economic process and their reversal. In short, production in the strict sense, consumption, not least as productive process, distribution and exchange are seen not only as analytically distinct but also as quasi-independent from each other—this means that each of them constitutes a separate segment of the process of generating value. Not enough with this, the determination of value is subjectivised and shifted to the sphere of exchange: instead of seeing the cost of production as core of the determination of value, it is now the level of exchange, i.e. demand and supply are considered to be the ultimate determinants of value. While this is misleading, the grain of truth is that it considers the role of exchange as part of the process of generating value. In a nutshell, one might say that the problem of a narrowly taken traditional Marxist perspective is given by fading out those areas that are at the periphery of the productive core, whereas the radical version of marginalist theory seems to be well capable to imagine value of something that has not been produced and does possibly not even exist. The key cannot be found by striking a balance; instead, it is necessary to overcome the separation by re-defining production, seeing it as matter of processuality and relationality concerning the whole life. This had been outlined earlier, suggesting that they are characterising the cooperative sector. Here, value is not a matter of marketable commodities, produced and consumed by individuals. Instead, cooperatives can be seen as organisational form, which utilises digitisation and AI as genuinely socialising auxiliaries, means of production that foster the development of a socio-individual marginal quality rate of production, emphasising its different elements as unity.

6 Cooperatives—The Economy of Building 'Castells'[11]

At this stage, it is time to correct the heading or to be more precise. Speaking of microeconomic development means to refer to an understanding of economic processes as being concerned with daily life, looking at mechanisms of production and allocation of goods and services, but also the overall distribution of time spent for the various dimensions of life: family, peers, political activities, including community activities, caring for others and the environment. Taking such perspective, the distinction between micro- and macro-economy becomes obsolete. Furthermore, the strict separation between different 'areas of life', the distinction between work and personal life, is withering away—however, this is not meant as subordination of all activities under the requirements of employment. Instead, coops are a roof under which the different activities merge as matter of 'creative integration into the environment' by way of coordinated activity in full acknowledgement of (cap)abilities

[11] This refers to the Catalan tradition of buidling human towers (see, e.g. EL PAÍS: Los 'castells', Patrimonio de la Humanidad; https://elpais.com/cultura/2010/11/16/actualidad/1289862002_850215.html; 2021/06/13).

and needs of each individual. Taking such view, we can conclude that a new micro-/macro-economy has to be a complex network of platforms, money not replaced but strongly complemented by a new currency: data. The way, every cooperative is performing—cooperation is about the permanent coordination based on communication, and communication as exchanging information about needs, abilities and also weaknesses—is now multiplied by lifting it on the macrolevel: the said network of platforms. This allows not least approaching the division of labour in a new way: as offering multiple activities to everybody instead of restricting everybody on one and only one specialised area.

Congratulations and Two Challenges

Congratulations at the end of a contribution to a Festschrift for a colleague and friend are surely appropriate. And having great trust in the celebre Hagen Henrÿ, I dare to add two challenges, hopefully being taken up in the near future. They are here formulated as questions:

- If we see 'life-world-capitalism', i.e. the concern with the 'production of every day's life', also as recognition of the value of lives beyond being workforce, which legal provisions are needed and possible to secure that such recognition is one of taking the 'full value' of the human beings as social being, into consideration?
- If cooperatives are [cl]aiming to be concerned not with profit-making and also not with distributing profit, but with the orientation of production on more and other than profit, what are the legal provisions needed and possible to secure that the transaction costs—being a central economic reason for setting up a cooperative—are fully recognised as social and thus not only treated separately in terms of taxation (especially tax exemption) but moreover covered by the public as direct beneficiary.

Bibliography

Arendt H (1958) The human condition. In: Canovan M (ed) Introduction. The University of Chicago Press, Chicago/London

Birch K (2017) A research agenda for neoliberalism. Edward Elgar, Cheltenham/Northampton

Brever J (2016) This is how capitalism works. https://artplusmarketing.com/this-is-how-capitalism-actually-works-b2907d1b4d78; 15/09/2019

Dürr H-P (2010^{3}) Warum es ums Ganze geht. Neues Denken für eine Welt im Umbruch; Herausgegeben von Dietlind Klemm und Frauke Liesenborghs; München: oecom Verlag

Hall, Soskice (eds) (2001) Varieties of capitalism: the institutional foundations of comparative advantage. Oxford University Press, Oxford

Haug F (2008/2009^{2}) The "Four-in-One Perspective": a manifesto for a more just life. Socialism Democracy 23(1):119–123. https://doi.org/10.1080/08854300802635932; https://warwick.ac.uk/fac/arts/english/currentstudents/undergraduate/modules/fulllist/second/en229/haug_manifesto_pdf; 18/09/2019

Herrmann P (2012) Four-in-one-perspective—or one divided by four equals one. https://wp.me/p1qrWe-h9; 25/07/18

Herrmann P (2011) Background paper: austerity policies—yes, no, or where to go with it? In: Background paper to the 17th workshop on alternative economic policy in Europe [Euromemo], 16–18 September 2011. Vienna. http://www2.euromemorandum.eu/uploads/background_paper_herm ann_crisis.pdf; 12/11/2019

Marx K (1867) Capital. A critique of political economy. In: Marx K (ed) (2010) Marx&Engels. Collected works, vol 35. Capital Volume I. Lawrence&Wishart, London

Marx K (1857) Economic manuscripts of 1857–1858. (First Version of Capital). A) Introduction: I. Production, Consumption, Distribution, Exchange (Circulation); first published in the journal Die Neue Zeit, Bd. I, Nos. 23–25, 1902–03; in: Karl Marx Frederick Engels: Volume 28: Marx 1857–61; London: Lawrence & Wishart, 2010: 17–48

van der Maesen LJG, Walker A (2012) Social quality and sustainability. In: van der Maesen LJG, Walker A (eds) (2012) Social quality: from theory to indicators. Macmillan, Basingstoke, pp 250–274

von Jhering R (1879) Fifth German edition: Kocourek A (ed) The Struggle for Law, with an Introduction (trans: Lalor JJ). Callaghan & Co., Chicago

The Relationship Between State and Cooperatives in the Legislation of Uruguay—The Development of Public Policies Under the Influence of the Doctrine, Which Inspired the Promotion of Cooperatives in the Twenty-First Century

Graciela Fernández Quintas

It is a pleasure for me, as a representative of the American Continent, to humbly write a contribution to the recognition of the greatness of the theoretical reflection on the wide range of legal topics that the Dr. Hagen Henrÿ's has raised in the last decade about the organization and contents of the cooperative legal framework that nowadays can be studied thanks to the enormous amount of legal literature existing regarding the author.

But let me above all to emphasize that Dr. Hagen Henrÿ's opinions have served us as a guide to exercise the Law with a critical function, because it is one of the characteristics of this distinguished professor engaged with the dissemination of the cooperative model, implementing a scientific doctrine from a philosophical point of view when he analyzes the convergence of legal norms with the justice and the purposes of the Law.

For the reason mentioned above and within the historical context of the 25 years of the declaration of Cooperative Identity, it is duly appropriate, while preparing ourselves for the International Congress of Cooperative Law to be held in Korea Seoul at the end of this year 2021, to coordinate and compare the existing legal texts on the cooperative Law and try to investigate its historical and sociological evolution under in light of Dr. Hagen Henrÿ's guiding ideas about the legal thinking.

Dr. Hagen Henrÿ has embodied the function of creating proposals that have formed an advanced knowledge of cooperative law and his contribution influenced the formulas that the legislators have translated into most of the Latin American

G. F. Quintas (✉)
Co-operatives of the Americas, Region of the International Co-operative Alliance, San José, Costa Rica
e-mail: presidencia@aciamericas.coop

W. Tadjudje and I. Douvitsa (eds.), *Perspectives on Cooperative Law*,
https://doi.org/10.1007/978-981-19-1991-6_18

cooperative legislations: let me quote and refer specifically to the Guidelines for Cooperative legislation published in 2012.

But the major recognition we have to pay to Dr. Hagen Henrÿ's is that he clearly understood, together with leaders of the cooperative movement, the raising attention the ILO was developing towards the Cooperative Law: this fact led to the ILO's Recommendation 193 on the Promotion of Cooperatives, which represents a milestone for the cooperative Law, opening for the promotion and declarations of National Interest all countries, as well as for the implementation of public policies.

Dr. Hagen Henrÿ managed to advocate for the essential concepts that all cooperative national regulatory frameworks must contain: the translation of cooperative values and principles into legal rules, thus making structural the difference existing between the cooperatives and other kinds of companies. He did so by pounding in all his conferences, the specific characteristic of the cooperative model, namely the Democratic Participation of the members, which in the current situation also represents a key axis to achieve a Sustainable Development.

Everything he did, everything resumed above has been of greater support in the Americas region and it had a keen relevance for the development of cooperative regulatory legal frameworks especially in our country, the Oriental Republic of Uruguay.

1 The Cooperative Movement in Uruguay and the Legal Framework

Since 2008, with the approval of Law n. 18407 about the Cooperative System, Uruguay has registered a series of structural changes that have impacted the relationship between the cooperative movement and its public policy.

All these changes were based on the creation of those legal mechanisms that influence the way the processes of cooperative promotion and development are drawn up, discussed, and executed in a permanent dialogue between the government bodies and the cooperative movement.

Thus, the participation of cooperative organizations in the process of drafting public policies has become essential of this.

From its Law n° 18407 onward, the Uruguayan cooperative movement has its institutional framework strengthened. Then, with the creation of the INACOOP—National Institute of Cooperatives, made up of representatives both of the government and of the cooperative movement itself, the State begins adopting the promotion and development of cooperatives as a permanent public policy.

The Law n° 18407 also deals with the recognition of new types of cooperative, institutionalizes the cooperative act, recognizes the cooperative law, creates instruments for capitalization and access to financing, and improves its control and promotion mechanisms: in this sense, the Law 18,07 is the milestone of the national cooperative movement, over which the development of public policy stands.

In the last 10 years, Uruguay has starred in a continuous and cumulative process of changes in its legal system, creating a huge variety of legal mechanisms to address structural topics related to social and economic development: this process would not have been possible without taking into consideration the Law n. 18407 about the Cooperative System.

The changes that have taken place can be classified as follows, in three main areas: (a) labor relations, (b) access to financing, and (c) education and competitiveness.

(a) **The labor relations**

The collective bargaining system has historically been based on classical tripartite relation, where Government, employers' organizations and unions participate in the negotiation process that regulates the working conditions. The ILO in its governance structure repeats precisely this approach.

However, the tripartite approach obliges the cooperative system to accept a logic of production relations typical of the traditional capitalism. Although labor relations can be conceived as ordinary to any type of organization, it is not possible to establish as the only accepted form, which uses the hierarchy principle, either by legal mandate (in the case of the public sector) or by being the owner of capital (case of the private sector), on which the relations of production are structured.

As Mintzberg points out,[1] the plural sector, of which cooperativism is part of, has its governance based on a horizontal structure whose decision-making process is focused on the democratic participation of its members, clearly expressed in the precept of one person one vote (which identifies the cooperative democratic consciousness).

Therefore, accepting the triparte model, where a cooperative is considered as the same as either a business chamber or a trade union movement means not to recognize the cooperative identity as a model apart from the ones based either on the ownership of factors of production or on the relationship between the roles and categories of employer versus worker.

In the case of Uruguay, the cooperative movement claims to have a representative in the highest governing body of the collective bargaining system (Consejo Superior Tripartito): not in the sense of being part of any of the representations of employers or workers, but as a member that represents its own sector, outside of the classical forms on which the organizations and entities of collective bargaining system have been organized their representation and connection with the labor relations.

The first step of this cultural change in Uruguay took place with the integration of a representative of the cooperative and social economy (whose most representative entity is CUDECOOP) as a member of the Board of the National Institute of Employment and Professional Training (INEFOP), the public body in charge of the design and implementation of training policies for workers and employers at national level: although our representative has a voice but cannot vote, the State, giving us this opportunity recognized the cooperative movement as a different entity, which

[1] Mintzberg (2015), p. 34.

cannot be assimilated to other type of organization that brings together employers and workers.

(b) **Access to financing**

For the sociologist Geoffrey Ingham,[2] capitalism leans on a series of institutions providing it with a sense: the money, the commercial exchange, the company, the capital, the financial markets, and the State. At the same time—points out the author—the economic development is associated to the division of labor, the technology, the growth of the population, the property rights, among other factors: all these factors, mixed up explain the current dynamics of exchange and planning of the economic processes of states and organizations.

Let bear in mind that economic development cannot be an objective in itself; it must be directly related to a "why" determined by the idea of social justice, and for this, the participation of an organized social movement is essential when it comes to the implementation of public policies.

In this sense, we cannot ignore the importance of money in the economic processes. Concretely, we use it as a measure to quantify the success or failure of an entrepreneurial project. But the danger of this purely descriptive and quantitative vision lies in the strengthening of a discourse and a practice that separates economic relations from social relations. It means that this vision sunders the economic outside the social and measures the success or failure in the income levels of a person or a group.

Money, in its instrumental feature, has a dual nature. As a social technology, it expands the infrastructural power of society, which is the institutional capacity of a State to exercise its jurisdiction over its entire territory, being able to implement specific decisions; but some particular interests—as INGHAM affirms[3]—could be interested in getting appropriated of its collective capacity and use the money "despotically" as a means of domination. When we see in the OXFAM[4] report that only eight people "specifically eight men" have the same wealth as the poorest half of the world's population, that is, 3.6 billion people we can visualize the degree of distortion of values of coexistence and social development that we are talking about.

Therefore, the development of cooperativism in the processes of inclusion and social mobility also depends on the access to financing. This is access to money-credit, which takes the form of indebtedness—mainly banking—which has the power to finance production, consumption, but also speculation.

Under this angle Uruguay in 2014 approved the creation of its DEVELOPMENT FUND, which 2 years later, in 2016, turns into a new institutional framework, the FONDES—INACOOP, an entity led by representatives of the government, the cooperative movement, and workers buyout.

The recognition in the recent reform of the financial inclusion system of the priority in the system of withholdings on wages and pensions of certain cooperative

---

[2] Ingham (2010), p. 36.

[3] Ingham (2010), p. 42.

[4] Oxfam Report (2016).

acts is not of less importance, which determines the real possibility of financing cooperatives in the credit system, through direct collection mechanisms. Today, the movement has been discussing at the legislative level that such recognition is for all cooperative classes without exception.

Recently, with the reform of the financial inclusion system, the decision to include a certain degree of priority in the system of withholdings on wages and pensions of some cooperative sector is not of less importance, because it makes real the possibility cooperatives to get financing in the credit system, through direct collection mechanisms. Today, the movement is advocating at legislative level that such recognition has to be extended to all cooperative types and sectors.

(c) **Education and competitiveness**

Education is part of human development. But when we talk about human capital, it is associated with the factors of production and therefore with competitiveness in an economy. If the first is an end in itself, the second is an instrument at the service of another objective, which must also be associated—at least in the cooperative case—with the improvement of the values of coexistence and the generation of value not only economic, but social and cultural.

In relation to this point, Uruguay has advanced a lot: from the institutional design of programs aimed to strengthen the education to the dissemination of cooperative principles amongst the values of democratic living in a society, up to its promotion in the formal educational system until the need to get the management more democratic as a key factor for the production and competitiveness processes. In the latter case, the advocacy rose from those cooperative organizations participating in decision-making processes, namely, by the National Institute of Cooperativism (INACOOP), and the National Institute of Employment and Professional Training (INEFOP), a cooperative training program aimed at developing the competencies of the actors of the cooperative system through training and technical assistance.

As Amartya Sen[5] points out, the GDP per capita is a measure of the resources we have available to produce different living conditions for the population, but it is not a good way of evaluating human capacities to build them; and it is where public policy and the cooperative movement must engage in order to change the structural and cultural conditions that limit the cooperatives' capacity for action from their management models.

2 Conclusions

Public policy does not depend only on the Government but also on the active participation of an organized social movement, with the capacity for proposition and action.

[5] Sen (2000), p. 15.

But it also must be said that, if the process of economic growth of the cooperative movement is limited to the exclusive development of certain sectors, we would be adopting a partial and schematic vision of the movement's potential as a actor able to change the social conditions.

Intercooperation or cooperation amongst cooperative cannot be merely discursive, but has to turn into practice, especially when designing and executing programs that aims to minimize asymmetries, and enables the condition by which the wealth generated by cooperatives remains within the cooperative movement.

To do this, a set of special rules, jurisprudence, doctrine, and practices based on the principles that determine and regulate the actions of cooperative organizations and the other subjects participating into the cooperative movement are strictly necessary.

This was excellently pointed out by our honoree Dr. Hagen Henrÿ when he affirmed "*the need to emancipate cooperative law from its roots, which are the law applicable to associations and the law applicable to capital companies. That will not happen without an interest of the community of Jurists and on the adequacy of the very notion of Cooperative Law …*".[6]

References

Henrÿ H (2020) ILO COOP 100 interview. https://www.ilo.org/global/topics/cooperatives/news/WCMS_738559/lang--en/index.htm

Ingham G (2010) Capitalismo. Alianza Editorial

Mintzberg H (2015) La sociedad frente a las grandes corporaciones. La necesidad del equilibrio social. Editorial Libros de Cabecera

Oxfam Report (2016) Una economía al servicio del 1%; en www.oxfam.org (bp210-economy-one-percent-tax-havens-180116-es_0(1).pdf)

Sen A (2000) Desarrollo y libertad. Editorial Planeta

[6] Henrÿ (2020).

Cooperative Law and Sustainable Development

An Introduction to the Cooperative Law Concerning Intangible Cultural Heritage of Humanity

Santosh Kumar Padmanabhan

1 Introduction

The common goal of sustainable development has been recognized by the International Court of Justice since 1997 as a concept of public international law. A more harmonized approach by legislators as concerns cooperative law is vital, if cooperatives are to contribute to sustainable development.[1]

This paper is an introduction to the subject of the international law on intangible cultural heritage from the perspective of the inscription of the *Idea and Practice of Organizing Shared Interests in Cooperatives* in the UNESCO Representative List vide the decision[2] of the 11th session of its Intergovernmental Committee for the Safeguarding of Intangible Cultural Heritage of Humanity (ICH) in Addis Ababa, Ethiopia in the year 2016.

2 Cooperatives as Intangible Cultural Heritage

UNESCO included cooperatives to the Representative List of Intangible Cultural Heritage of Humanity based on the submission made by the German Hermann-Schulze-Delitzsch-Gesellschaft e. V. and the Friedrich-Wilhelm-Raiffeisen-Gesellschaft e. V in 2016. This marks an important turn in the history of the governing

[1] Henrÿ (2018).

[2] Decision 11.COM.

Views expressed in the paper are fully personal and not of ICA.

S. K. Padmanabhan (✉)
Director of Legislation, International Cooperative Alliance, 105 Avevue Milcamps, 1030 Brussels, Belgium
e-mail: Kumar@ica.coop

W. Tadjudje and I. Douvitsa (eds.), *Perspectives on Cooperative Law*,
https://doi.org/10.1007/978-981-19-1991-6_19

legal instrument namely, the UNESCO Convention for the Safeguarding of Intangible Cultural Heritage, 2003 (hereinafter referred to as the Convention) for, the recognition and the safeguarding of the idea and practice of cooperatives is not restricted to the people of one community or one country but extends to the practitioners of cooperation around the world and theoretically speaking, to the 3 million active cooperatives operating worldwide.

The Representative List of the Intangible Cultural Heritage of Humanity is intended to enhance the understanding as well as the awareness about cultural heritage, and to make the cultural inheritance clearly visible, and to promote a dialogue, which expresses itself with respect and attention to, cultural diversity. The key identifier of intangible cultural heritage is the test of *outstanding universal value* which UNESCO explains as "cultural and/or natural significance which is so exceptional as to transcend national boundaries and to be of common importance for present and future generations of all humanity."[3]

The Convention has evolved the 'notion of cultural heritage' and has continued to expand its scope from the original understanding in 1972, which encompassed only buildings, monuments and sites, meaning only 'tangible' cultural heritage, to its current form that represents more subtle forms of human expression in their purpose of addressing human aspirations. At the same time, the international community, through its congruence of global social, economic and cultural challenges, united in 2015 in determining 17 Sustainable Development Goals[4] or SDGs, as key to ensuring the present generation leave behind invaluable natural and human-made assets for the future generations and their prosperity. As a follow-up to the 15-year program on the 8 Millennium Development Goals[5] (MDGs) coined in the year 2000, SDGs also aim to inspire states, private sector and the civil society, to achieve relatively better standards of life, livelihoods, treatment of the environment and its constituents and human aspirations of a multi-stakeholder society grounded in peace, justice and inclusion.

3 Legal Basis

The UNESCO Convention for the Safeguarding of the Intangible Cultural Heritage, 2003[6] is the *legal basis* for understanding the scope and protections possible for cooperatives as part of the ICH.[7] The Convention binds state parties to take necessary measures to ensure the safeguarding of ICH and at the same time, identify and

---

[3] World Heritage Convention (2019).

[4] 2030 UN Agenda on Sustainable Development.

[5] United Nations Millennium Declaration.

[6] The General Conference of the United Nations Educational, Scientific and Cultural Organization at its meeting in Paris, from 29 September to 17 October 2003, at its 32nd session, adopted the Convention for the Safeguarding of the Intangible Cultural Heritage.

[7] Samanta (2014). The paper notes UNESCO undertook some measures for the protection of traditional and folk culture prior to the 2003 Convention, such as the UNESCO Collection of Traditional

define the various elements of the ICH present in their territories, with the participation of communities, groups and relevant non-governmental organizations.[8] The Convention, under Article 2 (3) defines 'Safeguarding' as "those measures aimed at ensuring the viability of the ICH, including identification, documentation, research, preservation, protection, promotion, as well as revitalization of the various aspects of such heritage."

Additionally, the two binding conventions on human rights—International Covenant on Civil and Political Rights and International Covenant on Economic, Social and Cultural Rights, 1966—also contribute to the above-mentioned legal basis and in developing the understanding of what may be included in the *international cooperative law on cultural heritage.* At the same time, the Promotion of Cooperatives Recommendation (No. 193) 2002 of the ILO, and all international legal instruments referred therein, as well as the UN Agenda 2030 on Sustainable Development, contribute centrally to developing the understanding on the cooperative law concerning cultural heritage.

The definition[9] of Intangible Cultural Heritage as per the Convention clearly implies their intergenerational aspect, and the same can be understood in the case of cooperatives in the context of '*the international cooperative movement*',[10] and the role it plays in advancing sustainable development. Thus, from a legal point of view,

---

Music of the World, the Red Book of Endangered Languages, the Living Human Treasures the Proclamation of Masterpieces of the Oral and Intangible Heritage of Humanity—all enabled the formation of the notion of intangible cultural heritage.

[8] Article 11 of the Convention, 2003.

[9] The definition of ICH as per the Article 2 of the Convention refers to those practices, representations, expressions, knowledge, skills—as well as the instruments, objects, artifacts and cultural spaces associated therewith—that communities, groups and, in some cases, individuals recognize as part of their cultural heritage. The definition goes on to explain that this intangible cultural heritage, transmitted from generation to generation, is constantly recreated by communities and groups in response to their environment, their interaction with nature and their history, and provides them with a sense of identity and continuity, thus promoting respect for cultural diversity and human creativity. The Convention considers solely such intangible cultural heritage as is compatible with existing international human rights instruments as well as with the requirements of mutual respect among communities, groups and individuals, and of sustainable development. Further, the manifestations of this 'Intangible Cultural Heritage', are given to include the following:

(a) oral traditions and expressions, including language as a vehicle of the intangible cultural heritage;
(b) performing arts;
(c) social practices, rituals and festive events;
(d) knowledge and practices concerning nature and the universe.
(e) traditional craftsmanship.

[10] New economic and social trends 1992, Paragraph 5 that invites government agencies, national organizations representing cooperatives, the specialized agencies and other organizations, especially the Committee for the Promotion and Advancement of Cooperatives, to maintain and increase their programs of support to the international cooperative movement, within existing resources;

the safeguarding of cooperative enterprise in its genuine form[11] is an issue of legal significance and warrants a careful analysis and a strategy for policy interventions by stakeholders such as the participants of the Committee on the Promotion and Advancement of Cooperatives.

The Expert Meeting[12] on the Criteria for inscription on the lists established by the 2003 Convention that took place in Paris, France in December 2005 concluded that elements proposed for inscription on the Representative List, as well as programs proposed for funding in accordance with Article 18[13] of the Convention, must meet the certain requisites including compatibility with international human rights instruments, mutual respect and sustainable development.

4 International Relevance

A key question that surfaces here is whether only the German practice of cooperation can be safeguarded under the Convention? The answer is no! Although a strict interpretation of the Convention and its operational guidelines might prima facie indicate protection for the intangible cultural heritage of the applicant state, in this case, Germany, there is ample scope for interpreting the Convention and reading it with other international legal texts directly and indirectly concerning cooperatives, as well as crucial observations made by the ICA,[14] that must allow legal minds to fruitfully explore the application of the Convention to cooperatives, globally. Instances of overlap between the cooperative ideas in the ICH space are provided in the next section.

The German Cooperative Societies Act, 1889 defined cooperatives as societies, the membership of which is not closed, which have the object to promote the economic activities of their members by means of a jointly operated enterprise. Legal definition of the term cooperative is a basic element of cooperative law, and in order to come to a clear and precise definition of the term, lawmakers have to analyze and derive

[11] See Promotion of Cooperatives Recommendation 2002, paragraph 8 (b) that urges governments to ensure that cooperatives are not set up for, or used for, non-compliance with labor law or used to establish disguised employment relationships, and combat pseudo cooperatives violating workers' rights, by ensuring that labor legislation is applied in all enterprises.

[12] Report of the Expert Committee (2005).

[13] Programs, projects and activities for the safeguarding of the intangible cultural heritage: On the basis of proposals submitted by States Parties, and in accordance with criteria to be defined by the Committee and approved by the General Assembly, the Committee shall periodically select and promote national, subregional and regional programs, projects and activities for the safeguarding of the heritage, which it considers best reflect the principles and objectives of this Convention, taking into account the special needs of developing countries.

To this end, it shall receive, examine and approve requests for international assistance from States Parties for the preparation of such proposals. The Committee shall accompany the implementation of such projects, programs and activities by disseminating best practices using means to be determined by it.

[14] 1997. Jaipur, India Ian MacPherson.

irrevocable[15] elements from the system of cooperative principles in addition to the other general rules deduced from the idea of protecting the members and business partners of such organizations. As mentioned before, the year 1995 witnessed in a sense a carefully considered proposal by the ICA, for a harmonious definition of the term cooperative, that reconciled the two different components[16] of the cooperative society—group and enterprise—with one another, and to give this organization a form that does not only correspond to the requirements determined by its double nature, but which enables it to bring about member promotion in the most effective way.

The 1995 definition of the ICA that explicitly includes the terms ‘cultural needs and aspirations’ aims not at defining the ‘perfect’ cooperative but is intended to offer a broad scope and freedom to members in how they organize their affairs.[17] The distinction between the term ‘social’ and ‘cultural’ was only slightly explored during the presentation of the Cooperative Identity Statement and was referred to, first in the context of cooperatives organized specifically among cultural groups, and thereafter in the context of the principles on Membership, Democratic Control, Education, and the Concern for Community, and in relation to role of cooperatives in employment and social integration. At this time in history, the legal protection and safeguards for the intangible cultural heritage were not as articulated as they have been since 2003.

5 Examples of Overlaps of the Cooperative Idea in the ICH Space[18]

This section enumerates five instances of UNESCO listings apart from the German one, and all were taken up in the last decade, which show the overlapping of cooperatives and ICH in the cases in these examples. The text used to describe the following are mainly from the corresponding UNESCO decision.

1. The culture of Jeju Haenyeo (women divers)—Inscribed in 2016 on the Representative List of ICH.[19] This is a tradition and practice of women divers who dive to collect shellfish in Jeju Island of the Republic of Korea. Prior to diving the

[15] Münker (1981).

[16] Münker ibid p. 25.

[17] The background paper on the ICA Statement on the Cooperative Identity presented by Prof. Ian MacPherson to the Centennial Congress of the ICA in Manchester in 1995. The 1992 book titled ‘Cooperative Values in a Changing World’ by Swedish cooperator Sven Åke Book who led an independent group of researchers in the effort, and the book Cooperative Principles: Today and Tomorrow by W.P. Watkins provided the theoretical context out of which the Statement on the Cooperative Identity was derived.

[18] Explanations to the sections are from the lists of Intangible Cultural Heritage on the website of UNESCO.

[19] 11th Session of UNESCO Intergovernmental Committee for Safeguarding Cultural Heritage (2016).

women offer prayers to Jamsugut—the goddess of the sea and while surfacing after the dive, the women make certain verbal sounds. This tradition is passed on in families and through fishery cooperatives, and this practice advances the status of women in the community and promotes environmentally friendly methods and management of fishing.

2. Ala-Kiyiz and Shyrdak, art of Kyrgyz traditional felt carpets—Inscribed in the List of ICH in Need of Urgent Protection.[20] The workers and craft-persons practicing the technique and the semantics of ornamentation, which currently is placed under a high-risk of disappearing, have organized themselves into cooperatives.
3. Traditional art of Shital Pati weaving of Sylhet in Bangladesh—Inscribed in the Representative List of ICH.[21] Weavers living in low-lying areas of greater Sylhet engage in collecting and processing green cane or Murta, and in the craft of weaving sitting and prayer mats and bed-covers. This practice tends to promote social harmony among men and women weavers of Bangladesh, and in recognition of which, the Shital Pati communities are being organized into cooperatives to ensure the craft's transmission to younger generations.
4. Artisanal processes and plant fibers techniques for talcos, crinejas and pintas weaving of the pinta'o hat in Panama—Inscribed in the Representative List of ICH.[22] Plant fibers are used to make hand-made hats by artisans who weave braids with designs. The products are worn during festivities throughout the country, and the practice of weaving the hats tends to promote solidarity among artisans and suppliers of planters, who are increasingly organized into cooperatives.
5. Argan, practices and know-how concerning the argan tree in Morocco—Inscribed in the Representative List of ICH.[23] The women in rural south-west Morocco tend to practice traditional methods to extract oil from the endemic species of the Argan tree. The cultural aspect of the process includes cultivation, extraction, developing recipes and producing value-added products, and these aspects are known to contribute to social cohesion, and in developing mutual respect among communities. A film showcasing cooperatives of women producing Argan oil has been produced in collaboration with the ICA.[24]

[20] 7th Session of UNESCO Intergovernmental Committee for Safeguarding Cultural Heritage (2012).

[21] 12th Session of UNESCO Intergovernmental Committee for Safeguarding Cultural Heritage (2017).

[22] 12th Session of UNESCO Intergovernmental Committee for Safeguarding Cultural Heritage (2017).

[23] 9th Session of UNESCO Intergovernmental Committee for Safeguarding Cultural Heritage (2014).

[24] https://aroundtheworld.coop/cooperatives-and-womens-empowerment/.

6 Safeguarding ICH by Supporting Cooperatives and Related Conclusions

The general guidance note for providing support for policy development in the field of intangible cultural heritage[25] notes that State parties to the Convention are to develop or modify ICH-related policy and legislation to help in the implementation of the Convention (Article 13). It also notes that sometimes, instead of focusing on new regulations, States could consider expanding the mandate of existing institutions and frameworks. Additionally, State parties are also obliged to report on the progress of the implementation of this Convention. Aside this, governments have been encouraged under the framework of the Convention to integrate the safeguarding into development plans and policies at all levels. This has resulted in some States like Japan, China, Georgia, Niger, develop specific policy and legislation on ICH, whereas some others like France, Morocco, Servia and Viet Nam integrate ICH in overall cultural legislation.

The approach to view the safeguarding of ICH through a cooperative sector lens, does appear new, and is an approach that the international cooperative movement could propose at appropriate levels, including at the level of the Committee of Experts on the Application of Conventions and Recommendations, the International Law Commission, and other related competent groups. The next paragraph aims to develop interim conclusion(s) based on the understanding of the cooperative enterprise idea, and the key issue of 'subject matters to be covered' arising in ICH-Policy making.[26]

The subject matter to that ICH-related policies should cover is diverse. Cooperative legislation, more often than not, tends to cover a large number of sectors and areas of enterprise where cooperatives can legally ply. Some estimates say one out of three national constitutions makes a reference to cooperatives in its text, thus guiding almost 75 countries in the world to support and nurture cooperatives. The object of legislation on cooperatives, the author would like to argue, can include or can be interpreted to include the safeguarding of various intangible cultural heritage of countries, for the first among many reasons that cooperatives carry in them inherent means of promoting and implicitly protecting the cultural needs and aspirations of members. Additionally, the consultative character of the State-cooperative relationship provides inter alia, important if not the only apparatus to stimulate a collective consciousness for identifying, recognizing and protecting ICH, through creative interpretation or/and frugal reforms to cooperative legislation. One such example is the definition of the term cooperative in legislation in Pacific Island States, which refers to the definition of cooperatives per the Cooperatives (Developing Countries) Recommendation, 1966 (No. 127)[27] that does not include the terms 'cultural needs

---

[25] https://ich.unesco.org/doc/src/Guidance_note_on_ICH_policy_advice_2018_EN.pdf.

[26] as has been cited by the UNESCO guidance notes on providing support for policy development in the field of intangible cultural heritage https://ich.unesco.org/doc/src/Guidance_note_on_ICH_policy_advice_2018_EN.pdf.

[27] https://www.ilo.org/dyn/normlex/en/f?p=1000:12100:1344122806895::NO::P12100_SHOW_TEXT:Y:

and aspirations' as is in the case of Promotion of Cooperatives Recommendation, 2002. This revision may potentially enhance the role of cooperatives, related government departments, and others in the Pacific, in identifying and recognizing their ICH where after using the cooperative idea to safeguard the same.

As mentioned at the start, this paper is a minuscule attempt to stoke ideas and thinking among legal minds to bridge, as much as possible, the legislative intent and implementation of laws aimed at safeguarding ICH and those protecting and promoting cooperatives. In conclusion of this paper, the author refers to the draft guidelines aimed at creating a supportive environment for the development of cooperatives.[28] These guidelines note the significance of cooperatives in improving lives while contributing to economic, social, cultural and political advancement of community and nation, and the major role of cooperatives in national and international affairs. They also state that the most effective organizational location for the responsible entity would be within a department already charged with broad strategic and coordinating functions, such as the office of a prime minister or president. This specific guideline appears crucial in light of the collaboration suggested for the law and policymakers on culture and, for those responsible for cooperatives in the interest of safeguarding ICH while promoting and protecting genuine cooperatives, and while implementing the global policy agenda on sustainable development, which the international cooperative movement had articulated its intention to strive toward, in the ICA resolutions of the 1992 World Cooperative Congress in Tokyo, Japan.

A simplified analysis that the author draws based on the general knowledge about historically comparable civil codes of Germany and Japan, and in light of the recently adopted and yet to be enforced cooperative law on associated work by the Japanese Diet in 2020, is that the German idea and practice of organized shared interests as a UNESCO ICH may reflect positively on the safeguarding of the Japanese cooperative idea and practice, particularly in the twenty-first century where a new legislation promoting a framework of industry and sector will be enforced at a time when the COVID-19 pandemic has substantially increased suffering among people, especially among the aged and solitary youths at physical and mental health levels.

As per these provisions of promoting the Promotion of Cooperatives Recommendation, 2002 paragraph 8 on National Policies, States have been recommended to ensure and promote the highest civil standard in management and leadership of cooperative enterprises. Notably, the application of labor legislation and International Labour Standards across sectors and across geographies within the international cooperative movement, arguably grants an immeasurable reach and legal basis for cooperatives to contribute collectively to sustainable development through interlinked focus on the seventh cooperative principle on Concern for the Community done at the international level through the sixth cooperative principle embodying inter cooperation. Cooperative laws need intercourse with other legislations through policy, and ICH is an idea for policy led legal reform in the interpretation and/or application of laws safeguarding ICH as well as those protecting the cooperative

[28] UN resolution A/56/73 E/2001/68.

idea, i.e., Act defining the term cooperative or/and cooperative identity, and operationalizing values and principles. If any, a model legislation on cooperative societies and enterprises may be justified to include provisions for the 'protection' of cooperatives, and in it, the cooperative identity, as an idea and practice recognized as an ICH, and at the same time contain enabling provisions for the law to be read in consonance with the legal framework on culture and in particular ICH.

Lastly, and most importantly, promotion of education at all appropriate levels per paragraph 8.f. includes legal education and training for members and staff, and per the language of the fifth cooperative principle, for young people and opinion leaders as well. This aspect, along with their irrevocable democratic character, provision for the creation of special funds part of which are indivisible, make genuine cooperatives pioneers in the social solidarity economy spectrum, especially the related legal spectrum! For example, Corporate Social Responsibility is, in several cases,[29] a legal obligation handed top down to the private sector, whereas common purpose funds creation and social work are commonplace in the cooperative reality. The versatility of cooperative enterprise and the diversity of sectors and areas of work it influences may enhance with legal education on cooperatives at all levels, including universities, secondary cooperatives, state departments, and international organizations and inter-agency groups.

Acknowledgments In addition, the legal safeguards guaranteed in the 2003 Convention for the Safeguarding of the Intangible Cultural Heritage of the United Nations Education, Scientific and Cultural Organization complement the aim of creating a supportive legal and policy environment for cooperatives by promoting new and strengthening existing cooperatives, organized by communities practicing and protecting traditional knowledge, unique expressions of art and performances.

Note The author is grateful to Prof. Hagen Henrÿ for his kindness in sharing his experience and wisdom with people like me across the globe.

References

1997. Jaipur, India Ian MacPherson. 'Understanding the ICA Cooperative Identity Statement'. Report of the Special Workshop on the ICA Statement on the Cooperative Identity—from Theory to practice
2030 UN Agenda on Sustainable Development. https://sdgs.un.org/2030agenda
Decision 11.COM 2. https://ich.unesco.org/en/10b-representative-list-00891
Decision 11.COM of the 11th Session of UNESCO Intergovernmental Committee for Safeguarding Cultural Heritage, 2016
Decision 7.COM of the 7th Session of UNESCO Intergovernmental Committee for Safeguarding Cultural Heritage, 2012
Decision 12.COM of the 12th Session of UNESCO Intergovernmental Committee for Safeguarding Cultural Heritage, 2017

[29] India became the first country to implement a CSR provision in the law. Amended Section 135 of Companies Act, 2013 http://www.mca.gov.in/SearchableActs/Section135.htm.

Decision 12.COM of the 12th Session of UNESCO Intergovernmental Committee for Safeguarding Cultural Heritage, 2017
Decision 9.COM of the 9th Session of UNESCO Intergovernmental Committee for Safeguarding Cultural Heritage, 2014
Henrÿ H (2018) Trends in cooperative legislation: what needs harmonizing? J Res Trade, Manag Econ Dev 5(1)
Münker Hans-H. Cooperative Principles and Cooperative Law. Marburg/Lahn 1974 Fourth Reprint 1981
Operational Guidelines for the Implementation of the World Heritage Convention. Paragraph 49 (WHC. 19/01 – 10 July 2019)
Promotion of Cooperatives Recommendation 2002 paragraph 8 (b)
Report of the Expert Committee 2005h. https://ich.unesco.org/doc/src/00035-EN.pdf
Samanta K (2014) Legal Protection of the Intangible Cultural Heritage. Societas Et Iurispriudentia 2014 II(3):79–95. Article 11 of the Convention, 2003
The role of cooperatives in the light of new economic and social trends, G.A. res. 47/90, 47 U.N. GAOR Supp. (No. 49) at 171, U.N. Doc. A/47/49 (1992)
UN A/Res/55/2 on United Nations Millennium Declaration. https://undocs.org/A/RES/55/2
UN resolution A/56/73 E/2001/68 https://www.un.org/esa/socdev/social/documents/AnnexE200168.pdf

Concern for Community: Contributions of the Cooperatives and *Fraternité* to Sustainable Development

Tapani Köppä

1 Introduction

The slogan of the French Revolution *liberté, egalité, fraternité* has been shared worldwide. In France, the slogan has been included in the constitution of the republic. The slogan *fraternité* has been connected with the cooperative values of the cooperative movement, *mutual self-help, self-responsibility, democracy, equality, equity, and solidarity*. The statement of the identity of cooperatives by International Cooperative Alliance (ICA) includes concern for community as the seventh principle of cooperatives. International Labour Organisation (ILO) has elaborated this statement to serve the implementation of national cooperative laws on coordinated international ground. The concern for community gives cooperative societies an asset to participate in community development activities, according to the interests of the members. Cooperatives as legal actors are already partners in several activities of UN Sustainable Development Goals programmes (MacPherson 1996; ILO 2002).

Notes on the past are presented in the following chapters of this article, concerning the role of solidarity and *fraternité* in the mainstream economic development (fossil age, welfare state, market economy). Ecologically, economically and socially sustainable targets are referred as increasing common interests of the international community (UN) and global development of the market economy recently. The sustainable future, combining private and common interests, is expected to rely more on a holistic emphasis on well-being than on sectoral profitability, diversity of viable communities before the dominance of "conqueror species" and cooperation applied side by side with fair competition. More emphasis will be given to the values of *fraternité* and solidarity, too.

T. Köppä (✉)
University of Helsinki Ruralia Institute, Helsinki, Finland
e-mail: tapani.koppa@helsinki.fi

W. Tadjudje and I. Douvitsa (eds.), *Perspectives on Cooperative Law*,
https://doi.org/10.1007/978-981-19-1991-6_20

2 Fossil Economy and Its Heirs: Outdated Manuscript?

The Age of Great Discoveries with the slave trade and inventions like gunpowder gave Western powers fresh impetus to conquer the world from the 15th hundreds onwards. The invention of the steam engine in 1769 became a starting signal for innovations leading the whole world into the age of the fossil economy during the following one quarter of a millennium.

Liberalism and socialism were heirs of the French Revolution, inspired by the slogans *liberté, egalité, fraternité*. As grand narratives of the industrial age, these three slogans also shared actually the same belief in the never-ending richness of natural resources to be used for the insatiable needs of humankind. Both were also optimistic concerning technological development as a solution to both ecological problems, economic growth and the welfare of the people. The difference between these ideologies concerned ownership: liberalism preached private property combined with free competition in the markets, while socialism favoured common ownership of the means of production and spoke for public control of capital and markets.

Inspired by the third revolutionary slogan, *fraternité*, experiments of societies based on solidarity were also organised early by anarchistic communists or utopian socialists as communes of equal and free individuals striving for peaceful and cooperative societies. In the middle of the nineteenth century, the first modern cooperatives were established as economic organisations based on voluntary membership with equal voting rights, mutual self-help and fair return of surplus.

The historical struggle between socialism and capitalism came to its worldwide culminations point during the Cold War and ended with the collapse of the Soviet Union. Liberalism took hegemonic role as an economic policy doctrine strengthening illusions of continuous economic growth. As a consequence of economic globalisation, the world economy has become dominated by the values and role models of economic profit-making. Economic growth has become an absolute value while striving for that goal: "the economic imperium of the world markets has destroyed the specific value systems putting material goods, cultural creations and natural landscapes on the same level" (Guattari 2000, 9–13). Felix Guattari strongly criticises the one-dimensional world view of economics and its hegemony, because it subordinates human, social and ecological values to instruments of economic profit-seeking.

3 Welfare State and Solidarity

The role of solidarity was important in the building phase of welfare state. In Finland, e.g. free public primary education and health care centres were built as universal nationwide services during 1960s. Later development of the welfare state has lost something from its shared will of care-taking towards more factional lobbying of benefits according to earned benefits. Cuts of social expenditures and outsourcing of public services have used to be carried out following trendy cost-efficiency models of the new public management, borrowed as an organisational isomorphism from business world.

Markku Lehto, former chief secretary of the Finnish Ministry of Social and Health Affairs, argued that f*raternité* has not been an issue of priority between dualistic public–private debates in welfare policy programmes. He refers to the funding crises of the welfare and social security policies caused by the increasing risks of the present development. According to Lehto, acceptance of more moderate lifestyles is needed to save our common tax revenues. This means rethinking, e.g., earned social benefits, applied by consensus to expand the welfare state in the name of equality. Reductions are impossible, however, if there is not enough solidarity and instead the cake is shared by first-hand rights. There are signs among the wealthiest people in Finland of increasing hostility to accepting social benefits, based on their belief that poverty as well as success is only dependent on personal will and talents (Kantola and Kuusela 2020). Solidarity is needed to solve urgent global problems, too. However, global solidarity is weak, because international competition means a temptation to compromise the targets of the common good. States fall for the race towards the bottom, blowing a hole in the original purpose. (Lehto 2018; Katajavuori 2018, 380).

Globalisation has raised challenges connected with the future of the welfare state. Financial markets have grown disproportionately compared with the real economy, causing instability and rising indebtedness in the world economy. The wealth of the richest 1% exceeds the wealth of the remaining 6.9 milliard people, while the national budgets get short to fund the increasing needs of social and health expenditures (Oxfam International 2021; Inequality.org 2021). Simultaneously, revolutionary changes in technology closed factories down resulting in severe unemployment. Production may be continued somewhere else on the globe, with lower working costs and fewer taxes.

Markets are running according to the capitalistic doctrine of a profit-seeking perpetuum mobile, called *creative destruction*. The concept was introduced by Joseph Schumpeter, describing the gusty breakthrough of new technologies substituting old fashioned practices by a new, entrepreneurship-based growth (Schumpeter 1934). Costs grow, however, if measured by social and health indexes. Technological innovations move faster than communities with human relations, local dependencies or cultural meanings (Köppä 2015, 74–75, 2019, 43–44).

4 Rehabilitating *Fraternité* and the Ability to Cooperate

Beyond COVID-19 and experiences of recent global economic crises, there might now be the right time to turn back, learn win–win skills and re-vitalise our forgotten know-how, experiences and competencies to co-operate. This theme has been a concern of fertile studies in, e.g., evolution biology, psychology, anthropology and history. Wilhelm Kaltenborn summarises the idea and concrete forms of cooperatives covering the history of human societies with the conclusion that cooperation has always been the necessary condition of survival for mankind, and cooperation still belongs to the future existence of human societies at least as much as competition (Kaltenborn 2016; Wright 1999; Ostrom 1996; Polanyi 2001; Köppä 2012, 25–26).

According to Frans Timmermans, Vice-Chair of the Commission of EU, international atmosphäre in politics as well as in market economy has become antagonistic. He wants to remind Europeans, how French author Victor Hugo saw the three levels of the basic values: *liberté*—it is justice, *egalité*—it is action and *fraternité* meaning solidarity—it is responsibility. If solidarity cannot be realised, both freedom and equality remain death letters (Timmermans 2016). Freedom without solidarity leads to the notion that might is right: "those with the longest teeth, are followed like in a herd of wolves", said Yrjö Kallinen, Finnish philosopher and legendary preacher of ideas on cooperation (Salminen 2011; Köppä 2015, 75). Equality without solidarity means the tyranny of the masses.

The evolution of the human species is not solely based on individual instincts and egoism, but on collective relationships and cooperation. There is a risk to be drawn into destructive crises, if learning win–win games peacefully fails (Wright 1999; Harari 2016). The new paradigm following the age of fossil economy will be built with international consciousness taking into consideration the global climate crisis and the necessity of learning more sustainable ways of life ecologically, economically and socially. For all these reasons, the third slogan of the French Revolution, *fraternité*, has to be placed high on the agenda of legislative reforms dealing with market economy, competition and company laws.

5 Our Common Planet

On the highest international policy level, political decision-makers have found common understanding of fighting global warming and accepted to work together for more sustainable ecological, economic and social development. Solidarity, *fraternité,* has been recognised and might have been accentuated during COVID-19, requiring joint activities to prevent the pandemic, too.

- In the 1970s, the Club of Rome published *Limits to Growth*, a report warning of the contradiction between population growth and the shortage of non-renewal material resources around the globe (Meadows et al. 1972).
- In 1987, the United Nations commission led by Prime Minister Gro Harlem Brundtland published its report *Our Common Future.* Its aim was to arouse international consciousness to strive towards sustainable development, safeguarding both economic growth and its just distribution as well as ecological survival of the earth for future generations (The World Commission on Environment and Development 1987).
- In 2015, the United Nations agreed on *The Sustainable Development Goals*, a blueprint to achieve a better and more sustainable future for mankind. They addressed the global challenges we face, including poverty, inequality, climate

change, environmental degradation, and peace and justice. Special attention has been devoted to the prevention of climate warming (UN SDG 2021).
- The United Nations Framework Convention on Climate Change (UNFCCC), agreed in 1992, is the main international treaty on fighting climate change. Its objective is to prevent dangerous man-made interference with the global climate system. The Paris Agreement adopted by all UNFCCC Parties in December 2015 is the first-ever universal, legally binding global climate agreement (UN Climate 2021).

International cooperation between governments will become more and more important during the implementation of the UN programmes of sustainable development and climate agreement. What happens in the market economy will be decisive to turn the course. Eyes have already turned from the age of fossil economy towards bioeconomy and recycling. Digitalisation with AI (artificial intelligence) has been seen as a new generator of economic growth. Meanwhile, the policy of creative destruction has gained support from those believing in the invisible hand of free competition as the key to economic life to solve the problems ahead.

Compared with the evolution of the fossil age to conquer the world by fighting and competing, human mankind needs today a common understanding of the necessity to cooperate. It means rediscovering *fraternité,* solidarity. This means a need to turn the market economy consciously towards changes challenging the narrow concept of economy as merely profit-seeking. According to critics like Polanyi and Guattari, the one-dimensional view of the "market society" or "economic imperium" subordinated ecological as well as social and cultural values to economics. As long as the market economy is only understood as a profit-seeking instrument for investors, common benefits are exposed to become excluded as unwanted meanings that do not concern business life. The consequences might be fatally transferred to the extreme separation of the elite and masses in the future dystopia ruled by AI technology and "Homo Deus" (Harari 2016).

6 Cooperatives for Sustainability

Assisting cooperatives has long been on the agenda of the UN and several of its member organisations. The Committee for the Promotion and Advancement of Cooperatives (COPAC) is a contact forum for the International Cooperative Alliance (ICA), the UN Department of Economic and Social Affairs (DESA), the International Labour Organisation (ILO), the Food and Agriculture Organisation of the United Nations (FAO) and the World Farmers´ Organisation (WFO). These are information channels for dispersing cooperative know-how, concrete experiences and advice worldwide. Attention given by the UN and its member organisations to further cooperatives as useful instruments to solve socioeconomic problems should be transferred to the needs of the sustainable development and climate change agreements (COPAC 2021).

The ILO Recommendation Nr 193 on cooperatives (ILO 2002) has given the most valuable contribution to the recognition of cooperative ideas, practices and legal meaning worldwide. It is reasonable to argue that there are good reasons to reassess the business laws in general if the UN goals for sustainability are taken for granted. Acts to be implemented are agreed, and they are ready to be raised on the agenda of legislation internationally and nationally (Henrÿ 2003, 2019).

Mainstream business laws follow investor ownership laws, reinforcing profit as the purpose of the firm. This means that principles established in and for the fossil economy age of continuous growth are still accepted as valid. The system is changing, however, meaning a serious need to reassess the old rules. Global agreements emphasise solidarity and common responsibility to save the globe from overuse and exploiting scarce common resources for private use, not to mention business profit. Therefore, the business laws should be revised in favour of recognising the meaning of economic activities (Sjåfjell et al. 2019). This means the need of reconciling private interests of business life with common goals.

7 Diversity Map of Socioeconomic Markets

The form of enterprise matters if the viability of communities and local economies are included in the aims of the economy at large. The repeated crises of the capital-driven market economy have led to a critical deepening and culmination of socioeconomic problems overall, waiting for the turn of the course towards more just contents and solidarity-based forms of the economic system.

Economic activities can be divided into profit, non-profit and not-for-profit types of organisations. For-profit organisations can be either private or public. It is difficult to include all economic activities to be compared according to similar criteria and the same schedule, of course. In spite of that, Matrix 1 is built to categorise different kinds of undertakings according to their inclination to behave in striving for private or common interests. Actor cases are placed in the matrix according to their intensity to concern for private interests and shared community interests, respectively.

Matrix 1 describes different types of economic undertakings. Some of them are usually included in the market economy, like corporations, family enterprises, cooperatives and mutual companies. There may also be undertakings like associations, foundations and voluntary groups as representatives of the so-called social economy. Particularly interesting models of cooperation and co-ownership are traditional forms, still existing as informal practices in our modern world, like the Finnish "work parties", *talkoot*, and varieties of the *Commons* as historical examples of people´s rights to use together, e.g. common land or water areas (e.g. Ostrom 1996). The idea of commons has been applied to innovative uses both as face-to-face activities and in the internet recently (see e.g. Bollier 2021; Paterson 2010). Public organisations are not directly placed on the map, but they are players of the game, too, and it is important to take their role into account. The future role of the state and local public

Matrix 1 Socioeconomic scaling of undertakings (e.g. energy, manufacturing, traffic, housing, food, banking and finances, …)

Concern for Private Profit ***Independence, flexibility, private wealth,*** **etc**	***Concern for Community Benefits*** ***Taking care of people and ecology, collective facilities, joint skills, trust and belongingness, community wealth,*** **etc**		
	High	*Middle*	*Low*
High	Employee ownership, corporate responsibility, "corporate citizens"	Family ownership of for-profit companies, employee ownership with user stakeholders "corporate citizens"	Capitalistic investor–ownership, for-profit stock market firms
Middle	Social entrepreneurship **Social Economy**	Cooperatives, mutual **Social Economy**	Markets of "ego-stories" as types of self-employment
Low	Foundations, non-profit charity associations, **Social Economy**	Voluntary work/inputs for community, **Social Economy**	**Exclusion:** Failures of private, as well as community concerns

authorities in the future would be important as a coordinator of bottom-up initiatives, anchor organisations and their networks as concern for community activities.

The matrix can be filled by the branches of the economy. Taking climate change and sustainable development into account, most relevant branches of economy are energy, manufacturing industries, traffic, housing and agro alimentary industries. Processes of all these cover raw-material accession, the processing of commodities, delivering and waste management. Changes towards sustainability also concern directly or indirectly the financial sector, social and health services institutions, and media and education. Unravelling of the impacts of the concern for community helps to gain a more holistic view of the economic system and its actors as subjects of the changing processes. Putting more weight on concern for community and less on private interests could most probably mean that the social and ecological impacts of economic activities could become recognised according to their meaning in and for the collective life and the environment. Concerning market regulation, there is still one serious problem connected with the relationships between business and public decision-making, namely, corruption. Is it possible, that common aims meant to fight, e.g. climate warming or sustainable development, could be better guarded against corruption in a decentralised, bottom-up system than centralised top-down system? How to avoid this problem by legislative means, defending community spirit against private greed?

Moving in the matrix from the box down left to the box upright, the interest of the actor shifts from community benefit to private gain. In the middle, the balance has been established with private and common interests. In practice, there may be changes of interest weights inside the boxes, as well as shifts from one to another box. For example, a cooperative retail trade shop or a mutual insurance company may be turned into a limited company, meaning abandoning care taking of the mutual interests of the members and giving more say to outside investor interests. This is called de-mutualisation. Or it is possible, and indeed happens in reality, that a private profit firm or investor owner of a capitalistic stock market firm makes a donation for some non-profit charity organisation. A family-owned SME may become employee-owned because of the lack of owner´s family members to continue. Connected with the framework of this article, i.e. moving together towards global sustainability, shifts from boxes on the right side towards boxes on the left would be welcome as signs of an increasing awareness of a common destiny and learning solidarity.

The diversity maps can be composed of information based on existing entities, villages, municipalities or platforms created in the Internet. Gathered data could be used as a development toolkit for the communities or particular undertakings. Contacts with other undertakings could be established, and common interests mapped. Local business development offices could become involved as links between undertakings and potential customers, subcontractors, etc. This is not a new matter. There are community development agents and statistical data available for relevant local units, such as geographical information statistics in Finland. Use of the toolkit encourages entrepreneurs to look for win–win solutions together, especially concerning the viability of the community as a shared interest (Köppä 2005, 168–172). Interaction between civil society actors, private and public organisations also create local awareness and help to give priority to local work, services and partnerships.

Recognised by UN sustainable goals and climate agreements, the planet cannot be run by the growing fossil economy as before. There is a striking contradiction between the common consciousness of the shared responsibility of the governments and the capitalistic market economy as a profit maximising *perpetuum mobile*. Instead of intensified competition of scarce resources and belief in technological progress with creative destruction, it is time to integrate the market economy more closely with the universal global goals of ecological, economical and social sustainability. It's time for win–win games in the market economy, too.

In its present form and composition, the market economy is deeply biased towards private profit incentives, leaving shared common benefits aside. This makes the sense and target of economic undertakings unsatisfactory to meet the needs of the sustainable future. Even among influential economic circles, worries about the mental climate of competition-driven markets have got louder coinciding with the climate warming on the planet. There are private family entrepreneurs who are not satisfied with the business law merely as a means to bring profit to their business activities. They want to have some meaning for their work and aims, not only money.

The social economy is a concept referring to cooperatives, mutuals, economic associations and foundations. There are among them non-profit charities and volunteer organisations as well as special limited companies, too. In the diversity map, undertakings belonging to social economy are dispersed in several boxes. Common to all of them is their primary aim and purpose to provide services and help to users, not investors.

There are real as well as virtual platforms including market innovations based on shared ownership and replacing private profits with common benefits. Economic evolution of the digital age cannot be based on the skewed concept of *homo oeconomicus*. In the name of solidarity, a less competitive profit maximiser model of man is needed, able and willing to share the targets with his sister and brother citizens towards a common good and human progress.

There is one box left in the diversity map that still deserves attention, namely exclusion. This box, placed right down in Matrix 1, gathers actors that fail to succeed or find their place in the community. Looking at the reasons for the failure turns one´s attention to the system. Could this residual box show us the key to repair the system? I guess, yes. The answer is round the next corner. It is a *universal basic income* (UBI; see see e.g. Van Parijs and Vanderborght 2017; Bregman 2014). There is raising awareness around the globe right now concerning this radical proposal to reform social policy. This is, however, not the place to introduce it (The UBI) here. It is important to illustrate its potentiality. It is also relevant to complain that the reform would touch not only those placed in this box but also everybody else. It would give people freedom to do something meaningful, participate in something interesting, and feel they are worth being trusted. Some years ago, I asked young students in a survey interview what they thought about the effects of basic income. They expected to become involved in cooperatives, taking care of the environment, doing some charity in the neighbourhood or abroad, or starting entrepreneurship. With less bureaucracy and less calculation, basic income would catalyse people to realise concrete utopias together, and be concerned about themselves, their fellow creatures and communities. Rebuilding a sustainable world cannot be based on freedom of maximum profit cumulation and equal participation to exploit the planet and human minds. Without *fraternité,* learning new win–win solutions cannot be realised.

8 Conclusion

The idea of a more cooperative world is a realistic and up-to-date possibility. The end of the age of fossil economy waits around the corner, and the transition towards a new era of bioeconomy with recycling and large-scale utilisation of AI (artificial intelligence) and digital platforms is developed furiously. The contract of market economy and welfare state is in transition, too. Markets are, however, still running according to the hegemony of the company law, based on profit-making as the purpose of the firm. The model is emphasised throughout education and mass media as the only one of reaching economic competitiveness. At the same time, on the contrary, UN works to fight climate warming and to further sustainable development goals based on unanimous agreements of the governments (UN Climate 2021; UN SDG 2021).

In the future, private profit and common benefits are no more a question of either or, but both and. Concern for community means counterweight to private profit-seeking as the only mission of the enterprise irrespective of the meaning and context.

Combining concern for community with private profit can be realised in diverse ways, like the diversity matrix of this text. Like biodiversity in the nature, diversity of human ecosystems is essential during systemic changes. On the threshold of the future, market economy needs more emphasis on furthering the collective interests of the people in a spirit of *fraternité.*

In the future, values of solidarity and *fraternité*, connected with sustainability are widely shared and rewarded compared with individualistic-egoistic ideals of the life in fossil age societies. Instead of centralised decision-making, the sharing of common interests needs more dispersed action plans of industrial and economic policy. Development based on bottom-up initiatives and horizontal cooperation means a shift from private profit-making towards taking care of the concern for community. Learning new cooperative win–win solutions combined with diffusion of technological innovations is emphasised during the transition from the fossil age to a new era of renewable energy, digitalisation and AI systems. Diversity of the market economy gets empowerment by various forms of voluntary economic cooperation meaning cooperatives, social enterprises, public–private partnerships, and local as well as virtual platform networks. Practices of *commons* as take-overs of people to use public places and virtual spaces for common uses are revived as reconstructions of ancient predecessors of our cooperative future.

References

Bregman RC (2014) Free money for everyone, and five big ideas that can change the world. De Correspondent, Amsterdam

COPAC (2021) http://www.copac.coop

David B (2021) News and perspectives on the commons. http://www.bollier.org/

Guattari F (2000) The three ecologies. Translated by Ian Pindar. The Athlone Press, London and New Brunswick, NJ

Harari YN (2016) Homo Deus. A Brief History of Tomorrow. Vintage. Penguin Random House, London

Henrÿ H (2003) Co-operative legislation and values worldwide. Trends in co-operative legislation worldwide. In: Köppä T (ed) Osuustoiminnan lainsäädäntö, arvot ja kansainvälinen solidaarisuus. Osuustoiminnan vuosikirja 2001–2003.Taloudellisen yhteistyön ja osuustoiminnan tutkimuksen seura Kooperatiivi ry, Helsingin yliopiston Maaseudun tutkimus- ja koulutuskeskus, Mikkeli

Henrÿ H (2019) Friedrich Wilhelm Raiffeisen and Cooperative Law, Chapter 17). In: Henrÿ H (ed) Reiffeisen Today. An excerpt from the lively exchange of the IRU members. International Raiffeisen Union e.V. Bonn

ILO (2002) ILO NORMLEX Information System on International Labour Standards, R193—Promotion of Cooperatives Recommendation, 2002 (No. 193). https://www.ilo.org/dyn/normlex/en/f?p=NORMLEXPUB:12100:0::NO::P12100_ILO_CODE:R193

Inequality.org (2021) https://inequality.org/facts/global-inequality/#global-wealth-inequality

Kaltenborn W (2016) Illusion and reality. The cooperative idea: a constant companion throughout the history of mankind. Zentralkonsum eG and Books on Demand GmbH, Berlin and Norderstedt

Kantola A, Kuusela H (2020) Huipputuloiset. Suomen rikkain promille. Vastapaino. Tampere

Köppä T (2005) Globalisation of cooperative movement. In: Gangopadhyay P, Chatterji M (ed) Economics of globalisation. Foreward by Kenneth J. Arrow; Preface by Jeffrey Sachs. Ashgate, England and USA, pp 163–177

Köppä T (2012) Co-operative entrepreneurship and the new humanism. In Heiskanen J, Henrÿ H, Hytinkoski P, Köppä T (ed) New opportunities for co-operatives: new opportunities for people. Proceedings of the 2011 ICA Global research conference, 24–27 Aug 2011, Mikkeli, Finland. University of Helsinki Ruralia-institute

Köppä T (2015) Towards a renaissance of co-operativism or back to the beast capitalism? In: Laurinkari J, Unger F (eds) Justice and solidarity: the European utopia in a globalising era. Symposium in Kuopio. 2.-3.9.2014. European Academy of Sciences and Arts. Grano, Kuopio

Köppä T (2019) How to produce and share common humanistic values. Digitalisation and recognition of the social meaning of economic relationships. In: Laurinkari J, Unger F, Tefner Z (eds) Revisiting values and rights in a digitalising world. International symposium 18.09.2018 in Helsinki. European Academy of Sciences and Arts. Vienna Academic Press Verlag GmbH. Bad Vöslau, Österreich. https://www.euro-acad.eu/library?id=20

Katajavuori M (2018) Kuoleman ja elämän kysymys. Miten yksilöt, lajit ja yhteiskunnat altistavat itsensä tuholle. Atena Kustannus Oy

Lehto M (2018) Artikkeli. In: Kanava 7/2018. Otavamedia

Meadows DH, Meadows DL, Randers J, Behrens III WW (1972) A report for The Club of Rome´s Project on the Predicament of Mankind. New York 1972. https://www.clubofrome.org/publication/the-limits-to-growth/

Ostrom E (1996) Crossing the great divide: co-production, synergy & development. World Dev 24(6):1073–1087

Oxfam International (2021): https://www.oxfam.org/en/what-we-do/issues/extreme-inequality-and-essential-services

Paterson A (2010) Rural cooperation and the online swarm. article: a buzz between rural cooperation and the online swarm. In: Paterson AG (ed) Special Issue: Affinities Journal, vol 4, no 1: The new cooperativism. https://wiki.p2pfoundation.net/Rural_Cooperation_and_the_Online_Swarm

Polanyi K (2001) The great transformation: the political and economic origins of our time, 2nd edn. Foreword by Joseph E. Stiglitz. Beacon Press, Boston

Salminen M (2011) Yrjö Kallisen elämä ja totuus. (The Life and Truth of Yrjö Kallinen). Into

Schumpeter JA (1934) The theory of economic development, 1983rd edn. Transaction Publishers, London

Sjåfjell B, Mähönen J, Taylor MB et al (2019) Supporting the transition to sustainability: SMART reform proposals. University of Oslo Faculty of Law Research Paper No. 2019-63. Nordic & European Company Law Working Paper No. 20-05

The World Commission on Environment and Development (1987) Our common future. Oxford University Press

Timmermans F (2016) Fraternité. Retisser nos liens. Editions Philippe Ray

United Nations Framework Convention on Climate UN Climate Climate Change (2021). https://unfccc.int

UN SDG (2021) United Nations Sustainable Development Goals https://www.un.org/sustainabledevelopment/

Van Parijs P, Vanderborght Y (2017) Basic income: a radical proposal for a free society and a Sane Economy. Harvard University Press

Wright R (1999) Nonzero: the logic of human destiny. In: Pantheon Books. (The New York Times Book Review Notable Book in the year 2000)

Cooperative Governance and Sustainability: An Analysis According to New Trends in European Cooperative Law

Deolinda Meira

1 Introduction

António Sérgio, a Portuguese thinker, educator and politician, described cooperativism as "a movement of moral ascension and social reform, which serves as an instrument to the economic needs of men".[1] In his statement, António Sérgio summarizes the specificities of the cooperative phenomenon, namely, that it has always combined strong social and economic dimensions, which translate into the satisfaction of the interests of its members. There are many challenges facing cooperatives today, including holding on to the cooperative identity, competing with profit-making entities in an open economy and achieving sustainability. This paper will focus on this last challenge.

The theme connecting "cooperative" and "sustainability" in the global context and the current deep crisis in terms of sustainability can be found, in the words of Rui Namorado, "in the intimate tension between pragmatism that everyday business requires, and the utopian dimension that a persistent struggle for a better world is not exempt".[2] The cooperative, by virtue of its civic vocation, democratic character and participatory and supportive virtues, is a vehicle that can drive the demand for a different world. While today's search for sustainability is not exclusively the prerogative of cooperatives, the cooperative is sustainable and is driving sustainable development. The cooperative DNA is based on its own rationality, principles,

[1] Sérgio (1958), p. 235.

[2] Namorado (2005), p. 154.

[3] See Henrÿ (2012), p. 16 ff.

Present Address:
D. Meira (✉)
CEOS/ISCAP/Polytechnic of Oporto, Rua Jaime Lopes Amorim, S/N, 4465-004 São Mamede de Infesta, Portugal
e-mail: meira@iscap.ipp.pt

W. Tadjudje and I. Douvitsa (eds.), *Perspectives on Cooperative Law*,
https://doi.org/10.1007/978-981-19-1991-6_21

structural features and normative and ethical references that are consistent with the concept of sustainability.[3]

The pursuit of sustainable development by cooperatives has a solid tradition that is not the result of current fashion, but was born from the specificities of the cooperative phenomenon, combining a strongly social aspect with an economic one, translating into the satisfaction of the interests of its members. In 1935, George Fauquet emphasized this dual aspect of cooperatives, stating "It must be distinguished in the cooperative institution, a social dimension and an economic one, since it is: (1) An association of people who recognize, on the one hand, the similarity of certain needs and, on the other hand, the possibility of meeting them better through a joint venture than individually; (2) A joint venture whose particular goal responds precisely to the needs to be met".[4]

International institutions are recognizing the important role of cooperatives in economic, social, cultural and environmental development. Cooperatives are fuelling employment, mobilizing human resources, increasing social participation and a more equitable distribution of the benefits of globalization. In doing so, they are contributing to sustainable human development and combating social exclusion. The International Labour Organization's (ILO's) report "Cooperatives and the Sustainable Development Goals: A contribution to the 2030 Agenda for Sustainable Development" highlights that "Cooperatives are sustainable enterprises that are owned and run by their membership, and are built on values that encourage cooperation, empowerment and solidarity, rather than just profits".[5] In the same vein, the International Cooperative Alliance's (ICA's) "Blueprint for a Cooperative Decade" states that "Collectively members own their cooperative, and through democratic arrangements they participate in its governance. Individually they have a right to information, a voice, and representation". [6] Finally, the United Nations recognizes the role of cooperatives in the realization of the Sustainable Development Goals by including cooperatives in its indicators, targets and funding mechanisms.[7]

Cooperatives are best described as organizations of an atypical entrepreneurial nature. This atypicality is evidenced by: the primacy of social objectives over a return on capital; the importance of democratic governance; the combination of the interests of the members and the general interest; the defence and implementation of solidarity and responsibility values; the reinvestment of surplus funds in long-term development objectives or in providing important services to members or in the general interest; voluntary and free membership; and autonomous and independent management. These atypical features are reflected in the "Statement of Cooperative Identity" defined by the ICA in Manchester in 1995, based on a set of seven principles

---

[4] Fauquet (1980), p. 26.

[5] Available at https://www.ilo.org/global/topics/cooperatives/areas-of-work/WCMS_445131/lang--en/index.htm.

[6] ICA (2013), "Blue Print for a Cooperative Decade", available at http://ica.coop/sites/default/files/media_items/ICA%20Blueprint%20-%20Final%20-%20Feb%2013%20EN.pdf, accessed on 22 March 2014.

[7] Available at https://www.un.org/sustainabledevelopment/sustainable-development-goals/.

(Cooperative Principles)[8] on a set of values (Cooperative Values)[9] that shape those principles, and on a definition of a cooperative.[10]/[11]

Cooperative principles reflect what is most specific to the cooperative, containing the essence of the cooperative identity.[12] However, cooperatives currently face many challenges, which may force them to reinvent themselves from a legal point of view. Any legal reinvention of the cooperative model must deal with concerns about preserving cooperative identity in the face of seduction exercised by the legal form of commercial companies. In some legal systems, this seduction has led to the excessive liberalization of the cooperative legal regime (*companization*).[13] On the other hand, reinvention may be required to respond to a need to maintain the attractiveness of cooperatives and to strengthen their sustainability.

It is in this context and with these concerns that the "Principles of European Cooperative Law (PECOL)" project was undertaken. PECOL are a set of norms that are presented as "ideals" in the regulation of European cooperatives and reflect their most characteristic features. These standards were developed by a small team of legal scholars, Study Group on European Cooperative Law (SGECOL), following a comparative investigation of cooperative law and best practice in seven European legal systems (Germany, Spain, Finland, France, Italy, Portugal and the United Kingdom).[14] The PECOL project did not have the specific objective of promoting the harmonization of national legislation on cooperatives, but that these principles can be recognized and assumed by cooperative organizations and can be a reference for the legislator when regulating cooperatives.[15]

2 Cooperative Governance and Sustainability

This paper will focus on cooperative governance and sustainability in light of new trends in European cooperative law and will follow PECOL on this subject. These

[8] These Principles are as follows: Voluntary and Open Membership, Democratic Member Control, Member Economic Participation, Autonomy and Independence, Education, Training, and Information, Cooperation among Cooperatives, Concern for Community. See Namorado (1995).

[9] Cooperatives are based on the values of self-help, self-responsibility, democracy, equality, equity and solidarity. In the tradition of their founders, cooperative members believe in the ethical values of honesty, openness, social responsibility and caring for others. See Moreno (2014), pp. 371–393.

[10] ICA has established that "A cooperative is an autonomous association of persons united voluntarily to meet their common economic, social, and cultural needs and aspirations through a jointly-owned and democratically-controlled enterprise".

[11] See Fici (2013), pp. 37–64.

[12] See Meira and Ramos (2015), pp. 401–428 and Namorado (2018), pp. 28–36.

[13] See Henrÿ (2012), p. 9 ff.

[14] The Study Group on European Cooperative Law (SGECOL) aims to conduct comparative research on cooperative law in Europe. Principles of European Cooperative Law (PECOL) was his first project. See Fajardo et al. (2013), pp. 331–350.

[15] See Hiez (2017), p. 1, ff.

principles in terms of governance start from the realization that the cooperative does not have an autonomous purpose vis-à-vis its members, but rather it is an instrument to satisfy the individual needs of each and every member, and who will use it as cooperators to work, consume, sell and/or provide services. For this reason, it is said that cooperatives have a mutualistic scope, which distinguishes them from other entities. The absence of a profit scope is not unique to cooperatives, as there are other entities that do not have profit as their main purpose. What truly distinguishes the cooperative is the absence of an autonomous scope that differs from the interests of its cooperators. The mutualistic scope of the cooperative means that each cooperator will assume an obligation to participate in the cooperative activity, cooperating mutually and helping each other in obedience to the cooperative principles.

Because of this mutualist vocation, the performance of the cooperative's governance organs will necessarily and primarily be oriented towards the promotion of the cooperators' interests, that is, to the satisfaction of their economic, social and cultural needs.

In PECOL it is stated as a general principle of cooperative governance that "the governance organs of a cooperative are structured to pursue economic activities mainly in the interest of their cooperator members" (Section 2.1. (3)). The principle says "mainly" rather than "exclusively" because the social object of the cooperative is not limited to meeting the needs of its members and must also consider the interests of the community where the cooperative develops its activity. In this regard, all aspects of cooperative governance should be consistent with the ICA principle "concern for community", so that "cooperatives work for the sustainable development of their communities through policies approved by their members". Although primarily focussed on the needs of their members, cooperatives work to achieve sustainable development of their communities, under criteria approved by their members. In this respect, the governance of cooperatives is not restricted to its internal relations. The cooperative governance paradigm should also be aligned with the fundamental principles of Corporate Social Responsibility (CSR) and based on the adoption of best practices in relation to the organization's equal opportunities, social inclusion and sustainable development.[16]

PECOL expressly assumes that CSR is not voluntary. Given the cooperative identity, in particular, the fact that their governance organs must take into account the principle of concern for community, it is argued that there is a legal obligation for the governance organs of the cooperative to incorporate the core values of CSR into their activity, which should be subject to control, both internally (by the general assembly and the supervisory board) and externally (audit). PECOL states, as a general principle of cooperative governance, that cooperative governance "facilitates operation based on universally recognised cooperative values and principles, including cooperative social responsibility" (Section 2.1. (2)).[17]

---

[16] See Meira (2012), pp. 127–144.

[17] See Snaith (2017), p. 47 ff.

The cooperative principle of concern for community is strongly connected with another cooperative principle, "voluntary and open membership". This is the traditional *open-door principle* and appears in the ICA cooperative identity statement in following terms: "Cooperatives are voluntary organizations, open to all persons able to use their services and willing to accept the responsibility of membership, without gender, social, racial, political or religious discrimination". This principle has two limbs: firstly, joining should be voluntary, depending exclusively on the will of the member; secondly, the cooperative must be open to all people who are able to benefit from the cooperative activity and accept the responsibilities of membership.[18]

The connection between these two principles is evident. The traditional open-door policy which the cooperative has adopted when accepting new members is justified by the willingness of the cooperative to service the community in which it is rooted. Taking new members from the area where the cooperative carries out its activity is consistent with an organization whose goal is to meet the needs of its community. This practice reveals cooperatives as generators of stable jobs. They are strongly rooted in the community and this means they are more likely to carry on activities that fuel the entrepreneurial spirit and do not allow them to relocate. In this sense, PECOL establishes that "(...) membership of a cooperative must be open to any person able and willing to accept the responsibilities of membership" (Section 2.2. (1)). It follows from this principle that "cooperative statutes shall ensure that: (a) membership applications are dealt with by a designated organ within a reasonable time; (b) reasons are given for refusal; (c) the applicant can appeal to the members' meeting if a different organ refused admission; and (d) the applicant has the right to be heard before a decision is made on the appeal" (Section 2.2. (2)).[19]

Another principle that is relevant to defending the claim that cooperative governance should promote sustainable development is the cooperative "principle of education, training, and information". The cooperative identity statement provides that "cooperatives will provide education and training for their members, elected representatives, managers and employees, so they can contribute effectively to the development of their cooperatives. They will inform the general public, particularly the young and opinion leaders, about the nature and benefits of cooperation". This principle emphasizes the obligation of cooperatives to guarantee the education and training of their members, representatives of the elected bodies, directors and employees in cooperative thought and action.[20] This principle includes the duty to inform the general public in order to raise awareness of the nature and benefit of cooperation, to encourage new and informed membership. This principle is materialized directly in PECOL through the provision for a "reserve fund for cooperative education, training and information" (Section 3.4. (3)).[21]

The establishment of reserves for education and training means that the cooperative is not only a business organization but is also an organization with social

[18] See Meira (2019), p. 75 ff.; and Hiez (2019), p. 8 ff.

[19] See Snaith (2017), p. 49 ff.

[20] See Münkner (2012), pp. 132–135.

[21] See Fajardo and Meira (2017), p. 83 ff.

and educational concerns. This reserve fund will bear the costs of activities beyond the satisfaction of purely individual interests of cooperative members. While these activities are not strictly economic in nature, they may result in direct or indirect, immediate or deferred economic benefits for the cooperative and the community where the cooperative operates. This reserve is one of the most distinctive features of the cooperative enterprise when compared with other types of enterprise. It generates capital that is allocated to social purposes and benefits its members, employees and the community.[22] The recognition of the importance of education and training is also reflected in PECOL in setting out the obligation to "participate in education and training provided for members" (Section 2.3. (1)(d)).[23]

Sustainable development requires democracy. Hagen Henrÿ notes that democratic participation is the mechanism by which social justice is regenerated and is an important dimension of sustainable development. Democracy is the only way to empower people to make sustainable choices.[24] The cooperative principle of democratic member control means that cooperative governance is also characterized as democratic governance. In PECOL, the first general principle of cooperative governance states that "cooperatives are directed and controlled by or on behalf of their members, who have ultimate democratic control through their governance system" (Section 2.1. (1)) and that "cooperative governance reflects their jointly-owned, democratically controlled and autonomous nature" (Section 2.1. (2)). Unless cooperative statutes provide otherwise: "(a) in small cooperatives all members participate directly in making every decision, and (b) in other cooperatives, governance is divided between a structure or organ giving members ultimate control of the organisation ('members meeting') and one or more boards or committees who are responsible for the day to day management of the cooperative and are accountable to its members" (Section 2.4. (2)).[25]

Voting in members' meetings is in principle based on *one member—one vote*, regardless of the capital held (Section 2.4. (7)). However, "when necessary for the better functioning of a cooperative, statutes may confer plural votes not related to capital contribution, and reflecting, for example, (a) participation in cooperative transactions; (b) the number of members in particular subdivisions; or (c) the balanced representation of different member groups" (Section 2.4. (8)). When cooperative statutes allow for the option of plural voting, they must ensure that investor members or a minority of cooperator members do not control the cooperative, "total plural votes held by any cooperator member can never exceed a certain percentage of all members' votes cast at any members' meeting at which they vote, as defined by the law". However, "investor members may have plural votes according to capital, limited to a total of a certain percentage of votes cast at the members' meeting at which they vote, as defined by the law" (Section 2.4. (9) and (10)).[26]

[22] See Meira (2017), pp. 57–72.

[23] See Snaith (2017), p. 53 ff.

[24] Henrÿ (2013), pp. 18 ff.

[25] See Snaith (2017), p. 59 ff.

[26] See Snaith (2017), p. 59 ff.

The democratic character of cooperative governance also rests on the fact that the members of the governance organs must be cooperators. In the context of PECOL, this is regarded as an important right of members. According to cooperative doctrine, this mechanism was designed by legislators to ensure that members of the cooperative's governance organs would focus on promoting the interests of members. By allowing the direct representation of members in administrative and supervisory bodies, they have experience in dual roles as both beneficiary and manager and are permanently aware of the importance of ensuring that the interests of the cooperators do not deviate from the main purpose of the cooperative. However, in the name of the professionalization of management, PECOL includes the possibility for non-members to be integrated into administrative and supervisory bodies.

Democratic governance must necessarily be transparent, recognizing a broad right to information for members. PECOL provides "(1) Board members and managers shall ensure that the cooperative operates with a high level of transparency and shall give members sufficiently clear information to enable them to control the cooperative. (2) In particular, they shall ensure that full annual accounts and, if appropriate, consolidated accounts are drawn up, audited, and published to members with an annual report and cooperative and financial audit reports as required by law. Such documents shall be available to the public at the cooperative's registered office at a price not exceeding their administrative cost. (3) Members and applicants for membership have a right to information on their obligations and rights" (Section 2.6. (1) (2) (3)).[27]

3 Final Considerations

In conclusion, cooperative practice, based on the concept of sustainability and explicitly present in PECOL, should be regarded as a regenerating element for current times. The dominant business logic seems to be devoid of ethical elements, an absence of close relationships with communities and a general indifference to their problems. In contrast, PECOL suggests a legal framework for cooperatives that is based on a paradigm that is in line with the various dimensions of sustainable development, and therefore this model should be valued.

Bibliography

Fajardo G, Fici A, Henrÿ H, Hiez D, Münkner H, Hiez D (2013) El nuevo grupo de studio en derecho cooperativo europeo y el proyeto "Los principios de derecho cooperative europeo". CIRIEC. Rev Jurídica Economía Soc Cooperativa 24:331–350

[27] See Snaith (2017), p. 71 ff.

Fajardo G, Meira D (2017) Chapter 3. Cooperative financial structure. In: Fajardo G, Fici A, Henrÿ H, Hiez D, Meira D, Muenker H, Snaith I (eds) Principles of European Cooperative Law: Principles, Commentaries and National Reports. Intersentia, Cambridge, pp 73–95

Fauquet G (1980) O Sector Cooperativo. Ensaio sobre o lugar do homem nas instituições cooperativas e destas na economia (tradução de F. Pinto). Livros Horizonte, Lisboa

Fici A (2013) Cooperative identity and the law. Eur Bus Law Rev 24:37–64

Henrÿ H (2012) Guidelines for cooperative legislation. International Labour Office, Geneve

Henrÿ H (2013) Superar la crisis del Estado de Bienestar: el rol de las empresas democráticas, una perspectiva jurídica. Ciriec España-Rev Jurídica Economía Soc Cooperativa 24:11–20

Hiez D (2017) Introduction. In: Fajardo G, Fici A, Henrÿ H, Hiez D, Meira D, Muenker H, Snaith I (eds) Principles of European Cooperative Law: Principles, Commentaries and National Reports. Intersentia, Cambridge, pp 1–15

Hiez D (2019) Voluntary membership: up to witch point do cooperatives support liberalism? Int J Coop Law 2:8–25

ICA (2013) Blue Print for a Co-operative Decade. http://ica.coop/sites/default/files/media_items/ICA%20Blueprint%20-%20Final%20-%20Feb%2013%20EN.pdf

Meira D (2012) Cooperative social responsibility: an intercultural analysis. In: Sarmento C (ed) Permanent Transit. Discourses and maps of the intercultural experience. Cambridge Scholars Publishing, England, pp 127–144

Meira D (2017) Reflexões em torno do regime jurídico da reserva de educação e formação cooperativas. In: Teixeira M, Teixeira M (eds) O Pensamento Feminino na Construção do Direito Cooperativo. Vincere Editora, Brasília, pp 57–72

Meira D (2019) Identidade cooperativa, admissão e demissão dos cooperadores. Realidades convergentes no direito português. In: Miranda J, Sousa L, Gadea E (eds) Direito Cooperativo e Identidade Cooperativa. Brazil Publishing, Curitiba, pp 71–96

Meira D, Ramos E (2015) Os princípios cooperativos no contexto da reforma do Código Cooperativo português. CIRIEC-España, Rev Jurídica Economía Soc Cooperativa 27:401–428

Moreno J (2014) Los valores según la Alianza Cooperativa Internacional (ACI). CIRIEC-España, Rev Jurídica Economía Soc Cooperativa 25:371–393

Münkner H (2012) Making co-operative promoters-40 years ICDC. Marburgo

Namorado R (1995) Os Princípios Cooperativos. Fora do Texto, Coimbra

Namorado R (2005) Cooperatividade e Direito Cooperativo. Estudos e pareceres. Almedina, Coimbra

Namorado R (2018) Artigo 3º. In: Meira D, Ramos E (eds) Código Cooperativo anotado. Almedina, Coimbra, pp 28–36

Sérgio A (1958) Sobre o socialismo de Oliveira Martins, Ensaios, tomo VIII. Guimarães, Coimbra

Snaith I (2017) Chapter 2—Cooperative Governance. Commentary. In: Fajardo G, Fici A, Henrÿ H, Hiez D, Meira D, Muenker H, Snaith I (eds) Principles of European Cooperative Law: Principles, Commentaries and National Reports. Intersentia, Cambridge, pp 47–72

Thinking Beyond the Principle—From an Attempt to Legally Substantiate the Principle of Sustainability Using the Example of Agricultural Cooperatives

Georg Miribung

1 Introduction

Much has been said about sustainability in the social and natural sciences and law, and also with regard to cooperatives. Hagen Henrÿ hypothesises that 'the legal structure of genuine cooperatives lends itself to making a contribution to sustainable development and that the companization of cooperatives weakens this capacity.'[1] This paper attempts to substantiate this statement by analysing some legal norms for agricultural cooperatives found in the Italian legal system. Basically, I consider the situation of an agricultural cooperative that owns land used for classical farming activities like animal breeding or land cultivation. However, such an analysis is inevitably subject to certain limitations, not least because the concept of sustainability or sustainable development is postulated as a principle and is therefore difficult to articulate legally, particularly as a legal provision.

The commonly accepted concept of sustainability defines sustainable development as development that 'meets the need of the present without compromising the ability of future generations to meet their own need.'[2] This principle refers to

[1] See Henrÿ 2012, 20.

[2] At a global level, the term 'sustainability' was first discussed extensively in 1972 in Stockholm as part of the United Nations Conference on the Human Environment. The so-called Brundtland Report proposed a more detailed definition, and the concepts described in the report formed the basis for the development of a comprehensive and an attempt at a global, political strategy. The 1992 UN Conference on Environment and Development held in Rio de Janeiro concluded with the following five documents, all dealing with sustainability to a greater or lesser extent: Rio Declaration on Environment and Development, United Nations Framework Convention on Climate Change (UNFCCC), Convention on Biological Diversity (CBD), Forest Principles and Agenda 21. On this issue, see also Monien 2014, Portney 2015, Guido and Massari 2013b, Härtel 2014, Manservisi 2014.

G. Miribung (✉)
Faculty of Science and Technology, Free University of Bozen-Bolzano, 39100 Bolzano, BZ, Italy
e-mail: gmiribung@unibz.it

W. Tadjudje and I. Douvitsa (eds.), *Perspectives on Cooperative Law*,
https://doi.org/10.1007/978-981-19-1991-6_22

three partially competing facets: (a) social sustainability, which refers to the standard of living, education, jobs and equal opportunities; (b) environmental sustainability, referring to the use of natural resources, biodiversity and the prevention of pollution and (c) economic sustainability, which refers, for example, to economic growth, the creation of profits and the saving of costs. Although this three-pillar concept is widely accepted nowadays, there is disagreement over the method of its implementation.[3] Above all, the fact that all three pillars must be applied in a balanced manner has been criticised, and it has been argued that, in the event of a conflict between these pillars and their contents, prioritisation may be required.[4] This is especially true if one considers ecological sustainability, which, due to its association with the environment, constitutes the basis for all human action. As agricultural activities are closely linked to the environment, this paper discusses ecological sustainability.

Regarding cooperatives and their relation to ecological sustainability, Henrÿ observes that 'the ecological balance is maintained more easily by cooperatives, which are not legally required to maximize the financial return on investments.'[5] Some arguments that support this assumption result from the democratic structure of a cooperative, which should imply that members, when determining how a cooperative shall promote their needs, not only consider monetary advantages but also consider other values and goods, like a healthy and sound environment or the sustainable use of natural resources. These open debates are seen as typical for cooperatives and are protected by specific principles and legal rules like, for example, ICA principles 2 and 7; Section 2.4 of the Principles of European Common Law (PECOL); or Article 2538, paragraph 2 of the Italian Civil Code (CC). These rules and principles ultimately influence the content of a cooperative's purpose inasmuch as they establish a democratic opinion-forming process, which is, in principle, open in its results.

According to Italian law, the purpose of an agricultural cooperative is linked to Art. 2135 CC, which defines agricultural activities. These activities can be divided into two categories, namely main activities and related activities.[6] Under the first category, the legislator specifically subsumes cultivation of the land (land management), forestry and animal farming; the second category refers to commercial activities that are classified as agricultural activities through the criterion of connectivity of agricultural activity.[7]

---

[3] On this issue, see, among many others, Pennasilico 2015, Guido and Massari 2013a, Portney 2015, 1 ff., Landini 2015, 614 ff., Gehne 2011, 11 ff. Also consider Mathis 2017, Norer 2005, 469 ff., Monien 2014, 150 ff., Landini 2015, 614 ff., Manservisi 2014, Bodiguel 2014, 196 ff., Jannarelli 2013, 35.

[4] Depending on the political view, the content of the notion of sustainability may vary to a certain degree, or specific criteria or facets may be prioritized, thereby disfavouring other criteria (see sources in note 2). Also consider Thiele 2013 and Giovannoni and Fabietti 2013.

[5] See Henrÿ 2012, 25.

[6] For details, see Costato and Russo 2015, 353 ff. and Germanò 2016, 82 ff.

[7] The law provides examples of activities such as working, preserving, processing, marketing and/or refining production/products that are obtained principally from cultivating land or forests and/or

To qualify as a farmer, an entity's main activity must be care and development of the biological cycle (or a necessary stage of such a cycle) of a plant-based or animal-based nature, for which land or forest or fresh, brackish or marine waters may be used.[8] For my discussion, it is important to stress that not only natural persons but also—under certain conditions—legal entities, e.g. a cooperative, can qualify as farmers.[9]

Aligned with the various activities listed in Art. 2135 CC, agricultural cooperatives can be categorised according to the generally used set of categories of workers' cooperatives, consumer cooperatives and service cooperatives. In the agricultural sector, a workers' cooperative is formed by the hypothesis of the joint cultivation of the members' land and the joint breeding of the members' animals—in Italian law, this is considered an *agricultural enterprise*, as it meets all the requirements set out in Art. 2135 CC. Consumer cooperatives are based on the hypothesis that the agricultural products are supplied by the members but sold to non-members. Service cooperatives might, for example, process members' products, as in the case of social cellars, social oil mills and social cheese factories.[10]

This paper considers an Italian agricultural workers' cooperative organised as a mainly mutual cooperative, implying that it performs a direct agricultural activity as determined by Art. 2135 CC, primarily by transacting with its members; third party transactions are of minor relevance.[11] Furthermore, I assume that the cooperative is the owner of the land/soil, using it to conduct its agricultural activity. This soil, amongst other assets (e.g. processing and storage facilities), constitutes the patrimony of the cooperative. This is relevant because, according to Italian cooperative law, agricultural cooperatives formed as mainly mutual cooperatives as determined by Art. 2512 ff. CC must accept specific bonds on their patrimony; so-called indivisible reserves are hereby established. As a result, this patrimony can effectively be used only for cooperative ends, corresponding to the principle of disinterested dissolution. Henrÿ observes that indivisible reserves strengthen the ability of a cooperative to foster sustainable development because they neutralise the role of capital and may thus help to balance environmental issues with profitability.[12]

The combination of these two concepts—indivisible reserves and the notion of biological cycle as determined by Italian law—defines a bundle of assets that can only be used in a sustainable way—at least in theory. By analysing the characteristics

from animal farming. On this issue, see Germanò and Rook Basile 2011, 776, Casadei 2009, 345 ff.

[8] May and not must; this is not necessarily obligatory. For details, see Germanò 2016, 65 ff. and Costato and Russo 2015, 324 ff.

[9] For details, see Germanò 2016, 118 f., Costato and Russo 2015, 374 ff.

[10] These latter two types of cooperative are agricultural enterprises by virtue of Art. 1, para. 2 of Legislative Decree No. 228 of 18 May 2001. This solution applies the principle of transparency, meaning that the legal personality of the cooperative cannot 'hide' the identity of the members who join together to carry out the last stage of their business activity. On this issue, see Carmignani 2011, 860, Carmignani 2013, 858 ff.

[11] See Art. 2512 CC ff.

[12] See Henrÿ 2012, 25.

of these two concepts, I argue that specific aspects of Italian private law that relate to the principle of sustainability—and in particular to its ecological aspect—can lead to a legal concept that shifts this principle towards legal rules, albeit with limitations.

2 The Indivisible Reserves

According to Italian law, the constraint of indivisibility,[13] which is mainly mutual cooperative encumbers *ex lege* on its patrimony, basically obliges the use of the resource for a specific cooperative purpose. This purpose is to provide members with a patrimonial advantage as a result of relations of exchange between the concerned cooperative and its members (Italian doctrine refers to it as internal mutuality).[14]

This indivisibility is irreversible and intangible under civil law.[15] In addition, the law determines that it is impossible to distribute assets among the members, even if the cooperative is dissolved, in which instance the assets must be devolved to a mutual fund for the promotion and development of cooperation.[16] Here, a concept of mutuality emerges that goes far beyond the relationship between the member and cooperative and frames all cooperatives in a single system.[17] This systemic mutuality is, however, not an accessory element of mutuality in general but rather a condition of identity. With it, the cooperative interest rises to a systemic level: its scope includes not only individual members or third parties as customers of a cooperative but is extended to an overall system of cooperatives and therefore may not be reduced to the activity of a single cooperative.[18]

Indivisibility does not, however, automatically imply unavailability. In fact, the assets set aside as an indivisible reserve remain available for the purpose of the cooperative, even if the law does not clarify within what limits. Article 2545 ter CC allows for the use of indivisible reserves, expressly specifying only that this use cannot correspond to distribution among members/shareholders. No other limits

---

[13] Through this capitalisation of part of the cooperative's profits, mutuality is indirectly protected, preventing the tax benefits granted to cooperatives with prevailing mutuality from being thwarted by a subsequent distribution of profits to their members. See Lolli 2010, 8 ss. and, in general, Lolli 2010, 67 ss. See also Santagata 2014, 438 ff.

[14] See Paolucci 2012a, 9 and Tatarano 2011, 66.

[15] The cooperative constraint is objective and creates an immutable destination. See Lolli 2010, 88 ff. and Lolli 2012, 160 ff. See also Tatarano 2011, 539 ff.

[16] See art. 2545 undecies CC and Art. 2514 CC. See. Art. 2514, para. 1, letter d), CC, which establishes that in the event of the dissolution of the cooperative, the entire cooperative's assets, less only the share capital and any dividends accrued, must be devolved to the mutual funds for the promotion and development of cooperation. The legislator assigns these funds a right to obtain the assets in case of devolution (see Genco 2003), 74. Thus, one can correctly argue that the specific current members are not the owners of the unavailable assets but are only managers of other people's assets (like managers of a foundation), given that the essential aim is also to guarantee the integrity of the patrimony in the future. See Costi 2001, 131.

[17] See Lolli 2010, 10 ff. and Paolucci 2012, 9 ff.

[18] See Bosi 2012, 64 ff. and Tatarano 2011, 62 ff.

are mentioned, and the law only identifies some specific usages.[19] It is important to specify that, in general, the indivisible reserves must be used in such a way that the cooperative fulfils its social function, as required by Article 45 of the Constitution. This limit cannot be exceeded.[20]

As such assets must be used for the cooperative's purposes, an intergenerational patrimony is also created in case of dissolution that is only indirectly available to the members, as it helps the cooperative to promote its members' needs. In fact, this patrimony aims to guarantee, over time, the performance of the concerned cooperative, independent of the fact that the structure of the membership base changes over time.[21] This intergenerational patrimony clearly reflects the very notion of sustainability, which tries to combine present needs with those of a future generation. I argue that with this set of rules, sustainability is clearly put into practice.

To safeguard the interest underlying the purpose that binds the cooperative's assets—and, with this, implicitly the observance of the principle of sustainability—the law, based on specific provisions of general commercial law, assigns specific tasks to the board of directors and the board of statutory auditors and assigns specific internal control instruments to the general meeting of members.[22] The monitoring process that is installed herewith, shall, in particular, cover the usage of the indivisible reserves. In addition, in compliance with the requirements of Art. 45 of the Constitution, the legislator has determined specific provisions aimed at ensuring that the indivisible reserves are used in the appropriate manner, i.e. in a manner consistent with the social function of the cooperative.[23] This also reflects the interest in protecting the whole cooperative sector, as well expressed in the notion of systemic mutuality. In this regard, a peculiar external control exists over the cooperative, which takes place within precise boundaries aimed at delimiting the discretion within which the public administration and its employees must move.[24] It should also be noted that an alternative to the public administration recognised associations representing the cooperative movement may also be authorised to conduct the external supervision. By means of this cooperative audit, they ascertain whether 'mutualistic requirements' (*requisiti mutualistici*) are fulfilled, i.e. the observance of the specific criteria fixed by the law, which, if respected, attribute to the cooperative social function as understood by Art. 45 of the Constitution. These 'mutualistic requirements' must include the mutuality of the (cooperative) system and the various criteria that put it into practice: consequently, the cooperative audit will also have to ensure that the indivisible reserves are managed with the appropriate expertise and in compliance

[19] As a safeguard against possible circumvention, the rule establishes a priority criterion in the use of reserves to cover losses: after having used all other available resources, the indivisible reserves can be used; among these, the legal reserve is the last type of reserve.. For details, see Lolli 2010, 86 ff. and Tatarano 2011, 538 ss. In general, see Fajardo and Meira 2017, 83 ff.

[20] See Cusa 2012, 224.

[21] See Bonfante 2004, 2609.

[22] For details, see, for example, Bonfante 2014b.

[23] See Tatarano 2011, 580 ff. In general, see Paolucci 2012b.

[24] See Cusa 2012, 226.

with the assigned function.[25] In the case of an agricultural cooperative organised as a mainly mutual cooperative, this implies that it should also be necessary to consider how soil is used to conduct agricultural activities. In fact, the economic value of the soil must be protected from the degradation of the soil that would lead to losses in production output, because these losses, in the worst case, might eat into the legal reserves and thus severely diminish the cooperative's patrimony.

To sum up, the resources that can be used to carry out a cooperative's activities are particularly important for its functioning: in mainly mutual cooperatives, this is primarily the patrimony bound to the cooperative purpose (indivisible reserves align with the principle of disinterested distribution). This patrimony is first of all a monetary value determined according to accounting standards and documented by the annual financial statements. Thus, from this perspective, the sustainability mechanism found in the principle of disinterested distribution focuses on an economic value. The weakness of the concept, however, might result from the fact that these economic assets shall be used for cooperative businesses, which implies that discretion exists on how the assets will eventually be used. Inherent in this is the risk that the value might be destroyed by poor entrepreneurial decisions, despite strong external mechanisms aimed at protecting these assets; this is, however, part of the economic system that human beings have created.

As will be seen in the next chapter, the legal regime applicable to Italian agricultural cooperatives adds specific rules that may strengthen the constraints on the assets, thus enhancing the sustainable use of resources.

3 The Agro-Biological Criterion

According to Italian law, the stipulated agricultural activities—the cultivation of the land, forestry and animal farming—aim to care for and develop a biological cycle (or a necessary phase of the cycle) of a plant-based or animal-based nature. It refers to a natural process as a result of which material entities with 'organic' life are born, grow and die and are able to reproduce (i.e. to generate, in turn, other material entities with life). Through this notion, the legislature has recognised that agricultural activity is oriented towards continuous agricultural development.[26] For example, no agricultural activities exist if only isolated activities such as ploughing or sowing are carried out.

However, the presence of a biological cycle alone is also insufficient. In fact, agricultural qualification is excluded from all activities—even if they are linked to the care and development of a biological cycle—that cannot be conducted according to a 'traditional' operational module, i.e. through the use of those natural phenomena represented by the soil, the forest, etc. Thus, this *agrarietà* (agrarianism) refers exclusively to all those activities of care and development of the biological cycle

[25] See Cusa 2012, 225 ff.

[26] See also Casadei 2009, 328 ff., Iannarelli 2012.

that are able (even if only in theory)[27] to be implemented through the use of the soil or other natural phenomena (such as a forest or freshwater or brackish water), regardless of whether the farmer has replaced these natural supports with other, technologically different, solutions.[28] The intention of the legislation was to place the action of humanity at the heart of this concept—evidence of behaviour directly capable of affecting the biological cycle of animal or vegetable organisms, an action that manifests itself in terms of 'care' and 'development' of the biological cycle.[29]

This shows that the concept of the biological cycle contains aspects that link agricultural activities to (environmental) sustainability considerations, which is conclusive, as agriculture depends directly on a 'healthy' environment. This is most easily illustrated by the example of forestry, but it should also apply to the two other main activities. The special feature results from the object, i.e. the forest, which not only enables the production of specific products (e.g. wood) but, due to its importance for soil strength, air purity and landscape conformity, can also be said to produce the environment as such.[30] To conduct their activities successfully (including in economic terms), farmers must conduct their activity in an environmentally sustainable manner, as their continuing income depends on an asset that is environmentally sound. A poorly managed forest will lose value, and farmers therefore tend automatically to protect the substance of the soil, thereby implying environmentally sustainable behaviour.

Apart from grounds based on individual motivation, the legislation safeguards this environmental aspect via specific legal norms (e.g. by determining rules of good practice and forest management plans).[31] In principle, these requirements are based on scientific evidence that provides information on how the environment should be used. Their application is either obligatory or based on incentives,[32] and the practice of the agricultural activity hereby becomes even more pre-determined. The legal framework establishing ecological sustainability as an essential feature of an agricultural activity also has a significant impact on how animal farming and the cultivation of land must be conducted. Thus, taken together and according to these considerations, agricultural activity in accordance with Art. 2135 CC can in principle (*ex lege*) only be carried out sustainably. Yet, if we consider discussions on climate change, we might doubt that this is entirely true—in this context, agricultural activities are described as an important driver of the phenomenon, and the question arises as to why. As it is acknowledged that the cultivation of land and, in particular, animal

---

[27] See note 9.

[28] See, among many others, Casadei 2009, 328 ff., Costato 2006, 93 f., Germanò and Rook Basile 2011, 768.

[29] See Iannarelli 2012.

[30] These functions have always been considered to be the most important. In this regard, see Germanò 2016, 70 ff. Accordingly, agricultural activities cannot destroy the environment, as the activity would destroy itself. Obliging a farmer to do so would be a contradiction and demonstrates the limit of the set of obligations and rights linked to the notion of agricultural activities.

[31] On this issue, see, for example, Grimm and Norer 2015, 11 f., and Paul 1997.

[32] On this issue, see, for example, List 2019.

farming have a particular influence on climate change, it may be useful to add some observations relating to climate change and animal husbandry.

Looking at the relationship between climate change—i.e. the anthropogenic greenhouse effect—and animal husbandry and, implicitly, at the extent to which animal husbandry is (or can/must be) ecologically sustainable, it can be seen that the relationship between the production of economic value—with its production of greenhouse gases—and the destruction of the environment—because of climate change—cannot be directly captured but is shown by using scientific models.[33] If one links this understanding to the legal observations made in this essay, one might argue that this is because the biological cycle inherent in animal husbandry is—compared to forestry, for example—shorter, while the consequences of unsustainable behaviour in the context of climate change are only felt in the long term (by the next generation).[34] It thus seems unlikely that (in this specific example) farmers (i.e. agricultural cooperatives) will move towards more sustainable behaviour. There is a link missing between present and future experiences of consequence; an asymmetry between market participants whose experience of consequence manifests over different timescales, where the damage caused by one generation is only felt by the next. This raises the question of why the former would voluntarily change their behaviour at all—it seems more likely that market participants will switch to environmentally friendly behaviour only if/when they experience the negative consequences directly. This logic is no doubt equally applicable to forestry and other activities that use the soil as a medium of production to create economic prosperity. Thus, it can be assumed that farmers will pay special attention to environmental sustainability as long as the environmental consequences of agricultural activities more or less directly correlate with the biological cycle. However, if there is a delay in the correlation, and if that delay increases, environmentally sustainable behaviour on a voluntary basis is likely to be reduced.

4 Final Observations

According to Italian law, the activities of an agricultural cooperative (organised as a mainly mutual cooperative) using its own land to conduct one of the main agricultural activities are determined by specific rules that oblige it to conduct the activity in an environmentally sustainable manner. Specific constraints exist on the cooperative's patrimony, which in this fictive case also encompasses the land/soil used for agricultural activities.

---

[33] See, among many, Ermann et al. 2018, 81, Schmitz et al. 2012, 22, Härtel 2014, FAO 2016. See also Steinfeld 2006.

[34] It is also important to note that intensive livestock farming, particularly of cattle and pigs, requires huge amounts of water and uses vast areas of land to grow cereals for feed, which has serious effects on the environment. It should be noted that the focus on so-called zero-kilometre agriculture favours the reduction of transport and therefore leads to a significant reduction in CO_2 emissions.

One such constraint concerns the economic value of the patrimony, which may only be used for the cooperative's aim. In order to guarantee the sustainable fulfilment of this aim, the legislator designs a specific external monitoring instrument; through this, the proper usage of the patrimony is safeguarded. But sustainability cannot be perfectly safeguarded, because, like any entrepreneurial endeavour, mismanagement of the cooperative may diminish the economic value.

Another constraint concerns the activity, and thus the aim, of the cooperative. This constraint is legally linked to the dynamics of natural forces and is therefore also exposed to the risk that the activity might be severely affected by acts of nature. In order to achieve sustainability, specific rules exist that require that the activity be conducted in alignment with current scientific knowledge. This, too, will foster sustainable behaviour.

Using agricultural cooperatives as an example, I argue that Italian private law contains some interesting features—specific constraints on the patrimony—that might help to better conceptualise legal rules that aim to make the principle of sustainability more concrete and—maybe—ultimately legally enforceable. Both constraints rely on external advice, yet both have their shortcomings—in specific situations, it is hardly possible to foresee future consequences of present behaviour. As regards sustainable agricultural activities, this knowledge gap could be reduced to some extent if one considers the latest scientific evidence[35]; legislation could focus on this. The relevance of such considerations becomes clear when one considers that modern agro-food production contributes significantly to climate change—and this also concerns agricultural cooperatives.

References

Bodiguel L (2014) Agricoltura sostenibile: il sogno di un diritto. In: Nappi P, Sgarbanti G, Borghi P, Russo L, Fioravanti C, Agostini C, Manservisi S, Borraccetti M, Rizzioli S (eds) Studi in onore di Luigi Costato. Jovene, Napoli, pp 191–198

Bonfante G (2004) 2545 ter. In: Il nuovo diritto societario. Zanichelli, Bologna, p 2608

Bonfante G (2014) Il controllo amministrativo e giudiziario. In: Bonfante G (ed) La società cooperativa. Cedam, Padova

Bonfante G (2014) Le forme organizzative. In: Bonfante G (ed) La società cooperativa. Cedam, Padova

Bosi G (2012) I fondi mutualistici. Il mulino, Bologna

Carmignani S (2011) Le società agricole. In: Costato L, Germanò A, Rook Basile E (eds) Trattato di diritto agrario: I. UTET, Torino, pp 231–262

Carmignani S (2013) 2135. In: Gagnasso O, Vallebona A (eds) Dell'impresa e del lavoro. UTET, Torino, pp 858–873

Casadei E (2009) La nozione di impresa agricola dopo la riforma del 2001. Riv dir agr, 309–358

Costato L (2006) L'imprenditore agricolo. Riv Dir Civ 89–100

Costato L, Russo L (2015) Corso di diritto agrario italiano e comunitario, 4th edn. Giuffrè, Milano

[35] On this issue, FAO-IPCC EXPERT MEETING ON CLIMATE CHANGE, LAND USE AND FOOD SECURITY» https://www.ipcc.ch/site/assets/uploads/2018/05/EM_FAO_IPCC_report.pdf.

Costi R (2001) Proprietà e impresa cooperative nella riforma del diritto societario. Giur. Comm. 128–132
Cusa E (2012) Il controllo amministrativo sulle cooperative. Giur Comm 39:220–253
Ermann U, Langthaler E, Penker M, Schermer M (2018) Agro-food studies. Böhlau, Köln
Fajardo E, Meira D (2017) Cooperative financial structure. In: Fajardo G, Fici A, Henrÿ H, Hiez D, Meira D, Münkner H-H, Snaith I (eds) Principles of European Cooperative Law. Intersentia, Cambridge
FAO (2016) Climate change, agriculture and food security. FAO, Rome
Gehne K (2011) Nachhaltige Entwicklung als Rechtsprinzip. Mohr Siebeck, Tübingen
Genco R (2003) La struttura finanziaria. In: Genco R (ed) La riforma delle società cooperative. IPSOA
Germanò A (2016) Manuale di diritto agrario. Giappichelli, Turin
Germanò A, Rook Basile E (2011) L'impresa agricola. In: Costato L, Germanò A, Rook Basile E (eds) Trattato di diritto agrario: I. UTET, Torino, pp 757–797
Giovannoni E, Fabietti G (2013) What is sustainability? In: Busco C, Frigo ML, Riccaboni A, Quattrone P (eds) Integrated reporting. Springer, Cham, pp 21–40
Grimm C, Norer R (2015) Agrarrecht, 4th edn. Beck, München
Guido G, Massari S (2013) Introduzione. In: Guido G, Massari S (eds) Lo sviluppo sostenibile. Angeli, Milano, pp 3–10
Guido G, Massari S (eds) (2013) Lo sviluppo sostenibile. Angeli, Milano
Härtel I (2014) Vom Klimawandel bis zur Welternährung. In: Härtel I (ed) Nachhaltigkeit, Energiewende, Klimawandel, Welternährung. Nomos, Baden-Baden, pp 13–70
Henrÿ H (2012) Guidelines for cooperative legislation, 3rd edn. ILO, Geneva
Iannarelli A (2012) Impresa agricola. diritto-on-line
Jannarelli A (2013) Il divenire del diritto agrario italiano ed europeo tra sviluppi tecnologici e sostenibilità. Riv dir agr 11–35
Landini S (2015) Clausole di sostenibilità nei contratti tra privati. Diritto Pubblico 611–636
List M (2019) Nachhaltigkeit der Gemeinsamen Agrarpolitik der EU im Lichte der aktuellen Reform. In: Fang X, Martínez J, Qi X (eds) Nachhaltigkeit und Landwirtschaft in China und Deutschland. Nomos, Baden-Baden, pp 129–142
Lolli R (2010) Le riserve divisibili e indivisibili nelle società cooperative. Cedam, Padova
Lolli R (2012) I mezzi propri delle cooperative e i bilanci. In: Paolucci LF (ed) Le società cooperative, pp 147–179
Manservisi S (2014) Il principio dello sviluppo sostenibile. In: Borghi P, Germanò A, Casadei E, Sgarbanti G (eds) Il divenire del diritto agrario italiano ed europeo tra sviluppi tecnologici e sostenibilità. Giuffrè, Milano, pp 175–224
Mathis K (2017) Sustainable development, economic growth and environmental regulation. In: Mathis K, Huber BR (eds) Environmental law and economics. Springer, Cham, pp 3–42
Monien J (2014) Prinzipien als Wegbereiter eines globalen Umweltrechts? Nomos, Baden-Baden
Norer R (2005) Lebendiges Agrarrecht. Springer, Vienna
Paolucci LF (2012a) Definizione e aspetti caratterizzanti. In: Paolucci LF (ed) Le società cooperative, pp 1–24
Paolucci LF (2012b) La vigilanza. In: Paolucci LF (ed) Le società cooperative, pp 221–237
Paul F (1997) Ordnungsgemäße Landwirtschaft. Berichte Über Die Landwirtschaft 75:539–561
Pennasilico M (2015) Sviluppo sostenibile, legalità costituzionale e analisi "ecologica" del contratto. Pers Merc 37–50
Portney KE (2015) Sustainability. MIT Press essential knowledge series, MIT Press, Cambridge, Massachusetts
Santagata R (2014) 2545 quater. In: Delle società, dell'azienda, della concorrenza. UTET, Torino
Schmitz C, Biewald A, Lotze-Campen H, Popp A, Dietrich JP, Bodirsky B, Krause M, Weindl I (2012) Trading more food: Implications for land use, greenhouse gas emissions, and the food system. Glob Environ Chang 22:189–209. https://doi.org/10.1016/j.gloenvcha.2011.09.013

Steinfeld H (2006) Livestock's long shadow. FAO, Rom
Tatarano MC (2011) La nuova impresa cooperativa. Giuffrè, Milano
Thiele LP (2013) Sustainability, 1st edn. Wiley, New York

Energy Cooperatives and Sustainable Development

Emanuele Cusa

1 Sustainable Development and Energy Consumption

In 1987, the United Nations (UN) defined the phrase "sustainable development" in the so-called Brundtland Report,[1] as "a process of change in which the exploitation of resources, the direction of investments, the orientation of technological development and institutional change are all in harmony and enhance both current and future potential to meet human needs and aspirations". As proposed in Annex 1 of the report, "all human beings have the fundamental right to an environment adequate for their health and well-being" and "States shall conserve and use the environment and natural resources for the benefit of present and future generations". Aiming for sustainable development implies engaging in a complex activity because three goals have to be pursued simultaneously: (i) economic growth; (ii) social development; and (iii) environmental protection.[2]

[1] This report, prepared by the World Commission on Environment and Development (chaired by G.H. Brundtland), was entitled *Our Common Future* and corresponds to the Annex to UN General Assembly document A/42/427, *Development and International Co-operation: Environment*, dated 2 August 1987. The said report was approved by the UN General Assembly on 11 December 1987 (A/res/42/187).

[2] According to Henrÿ (2013b), p. 813, sustainable development is achieved through economic security, ecological balance, political stability and social justice. This last holds a pivotal position, because, without it, sooner or later there will be political instability and economic insecurity. In H. Henrÿ's opinion, to have social justice, people should be able to exercise their human right to participate democratically in concrete forms (i.e. into political, social, and economic institutions) of action. On social justice and how it relates to sustainable development and different forms of enterprises, see Henrÿ (2015), pp. 81–96.

E. Cusa (✉)
Business Law, Università degli Studi di Milano-Bicocca (University of Milano-Bicocca), Milan, Italy
e-mail: emanuele.cusa@unimib.it

W. Tadjudje and I. Douvitsa (eds.), *Perspectives on Cooperative Law*,
https://doi.org/10.1007/978-981-19-1991-6_23

All development consumes energy, but sustainable development requires that the energy consumed is accessible to all human beings without damaging (or doing the least possible damage to) the environment.

The current UN programme for universal sustainable development—*Transforming Our World: The 2030 Agenda for Sustainable Development* (hereafter 2030 Agenda), adopted by the UN General Assembly on 25 September 2015[3]—features one goal of particular interest among the 17 Sustainable Development Goals (hereafter SDGs) established. Goal 7 (hereafter SDG7) aims to "ensure access to affordable, reliable, sustainable and modern energy for all". According to the last UN report on the implementation of the SDGs,[4] "the proportion of the global population with access to electricity increased from 83% in 2010 to 90% in 2018, meaning that over 1 billion people acquired this essential service", but "still, 789 million people—85% in rural areas—lacked electricity". In addition, "the share of renewable energy in total final energy consumption reached 17.3% in 2017, up from 17.0% in 2015 and 16.3% in 2010". Moreover, achieving SDG7 means spending a large amount of money.[5] More generally, the "2030 Agenda can only be realized through a whole-of-society approach, with actors beyond Government embracing the paradigm shift behind the Agenda, aligning their own systems with the Sustainable Development Goals, actively participating in implementation efforts and becoming champions for continued improvement".[6]

Among the social actors, enterprises, in their different forms and sizes,[7] as monitored by socially conscious and informed consumers that vote with their wallets, play a key role in achieving sustainable development.

2 Sustainable Development and Cooperatives

Within the economic private sector, the cooperative movement definitely holds an important position in implementing the 2030 Agenda, as the International Labour Organization (ILO) asserted even before the approval of the 2030 Agenda,[8] and this applies to the energy divide in particular.[9]

---

[3] UN General Assembly, *Transforming Our World: The 2030 Agenda for Sustainable Development*, 21 October 2015, A/res/70/1.

[4] UN, *The Sustainable Development Goals Report 2020*, UN, New York, 2020, pp. 38–39.

[5] On this point, see Tracking SDG7: The Energy Progress Report 2020, The World Bank, Washington, 2020.

[6] UN Economic and Social Council, *Special Edition: Progress Towards the Sustainable Development Goals. Report of the Secretary-General*, 8 May 2019, E/2019/68, para 67.

[7] See UN General Assembly, *Transforming Our World: The 2030 Agenda for Sustainable Development*, 21 October 2015, A/res/70/1, para 67.

[8] Wanyama (2014).

[9] ILO, *Providing Clean Energy and Energy Access Through Cooperatives*, ILO, Geneva, 2013.

Therefore, as the UN has repeatedly confirmed,[10] there is a general consensus at the international organization level that cooperatives may contribute positively to achieving sustainable development.

The same international cooperative movement is conscious of being an actor of collective action in achieving the 2030 Agenda, as attested by the current action of the International Co-operative Alliance (ICA).[11]

A true cooperative[12]—as representative of true (i.e. sustainable) development—should combine economic, social and environmental dimensions in its actions, woven together through the democratic participation of its members. Clear proof of the fact that cooperatives and their activities are synergic with sustainable development is represented by the following seventh principle (referred to as *Concern for Community*) included in the updated ICA *Statement on the Cooperative Identity* (hereafter ICA Statement, corresponding to a worldwide *vademecum* for true cooperatives) approved in 1995: "co-operatives work for the sustainable development of their communities through policies approved by their members".[13] According to the ICA Statement, a true cooperative, besides its compulsory and main purpose (i.e. meeting the "common economic, social, and cultural needs and aspirations" of its members, or the so-called "mutual scope"),[14] should pursue a secondary purpose, which is to contribute to sustainable development.

---

[10] See, for instance, *The Future We Want*, corresponding to the final declaration on sustainable development and a green economy adopted at the UN Conference on Sustainable Development in Rio de Janeiro, 19 June 2012, A/conf.216/L.1, para 154.

[11] ICA is an international non-governmental organization, founded in 1895, that, through its members, unites, represents and serves more than one billion cooperative members on the planet.

[12] On the above notion, see para 3.

[13] ICA, *Guidance Notes to the Co-operative Principles*, ICA, 2015, explains two important points: *(i)* the "7th Principle was first stated as a separate and distinct Co-operative Principle in the reformulation of the Co-operative Principles agreed by the members of the Alliance at its General Assembly in Manchester in 1995. Prior to 1995, concern for communities was part of the 6th Principle, Co-operation among Co-operatives which, in the 1966 clarification of the Principles by the Alliance, stated that: 'Co-operatives, to best serve their members and communities, should co-operate with each other, both at home and abroad'"; and *(ii)* the concept of sustainable development used in the said principle derives from and refers to the same concept defined by the UN in the Brundtland Report. On the ICA's seventh cooperative principle, see MacPherson (2012), who coordinated the lengthy process of consultation (involving thousands of co-operators around the world) finalized in a proposal that became in 1995 the actual ICA Statement.

[14] More precisely, from the legal point of view, see the mutual purpose definition contained in Art. 1, para 3, regulation (EC) 1435/2003 of 22 July 2003 *on the Statute for a European Cooperative Society* (SCE).

3 ICA Statement on the Cooperative Identity and True Cooperatives

The ICA Statement integrates public international law not thanks to its reference in the UN General Assembly resolution 56/114 (*Cooperatives in Social Development*) of 19 December 2001,[15] but thanks to its insertion into *The Promotion of Cooperatives Recommendation, 2002*, adopted by the ILO General Conference on 20 June 2002 (hereafter ILO Recommendation).[16] Therefore, there is the following rule of (hard) international law (whose infringement, unfortunately, does not result in any international sanctions against the lawbreaker): ILO Member States "should adopt specific legislation and regulations on cooperatives, which are guided by the cooperative values and principles set out in Paragraph 3 [corresponding to those contained into the ICA Statement, whose principles are inserted into the Annex of the ILO Recommendation], and revise such legislation and regulations when appropriate" (paragraph 10, ILO Recommendation).

Pursuant to the above-mentioned international legal rule, if cooperatives—operating in one of the 187 ILO Member States, which includes all EU Member States,[17] because the ILO Recommendation is undoubtedly legally binding[18]—complied with the ICA's seventh principle and observed the entire ICA Statement, they would contribute to sustainable development to different degrees, depending on their sizes and their activities. Indeed, the ICA's seventh principle cannot be considered part of the soft international law related to the corporate social responsibility (CSR) approach, but it is a mandatory purpose of a specific enterprise model: that of

---

[15] UN General Assembly, *Cooperative in Social Development*, 18 January 2002, A/RES/56/114. The above-mentioned UN resolution (according to which Member States should consider the ICA Statement "in developing or revising their national policies on cooperatives") refers to the ICA Statement via paragraph 11 of the *Draft Guidelines Aimed at Creating a Supportive Environment for the Development of Cooperatives*, corresponding to the Annex of *Cooperatives in Social Development. Report of the Secretary-General*, 14 May 2001, A/5673-E/2001/68; this last report is cited in the resolution 56/114.

[16] I follow Henrÿ (2013a), p. 66, when he considers only the ILO Recommendation as a source of public international law, because of its universal applicability and its binding nature; as a matter of fact, it is normally maintained [cf., *ex multis*, Conforti (2018), pp 8, 199 ff] that public international law (that is hard international law) is formed from mandatory rules only, limiting the (external and/or internal) power of States.

[17] In my opinion, EU Member States' national cooperative law should be compliant with the ICA Statement in support of the ILO Recommendation only and not of the European Commission Communication of 23 February 2014 *On the Promotion of Co-operative Societies in Europe* (COM[2004]18 final) as well because the European Commission, with this document, simply "invites [EU] Member States to be guided, when drafting national regulations governing cooperatives, by the "definition, values and co-operative principles" of the above-mentioned Recommendation [i.e. the ILO Recommendation] but also to be sufficiently flexible in order to meet the modern needs of cooperatives".

[18] The related demonstration is offered by Henrÿ (2013a), pp. 67–76.

the true cooperative, namely, cooperatives that are compliant with the ICA Statement.[19] Therefore, as sustainable development became a concept of international law in 1997,[20] since 2002, a true cooperative has become an enterprise model with an internationally obligatory purpose: implementing sustainable development.[21] Of course, the respect of the said obligatory purpose should be controlled not only by the ILO Member State but also by the cooperatives association (often referred to as the federation) to which cooperatives belong, providing that the said association is part (even indirectly) of the ICA; as a matter of fact, all cooperative associations that are members of the ICA must (in force of a contractual obligation) check if their members respect the ICA Statement.[22]

4 Technology, Energy Cooperatives and Sustainable Development

Energy cooperatives (hereafter cooperatives that produce energy and/or energy services)[23] are already a worldwide phenomenon with strong growth that are located in rural and urban areas in both developing and developed countries.[24]

Technology makes the diffusion of energy cooperatives easier and energy cooperatives contribute to sustainable development. Technology helps energy cooperatives in at least five ways:

(i) It decreases the costs of energy production, making it affordable for almost all people to produce and/or consume energy[25];
(ii) It allows an energy enterprise to be set up using less financing than in the past[26];

---

[19] Henrÿ (2013c), p. 61 ff., defends the functional relationship between the legal structural features of cooperatives and sustainable development (named cooperative social responsibility or CoopSR) capable of strengthening and complementing the CSR approach.

[20] Defined as the "need to reconcile economic development with protection of the environment" in the International Court of Justice judgment of 25 September 1997 (GabCikovo-Nagymaros Project [HungarylSlovakia], Judgment, I.C.J Reports 1997, p. 7, paragraph 140).

[21] That is, from the approval of the ILO Recommendation.

[22] The above-mentioned obligation derives from the ICA articles of association (see, in particular, Art. 3 and 6).

[23] Normally, the said cooperative can be a qualified consumer cooperative, but it can also be a worker cooperative or a mixed cooperative, according to the mutual relationships (exchange agreements) between the co-operators and the cooperative that characterizes its governance.

[24] See again ILO, *Providing Clean Energy and Energy Access Through Cooperatives*, ILO, Geneva, 2013.

[25] In developed countries, mainly because of the corruption of public authorities, a significant proportion of people needs non-repayable (public or private) capital to at least consume energy.

[26] Above all, in developing countries (but also in developed countries), public finance is needed to (at least) implement (and maintain) an energy distribution system, but if that is combined with the promotion of energy cooperatives, it is possible to extend electrical service (and to maintain its

(iii) It facilitates the decentralization of energy production, thereby offering many advantages for sustainable development, such as the utilization of local energy sources, increased local security of the energy supply, shorter transport distances, reduced energy transmission losses and the fostering of community development and cohesion (thanks to the related income sources and jobs supplied locally);
(iv) It permits some productions or storage of energy that were impossible or too expensive in the past;
(v) It allows for the exchange, distribution (for instance, via blockchain) or monitoring (e.g., using smart metering systems) of energy that was impossible or too expensive in the past, thanks (mainly) to the information and communications technology.

Moreover, energy cooperatives contribute to sustainable development in at least nine ways:

(i) They are the best tool for groups of energy prosumers (those who are consumers and producers at the same time), because of their compulsory mutual purpose (in the sense of the self-help principle); as a matter of fact, cooperatives are user-owned and not investor-owned[27]; such a purpose, indeed, forces people to become (collective, through their cooperative) producers (intermediate aim) in order to have better economic conditions as (individual) consumers (final aim);
(ii) They offer an incentive to reduce energy consumption because their members (oppositely from the members of traditional companies producing energy) are interested in spending less money to buy energy,[28] either by reducing the price of energy, by reducing energy consumption by acting with restraint, or by increasing energy efficiency (thereby reducing energy expenses through less energy consumption);
(iii) They facilitate raising capital among ordinary people that want to optimize their energy expenses, eventually by increasing their energy efficiency, and thus they get many small savers directly involved in the energy sector;
(iv) They combine democracy (and, if real and effective, participation) and production (of energy and/or of energy services), which is a strategic factor in the energy sector, thanks to their mandatory democratic structure; thus, energy cooperatives foster the involvement and the awareness of citizens in achieving sustainable development, facilitate the uptake of the related

efficiency) in rural (or less developed) areas, as it happened in rural areas in the U.S.A., under the Roosevelt administration, thanks to the Rural Electrification Act of 1936.

[27] That a true cooperative must have a mutual purpose explained above is clearly expressed in the ICA Statement (see, in particular, cooperative definition, cooperative values and the first cooperative principle therein). The same obligation is required for all Italian cooperatives, even the social ones, as explained by Cusa (2019), pp. 963–965.

[28] The same idea was already expressed by Henrÿ (2012b), p. 25.

new technologies and consumption patterns and increase local acceptance of renewable energy[29];

(v) They are interested in the territories in which they are located because their members' seats/centres of interest are in the place where their cooperative runs its business;

(vi) They are interested in poor or vulnerable consumers and tenants, thanks to the dividend cap, the open-door principle and the values pursued, which are all characteristics of true cooperatives; therefore, cooperatives help fight energy poverty, for example, through on-bill energy financing programmes reserved for their members[30];

(vii) They mainly produce energy from renewable energy sources (RES), above all from photovoltaic (PV) systems (the visible part of which are their solar panels) and wind turbines, by converting sunlight and wind (RES is at the disposal of the greatest segment of the world's population) directly into electricity; thus, energy cooperatives may contribute to eliminating (or, at least decreasing) the energy divide and to improving the climate and reducing greenhouse gases (a group of gases contributing to global warming and climate change), particularly carbon dioxide (CO_2), thanks to the replacement of fossil energy sources with RES;

(viii) They increase their capacity to respond to the needs (mainly economic, but not only) of their members not through concentration, but through collaboration, mainly thanks to federations[31] or second-tier entities,[32] thereby preserving the diversity of enterprise models and pluralism in the market in favour of the sustainability of the same market[33];

---

[29] If social justice is a key aspect of achieving sustainable development and the most effective mechanism by which to secure social justice is democratic participation, then cooperatives contribute to sustainable development by engendering democratic participation. See Henrÿ (2013b), pp. 813–816.

[30] That is financing (eventually with public support, e.g., only with a guarantee scheme) energy improvements that are repaid by a utility customer on their monthly utility bill. In these cases, if the monthly payments of the debtor are spread over many years, it is even possible that the bill savings (thanks to the energy efficiency obtained using the said loan) are greater than the costs of repayment of the debt.

[31] Just two examples of energy cooperatives federations: (i) REScoop.EU represents about 1.500 European energy cooperatives; (ii) the National Rural Electric Cooperative Association represents more than 900 U.S.A. local electric cooperatives.

[32] Normally, in the form of cooperatives, the second-tier energy cooperatives are well represented in the U.S.A. by the so-called generation and transmission (G&T) cooperatives (about 60) that provide for the wholesale energy power needs of their energy distribution cooperatives members (all together, around 600); the latter cooperatives serve end-users.

[33] Also, Henrÿ (2012b), pp. 21–22, points out the linkage between the principle of the diversity of enterprise types (that prevails in the preservation of existing types of enterprises) and sustainable development.

(ix) They can become an institutional vehicle of collaboration between public and private entities to implement renewable energy projects of public interest,[34] through the direct membership of local authorities in these cooperatives, as many examples around the world demonstrate.

In conclusion, energy cooperatives, if they respect the ICA Statement (by becoming true cooperatives), contribute to *sustainable* development because they are themselves *sustainable* economic organizations.

5 The New EU Law on Energy Communities

The EU has its own competence (concurrent with that of the EU Member States respecting the principles of subsidiarity and proportionality, according to article 5 of the Treaty on European Union) on energy (the EU policy on energy), "in the context of the establishment and functioning of the internal market and with regard for the need to preserve and improve the environment", consisting, among others, of promoting "energy efficiency and energy saving and the development of new and renewable forms of energy" (article 194, paragraph 1, letter *c*, Treaty on the Functioning of the European Union, or TFEU). Pursuant to article 194 TFEU the EU has approved the following two important directives, helping Europe to achieve its SDGs: directive (EU) 2018/2001 of 11 December 2018 *On the Promotion of the Use of Energy from Renewable Sources* (so-called RED II); and directive (EU) 2019/944 of 5 June 2019 *On Common Rules for the Internal Market for Electricity* (so-called IME).

These directives are important for my reasoning because they introduced into EU law (and, consequently, into the national laws of all EU Member States) two new (due to their membership, structure, governance requirement and purpose) enterprise models to set up energy communities:

(i) The renewable energy community (REC), according to the directive (EU) 2018/2001, whose national laws (implementing this directive) shall be brought into force by the EU Member States by 30 June 2021;
(ii) The citizen energy communities (CEC), according to the directive (EU) 2019/944, whose national laws (implementing this directive) shall be brought into force by the EU Member States by 31 December 2020.[35]

The intention of the EU legislation is that energy communities can help the EU Member States to achieve the objective of the 2015 Paris Agreement on climate change (and, consequently, reach targets directly related to some SDGs). More

---

[34] Such as when a municipality leases the roofs of its own public buildings (like schools) to install PV systems, owned by an energy cooperative, of which the municipality is a member, in order to collaborate with its citizens.

[35] For a first comment on the above-mentioned energy communities, see Fajardo (2019), pp. 116–119, Cusa (2020), pp. 71–126 and RESCOOP.UE & ClientEarth (2020), *Energy Communities under the Clean Energy Package. Transposition Guidance,* Rescoop, Brussels.

precisely, the EU law on energy communities has been thought to support the EU in achieving its binding goal by 2030: which is that at least 32% of gross final energy consumption in the EU will be covered by RES.

RECs and CECs should not be confused with the general phenomenon of energy self-consumption (*rectius*, with collective energy self-consumption and, therefore, with possible collective self-consumption schemes), as defined in the two directives above, for at least the following reason. If RECs and CECs are legal entities distinct from their members, no legal coincidence is possible between the producer (the energy community) and the consumer (its members); therefore, RECs and CECs themselves (and also their members, at least for the energy produced by plants owned by their community) cannot be qualified (strictly speaking, according to EU law) as prosumers with regard to their energy activities. Nevertheless, energy communities may be included in the legal tools envisaged by EU law to implement one of the principles that shall govern the European internal market of energy: the empowerment of consumers to act as market participants in the energy market and the energy transition.

6 The EU Model of a Renewable Energy Community as a True Energy Cooperative

The REC will be a relevant European model of energy cooperative for the following two reasons.

Firstly, as a CEC, REC has as its primary purpose "to provide environmental, economic or social community benefits for its shareholders or members or for the local areas where it operates, rather than financial profits" (article 2 [16] [c] directive [EU] 2018/2001). Therefore, the cooperative model, with its primary mutual purpose, is perfect to provide (at least) economic benefits for (not necessarily only) members of the REC.

Secondly, differently from a CEC, REC must be an autonomous legal entity, in the sense that it "should be capable of remaining autonomous from individual members and other traditional market actors that participate in the community as members or shareholders, or who cooperate through other means such as investment" (recital 71 of directive [EU] 2018/2001). Consequently, the REC should be a democratic economic organization. Therefore, the ideal (not the unique) business model with which to set up the REC is as a cooperative.

REC should be "located in the proximity [it seems to be interpreted not as virtual or metaphoric, but as literal proximity] of the renewable energy projects [such as a wind power plant, a storage plant, a solar farm, or an electrical grid] that are owned and developed by that legal entity" (article 2 [16] (a) directive [EU] 2018/2001). However, more RECs, that are not necessarily located in close proximity, "should be able to share between themselves energy that is produced by their community-owned installations" (recital 71 of directive [EU] 2018/2001). Hence, a REC member may consume the energy produced by another REC that is distant from the said member, thanks to the possible horizontal integration among RECs.

Only subjects of the following categories will be able to become members of a REC: "natural persons, SMEs or local authorities, including municipalities" (article 2 [16] [b] directive [EU] 2018/2001). As regards local authorities, they will be members not necessarily (i.e. it will be lawful to have a REC without a local authority among its members), but they will be encouraged to join (so, clearly, article 22, paragraph 4 (h), directive [EU] 2018/2001).

According to the definition of a REC, it seems impossible for a cooperative whose members are only or mainly RECs to qualify as a REC; nevertheless, such a second-tier cooperative may exist legitimately and can supply services directly to its members and/or the members of its members.

EU law rules that the Member States "promote and facilitate the development of" RECs in their territories, *inter alia*, by supporting public authorities "in enabling and setting up renewable energy communities, and in helping authorities to participate directly", without prejudice to articles 107 and 108 TFEU (article 22, paragraphs 4 and 7, directive [EU] 2018/2001).

This means that REC, an entrepreneur necessarily promoted, if it is a cooperative, has to be a true cooperative, as the European Court of Justice (ECJ) pronounced in the famous Paint Graphos case (judgment of 8 September 2011 [Joined Cases C-78/08 to C-80/08]).[36] Otherwise, if a Member State allowed RECs in the form of a cooperative to act not as a true cooperative, then the same Member State could infringe EU State aid law (with all the negative consequences for that State). Indeed, only if a true cooperative is promoted, the related measure is not a State aid, because it is not selective.

According to Paint Graphos, the characteristics (listed in paragraphs 55–62 of the said judgment) of a true cooperative (i.e. with the ECJ describing cooperatives as those that "truly pursue an objective based on mutuality"), mostly deducted from recital 10 of regulation (EC) 1435/2003 on SCEs, are the following six: *(i)* "in the light of the principle of the primacy of the individual" there should be coherent rules "on membership, resignation and expulsion" of the members, the activities of the cooperatives "should be conducted for the mutual benefit of the members, who are at the same time users, customers or suppliers, so that each member benefits from the cooperative's activities in accordance with his participation in the cooperative and his transactions with it", cooperatives should "act in the economic interest of their members" and their relations with members should be "not purely commercial but personal and individual, the members being actively involved in the running of the business and entitled to equitable distribution of the results of economic performance"; *(ii)* the "control of cooperatives should be vested equally in members, as reflected in the 'one man, one vote' rule"; *(iii)* during the life of the cooperatives their reserves and assets should be "commonly held, non-distributable" and should "be dedicated to the common interests of members"; *(iv)* "net assets and reserves

[36] In European Court Reports, 2011, I-7611. On the said judgment and its importance for the cooperative law in the EU and in the EU Member States, see Cusa (2013a), pp. 51–64.

should be distributed on winding-up to another cooperative entity pursuing similar general interest purposes"; *(v)* cooperative shares should not be listed; *(vi)* a limitation on financial remuneration on loan and share capital should make "investment in a cooperative society less advantageous" than in a for-profit company.[37]

7 Conclusion

If it were set up in compliance with national law implementing EU law on RECs, a European energy cooperative would respect not only the international and vague model of a true cooperative laid down in the ICA Statement but also the European and more precise model (derived from the related ECJ case law model) of a true cooperative laid down in national laws implementing directive (EU) 2018/2001. Therefore, a REC, being a truer cooperative than the international true energy cooperative, should contribute to *sustainable* development better than the latter, since it is a more *sustainable* economic organization.

Hopefully, national laws implementing EU law on RECs invert the international tendency to lack an interest in cooperative law and to engage in the companization of cooperative law.[38] Thus, a well-conceived national law on RECs would demonstrate that a cooperative may be a useful business model, as an alternative to the company model, to achieve sustainable development more quickly.

References

Conforti B (2018) Diritto internazionale, 10th edn. Editoriale Scientifica, Napoli

Cusa E (2013a) Le forme di impresa private diverse dalle società lucrative tra aiuti di Stato e Costituzioni economiche europee. Giappichelli, Torino

Cusa E (2013b) State aid law and cooperatives in Europe. In: Brazda J, Dellinger M, Rößl D (eds), Genossenschaftes im Fokus einer neuen Wirtschaftspolitik. IV, LIT, Wien, pp 1105–1119

Cusa E (2019) Le cooperative sociali come doverose imprese sociali. Nuove Leggi Civili Commentate 42(4):948–989

Cusa E (2020) Sviluppo sostenibile, cittadinanza attiva e comunità energetiche. Orizzonti del Diritto Commerciale 1:71–126

Fajardo-García G (2019) New perspectives for the cooperativism of renewable energies: legal recognition and promotion. Int J Cooperative Law 2:111–126

Henrÿ H (2012a) Basics and new features of cooperative law—the case of public international cooperative law and the harmonisation of cooperative laws. Uniform Law Review 17(1):197–233

Henrÿ H (2012b) Guidelines for cooperative legislation, 3rd edn. ILO, Geneva

Henrÿ H (2013a) Public International Cooperative Law. In: Cracogna D, Fici A, Henrÿ H (eds) International handbook of cooperative law. Springer, Berlin-Heidelberg, pp 65–88

Henrÿ H (2013b) Trends and prospects of cooperative law. In: Cracogna D, Fici A, Henrÿ H (eds) International handbook of cooperative law. Springer, Berlin-Heidelberg, pp 803–823

[37] So Cusa (2013b), p. 1115.

[38] On the above-mentioned tendency, see Henrÿ (2012a), pp. 198 ff.

Henrÿ H (2013c) Sustainable development and cooperative law: corporate social responsibility or cooperative social responsibility? 10 Int Comparative Corporate Law J 3:58–75

Henrÿ H (2015) Social justice through enterprises. the end of the 1972/1973 conjuncture? a legal perspective. Int J Soc Quality 5(2):81–96

MacPherson I (2012) Cooperative's concern for the community: from members towards local communities' interest. Euricse Working Paper n. 46|13

Wanyama F (2014) Cooperatives and the sustainable development goals: a contribution to the post-2015 development debate. ILO, Geneve

The Wasted Potential of Cooperative Societies in Africa: Focus on Rural Development

Willy Tadjudje

1 Introduction

Conventionally, a cooperative is defined as an autonomous association of people voluntarily united to meet their common economic, social and cultural needs and aspirations through an enterprise whose ownership is collective and where power is exercised democratically. This definition is reflected in the International Cooperative Alliance's (ICA) Statement on International Cooperative Identity.[1]

The cooperative formula in Africa, in its modern form, was introduced through colonisation. At the time of colonisation, colonial administrations seem to have diverted the cooperative or communitarian spirit that they found on the continent. By law or regulation, they introduced biased and flowed features in the cooperatives so that they would only serve selfish interests. As a result, those "first-generation" cooperatives were effectively controlled by the colonial administration.[2]

Later, at the time of independence, most of the newly created African States validated and maintained that colonial legislation for two reasons, one being political in nature and the other socio-economic. Politically, colonial legislation was seen as favoring a better control of the population. Economically, the cooperative framework enabled the young governments to set up rural development programs that would be monitored and controlled through cooperatives, which were actually managed by civil servants. This is what we can call the "second generation" of African cooperatives.

In most African countries, significant developments have occurred in the meantime. A cooperative revival emerged around the 1990s, with the advent of autonomous

[1] Henrÿ (2013a), p. 65.
[2] Holmén (1990), p. 23.

W. Tadjudje (✉)
Université Catholique de Louvain, Ottignies-Louvain-la-Neuve, Belgium
e-mail: willy.tadjudje@uclouvain.be

W. Tadjudje and I. Douvitsa (eds.), *Perspectives on Cooperative Law*,
https://doi.org/10.1007/978-981-19-1991-6_24

and independent cooperatives, in contrast with the state-controlled model that had prevailed since the colonial period and was reconducted at the beginning of independence. This is called the "third generation" of African cooperatives.[3]

Cooperatives currently exist in all African countries and have enormous potential as vectors for development, especially in rural areas.

As noted by authors,[4] men and women faced debilitating problems of poverty, exclusion and inequality invented, almost 300 years ago, new ways of meeting their needs: the cooperative and the mutual. The model, inspired by the ideas of equality, democracy, freedom, equity, solidarity and care, and aiming toward a balance among those values, has evolved between practice and ideals. The organisational innovation brought forward through the cooperative project is shaking up our conceptions of the economy and business management.

Similarly, Charles Gide, a great French academic and theorist of consumer cooperatives, believes that cooperatives are "daughters of misery and necessity".[5] The author emphasises that, for those who lack financial means, regrouping in cooperatives is the only weapon available. The basic idea is to find ways, through cooperatives, to allow the poorest to make a dignified and respectable place in society for themselves, in order to escape exclusion and poverty.

Cooperatives have economic, social and cultural potential and can be decisive tools for positive transformation in the rural areas in Africa. In an analytical methodological approach, we will first present the potential of cooperatives in terms of improvement of living and working conditions in rural areas and, then, we will examine the possible strategies for a more efficient promotion of cooperatives to enable them to fulfill their development mission more effectively.

2 The Great Potential of Cooperative Societies for Rural Development in Africa

Cooperatives have always made it possible for men and women to access goods and services without being exploited. They can be seen as models of humanisation and sustainability of economic activities, thus introducing new approaches to corporate governance. By focusing primarily on human needs, cooperatives are an answer to today's sustainable development crises and deliver a distinct form of shared values that can be translated into economic, social and ecological terms.[6]

[3] Tadjudje (2015a), p. 36.

[4] Lafleur and Merrien (2012), p. 1.

[5] Gide (1904).

[6] ILO/ICA (2015), p. 20.

2.1 *Bettering Living and Working Conditions*

One of the most aggravating economic issues facing Africa, which does affect rural areas more seriously than cities, is the informality of a sizeable portion of the economic activity. According to the definition given by the International Labor Office (ILO) in 2002, the expression "informal economy" refers to all economic activities of workers and economic units that are not covered—under legislation or practice—by formal provisions. These activities do not fall within the scope of the law, which means that these workers and units operate outside the law; or they are not covered in practice, which means that the law is not applied to them even though they operate under the law; or the law is not respected because it is inappropriate, restrictive or imposes excessive burdens.[7]

The actors of the informal sector suffer from heightened vulnerability, especially in rural areas. They work extensively, but without always seeing much improvement in return as to their living and working conditions. For these reasons, the organisation of actors, especially in the form of a cooperative society can be the beginning of a solution. Knowing that cooperatives are entities recognised by the law, at least the activities organised in groups (within the framework of the cooperative) will allow rural actors to re-enter the frame of legality, and therefore dramatically strengthen the recognition, and then enforceability of their rights.

That is the reason why Hagen Henry underlines that, over the past 160 years, cooperatives have proved their worth as a way of promoting informal sector actors into the formal economy in many countries around the world. Cooperative law and policies facilitate the recognition of cooperatives as legal persons enjoying the same rights and obligations as those of other legally recognised economic entities. Appropriate legislation, which also regulates the taxation of cooperatives, takes into account the difference between profit and surplus, the rationale for patronage refunds, the constitution of indivisible reserve funds and the application of appropriate accounting standards are very effective measures in deterring informal economy's actors from tax evasion and the failure to pay social contributions.[8]

The formalisation of economies (through the development of cooperatives) can contribute to the promotion of decent jobs in rural areas.

According to the ILO, the concept of "decent work" is a good approximation of workers' aspirations, namely the possibility of productive, well-paid work with safe working conditions and social protection for the worker's family.[9] Decent work gives people the opportunity to flourish and integrate into society, as well as the freedom to express their concerns, trade unionise and take part in decisions that will affect their lives. It assumes equality of opportunity and treatment for women and men.[10]

To promote decent work in Africa through cooperatives, it is important to establish public and institutional policies that enable actors to pool their efforts, the purpose

---

[7] ILO (2002), p. 133.

[8] Henrÿ (2013b), p. 106.

[9] ILO (2013), p. 257.

[10] Ghai (2003), pp. 121–157.

being of course economies of scale. In the agricultural field, for example, the challenge is to maximise the added value of the products, instead of selling them in their raw state. Organising industrial units can be difficult for an isolated economic actor, exactly because such economies of scale are limited, but feasible as part of a collective and concerted project (within the framework of a cooperative).

Another critically important condition for decent work is the possibility of trade unionisation. One of the particularities of cooperatives consists in their faculty to organise themselves into apexes (umbrella cooperatives), including unions of cooperatives, federations and confederations. Traditionally, unions of cooperatives aggregate grassroots cooperatives, federations integrate unions and the confederation is a collection of federations. The purpose of this pyramid organisation is, on the one hand, economic: for grassroots cooperatives, it is a question of associating together to make, as part of a union, what would be more difficult to consider individually. This may involve marketing, accounting, setting up a processing unit or setting up a common point of sale, etc. On the other hand, cooperatives have a political mission. They act in defense of the rights of their members and represent them in all instances. From this point of view, the grouping into a cooperative integrates the possibility of organising to defend professional rights. In this sense, the mission of cooperative apexes may comprise the objectives of a trade union.

By design, cooperatives are managed democratically. Consequently, no matter how many shares one holds, votes are expressed at a general meeting following the "one person, one vote" rule. If anything matters in a cooperative, it is the work done by members and not the amount of contribution to the share capital. This is the reason why cooperatives distribute not dividends (like in corporations), but patronage refunds, in proportion to the economic operations carried out by each member. The democratic nature of cooperatives makes them an ideal school of democracy and equality.

A final (and vital) feature of decent work is social and health protection. In various African countries, health cooperatives are created to meet the health needs of the population, because of the general inability, on the part of the state, to provide adequate social services, especially in rural areas.[11]

2.2 Developing Social and Cultural Services

Among the negative social effects generated by the current strand of capitalism are certain problems, such as inequality and exclusion. The individual owner of economic capital has the essential tool to produce wealth. This wealth is acquired and exploited individually where it could have benefited an entire community in the context of a cooperative. In cooperatives, members favor equality through a diversified methodology for managing the benefits generated by the activities undertaken, as well as a democratic culture for decision-making.

[11] Girard (2014), p. 31.

Unlike corporations, cooperatives are directly and organically concerned with the needs of the poorest and the community, in compliance with their nature as non-profit enterprises. Therefore, the term "profit" is inappropriate in cooperatives: it is more accurate to think of the supplemental value created in that frame as "surplus". Similarly, members receive "patronage refunds" and not "dividends" as they would from corporations. In doing so, cooperatives place human beings at the center of their operations. The human being is rewarded for his/her work and not for his/her economic capital. Equality is consecrated above all other criteria.

The most visible cooperative sector in Africa, evidently in rural areas, is agriculture. Increasingly, when agricultural cooperatives gain strength, they engage in activities in social sectors abandoned by the government or ignored by corporations, mainly health, education and microfinance. Cooperatives thus replace the state in order to address, at least partly, the needs of the community, while they remain private enterprises. A good example comes from Ethiopia with the Oromia Coffee Farmers' Cooperative Union (OCFCU)[12] taking into consideration their work to improve the life in their community, through the building and establishment of social infrastructures.

2.3 *Improving Ecological Balance and Sustainability*

2.3.1 Ecological Balance

Cooperatives generally have a positive ecological balance. An important advantage for cooperatives lies in their territorial anchorage, which induces a very central principle, to wit, that of commitment to the community. Commitment to the community has been embedded in international cooperative law since 1995, following the revision of the International Statement on Cooperative Identity by the International Cooperative Alliance (ICA).

For cooperatives, it is about adopting internal measures so that the surrounding community can benefit from the repercussions of their investments, which is done daily, perhaps unconsciously, through various mechanisms. Commitment to the community, in the same direction, would aim to preserve the integrity of the surrounding environment, through responsible ecological attitudes.

[12] Oromia Coffee Farmers' Cooperative Union (OCFCU) is a smallholder coffee-growers-owned cooperative union established on June 1, 1999, by 34 cooperatives with 22,691 farmers. Today, there are 405 cooperatives with over 400,000 members and $20,000,000 share capital.

2.3.2 Sustainability

The investor-owned business was at the center of the financial crisis, with investors acting in their own interest and that of a handful of stakeholders. This is the manifestation of a possible adverse consequence of individual, though shared, property. For their part, cooperatives introduce the notion of common property as an approach to sustainable development in economic terms. This property results in the establishment of a common heritage.[13]

The common heritage of cooperatives is essentially constituted through the obligation to establish legal reserves that cannot be shared or distributed.[14] Furthermore, there are other aspects related to the restriction of the economic rights of members, knowing that the cooperative is not created to yield profit, but to improve the living and working conditions of its members. The reserves are an integral part of the cooperative's common heritage, and that role is safeguarded by the impossibility to share them in the course of social life. This indivisibility of the reserves becomes a manifestation of the questioning of any privative appropriation of the elements of the common heritage by the present or outgoing members.[15]

The cooperative, beyond being an instrument of development at the service of current members, is also a vector for solidarity and intergenerational support. The indivisibility of reserves, both during the life and at the dissolution of cooperatives, appears as a "sustainable development practice developed and applied to the field of business management, because this practice makes it possible to better respond to needs of the present while increasing the ability of future generations to meet their own needs. From this point of view, cooperatives can inject new methods of management, so as to ensure sustainability, while respecting the traditions and well-being of all".[16]

3 The Currently Unused Potential of Cooperative Societies for Rural Development in Africa

The necessity to efficiently promote cooperatives societies in Africa is justified by the current state of the cooperative movement. Possible solutions must be proposed.

---

[13] Touzard and Vandame (2009), pp. 36–57.

[14] At the end of each fiscal year, cooperatives must, before any distribution of patronage refunds, pay part of the annual net surplus in the form of indivisible reserves. This rate is between 10 and 20% depending on the country.

[15] Hiez (2008), p. 361.

[16] Lafleur and Merrien (2012), p. 12.

3.1 *Current State of the Cooperative Movement in Africa*

Cooperatives benefit from various frameworks through which they can defend the interests of farmers and rural people. Committed to improving the living conditions of their members, they usually remain at the forefront of social change. Despite the robustness of these existing frameworks, cooperative movements in Africa remain relatively weak. This can be explained by various reasons.

3.1.1 Negative Perception and Image of the Cooperative as a Tool

Most of the potential actors still have the mental image of cooperative as village associations of indigent people.

This attitude can be explained by ignorance, and also by a lack of training. A cooperative is a place of emancipation and that is why training is a core principle of its operation. However, this lack of training results from an insufficiency of human and financial resources. Unfortunately, cooperative studies are not included in African schools and academic curricula.

This perception of cooperatives has consequences, including the recurrence of the phenomenon of parallel sales of crops by members of agricultural cooperatives. The cooperative is set up, among other purposes, to allow producers members of the cooperative to sell at the best possible price by pooling their efforts within their cooperative. This is the reason why, in order to guarantee its contractual negotiation capacity, the cooperative passes with each cooperator, a contract of delivery of the exclusivity or a determined part of the harvest. In practice, producers tend to break the contract; however, when cooperative producers decide to sell in parallel, they weaken the contractual and commercial capacities of their cooperative.

3.1.2 Inefficient Management and Functioning

A successful business must be both efficient and effective. It is effective when it achieves the goals it has set for itself. It is efficient when it minimises the means implemented to achieve the objectives it has set itself.

In the context of Niger, for example, it was noted that in the elections of the members of the Board, the same people kept being re-elected, even if their previous management was not positive. The social constraint is such that young people and people with little money do not dare to run against the president of the cooperative who enjoys high notoriety in the village, either because he is wealthy or because he is a member of the family of the village chief, still because he militates in favor of the political party in power. Even an elder does not dare to challenge the president and run the risk of tainting the family relationships that bind them.[17]

---

[17] Bontianti (2003), pp. 103–118.

In this perspective, misappropriations become increasingly likely in cooperatives. These misappropriations are thus orchestrated by leaders, and this could be a strong incentive, among other things, for some to remain in the management functions. Indeed, "in many rice cooperatives in the department of Tillabéry (West of Niger), the peasant farmers struggle to pay the royalties at the end of the rice season simply because the managers of the cooperatives embezzle funds and overtax the peasants to try to hide the traces of their diversions. It is common that at the end of a campaign, the farmer is asked to repay more than he has incurred debts: the repayment is in kind. For example, a farmer is asked to repay 8 bags of rice, even though he has only harvested 5 bags".[18]

Such behaviors are therefore related to poor information about the real nature of cooperatives. As things stand, they are real societies, with all the constraints attached to enterprises. To reinvigorate cooperatives, especially in rural areas, it is imperative to strengthen training and awareness-raising actions. This would be an opportunity, for example, to let people know that leaders are responsible and that the actions they take, within their mandate, can lead to sanctions.[19]

3.1.3 Poor Access to Funding

One of the missions of cooperatives is to achieve economies of scale in the interest of their members. The full realisation of economies of scale depends heavily on the ability of members to contribute. In agricultural cooperatives, the debate is whether the cooperative collects members' products, sells them before paying the price to the cooperator or the cooperative pays the cooperator directly for the delivery of the product.

In the first case, the cooperator has to wait, and sometimes he or she cannot afford to, and therefore ends up making transactions with independent traders. In the second case, if it is necessary to pay directly at the time of the reception of products, very often the cooperative does not have enough cash to honor such an engagement. At times, cooperatives solicit loans from industrial groups that buy their products to finance the campaign.[20]

It is understandable that all those difficulties occur where the cooperative is not sufficiently funded. However, normally, at the creation of the cooperative, after the definition of needs, the cooperators must provide the necessary means to allow the cooperative to work. It is this participation that will allow the cooperative to achieve economies of scale in order to effectively meet the needs of its members.

Nevertheless, in practice, "rarely, an organisation has been the result of collective solutions to common problems identified by members with a relevant strategy of self-financing. The fact is that most organisations are not able to properly perform

---

[18] Sambiani (2001), pp. 109–121.

[19] Simmons (2008), pp. 2131–2140.

[20] Tadjudje (2020), p. 178.

economic functions for the benefit of members who pay little contribution. Moreover, the share capital of the majority of peasants' organisations consists mainly of membership fees and contributions seem derisory to support economic activities".[21] Thus, there are cooperatives bringing together actors who for some have never released a single share, but consider themselves members of the cooperative. There are also actors hostile to any form of contribution, but still demanding services.

3.1.4 Weak Structuring and Unproductive Dialogue with the State

In order to achieve economies of scale, cooperatives usually come together in unions, federations and confederations. Nevertheless, on the African continent, those umbrella organisations are endemically weak, which is usually attributable to leadership quarrels. Many aspire to the position of president of the confederation and, eventually, the project of creation never materialises. Another common cause of failure is a lack of financial resources to mobilise the actors or make the new structure work.[22]

However, it seems that the training problem is the most easily solvable and that the others would only come from the goodwill of the actors. Once structuring is assured, cooperatives should organise their representativeness. African cooperatives are not only weakly structured. They are also underrepresented in the various forums where they should normally make their voices heard. These are grounds for legislative processes and government actions. In some countries, it has been found that cooperative laws and agrarian reforms have been adopted without the proper consultation of cooperative actors. The same is true of government actions taken without prior notification of the cooperative movements. Therefore, there is a risk of applying rules contrary to the needs and interests of cooperatives and therefore farmers and rural people.[23]

3.2 *The Necessity to Promote Effective Cooperative Societies for Rural Development in Africa*

According to the Blueprint for a Cooperative Decade,[24] to improve and promote a strong and reliable cooperative movement, it is necessary to focus on five critical interlinked themes and establish implementation strategies in relation to each of them:

1. Elevate participation within membership and governance to a new level;
2. Position cooperatives as builders of sustainability;

---

[21] Onate (2012), p. 23.

[22] Tadjudje (2020), p. 178.

[23] Münkner (1987), p. 1.

[24] ICA (2013).

3. Build the cooperative message and secure the cooperative identity;
4. Ensure supportive legal frameworks for cooperative growth;
5. Secure reliable cooperative capital while guaranteeing member control.

3.2.1 Elevation of Members' Participation

The individual member has an idiosyncratic role to play in a cooperative which goes beyond the basic economic relationship of customer, worker or producer. Collectively, members own their cooperative, and through democratic arrangements they participate in its governance. Individually they are entitled to information, voice and representation.

If being a member of a cooperative does not result in visible and tangible benefits to members, there is no incentive for membership. Cooperatives are established to provide solutions to the needs and aspirations of members. Therefore, if a cooperative does not develop services in return for the contributions of the cooperators, the latter will see no advantage in pooling their efforts within the framework of a cooperative. On the other hand, in the event that the members enjoy benefits resulting from their membership in a cooperative, they are therefore encouraged to continue their participation in the activities of the cooperative and other persons may be encouraged and motivated to become members.

In this way, the process of self-promotion of the cooperative can become fruitful: participation in the activities of the cooperative produces benefits for the member, who is therefore motivated to continue and intensify his/her participation in the life of the cooperative.

Roughly speaking, where the new rules of collaboration under the cooperative are not known, accepted and respected by the cooperators, the norms and rules of capitalism could penetrate the cooperative societies. In this case, the cooperative will not be able to function effectively. Information, education, training and awareness-raising about the principles and practical rules of cooperative action are essential conditions for bringing individuals to understand the process of self-promotion and master the organisation of work in cooperative societies.

Investment in education, training, information and awareness is simultaneously a direct investment in the mobilisation of human resources for the development and animation of the cooperative society. In this movement, umbrella cooperatives can play an important role in organising training courses in affiliated cooperatives with a view to pooling efforts. In some experiments, leaders are trained to serve as grassroots trainers, in order to take into account cultural realities, including the possibility of restoring mother tongue knowledge in rural areas.[25]

[25] Münkner (1988), p. 1.

3.2.2 Focusing on Sustainability

The Blueprint for a Cooperative Decade underlines that cooperatives have always set out to enable people to have access to goods and services, without exploitation. This has meant trading in accordance with a set of values approximating to a great extent what we would today call sustainability. By placing human needs at their center, cooperatives respond to today's crises of sustainability and deliver a distinctive form of "shared value". Quite simply, a cooperative is a collective pursuit of sustainability. Cooperatives seek to "optimise" outcomes for a range of stakeholders in the long term, without seeking to "maximise" the benefit for any single stakeholder.

Building economic, social and environmental sustainability must therefore be one of the over-arching motivations and justifications for a growing cooperative sector. It offers an answer to the question of why cooperatives are necessary and beneficial at this historical juncture. Put simply, cooperatives are more efficient than investor-owned businesses, once a more complete range of costs and benefits (present and future) is taken into account.

The emphasis on sustainability should also be increased, for example in the field of land, knowing that this issue poses enormous problems in rural Africa. Cooperatives can organise themselves to promote new mechanisms for securing their land, in order to avoid conflicts. More concretely, they will have to fight land-grabbing when necessary so that the actors present in rural communities can live and draw sufficient economic resources by the exploitation of their lands, which they exploit rationally while respecting the life cycle of nature.[26]

3.2.3 Protecting Cooperative Identity

According to the Blueprint for a Cooperative Decade, a great advantage that cooperatives possess is having Cooperative principles. Cooperatives don't simply appear different, thanks to some image makeover—they fundamentally are different. Their abiding values of participation and sustainability are not just bolted on to a conventional business model, but structure how they are owned, governed, managed and evaluated. With consumers increasingly cynical about the ethical "green-washing" of corporate brands, cooperatives have an authenticity that no other ethical business model can match.

An effective way to protect the identity of cooperatives is to include cooperative education courses in college and university programs. In most African countries, all forms of organisation and enterprise are included in training programs, *except* cooperatives. This is very likely to be the starting point of the widespread confusion regarding the specificity of cooperatives.

[26] Tadjudje (2015b), pp. 135–265.

3.2.4 Providing and Ensuring Supportive Legal Framework for Cooperative Growth

The view that cooperatives are a marginal form of enterprise is not uncommon. There is often a failure to understand precisely how they work or the benefits they deliver, and the misunderstanding is often exacerbated by the general lack of coverage of the cooperative sphere in the education and training of those going into the business world. These factors contribute to financial, legal and regulatory infrastructures that are essentially designed for the greater majority of businesses, which are profit-oriented and shareholder-owned but are inappropriate for cooperatives in certain important respects.

In addition to this reality, there is also, in the context of Africa, an *instrumentalisation* of cooperatives by the public authorities. This dates from the colonial period in which cooperatives served as a tool for implementing public development plans. Since the beginning of the 1990s, most African states have developed cooperative legislation that favors the independence and autonomy of cooperatives vis-à-vis public authorities. This is why the ILO summarises the role of the state in the development of cooperatives as follows: "States should restrict the role of government to a regulatory function of cooperatives to:

1. establishing a policy and legal framework based on cooperative principles;
2. the establishment of an institutional framework for rapid and simplified registration of cooperatives;
3. the establishment of a policy and legal framework to promote a vertical cooperative structure that meets the needs of cooperative members;
4. the adoption, for the supervision of cooperatives, of measures equivalent to those applying to other forms of enterprise".[27]

It is important for cooperatives themselves to resist any tendency to mimic investor-owned enterprises in operational, management and governance practices, which do not reflect the distinctiveness of cooperatives. This can often be the easier option when operating within infrastructure designed for investor-owned businesses, but unless cooperatives resist and fight for appropriate recognition and treatment they risk losing their distinctiveness and commercial advantages through isomorphic behavior. Managers need to be supported and encouraged in their efforts to achieve and maintain those objectives.

3.2.5 Securing Reliable Capital Without Sacrificing Autonomy and Independence of Cooperatives

According to the Blueprint for a Cooperative Decade, investor-owned businesses raise capital from those who are looking for a financial return. This may be in terms of income from dividends, or capital growth in the value of the business over a period of

[27] ILO (2001).

time, or a combination of the two. Traditional "equity capital" provides these benefits and relies on the principle that ownership of a share entitles the investor to a proportionate share of the underlying capital value of the company, and a proportionate share of any profits distributed by way of dividend.

Cooperative capital is different in relation to both of these principles. First, a member is generally only entitled to receive back from the society the amount of money deposited or subscribed for shares. So there is no entitlement to a share in the endeavor's underlying value. Second, whilst cooperatives can pay interest on capital, under the third Cooperative principle members receive "limited compensation, if any, on capital subscribed as a condition of membership". To the extent that profits or surplus is distributed to members, that distribution is in proportion to the members' trade with the society.

When compared with company equity capital, cooperative capital does not offer investors comparable economic benefits. As a result, it is not as economically attractive and is of little interest to investors.

From this point of view, banks are reluctant to extend credit to cooperatives, so they are forced to gain a way to access finance by themselves. Instead of abandoning their pursuit, they can rely on the existing techniques and strategies. One of them consists of resorting to internal contributions, in the form of *tontine*. This has been observed in Mali where women selling fresh fish have been confronted at one point with a very specific problem. The latter bought fish daily from fishermen and sold them in markets. Early on, they faced a problem of fish conservation, as they were unable to sell everything they bought from fishermen before the end of the day. After reflection, they had the choice between buying a freezer, or the use of the technique of smoking. The second solution proved to be the most practical. They assessed the costs of acquiring a fish-smoking unit and this was out of their immediate range. Knowing that they were not eligible for bank credit due to the lack of collateral, they decided to use the savings technique. Every day every woman should pay a small amount. By adding up these contributions over time, they were able, in a short time, to raise the necessary budget to acquire their fish-smoking unit. Thanks to this acquisition, they have considerably improved their living and working conditions.

In practice, women's contributions have been converted into shares, as part of an increase in the share capital of their cooperative. This practice is to be encouraged. In most cases, cooperatives set the amount of their share capital without referring to any budgeted needs assessment. Moreover, they do not always think of increases in share capital (the main source of funding for the cooperative) during their social life, in order to be able to provide services to members.

Most cooperatives resigned themselves to remaining poor and unproductive as if their financial situation was a foregone conclusion. The reality is that the members have not formed their cooperative taking into account its purpose which is the resolution of the problems they face.

References

Bontianti A (2003) Mouvement coopératif et organisation du monde rural au Niger: bilan, perspectives et propositions pour l'avenir. Les Cahiers D'outre-Mer 221:103–118
Ghai D (2003) Travail décent: concept et indicateurs. Rev Int Trav 2:121–157
Gide C (1904) Les sociétés coopératives de Consommation. Biblithèque du musée social
Girard J-P (2014) Better health & social care-how are co-ops & mutuals boosting innovation & access worldwide? An International Survey of Co-ops and Mutuals in the Health and Social Care Sector. http://productionslps.com/wp-content/uploads/2014/10/International-survey-co_op-and-mutual-Health-and-social-care-CMHSC-14.pdf.
Hiez D (2008) La propriété commune de la coopérative, un modèle de développement durable. In: Draperi JF (ed) Défis coopératifs, Alimentation, crédit, démocratie, développement, l'Harmattan, p 361–382
Holmén, H (1990) State, cooperatives and development in Africa. The Scandinavian Institute of African Studies. Research report no. 86
Henrÿ H (2013a) Public international cooperative law. In: Cracogna D et al (eds) International handbook of cooperative law. Springer, Heidelberg, pp 65–88
Henrÿ H (2013b) Guidelines for cooperative legislation. International Labor Organization
ICA (2013) Blueprint for a cooperative decade. International Cooperative Alliance
IFAD (2016) Rural development report 2016—Fostering inclusive rural transformation, IFAD
ILO (2001) Promotion of cooperatives, 5th question at the agenda of the 89th session of the international labour conference. International Labour Organisation
ILO (2002) Decent work and the informal economy. International Labour Conference
ILO (2011) Des coopératives pour un développement rural axé sur les personnes. International Labor Organisation
ILO (2013) Decent work indicators—Guidelines for producers and users of statistical and legal framework indicators. International Labor Organisation
ILO/ICA (2015) Cooperatives and the sustainable development goals—a contribution to the post-2015 development debate—a policy brief. International Labor Organisation/International Cooperative Alliance
Lafleur M, Merrien A-M (2012) Impact socio-économique des coopératives et des mutuelles—Quand le passé inspire le futur: contribution des coopératives et des mutuelles à un monde meilleur. University of Sherbrooke
Mercandalli S, Losch B (2017) Rural Africa in motion—dynamics and drivers of migration South of the Sahara. FAO and CIRAD
Münkner H (1987) Strengths and weaknesses of the co-operative movement in West Africa—conditions for its development. Terre Et Progrès 71:16–18
Münkner H (1988) Pourquoi les coopératives sont-elles importantes pour les pays en voie de développement ? Comment peuvent-elles être efficaces ? Genossenschaftsforum 1
Onate S (2012) Les organisations de producteurs en Afrique de l'Ouest et du Centre : attentes fortes, dures réalités. Le cas du Burkina Faso. FARM/IRAM
Sambiani D (2001) Réflexions sur les obstacles aux organisations paysannes en Afrique: un exemple emprunté du centre rizicole de Zio du sud-Togo. Rev CAMES 002:09–121
Simmons R (2008) The role of co-operatives in poverty reduction: networks perspectives. J Socio-Econ 37:2131–2140
Tadjudje W (2015a) Le droit des coopératives et des mutuelles dans l'espace OHADA. Larcier
Tadjudje W (2015b) L'accès durable des paysans à la terre: quel peut être l'apport des coopératives à la lutte contre l'accaparement des terres en Afrique ? Revue des mutations en Afrique—Réflexions sur les politiques et les pratiques 1:135–156
Tadjudje W (2020) Les conditions de l'efficacité des coopératives en Afrique. Academia
Touzard J-M, Vandame R (2009) La coopérative comme outil du développement durable : le cas des coopératives d'apiculteurs au Mexique et au Guatemala. RECMA 313:36–57

Legal Developments Regarding Cooperatives' Activities and Governance

The Multi-activity, Multi-stakeholder and Community Interest Cooperative and Their Legal Regulation

Gemma Fajardo-García

In honour of Professor Hagen Henry for his friendship, teaching, and persistent and successful commitment to Cooperative Law

1 Introduction

Cooperatives emerge as an organisational and operational model of a group of people who, having common needs, unite to meet those needs through the common development of economic activities.

We initially know the organisational and operational model through the literature and its materialisation in social statutes such as the Statutes of the Rochdale Equitable Pioneers Society, the most characteristic rules of which are identified with the subsequently named cooperative principles.

The cooperative emerges as an original model which is different from the current private organisational models, at the moment, which are mainly commercial companies. It is true that the Rochdale Pioneers were inspired by the statutes of a mutual benefit society, the Manchester Sick and Burial Benefit Society,[1] and though they took essential characteristics such as open door, democratic management or the participation of the associates in the activity from these, the fact is that their corporate purpose went beyond social security. The people who establish a cooperative do so to meet their common economic, social or cultural needs. As the definition of the

[1] See Holyoake (1975).

This work is the result of the research project: Social Economy, Self-management and Employment (DER2016-78732-R) Financing: Ministry of Science, Innovation and Universities of Spain, State Research Agency and European Regional Development Fund (ERDF).

G. Fajardo-García (✉)
University of Valencia, Valencia, Spain
e-mail: fajardo@uv.es

W. Tadjudje and I. Douvitsa (eds.), *Perspectives on Cooperative Law*,
https://doi.org/10.1007/978-981-19-1991-6_25

ICA cooperative states, these needs can be unique and limited or they can be diverse, but in any case they are the central reason why the cooperative exists.

Since its origins, the cooperative has been adapted to meet multiple needs and this has resulted in various cooperative models. Some laws qualify cooperatives by types or trades, depending on the members' function as stakeholders (workers, consumers and producers), or the economic activities carried out (credit, insurance, agriculture, transportation, teaching and housing). This allows specific standards to be established for each type of cooperative and facilitates their integration into cooperative federations that represent their particular interests. These different types are usually regulated by special laws or particular standards within a general law on cooperatives.[2]

However, in their growth, the cooperatives should not be limited by the existence of predetermined classes and they must be able to adopt the cooperative form whatever the new need to be met. When there is no expressly adequate typology to regulate the new model, it is common for the new cooperative to submit to the most similar cooperative model established by law.

The possibility of having a flexible instrument such as the cooperative to meet the needs of its members has favoured the creation of new cooperatives to meet new needs as well as the extension of the corporate purpose of existing ones to respond to new needs. Therefore, by dealing with the corporate purpose of cooperatives, we can differentiate several cooperative models.[3]

(a) Cooperatives are created to meet a specific need of their members, which constitute a homogeneous group, such as a credit cooperative, whose activity is to provide credit services to its members (users of such services). This would be the case of a specialised cooperative, also called mono-active or uni-active.
(b) Cooperatives are created to meet various needs of their members, which constitute a homogeneous group, such as a consumer cooperative that in addition to credit activities performs other activities such as the construction of homes for its members. This would be the case of a multi-activity cooperative.
(c) Cooperatives are created to meet the needs of their members, which constitute a heterogeneous group, such as a cooperative that supplies food to its consumer members, with the work of its worker members. This would be the case of a multi-stakeholder cooperative.

The previous classification reflects the possible existence of various corporate purpose models of a cooperative based on the combination of activities and member categories, but in any case, they are cooperative models which have meeting the needs of their members as their priority purpose. That is, all of them are cooperatives for mutual purposes, members may be homogeneous or not, and the needs singular or plural, but in any case their satisfaction is the priority objective of the cooperative.

---

[2] See Münkner (2015).

[3] Colombian Cooperative Law (Law No. 79 of 1988) states that due to the development of their activities, cooperatives may be specialised, multi-activity and multi-stakeholder.

Together with these cooperatives, other models have been developed in recent years that focus on meeting the needs of a group of people, whether or not they are members of the cooperative. In these cases, the general interest of the said group of people or community becomes relevant to the mutual interest of the members. These cooperatives can be called community interest cooperatives. This would be the case of a rural development cooperative that integrates various groups of people as members whether or not they participate in their economic activity, but that seeks to benefit the interests present in a given territory from this activity.[4]

This evolution has been natural and reflects the way in which civil society is organised to meet the needs that are not met by the state or the market; or that are not met enough. However, these social innovations are not always accompanied by the corresponding legal recognition and their necessary adaptation to the cooperative legal regime.

In the following pages we will briefly analyse these cooperative models in order to identify what economic function they meet if they have a presence in the legal systems, and what their main characteristics would be.

2 Multi-activities and Multi-stakeholder Cooperative

As we have seen, multi-activity cooperatives go against specialised cooperatives. These seek to meet a specific need shared by a homogeneous group of people. These people are integrated as members of the cooperative in order to participate in their economic activity, thanks to which they hope to meet their needs. For example, if it is a worker cooperative, its need will possibly be to obtain a stable and satisfactory job; and if it is a consumer cooperative, the acquisition of certain goods or services in the best possible conditions. Participation in the cooperative activity is the main right and duty that the member has when entering the cooperative (they participate by working, acquiring, transforming or marketing their goods or services through the cooperative); but in addition, it assumes the responsibility of its management, in the terms agreed in its statutes, and the management must always be democratic. Any person who shares the same need, wants to participate in the cooperative activity and meets the requirements established in the statutes, must be able to access the cooperative requirement, without obstacles or limitations that are not justified or discriminatory. However, it is possible that the cooperative accepts that non-members can participate in the said cooperative activity (non-member users) as long as the legislation and the statutes of the cooperative authorise it and under the conditions of the said authorisation.

A multi-activity cooperative is one that carries out various economic activities to meet the plural needs of a homogeneous group of members; for example, a consumer cooperative that supplies its members with food products, and also provides them

[4] See Solarino (2020), p. 109.

with financial, social and cultural services. An example of a multi-activity cooperative would be agricultural cooperatives.[5] In all of them, the members are owners of an agricultural business or of agricultural interests, and the activities that these cooperatives carry out may consist of acquiring and producing for the cooperative or for the business of their members, animals, feed, fertilisers, plants, seeds, insecticides, materials, instruments, machinery, facilities and any other elements necessary or suitable for agricultural production and development; conserve, typify, manipulate, transform, transport, distribute and market, even directly to the consumer, the products coming from the cooperative's business and their members in their natural or previously transformed state; acquire, plot, clean and improve land for agriculture, farming or forests, as well as the construction and operation of the works and facilities necessary for these purposes; any other activities that are necessary or suitable or that facilitate the economic, technical, labour or ecological improvement of the cooperative or of the holdings of the members, etc.

These cooperatives can also carry out additional activities for their members and other people in their environment, as well as activities aimed at promoting and improving the agricultural population and the rural environment in general, as well as a manifestation of interest by the community that characterises the cooperatives.

A multi-stakeholder cooperative would be one that carries out one or several economic activities to meet the needs of two or more member groups. This would be the case of a transport cooperative that carries out the transport activity with transport members (producer), and worker members, therefore integrating a business services cooperative and a worker cooperative; or a production and distribution cooperative that integrates consumer and producer members (farmers). In Article 105 of Spanish Law on Cooperatives 27/1999, multi-stakeholder cooperatives are described as "those that, regardless of their type, have double or plural cooperative activity, fulfilling the purposes of different types of cooperatives in the same society,... and in compliance with what is regulated for each of these activities. In such cases, its corporate purpose will be plural and they will benefit from the legal treatment that corresponds to it for the fulfilment of said aims. In the corporate bodies of the integrated cooperatives there must always be representation of the integrated activities in the cooperative. The Statutes may reserve the position of President or Vice President to a certain type of member".

Returning to the agricultural sector, a multi-stakeholder cooperative could be a cooperative that integrates both the owners of farms or agricultural interests as owners, as well as the workers of the cooperative,[6] or members who do not participate in agricultural activities but activities of another nature (tourism, renewable energies, etc.). Portuguese legislation calls these "multisectoral agricultural cooperatives" and they will be agricultural, provided that they have at least one specific activity of the

---

[5] This is expressed by Spanish Law 27/1999 (Art. 93) in relation to agricultural cooperatives; the French Rural Code in relation to agricultural cooperative societies (Art. L.521-1 and L.522-1) and Portuguese Decree-Law No. 335/99 (Art. 13 et seq.) on "Cooperativas agrícolas polivalentes e multissectoriais".

[6] In Italy it would be the case of a cooperative that integrates the two types of agricultural cooperative: "*cooperative di produzione*" and "*cooperative de conferimento*".

agricultural industry in their corporate purpose and their members, registered in the agricultural activity, are more than half of the total members of the cooperative.[7]

Multi-activity and multi-stakeholder cooperatives have a long-standing tradition. The cooperative of the Rochdale pioneers was created from its origin as a cooperative of this nature since its statutes provided for the opening of a warehouse for the sale of provisions, clothes, etc. for its members; the purchase and construction of a certain number of houses for its members; the start of manufacturing of the articles that society deems appropriate to provide work for members who are unemployed or subject to repeated reductions in their wages; and the purchase of land to be cultivated by unemployed members or whose work was poorly paid.[8]

Multi-activity cooperatives are very common in Latin America.[9] Most of them begin as specialised cooperatives, usually savings and credit cooperatives, and over time and due to the demand of their own members they incorporate other services such as health, education, sport, recreation, consumption, etc. into their purpose.[10] According to Rymel Serrano, these cooperatives were developed in Colombia in 1930 and were promoted by companies in order to improve the living conditions of their workers through them and simultaneously, remove much of the worker pressure on the company.[11] In this way the cooperative emerged to meet the consumption of workers, but it also offered them credit services and housing further down the line, as well as recreation and education activities, etc. Another case of a multi-activity cooperative developed especially in Argentina is the so-called public service cooperatives, which were initially created to provide necessary services but were not profitable for commercial companies such as electrification, water, gas, sewers, drains and roads; over time they began to provide other services (funeral, health, social assistance, telephony, radio, television, internet, conservation of rural roads, etc.).[12] The public services cooperative has several variants and according to García Müller,[13] they can be not only specialised or multi-active cooperatives but also of users of public services, service providers or mixed (multi-stakeholder). Sometimes public service cooperatives acquire greater public relevance, as they are promoted and owned by public administrations or controlled by them, as in the Valencian Community (Legislative Decree 2/2015, Art. 99) or Bolivia.[14]

---

[7] Decreto-Lei 335/99, Art. 19 et seq.

[8] See Holyoake (1975), p. 20.

[9] See Silva (2008), p. 115.

[10] See García Müller (2018), p. 101.

[11] Serrano (2018), p. 21.

[12] See Fernández (2017) and Moirano (2008), p. 8.

[13] García Müller (2008), p. 137.

[14] According to the Political Constitution of Bolivia (7 February 2009, Art. 335): "*Public service cooperatives are non-profit organisations that have collective interest, are under government control and are democratically managed. The selection of their administration and supervisory authorities will be carried out in accordance with their own statutory regulations and supervised by the Plurinational Electoral Body. Their organisation and operation will be regulated by law*".

3 Community Interest Cooperatives

Community interest cooperatives can be considered an evolution of multi-activity and multi-stakeholder cooperatives since the interest they seek to satisfy goes beyond the interest of the various associated groups, until they are identified with the interest of the community.[15]

It is true that the interest in the community has always been present in the cooperative, and not only since it is explicitly recognised as another cooperative principle.[16]

However, a new principle was incorporated in the revision of the cooperative principles approved in "The ICA Statement on the Cooperative Identity" in 1995 (7th Principle. Concern for Community). According to this principle: "Cooperatives work to achieve the sustainable development of their communities through public policies approved by their members." This principle is based on the value of solidarity and shows that although cooperatives exist primarily for the benefit of their members, they are also closely linked to the communities in which they are in, so they have a responsibility for the development of the community from an economic, social, cultural and environmental point of view. But the scope of this commitment, as the Report that accompanies the ICA Declaration says, must be determined by the members. The members have to decide how deeply and in what specific way a cooperative should make its contributions to its community.[17] Indeed, the commitment that a cooperative assumes to its community can be very intense, but it will be subject to the decision of its members, so it can be concluded that the predominant interest in the cooperative remains the interest of its members.

The novelty presented by what we call cooperatives of community interest is that they equate community interest with the interest of the cooperative members and even prioritise it. This relevance has led to the admission, both in the legislation and in theory, that the cooperative can have the interest of its members (mutual purpose) or the interest of the community as its purpose, also identified as the general interest of the community.[18]

The word "community" comes from the Latin *commūnitās*, which means "quality of the common, a group of people who live together, who have the same interests or who live under the same rules". The Dictionary of the Royal Spanish Academy defines community as a group of people from a town, region or nation, and as a

---

[15] See Mori (2014), p. 347.

[16] See Uribe (2002), p. 380.

[17] As Uribe (2002), p. 376, explains, the original text of this principle put both interests at the same level ("At the same time that they focus on the needs and desires of the members, cooperatives work to achieve the sustainable development of their communities"); but at the initiative of the German delegation, it was reconsidered that the promotion of the members should prevail, as well as the socio-user identity.

[18] This is described in the Law on Social Cooperatives as we will see and is included in the study on the Principles of European Cooperative Law. See Fici (2017), p. 19. According to the proposed definition of cooperative in these principles: "Cooperatives may also be established to carry on an economic activity mainly in the general interest of the community ("general interest cooperatives")".

group of people linked by common characteristics or interests, among other meanings (www.dle.rae.es).

A cooperative of community interest would be one that therefore seeks the satisfaction of the needs of people who belong to a community because they have the same interests or reside in the same area. This category could include social cooperatives, public services, local development, immigrants, youth, women, elderly people, etc., provided that its objective is to benefit all the people that make up that community with its activity, whether or not they are associated with the cooperative.

The idea of a cooperative that primarily addresses the general interests versus the interests of its members may seem contradictory to the definition of cooperative that we saw at the beginning; however, as we also saw, the cooperative principle of interest for the community accepts that it is the members of the cooperative that determine what their commitment to the community will be and how they will carry it out.

It is possible that the community interest coincides with the general interest of society, but this may not be the case. The general interest is identified more with the common good or general will, whose defence justifies the birth of the State, and that once recognised in the Constitution, it legitimises the adoption of decisions and public policies. The general interest in the regulations is usually identified with the public interest, an interest that transcends the specific interests of both citizens and groups of citizens. The community interest can coincide with the general interest when it seeks the well-being of people, the defence of the environment or the fight against social exclusion, for example. But it is also possible that the satisfaction of the needs of a specific community is carried out with actions that are not compatible with the general interest of society. Therefore, it seems more appropriate to use the expression of community or collective interest, which is more descriptive, than that of general interest; notwithstanding recognising that many activities carried out by cooperatives of community interest will in turn be of general interest.

There are different kinds of cooperatives of community interest that can be developed. In some cases, the beneficiary groups will be defined by their status (age, sexual orientation, ethnicity, religion etc.); by sharing the same circumstances (patients, migrants, refugees, disabled, social exclusion and unemployed); the same interests (professional, sports, recreational, cultural etc.) or by their location in the territory (neighbourhood, municipality, region etc.). All of them would have in common that their corporate purpose is aimed at satisfying the needs and interests (singular or plural) of certain groups or communities, by conducting business activities that are organised in accordance with cooperative values and principles.

Some legal systems have provided specific cooperative models that respond to these characteristics. This would be the case in France of the Collective Interest Cooperative Societies and the Agricultural Collective Interest Society; and in Italy, of the Social Cooperative and Community Cooperative.

(a) Collective Interest Cooperative Societies. Regulated in Law No. 47-1775 of 10 September on the Statute of the Cooperation (Arts. 19 quinquies to 19 sexdecies), they are defined as variable capital companies and their purpose is the production or supply of goods and services of collective interest and social utility,[19] normally within the framework of international solidarity and development aid projects. Non-members can benefit from the products and services of this cooperative. Members may be any natural or legal person who contributes to their activity in any way, mainly the people who produce the goods and services, the employees of the cooperative, who usually benefit, free of charge or onerously, from the activities of the cooperative, volunteers and public persons. The cooperative must incorporate at least three categories of members, which will necessarily include the people who benefit from its activities and the workers, and in their absence, the producers of the goods and services of the cooperative. The territorial public entities (territorial collectivities, their groupings and territorial public establishments) can collectively hold up to 50% of the capital of each cooperative.

Each member has one vote in the assembly, or when applicable, in the panel to which they belong. The statutes may expect that members are distributed based on their participation in the activity of the cooperative or their contribution to its development in three or more panels. Each panel has an equal number of votes to the general assembly unless the statutes provide otherwise. In the event that the statutes determine the distribution of members by panels and the number of votes that each panel will have in the assembly, no school may have more than 50% of the total votes or less than 10%, and contribution to capital may not be the weighting criterion.

The bylaws must allocate the annual budget to a statutory reserve. This cannot be less than 50% of the sums available after the provision of legal reserves. The total amount of interest on capital contributions cannot exceed the amounts available after the previous allocations. Subsidies, grants and other financial measures provided to the cooperative by territorial public entities and associations will not be taken into account for the calculation of interest payable to social parties. The norms by which the benefits generated by the clients are not distributable and those that determine that the distribution of the surpluses must be made in proportion to the participation in the cooperative activity, are not applicable to these cooperatives, nor those that allow the capital charged to reserves to be increased. Upon dissolution of the cooperative and after liquidating the liability, the assembly may decide to reimburse the capital contributed by the members, and the rest, to other cooperatives, cooperative unions or companies of the social and solidarity economy.

(b) Agricultural Collective Interest Companies, regulated in the Rural Code (Art. L531-1 and L532-1) are cooperatives constituted as civil or commercial companies, which are intended to create or manage facilities and equipment, or

[19] Social goods and services are those that meet at least one of the following three conditions: aim to provide support to people in a fragile situation, "contribute to the fight against exclusion and health, social, economic and cultural inequalities, to education for citizenship, the preservation and development of the social link or the maintenance and reinforcement of territorial cohesion", or they contribute to sustainable development.

provide services, either in the interest of farmers in a given rural region, or more generally, to the inhabitants of that region without professional distinction.

Regarding the distribution of votes in the general meeting, the law wants 4/5 of the votes to be in the hands of farmers or foresters in the area of the cooperative, natural or legal persons who possess agricultural interests in the said area relating to the cooperative corporate purpose; agricultural groupings of community land exploitation; agricultural associations and unions and other agricultural cooperative societies, unions of these and societies of agricultural collective interest.

The above must mainly participate in the activities of the cooperative. At least 50% of the activities must be carried out with them.

(c) Social Cooperatives.

Social cooperatives, regulated by Law 381 of 8 November 1991, are characterised by the objective of "pursuing the general interest of the community" to human promotion and the integration of citizens through (a) the management of social, socio-sanitary and educational services, and (b) the development of diverse activities (agricultural, industrial, commercial and services) aimed at the employability of disadvantaged people. The condition of a disadvantaged person is determined administratively. The disadvantaged people of the cooperative (c) must represent at least 30% of the workers of the cooperative and must be members.

These cooperatives can expect the presence of volunteer members in their statutes, provided they do not exceed half of the members in number. It is also provided by the law that social cooperatives may accept public or private legal persons as members whose statutes provide for the financing and development of the activity of such cooperatives.

To be benefited fiscally, social cooperatives must meet the mutual requirements required by the Legislative Decree of 14 December 1947 (Art. 26) to all cooperatives: non-distribution of dividends above the legal interest; non-distribution of reserves among the partners; and reimbursement, in case of dissolution, of the equity, with the capital contributed deducted, for the purpose of public interest.

(d) Community Cooperatives

The so-called community cooperatives have been developed in Italy in recent years in order to improve living conditions in local communities affected by the economic crisis, depopulation and the abandonment of public services by the Public Administration.

There is not yet a state law that regulates these cooperatives,[20] but they have been the subject of attention by various regions, some of which have

[20] A bill was passed on 13 July 2017 and a bill submitted by several deputies on 23 May 2018. Spanish text is available at: http://documenti.camera.it/_dati/leg18/lavori/stampati/pdf/18PDL0003830.pdf.

passed special laws for their regulation,[21] while others have incorporated their regulation into the laws that regulate and promote cooperatives.[22]

Legacoop (Lega Nazionale delle Cooperative e Mutue) launched the project "*Cooperative di Comunità*" in 2010 in order to promote a network of cooperatives that improve local communities, encouraging autonomy and organisation of citizens. This organisation, which represents about 15000 Italian cooperative companies from all sectors and territories, presents a comparative analysis of this plural regulatory framework on its website from which the characteristics common to Italian community cooperatives can be deduced.[23]

From this comparative study, it follows that the explicit objective of the community cooperative is to favour the development and strengthening of local communities, developing economic activities aimed at the production of goods and services of and for the community, improving common goods, cultural traditions, territorial resources in a process of strengthening social cohesion and training of community members.

Community cooperatives can be constituted as cooperatives of producers, workers, users, social cooperatives, multi-stakeholders etc., where the important thing is not the type of activity but the purpose of improving the community of reference. For this same reason, natural and legal persons, third sector organisations and public entities can be members of a community cooperative.[24] This plurality of interests is reflected in turn in models of participatory and solidarity organisation and management. Apart from that, a community cooperative model cannot be defined because, as has been said, each community is different and unique; each will have its own needs and each will respond to them with its own resources and capabilities.

Given the social value generated by community cooperatives and their contribution to the common good, they are promoted in the laws. The following are among the measures with which the Public Administration contributes to promoting these cooperatives: capital contributions; personal resources; loans in favourable conditions; technical assistance and training; transfer of underused buildings or areas, etc.

---

[21] This is the case of the Puglia Regions (Law No. 23 of 20 March 2014); Liguria (Law No. 14 of 7 April 2015), Abruzzo (Law No. 4 of 24 September 2015), Sardinia (Law No. 35, of 2 August 2018) or Umbria (Law No. 2 of 11 April 2019). Other regions are currently developing their regulation, as in the case of Campania (Official Bulletin of 02/25/2019).

[22] In the case of the Region of Tuscany (Law No. 24 of 8 March 2014), Emilia Romagna (Law No. 12 of 17 July 2014) Basilicata (Law No. 12 of 20 March 2015) or Lombardy (Law No. 36 of 6 November 2015).

[23] http://www.legacoop.coop/cooperativedicomunita/sintesi-delle-leggi-regionali/.

[24] According to the Third Sector Code, approved by Legislative Decree No. 117 of 3 July 2017, entities of the Third Sector are voluntary organisations; social promotion associations; philanthropic entities; social enterprises, including social cooperatives; associative networks; mutual aid societies; recognised and unrecognised associations, foundations and other private entities that are not companies (Fici, 2020).

The review of some of the cooperatives that are identified as of community interest shows that in the corporate purpose of all of them the satisfaction of the needs of their members is present; therefore, the relevance that the general or community interest acquires in them does not overshadow the mutual interest that is still present. Both producers, as well as workers or users of goods and services produced or served by the cooperative, must be present among the members; and all this without prejudice to the fact that the cooperative's action directly benefits other members of the community (non-members) and indirectly the entire community, which improves their living conditions.

4 Conclusions that Can Be Drawn from This Brief Analysis of Multi-activity, Multi-stakeholder and Community Interest Cooperatives

The cooperative is an ideal instrument for meeting the individual and multiple needs of people, so anyone interested in it should be able to have access to the cooperative. This characteristic, which is described as the open door principle, reflects the supportive nature of the cooperative with its surroundings.

The classification of cooperatives by typologies should not hamper the development of new activities to meet new needs not stipulated by the legislator.

The cooperative also makes it possible for several groups of members with diverse needs and interests to integrate into the same entity. In these cases, the rights of minority groups that are part of the cooperative must be guaranteed.

All cooperatives must be able to meet the interests of the community to the extent agreed by the members in their statutes. The defence of collective and community interests is compatible with the defence of the interests of the associates, who also belong to the community.

In all the cases analysed, there is a diversity of activities and subjects involved. Therefore, this diversity must be taken into account in the internal management of the cooperative, both when determining and applying the economic results generated by the various activities as well as when making decisions about them. For these purposes, the so-called cooperative sections are a fundamental instrument, so it is not surprising that some laws force their constitution in these cases.[25] If sections are not constituted, panels must be created by categories of members to give each group representation in the general meeting, with regards to their involvement in the cooperative activity. It is also possible to consider the scope of action not only of the general assembly but also of the various sections when deciding on issues that mainly affect a group of members or specific activity. The self-management that characterises the cooperative must be reflected in the management of each one of the activities that it carries out, especially when not all the members participate in

---

[25] After defining what a multi-activity cooperative is, the Colombian Law on Cooperatives No 79 of 1988 states in its Article 63: "The services will be organised in independent sections, according to the characteristics of each specialised type of cooperative."

all the activities, and this, without prejudice that the main bodies of the cooperative ultimately have the competence to resolve internal conflicts and make decisions that are in the general interest of the cooperative, and minority members have ways to defend their rights.

When the interest in a cooperative reaches greater prominence in the community, it is normal that its corporate purpose also interests other groups that by design seek to satisfy interests of general scope, such as public administrations, the third sector or volunteering. This greater presence of general interests in some cooperatives is reflected not only in the participation of these entities among their associates but also in the increase in the results assigned to reserves (indivisible) and destined to fulfil the purposes of general interest of the community.

The community interest cooperative usually integrates various groups interested in the community of reference who participate in its economic activity as producers, workers or consumers/users (cooperators) and who collaborate for the good purpose of this activity and the fulfilment of its objectives (administrations, non-profit organisations, volunteers or other natural or legal persons who contribute to the good end of the cooperative through their contribution of capital or in any other way). This heterogeneous set requires the establishment of priorities and limitations.

Among other limitations, no group should exceed 50% of the votes in corporate bodies; cooperators should have a controlling interest in the business activity and in the decisions made by the cooperative, and potential funders should have a limited interest both in the corporate bodies and in the remuneration that they receive for their investment. Expansion in terms of business activities, stakeholders and objectives must be compatible with the cooperative identity, otherwise, the distinction between the cooperative and other legal structures becomes blurred.

References

Fernández de Andreani P (2017) Cooperativas prestadoras de servicios públicos. Astrea, Buenos Aires

Fici A (2017) Definition and objectives of cooperatives. In: Fajardo G, Fici A, Henrÿ H, Hiez D, Meira D, Münkner H, Snaith I (eds) Principles of European cooperative law. Principles, commentaries and national reports. Intersentia, Cambridge, pp 19–45

Fici A (2020) Enti del terzo settore: nozione, requisiti e tipologie. In: Bassi A (ed) Gli enti del terzo settore. Lineamenti generali. Editoriale scientifica, Napoli, pp 119–142

García Müller A (2008) El marco jurídico de las cooperativas multiactivas. In: Alvarez JF (ed) Naturaleza y especificidad de la cooperativa multiactiva. COOTRADIAN - Escuela de Economía Solidaria, Bogotá, pp 25–39

García Müller A (2018) Derecho Cooperativo, Mutual y de la Economía Social y Solidaria. AIDCMESS, Mérida

Holyoake JJ (1975) Historia de los Pioneros de Rochdale, 2nd edn. AECOOP - Aragón Colección Universitas, Zaragoza

Moirano AA (2008) Cooperativas multiactivas. In: Alvarez JF (ed) Naturaleza y especificidad de la cooperativa multiactiva. COOTRADIAN - Escuela de Economía Solidaria, Bogotá, pp 5–18

Mori PA (2014) Community and cooperation: the evolution of cooperatives towards new models of citizens' democratic participation in public services provision. Ann Pub Coop Econ 85(3):327–352

Münkner H (2015) Revision of co-operative law as a reaction to the challenges of economic, social and technological change. Ciriec Revista Jurídica De La Economía Social y Cooperativa 26:1–11

Serrano R (2018) Orígenes y características de la cooperativa multiactiva. In: Alvarez JF (ed) Naturaleza y especificidad de la cooperativa multiactiva. COOTRADIAN - Escuela de Economía Solidaria, Bogotá, pp 19–24

Silva Díaz JA (2008) La multiactividad en números. In: Alvarez JF (ed), Naturaleza y especificidad de la cooperativa multiactiva. COOTRADIAN - Escuela de Economía Solidaria, Bogotá, pp 115–124

Solarino S (2020) Las cooperativas comunitarias en Italia y su contribución al desarrollo rural. In Fajardo G, Escribano J (eds) Despoblamiento y Desarrollo Rural. Propuestas desde la Economía Social, 2nd edn. Ciriec, Valencia, pp 109–120

Uribe C (2002) Bases del Cooperativismo. Fondo Nacional Universitario, Bogotá

Cooperatives and Transport: A Complex and Unequal Reality. Approach of Spanish Law

Itziar Villafáñez Pérez

1 Introduction: The Complexity of Cooperativism in Transportation

The transport sector is undoubtedly a particularly interesting and complex area in relation to cooperativism, due to the multiple options it offers for the latter, at least on a theoretical level. At the same time, it is a question that raises several difficulties from a legal perspective, due to various elements that have to be taken into account jointly.

On the one hand, transport can be carried out through different modalities. That presents different realities and dynamics (such as the atomization or concentration of operators, the infrastructure necessary for the development of the activity, and the impact on the public interest, etc.).

We must also not lose sight of the different types of cooperatives in terms of the position of the members in relation to the cooperative activity. They could be working members of a cooperative that offers services of transport, users of the

[1] We don't include other cooperatives in which the link with transport is indirect, since neither the cooperative nor the partners are providers of the transport service (e.g., a worker cooperative that provides services to transport companies).

Work linked to the research projects "*El transporte ante el desarrollo tecnológico y la globalización: nuevos desafíos jurídicos del sector marítimo y portuario*" (DER2015-65424-C4-1-P) and "Nuevas tecnologías, transformación de mercados y Derecho de la Competencia" (RTI2018-094201-B-C21), funded by Ministry of Science and Innovation and ERDF. Consolidated research group of the Basque university system "La ética empresarial en las diversas manifestaciones del Derecho Mercantil" (IT 1146-16).

I. Villafáñez Pérez (✉)
Faculty of Economics and Business, University of the Basque Country (UPV/EHU), Lehendakari Agirre 83, 48015 Bilbao, Spain
e-mail: itziar.villafanez@ehu.eus

W. Tadjudje and I. Douvitsa (eds.), *Perspectives on Cooperative Law*,
https://doi.org/10.1007/978-981-19-1991-6_26

transport services of a cooperative or transporters who use the services offered by a cooperative for the development of their activity.[1]

This diverse scenario is also accompanied by different legislation for each mode of transport, in addition to being a highly regulated and controlled sector, due among other issues to the general and strategic interests affected. For the same reason, public intervention in relation to transport is very important, especially in terms of the infrastructure needed to carry it out. Sectoral legislation, besides, must be applied in conjunction with cooperative legislation, which generally contains brief references to cooperatives in the transport sector, and which in the case of Spain presents some complexity as at present there are 16 cooperative laws from the autonomous communities and State law.[2]

The globalization and liberalization of the economy (including, progressively and unevenly, the liberalization of transport services in their different modalities), especially in the European Union, also has a direct impact on the reality of transport and its regulation. In this sense, we must underline the changes that this entails in the dynamics of transport and its operators (obviously when introducing new competitors), as well as different supra- or international legislation, such as the norms of different nature of the European Union, or the applicable international conventions.

Finally, new technologies pose numerous challenges for companies operating in the transport sector, particularly from the perspective of cooperatives. This is notable in relation to the provision of transport services and the emergence of internet platforms for their management.

All of the above presents a difficult panorama to address. However, in this essay we humbly intend to make some notes on the interrelationships between cooperativism and transport, basically taking as a reference the Spanish legislative framework (both cooperative and sectoral legislation), and focusing mainly on the possibility of constituting different types of cooperatives in different kinds of transport. Finally, we make a brief reference to the incidence of new technologies.

2 Typology of Cooperatives in the Transport Sector

As anticipated, one of the aspects that give interest and complexity to the subject under study is the wide range of possibilities that, at least theoretically, arise from the perspective of transport and cooperativism. The practice demonstrates the versatility of cooperatives, which are a valid instrument to carry out very diverse economic activities following the values and principles of cooperativism. Let's not forget the broad definition of cooperative according to ICA: "A cooperative is an autonomous association of persons united voluntarily to meet their common economic, social, and cultural needs and aspirations through a jointly-owned and democratically-controlled enterprise". In this same line, according to art. 1.2 Law 27/1999, of July 16, on

[2] Plus laws on specific classes or on specific aspects of cooperatives nor their development rules.

Cooperatives (statewide cooperative law; LCoop) any lawful economic activity may be organized and developed through a cooperative incorporated under this law. Thus, as long as a special rule doesn't directly or indirectly prohibit the development of an activity to cooperatives, they could develop any economic activity.

Following a classification of cooperatives based on the cooperative activity, in the field of transport we could find three types of cooperatives: (A) Worker transport cooperatives: members provide their personal work in the cooperative, which provides transportation services. That is, the cooperative is a carrier; (B) Transport user cooperatives: members are users of the transport services provided by the cooperative, which as in the previous case is a carrier; (C) Transport providers cooperatives, or transporter/carrier cooperatives: members are providers of the transport services (that is, the carriers), and at the same time users of the cooperative's services, which can have diverse nature (cargo search, logistics, fuel supply, etc.).

This classification must be combined with that relating to the different modes of transport in terms of the means of transport in question (the main ones being road, rail, air and sea transport, without forgetting multimodal transport, with its added problems), as well as for the purpose of transport (goods, people or mixed).

3 Approach to the Regulation of Transportation Sector Cooperatives

3.1 Transportation Cooperatives in Cooperative Legislation and Road Transport

Spanish legislation reflects the existence of cooperatives in the transport sector mainly in cooperative legislation, given that in sectoral legislation mentions of cooperatives are scarce or non-existent.

Art. 100 LCoop expressly refers to the cooperatives of carriers, its purpose being "the provision of services and supplies and the performance of operations, aimed at the economic and technical improvement of the operations of its partners", which have the legal consideration of carriers. The same provision also refers to the possibility of carrying out the activities expressly authorized by the Land Transportation Law.[3] It is, therefore, a cooperative which provides various services to partners, who are the ones who do the transportation and, as said, have the legal consideration

[3] Law 16/1987, of July 30, on Land Transportation Planning (LOTT). See in particular articles 22.2.III and 119.1 LOTT on intermediation in the contracting of transport. Also art. 159.1.c Royal Decree 1211/1990, of September 28, which approves the Regulation of the Land Transportation Law (ROTT).

of carriers.[4] This provision is not limited to a specific mode of transport, so transport cooperatives are possible in any transport sector. The explicit reference to land transport regulations should not be understood as excluding other forms of transport. However, most transport cooperatives operate in the field of road transport. In fact, as we show in this work, within the sector regulation, the regulation on road transport is the only one that expressly refers, even briefly, to cooperatives.[5]

On the other hand, although generally not expressly regulated, cooperative legislation also covers the possibility of other types of cooperatives in the field of transport. Thus, as regards worker transport cooperatives, when not expressly regulated, it must be understood that they are included under the general figure of worker cooperatives. Some cooperative laws, meanwhile, regulate them to a greater or lesser extent. For example, in Valencian legislation,[6] art. 97, on "transport cooperatives" (those cooperatives that aim to "organize or provide transport services or carry out activities that make this object possible"), indicates that they may take three different forms: (a) "worker cooperative or, properly, transport cooperative", that is, the "group of carriers, drivers or other personnel, in order to carry out the corporate purpose"[7]; (b) "services or carriers cooperative", with the "purpose of facilitating business activity by carrying out tasks such as organizing transport, administration and workshops"[8] and (c) "mixed transport cooperative", modality "which may include exclusively

---

[4] The same precept also authorizes the development of operations with non-partner third parties if a specific rule authorizes it. Art. 26.4 also allows the weighted plural vote in these cooperatives in proportion to the volume of cooperative activity, with limitations.

In similar terms (in some cases also recognizing the possibility of plural or weighted voting, and usually also referring to land transport regulation): Castile and León (art. 115 Law 4/2002), Asturias (arts. 174–175 Law 4/2010), La Rioja (arts. 124 Law 4/2001), Murcia (art. 123 Law 8/2006), or Balearic Islands (art. 130 Law 1/2003).

Generally, in the cooperative laws of the autonomous communities, we find some reference to the cooperatives of carriers, with this denomination or a different one: Madrid (arts. 110 and 120 Law 4/1999), Catalonia (art. 129.4 Law 12/2015), Cantabria (art. 122 Law 6/2013), Navarre (art. 74 Foral Law 14/2016), Extremadura (art. 144 Law 9/2018), in addition to the laws that are indicated in this section below (Basque, Valencian, Castilian-La Mancha, Galician, Andalusian and Aragonese laws, which also make more or less direct reference to the worker transport cooperatives).

[5] The doctrine has especially studied these cooperatives and the reasons for their success, underlining some elements that explain the suitability of the cooperative model in the transport of goods by road: the liberalization of the European market, the high level of business atomization and dependence on transport agencies, the difficulty of contracting loads during transport, the imbalance between supply and demand, the low training that workers in the sector generally have (notably in terms of company management), etc. García Villalobos (2000 and 2001). In the area of transportation of people, we emphasize taxi drivers' cooperatives.

[6] Legislative Decree 2/2015. In similar terms, the Cooperative Law of Castilia-La Mancha (art. 129 Law 11/2010). Other cooperative laws that expressly regulate worker transport cooperatives, in addition to the cooperatives of carriers: Galicia (art. 116 Law 5/1998), Andalusia (art. 95 Law 14/2011, see also art. 101.2), Aragon (art. 75 Legislative Decree 2/2014, see also art. 79), Basque Country (art. 129 Law 11/2019).

[7] The law develops the regulation applicable to these cooperatives, in particular as regards the provision of vehicles by members, and the admission of new members.

[8] Valencian law also recognizes transport cooperatives in art. 95.2 (business or professional services cooperatives).

service members and others that, not having the title of carrier, can carry out the activity with vehicles belonging to the cooperative or provided by the partner".

Regarding the sector legislation, after the modification introduced in LOTT by Law 9/2013,[9] express references to worker transport cooperatives (which previously were regulated with a certain degree of detail) have been removed from it, so it only refers expressly to carriers cooperatives. However, it must be understood that worker cooperatives can still operate as carriers, provided they meet the requirements of companies operating in the sector. After the modification of LOTT, the previous prohibition of the existence of mixed cooperatives in road transport has disappeared.

The distinction between carrier cooperatives and worker transport cooperatives has important legal implications. It must be taken into account that the legal consideration of the carrier has consequences regarding the need for authorizations, the possibility of carrying out transport contracts, the liability derived from them, etc. We must add that the legal nature of the mutualist relationship between the cooperative and its members is considered corporate (not properly contractual),[10] also concerning worker cooperatives, in which working partners are not subject to the cooperative for an employment relationship.

All of the above is related to the phenomenon of so-called false cooperatives or "screen" companies. We are referring to the fraudulent use of cooperatives in the field of transport, particularly through the establishment of worker transport cooperatives with the purpose of avoiding both the application of the legislation applicable to labour relations,[11] and the regulations to which the partners would be subject in case of having the legal qualification of carrier (authorizations, billing, responsibility, etc.).[12]

Finally, we must refer to the transport cooperatives in which the members are users of the transport services. This possibility is barely expressly envisaged in cooperative legislation, except in some cases, as happens in a very partial way with the agricultural cooperatives (e.g., art. 93 LCoop). It seems that this option would fit among the service cooperatives, to the extent that they may have as their object, among others, the provision of supplies and services (which may include transportation) for their members, who would be natural or legal persons, owners of industrial or services holdings, and professionals or artists who exercise their activity on their own (art. 98 LCoop). Likewise, consumer and user cooperatives could also have as object the provision of transport services to their members (which may be natural persons or

---

[9] This law abolished the precepts expressly dedicated to the different types of cooperatives in transport in LOTT, ROTT and Order of July 23, 1997 (of development of ROTT in matters of transport cooperatives and marketing companies). See Mundo Guinot (2014). More extensively about these cooperatives: Mundo Guinot (2013). See also Villafáñez Pérez (2010).

[10] In the case of road freight, the sector legislation itself underlines this aspect (art. 5.3 of Land Freight Contract Law (Law 15/2009).

[11] For example, Supreme Court's decision, STS (Sala de lo Social) 2263/2018, May 18. About this judgment and, in general, the problem of false worker cooperatives with the purpose of avoiding the application of labor law: García Jiménez (2018).

[12] Among others, STS (Sala de lo Contencioso-Administrativo, Sección 3ª) 5 February 2008.

entities that are final recipients) through third parties or directly (art. 88 LCoop).[13] In any case, for the exercise of transport directly by the cooperative, it is necessary to comply with the sectoral regulations and to have the legal status of the carrier. For all these reasons, without excluding such a possibility, it seems more plausible that these cooperatives manage transport services provided by third parties for members, rather than directly.

3.2 Sea Transport

We do not find in the cooperative legislation specific norms for cooperatives in the field of maritime transport, so what is indicated in the previous section must be taken into account, where appropriate.

As regards the sector legislation (reference law is Law 14/2014, of July 24, on Maritime Navigation; LNM), there isn't a specific regulation of cooperatives in this area, but neither, in principle, is access to cooperatives, as ship-owners and/or shipping companies, restricted.[14] In this sense, the existence of cooperatives of different types in relation to these activities should be accepted, complying with the general legal requirements: worker cooperatives[15]; cooperatives in which members are users of maritime transport services; or cooperatives in which the partners (shipping companies and/or ship-owners) obtain different services for the development of their activity.

Regarding the latter, it is necessary to make some notes. On the one hand, Law 14/2014 itself regulates some auxiliary navigation contracts, the content of which could be carried out under a cooperative regime (arts. 314 *et seq.*), such as the naval management contract, the consignment contract for ships or the port handling contract. However, what has already been mentioned regarding the corporate legal nature of the mutual relationship must be taken into account when considering whether such a possibility is legally possible and, if so, what legal regime would be applicable to the mutual relationship. This reflection is applicable to other cases, such as ship-use contracts (arts. 188 *et seq.*), for example as regards a possible charter contract (arts. 203 *et seq.* LNM), properly transporting goods by sea (if this is the cooperative activity). In any case, as indicated, it is necessary to make clear the kind

[13] Without forgetting other options, such as educational cooperatives, providing transport services as an activity related to teaching services, to which the standards for consumer and user cooperatives are actually applicable (art. 103 LCoop).

[14] To our knowledge, when art. 146 LNM indicates that "The ship-owner who dedicates the vessel to navigation for business purposes must register in the Mercantile Registry" does not mean that there is a prohibition for cooperatives, even though these in principle are registered in the Register of Cooperatives.

[15] See Díaz De la Rosa (2009), who presents a detailed analysis of the legal regime applicable to a possible cooperative shipping company, in particular in the case of a worker cooperative. It also refers to a possible cooperative of shipping companies (which would be its partners).

of cooperative in question, as well as the relationship between it and its partners, also for reasons such as the determination of who is the carrier, liability regime etc.

On the other hand, it is necessary to take into account the necessary infrastructures for the development of this transport (fundamentally the ports, besides the ship) and its subjection to general and strategic interests. Despite being a sector in process of liberalization, it is a highly regulated issue, precisely to ensure the provision of services. In this regard we have to take into account Royal Legislative Decree 2/2011, of September 5, which approves the Consolidated Text of the Law on State Ports and Merchant Marine. The arts. 104 *et seq.* regulate the provision of services in ports, and although competition between companies is liberalized and promoted, it is subject to public control. Among the public service obligations which must be accepted by all service providers is universal coverage, with the obligation to meet any reasonable demand, under non-discriminatory conditions, except for the cases of private passenger and goods terminals. Likewise, when appropriate, the submission to the tariff authority of the Port Authority is envisaged. These precepts do not facilitate (even they do not prohibit it) the provision of these services under a cooperative regime, with the exception of private use terminals and the self-provision of services therein.

Finally, the existence of cooperatives dedicated to maritime transport[16] does seem to have a place in the field of short distance transport, for example to and between the islands, passenger transport between nearby ports, and tourism or leisure transport.

3.3 *Rail Transport*

Contrary to what happens in other types of transport, in the field of the railway sector the State regulations (Law 38/2015, of September 29, of the Railway Sector; LSF) reserves the possibility of obtaining a railway license for companies that, among other requirements, have the legal form of a public limited company (art. 50.1.a LSF), although, at the same time, it is recognized that "Railway company licenses granted by the other States of the European Union will produce all their effects in Spain" (art. 49.4 LSF), in a context of liberalization of rail transport. Therefore, there is an obvious limitation to the use of the cooperative formula for rail transport. This is a questionable rule since the creation of a cooperative in this area could be considered as long as it complies with legal general requirements. The difficulties that in practice could be found by companies that consider opting for the cooperative model do not seem to justify the legal prohibition of this possibility.[17]

In any case, some realities of this type of transport cannot be ignored, such as the small number of operators in it (particularly in the Spanish State), given that

---

[16] Or river transport, which is not very common in Spain due to lack of navigable rivers.

[17] In fact, we found some cooperative experience in the sector, such as, for example, Go-op in the United Kingdom, whose constitution has not been easy (http://www.go-op.coop/), or, recently, Railcoop, in France (https://www.railcoop.fr/).

its liberalization in the European Union is not very advanced. It is also a transport highly conditioned by the necessary infrastructure for the realization of the transport itself. Similarly, railway infrastructures (roads, stations, etc.) are generally of public interest (when not strategic), their management and decision-making around them falling to the Public Administrations.[18]

As proposed for maritime transport, the possibility of establishing cooperatives in relation to the provision of common services to railway companies, in which private initiative is recognized, could be considered. Thus, for example, it could be an option in terms of service facilities (art. 42 LSF). According to the different types of cooperatives, we could think, at least in theory, of a cooperative constituted by the railway companies themselves to obtain common services. However, it must be taken into account that the regulation itself seeks to guarantee the independence of companies that provide rail transport services against companies that use their facilities when they are under their control, in cases where they have a dominant position in relation to the provision of rail transport services.[19] In addition, they must facilitate, in a non-discriminatory manner, access to all railway companies and other candidates to such facilities and the services provided in them (art. 43 LSF).

For its part, art. 45 LSF refers to the provision of services in facilities owned by the general managers of railway infrastructures of general interest. It is noted that the provision of complementary and auxiliary services in these will be carried out under private law, and it is indicated that it is possible that railway companies can provide for themselves or in collaboration with other railway companies, directly or through contracts with third parties, such auxiliary services. It seems that a path to cooperation between different railway companies in the provision of such services can be opened. In any case, it will be the practice which demonstrates the extent to which it is a theoretical or a real possibility.

3.4 Air Transport

Air transport and its regulation are also highly conditioned by its implications for the general interest and the infrastructure necessary to carry out the activity. In this sense, we refer to a large part of the reflections of the previous pages. However, in this area we do not find a formal restriction on airline companies having a cooperative form. Being a largely liberalized activity in the European Union (with few exceptions), Regulation (EC) No. 1008/2008 of the European Parliament and of the Council of 24 September 2008, on common rules for the operation of air services in the Community, does not impose the adoption of a specific legal form to obtain an operating license, so a cooperative that complies with the requirements of arts. 4 and 5 (general requirements

[18] The private railway lines are recognized by Law 38/2015, but with a very limited scope (art. 40), and always conditional on the public interest.

[19] Such independence could be achieved by organizing different divisions within the same legal entity (art. 42.3 LSF).

and financial conditions) could obtain it. Nor does State legislation impose a specific legal form, referring to an individual or collective companies (arts. 70 et seq. of Law 48/1960, of July 21, on Air Navigation; LNA).[20]

A different thing is the difficulty that may arise in meeting these requirements. However, the above cannot be an impediment to envisaging cooperatives in the field of air transport, the different schemes that we have proposed being valid (and, in fact, throughout the world there are cooperative experiences in the sector of great interest): air transport worker cooperatives,[21] cooperatives of users of transport services or cooperatives of carriers.[22]

Again, the cooperative model could have a special development in the field of air transport also in relation to private flights, in smaller airplanes or by helicopter.

4 Brief Reference to the Incidence of New Technologies and Digitalization

There is no doubt that new technologies and digitalization have consequences in terms of internal and external relations of companies, which generates numerous opportunities and challenges, as well as difficulties and conflicts. In this sense, it would be of interest to analyze how these can affect the internal functioning of cooperatives in the transport sector, which operate in a sector characterized by definition by mobility.[23]

At this time we underline the incidence of the emergence of internet platforms related to transport services, which have led to a revolution in the way of contracting. Different factors explain the above: the ease and closeness in terms of the use of new

---

[20] The references of these articles to the shares, typical of the limited public corporations, are applicable only to cases in which this legal form has been chosen. We deduce it from the text of the arts. 75 or 80.first *in fine* LNA.

The Ministerial Order of March 12, 1998, which establishes the rules for the granting and maintenance of operating licenses to airlines, the references to the Mercantile Registry, shares… cannot be accepted as a basis for the exclusion of cooperatives but should be applied to them according to their financial, patrimonial and organizational scheme (since, for example, the right to vote in cooperatives and their control does not depend on participation in the capital).

[21] We highlight at this point Brascoota (http://www.brascoota.com.br/), a Brazilian freight and passenger transport cooperative created in 2014. We can also mention the brief and failed experience of the Alas de Uruguay Cooperative, created by former Pluna workers with government support.

[22] In fact, it is common for them to make cooperation agreements and organize themselves in alliances sharing staff, infrastructure, logistics centers, routes… Nor can we fail to mention SITA (Société Internationale des Télécommunications Aéronautique, S.C., registered in Belgium; www.sita.aero) in technologic development and telecommunication services.

[23] Consider, for example, the implications that telematic voting can have on a cooperative of carriers dedicated to the transport of goods by road that carries national or international transport.

Apart from that, we cannot forget that the development of new technologies in transportation is posing new challenges, also legal, for example in relation to unmanned and autonomous vehicles for transport purposes.

technologies, the immediacy of the service, or making it possible to put people in touch with a wide range of others.[24] Although they have an immense potential for the development of society and well-being, at the same time their use is the source of important social conflicts. This is notorious from the point of view of competition and labour law. As has been pointed out, the determination of who has the legal status of a carrier is also relevant, since it must assume the requirements and liabilities derived from transport.

In this context, without losing sight of the potential that platforms may have for cooperatives and their development (management, hiring, more independence, customer search etc.), cooperativism itself is a valid alternative in such situations. Thus, these types of platforms and other technologies are beginning to be promoted from the cooperative model, adapting the idea of cooperatives to the platform economy, cooperativising the ownership of digital platforms, and applying cooperative principles to it, among them the cooperation among cooperatives (e.g., in order to save technological costs).[25] However, it is necessary to warn that the experiences in Spain are, today, scarce and very limited.[26]

5 Conclusions

Cooperativism in the field of transport presents a complex, unequal and, at the same time, rich reality, raising many possibilities for development. All this is conditioned by the structure of the sector and of each type of transport, including liberalization, the necessary infrastructure and the existing conditions for carrying out the service, and the consideration of public and even strategic interest that often precede the transport itself, including the incidence of the legal framework.

In any case, it should be stressed that cooperativism, in its different modalities, is a valid model for diverse transport. Although throughout the world we find several experiences of larger or smaller cooperatives that certify it, it is, however, an issue that is still largely to be explored and developed. We consider of great interest the extension of the cooperative model, with the principles and values that identify it, to the different forms of transport. The characteristics of the sector imply that, together with the study of national systems, the international perspective must be emphasized. Likewise, special attention should be given to the implications of the digitalization of the economy.

[24] Facilitating issues such as finding with whom to share transport costs, in what would originally be called "collaborative economy".

[25] An interesting experience is CoopCycle (https://coopcycle.org/en/), a federation of bike delivery coops which, among other things, has developed a software to manage their activity.

[26] For example, La Pájara (Madrid), Mensakas (Barcelona), Botxoriders (Bilbao) or Eraman (Vitoria-Gasteiz, https://eraman.coop/).

References

Díaz De La Rosa A (2009) El naviero cooperativo. Aranzadi – Thomson Reuters, Cizur Menor

García Jiménez M (2018) Falsas cooperativas, usos abusivos y derechos de los trabajadores. Análisis jurisprudencial y propuestas de actuación. CIRIEC España. Revista Jurídica De Economía Social y Cooperativa 33:185–222

García Villalobos JC (2000) Las sociedades cooperativas en el transporte de mercancías por carretera en España. Consejo Económico y Social, Madrid

García Villalobos JC (2001) Las sociedades cooperativas de transportistas en España. REVESCO 72:49–68

Mundo Guinot ME (2013) Las sociedades cooperativas de transporte: régimen jurídico y aspectos controvertidos. Marcial Pons, Madrid

Mundo Guinot ME (2014) Principales novedades en las cooperativas de transporte de mercancías por carretera tras la reforma de la normativa de ordenación de los transportes terrestres. Revista De Derecho Del Transporte 13:93–122

Villafáñez Pérez I (2010) Problemas actuales del régimen jurídico de las cooperativas en el ámbito del transporte por carretera. Una revisión actualizada. Revista De Derecho Del Transporte 5:11–42

Conclusion: Current Prospects of Cooperative Law

Willy Tadjudje and Ifigeneia Douvitsa

This honorary volume has not been preconceived in its structure. It was structured based on the content of the contributions received from the authors. Indeed, an invitation to contribute was shared, with the only instruction to propose a paper related to cooperative law, and contributions followed. This may explain a completely different physiognomy from what is usually found in most collective books, i.e. a preliminary orientation and structuring of the content.

This freedom offered to the authors to work on any topic of cooperative law was a risk for the editors, as the contributions could arrive without any direct link or relationship between them. Nevertheless, the editors did not have much choice, since Hagen Henrÿ, in the course of his rich professional career, has dealt with practically all areas of cooperative law (substantially and geographically), so it was not necessary, at the outset, to pre-orientate the content of the authors' contributions. However, as we have seen, there are many convergences between the analyses, beyond cultural or historical specificities.

Major themes were addressed, such as the history of cooperative law, its constitutionalisation, social and solidarity economy law and cooperative law, legal specificities and essence of cooperatives, cooperative law and sustainable development, activities and governance of cooperatives. Overall, the authors have largely questioned the phenomenon of companisation of cooperatives that is occurring in almost all regions of the world.

Beyond these topics, all of which are quite relevant and need not be revisited, we would like to lay out two perspectives on cooperative law. Around the world, more and more countries are adopting laws governing the social and solidarity economy and this sometimes has important influences on cooperative law. Also, the whole planet has been hit by the health crisis and it is obvious that the said crisis affects the effectiveness of cooperative law. In this sense, digitalisation can provide solutions.

W. Tadjudje and I. Douvitsa (eds.), *Perspectives on Cooperative Law*,
https://doi.org/10.1007/978-981-19-1991-6

Social and Solidarity Economy (SSE) Law and Cooperative Law

From a legal-institutional point of view, the SSE is generally defined according to a double approach. The first one focuses on the identification of organisations, independently of their legal status. What is important in this approach is the conformity of the rules of operation to a set of values and principles, which corresponds to a normative approach to SSE. The second approach is based on an exhaustive inventory of existing legal statuses using various assessment criteria, in particular the absence of profit maximisation, which is an enumerative approach to SSE.[1]

This is the reason why some authors consider that SSE laws are umbrella laws.[2] They are all more so because they integrate provisions relating to a set of legal forms of organisation, whereas the latter is already, most often, the subject of specific legislation. In this sense and according to Caire and Tadjudje, an international comparison of SSE laws reveals five possible conceptual approaches.[3]

1. **General umbrella law**. Federation of already regulated legal forms of enterprise and/or organisation (e.g. cooperatives, mutual societies, associations, etc.), all of whose entities are *de jure* classified as SSE enterprises or organisations. The general umbrella law does not modify any provision of the laws specific to each legal form of enterprise or organisation. For example, the Quebec law (Social Economy Act, 10 October 2013).
2. **Umbrella law providing distinctions**. Laws that federate legal forms that are already regulated, and that do not modify any provision of the laws governing each of them. However, they distinguish, for one or more legal forms, entities that benefit by right from the status of SSE enterprise or organisation, from those that are eligible under certain conditions. For example, the Spanish law (Ley 5/2011, de 29 de marzo, de Economía Social).
3. **Umbrella law including extensions**. Federation of already-regulated legal forms that do not modify any of the provisions of the laws governing each legal form, and that add a new legal form (e.g. social enterprise). The rules specific to the new legal form may be incorporated into the framework law, possibly with a reference to a decree for the details, or they may give rise to

[1] Caire and Tadjudje (2019).

[2] Hiez (2021).

[3] Caire and Tadjudje (2021). According to these authors, the common point of the five conceptions is that of legal subsidiarity: a cooperative remains first a cooperative, an association "remains first" an association, etc. and the attributions of the ministries in charge of the various legal forms and sectors remain. It is not about creating a new status of SSE organisation or enterprise, nor is it about creating a new overarching policy, bringing together all existing statutory and sectoral policies. The role of the SSE framework law is that these structures are recognised in addition to social and solidarity economy, that they can be represented as such to the competent authorities and that they are taken into account in the sectoral strategies in order to benefit from common favorable public provisions.

the subsequent drafting of a specific law. For example, Cape Verde law (Lei n.º122/VIII/2016 estabelece o regime jurídico da economia social).

4. **Umbrella law bringing changes**. Federation of legal forms that are already regulated, and that incorporate modifications to certain provisions of the laws specific to each of them. There are three possible reasons for this: bringing the provisions of the laws governing the legal forms into line with the SSE law (Type 1), creating a new variation on an existing legal form (Type 2) or modernising provisions specific to a legal form (Type 3). For example, Type 1—Ecuador Law (Ley organica de economia popular y solidaria y del sistema financiero popular y solidaria, Registro Oficial 444 de 10 May 2011). Type 2—France law (Law of 31 July 2014 on the social and solidarity economy). Type 3—Wallonia-Belgium decree (Decree of 20 November 2008 on the social economy).
5. **Umbrella law instituting a label**. Laws that institute a label or an SSE approval imply for the interested entities, whatever their legal form, to carry out a specific step aiming at the conformity of their activity and their functioning to prescribed standards. For example, Luxembourg law (Law of 12 December 2016 on the creation of societal impact companies).

If we stop at category 4, we would understand how the SSE law can have an influence on cooperative law. Category 4 specifies three types of possible changes that the SSE law can bring. In Type 1, for example, in Ecuador law (Ley organica de economia popular y solidaria y del sistema financiero popular y solidaria, Registro Oficial 444 de 10 May 2011), the final part of the law incorporates various provisions introducing reforms in other laws, with the aim of adapting them, in order to build a certain coherence with SSE law. This necessarily concerns cooperatives. In Type 2, article 47 and following the French law (Law of 31 July 2014 on the social and solidarity economy) relate to the cooperative of activities and employment,[4] by amending the 1947 law on cooperatives.[5] In Type 3, Chapter 4 of the Walloon (Belgium) decree (Decree of 20 November 2008 on the social economy) refers to amending provisions with, in particular, its section one concerning the "Modificative provisions of the decree of December 18, 2003 relating to the conditions under which integration enterprises are approved and subsidised". These enterprises may be cooperatives.

These are just a few examples. In fact, even category 3 ESS laws can lead to difficulties, as can category 4 ESS laws. Indeed, the SSE law can promote, for example, a new form of cooperative, without this being in harmony with the general cooperative law (for the countries where it exists) or so that it complicates the landscape of cooperative law even more (notably in countries without general coordination of cooperative law).

The modification of the laws governing legal forms, including cooperative law by the framework law or the umbrella law (SSE law), may pose a problem of coherence

---

[4] In French *Coopérative d'activité et d'emploi.*

[5] This law of 1947 is the general law for all cooperatives in France. Besides it, there are various laws governing cooperatives according to the sectors of activity. For more details, see Hiez (2018).

of legislative policy. Ideally, the laws to be federated should be adapted first, before the framework or umbrella law is drafted so that the latter keeps its specificity.

In some countries, cooperative law is already quite scattered, due to a multitude of laws and decrees, sometimes without effective coordination between them, and needs to be harmonised. If, in addition, the modifications introduced by the SSE laws have to be added, the task can be even more difficult.

Covid-19, Cooperative Law and Digitalisation

Cooperatives were born out of the crisis and have always been able to demonstrate their ability to resist in times of crisis.[6] The Covid-19 health crisis is not the first challenge the cooperative movement has faced. In all circumstances, based on their ethics,[7] cooperatives have been able to find sustainable solutions to support men and women throughout the world.[8]

The Covid-19 pandemic has particularly affected the normal functioning of cooperatives.[9] Depending on the country, cooperatives are not always allowed to hold remote meetings, or at least the law does not provide for such rules. For example, in OHADA[10] law[11] on cooperative societies, article 215 of the Uniform Act[12] provides that "The draft statutes must be submitted to the constitutive general assembly for adoption. The cooperative members shall participate in person, under penalty of nullity, in the constitutive general meeting of the simplified cooperative society".

In the absence of planning rules for the current period, one may wonder how the cooperatives could be created and how the meetings could be held. Indeed, still according to OHADA law, general assembly meetings can only be held in person (there is, therefore, no possibility of virtual participation) even if absent members can give proxy to those present to represent them.[13]

---

[6] Münkner (2012).

[7] Münkner (2015).

[8] Birchall and Hammond Ketilson (2009), Aragón, Iturrioz and Narvaiza (2016).

[9] World Cooperative Monitor (2020), UNTFSSE (2020), Mohit (2021).

[10] Organisation fro the Harmonisation of Businees Law in Africa.

[11] For more details, see Tadjudje (2021), Hiez and Tadjudje (2013).

[12] The Uniform Act is the form through which the OHADA legislator produces its rules of law (acts of legislation), which are applicable in the same way in 17 countries of Central and West Africa, mainly French-speaking. Tadjudje and Labi (2020).

[13] The European legislator has taken measures in this sense, for the year 2020, through the adoption of a regulation. Council Regulation (EU) 2020/699 of 25 May 2020 on temporary measures concerning the general meetings of European companies (SEs) and of European Cooperative Societies (SCEs). Its Article 2 is related to "Temporary measure concerning the general meetings of European Cooperative Societies (SCE)" and states that "Where, in accordance with the first sentence of Article 54(1) of Regulation (EC) No 1435/2003, a general meeting of an SCE is to be held in 2020, the SCE may, by way of derogation from that provision, hold the meeting within 12 months of the end of the financial year, provided that the meeting is held on 31 December 2020 at the latest".

The law should not be an obstacle to the development of cooperatives. It would be good if legislators could provide mechanisms for virtual meetings in cooperatives, even if the technology is not always available in all countries of the world to achieve this. At the very least, legislators should allow cooperatives to choose between face-to-face and virtual meetings, or a combination of the two, with appropriate security rules in place. Some countries are ahead of the curve.[14] This is the case in Singapore. In 2020, the guidelines for cooperatives were adopted by the Registry of Cooperative Societies at the Ministry of Culture, Community and Youth, in relation to Covid-19 (Temporary Measures and Alternative Arrangements for Meetings for Charities, Cooperative Societies and Mutual Benefit Organisations). The guidelines were subsequent to an order.[15]

In general, digitalisation can play an important role in the development and management of cooperatives, as the authors have pointed out.[16] It is time to involve and integrate it as an important player in the promotion of cooperatives, especially in this time of the Covid-19 pandemic. "States all over the world have quickly amended legislation in order to help businesses conduct their activities remotely and online. (…) Regarding virtual shareholders' meetings and doing business online, there are legal questions, such as who bears the burden of liability for inadequate technical measures used for the meeting and whether shareholders are being deprived of certain rights. Unified authentication opportunities create the possibility of developing a secure online platform for conducting meetings. How can transparency be assured during a pandemic when board meetings and annual general meetings are not physically held and are held behind closed doors? Should governments continue to allow emergency solutions only or is this a time for a digital turn in company law?".[17]

[14] It should be noted that apart from the question of the holding of general meetings (on which we have focused in particular), other issues affect the proper functioning of cooperatives, in particular the frameworks for insolvency, or disclosure requirements. The OECD has investigated these three issues in 37 jurisdictions. OECD (2020).

[15] The guidelines are available online: https://www.mccy.gov.sg/-/media/MCCY-corp/Sectors/COVID-19_Alternative_Meeting_Arrangements_for_Co-ops_Guidelines_6May2020.pdf. They state that "The Guidelines incorporate the alternative arrangements prescribed in the Order, as well as other practices that cooperative societies should adopt given the inability of members or delegates to attend meetings in person. The Guidelines should be read together with the Order. Cooperative societies shall refer to the Order, the Cooperative Societies Act and their own by-laws, and seek legal advice if needed".

[16] Mannan (2018); Ciruela-Lorenzo (2020); Yang et al. (2021).

[17] Härmand (2021).

References

Aragón C, Iturrioz C, Narvaiza L (2016) Cooperatives' social responsibility in crisis time: how should they behave? REVESCO Revista De Estudios Cooperativos 123:7–36
Birchall J, Hammond Ketilson L (2009) Resilience of the cooperative business model in times of crisis. International Labour Organisation
Caire G, Tadjudje W (2019) Toward a global legal culture of the SSE enterprise? Int Comparison SSE Legislation RECMA 353:74–88
Caire G, Tadjudje W (2021) Guide pour légiférer sur le droit de l'économie sociale et solidaire. Food and Agricultural Organisation (publication in progress)
Ciruela-Lorenzo AM et al (2020) Digitalization of agri-cooperatives in the smart agriculture context. Proposal of a digital diagnosis tool. Sustainability 12:13–25
Härmand K (2021) Digitalisation before and after the Covid-19 crisis. ERA Forum 22:39–50
Hiez D, Tadjudje W (2013) The OHADA cooperative regulation. In: Cracogna D et al (eds) International handbook of cooperative law. Springer, pp 89–113
Hiez D (2018) Sociétés coopératives Création, organisation, fonctionnement. Dalloz
Hiez D (2021) Guide pour la rédaction d'un droit de l'ESS. Guidelines SSE-IF
Mannan M (2018) Fostering worker cooperatives with blockchain technology: lessons from the colony project. Erasmus Law Rev 3:1–14
Mohit D (2021) Resilient to crises: how cooperatives are adapting sustainably to overcome COVID-19-induced challenges. Int J Rural Manag 17:13–39
Münkner H-H (2012) Co-operation as a remedy in times of crisis. Agricultural co-operatives in the world. Their roles for rural development and poverty reduction. Marburg Stud Cooperation Cooperatives 58. https://www.euricse.eu/publications/1064/
Münkner H-H (2015) Co-operative principles and co-operative law. LIT Verlag Münster
OECD (2020) National corporate governance related initiatives during the Covid-19 crisis—a survey of 37 jurisdiction. OECD. https://www.oecd.org/corporate/National-corporate-governance-related-initiatives-during-the-covid-19-crisis.pdf
Tadjudje W, Labi C (2020) Business ethics in the OHADA zone: uniform law, uniform ethics? In: Frenkel DA (ed) An anthology of ethics. ATINER—Athens Institute for Education and Research, pp 47–62
Tadjudje W (2021) Le droit des coopératives en Afrique—Réflexions sur l'Acte uniforme de l'OHADA. Epure. Reims, France
UNTFSSE (2020) What role for the social and solidarity economy in post Covid-19 crisis recovery? United Nations Inter-Agencies Task-force on social and solidarity economy Statement. https://www.ilo.org/wcmsp5/groups/public/---ed_emp/---emp_ent/---coop/documents/publication/wcms_748794.pdf

W. Tadjudje and I. Douvitsa (eds.), *Perspectives on Cooperative Law*,
https://doi.org/10.1007/978-981-19-1991-6

World Cooperative Monitor (2020) Impact and reactions of cooperatives to Covid-19. In: Exploring the cooperative economy report 2020. Euricse/ICA. https://monitor.coop/sites/default/files/publication-files/covid-chapter-wcm-2020-1463679426.pdf
Yang D et al (2021) Do cooperatives participation and technology adoption improve farmers' welfare in China? A joint analysis accounting for selection bias. J Integr Agric 6:1716–1726

The manufacturer's authorised representative in the EU is Springer Nature Customer Service Centre GmbH, Europaplatz 3, 69115 Heidelberg, Germany. If you have any concerns regarding our products, please contact ProductSafety@springernature.com

Printed and bound by CPI Group (UK) Ltd, Croydon, CR0 4YY
30/09/2026
02225248-0006